Universal Human Rights
in Theory and Practice

UNIVERSAL HUMAN RIGHTS
IN THEORY
AND PRACTICE

Jack Donnelly

CORNELL UNIVERSITY PRESS

Ithaca and London

First published 1989 by Cornell University Press
First printing, Cornell Paperbacks, 1989

Printed in the United States of America

Library of Congress Cataloging-in-Publication Data

Donnelly, Jack
    Universal human rights in theory and practice / Jack Donnelly.
        p.   cm.
    Includes index.
    ISBN 0-8014-9570-9 (pbk. : alk. paper)
    1. Civil rights. 2. Human rights. 3. Cultural relativism. I. Title.
JC571.D75   1989   323—dc20   89-7057

Cornell University Press strives to use environmentally responsible suppliers and materials to the fullest extent possible in the publishing of its books. Such materials include vegetable-based, low-VOC inks and acid-free papers that are recycled, totally chlorine-free, or partly composed of nonwood fibers.

Paperback printing   10 9 8 7 6 5

Contents

Acknowledgments   ix

Introduction   1

PART I   Toward a Theory of Universal Human Rights   7

1 The Concept of Human Rights   9
   1 The Nature of Rights   9
   2 Special Features of Human Rights   12
   3 The Source of Human Rights   16
   4 The Subjects of Human Rights   19
   5 What Human Rights Do We Have?   21

2 The Interdependence and Indivisibility of Human Rights   28
   1 The Civil-Political, Economic-Social Dichotomy   28
   2 Basic Rights   37

PART II   Human Rights, Liberalism, and the West   47

3 Non-Western Conceptions of Human Rights   49
   1 "Human Rights" in Islam   50
   2 "Human Rights" in Traditional Africa and China   53
   3 Rights and Duties: The Soviet Union and
     "Human Rights"   55
   4 The Individual, Society, and Human Rights   57
   5 The Relevance of Human Rights   60
   6 Postscript: The West and Human Rights   63

4 Human Dignity, Human Rights, and Political Regimes   66
   by Rhoda E. Howard and Jack Donnelly
   1 Liberalism and Human Rights: A Necessary
     Connection   68
   2 Equality, Autonomy, and Communitarian Societies   75
   3 Human Dignity, Human Rights, and Political Regimes   84

5 Human Rights and Western Liberalism   88
   1 Locke and the Roots of Liberalism   88
   2 The Individual and Society   90
   3 Private Property and the State   93
   4 "Positive" Rights   100
   5 Economic and Social Rights   101
   6 Locke, Liberalism, and the Bourgeois Political
      Revolution   104

PART III   Human Rights and Cultural Relativism   107

6 Cultural Relativism and Universal Human Rights   109
   1 Defining "Cultural Relativism"   109
   2 Relativity and Universality: A Necessary Tension   110
   3 Varieties of Cultural Relativism   114
   4 Culture and Relativism   118
   5 Assessing Claims of Cultural Relativism   121

7 Human Rights and Cultural Values: Caste in India   125
   1 "Human Rights" and Traditional Indian Society   126
   2 Caste, Status, and Purity   127
   3 The Ontology of Caste   128
   4 Flexibility, Mobility, and Equality   132
   5 Caste and Cultural Relativism   135
   6 Caste and the Contemporary Struggle for
      Human Rights   137

8 Human Rights, Group Rights, and Cultural Rights   143
   1 Human Rights and Peoples' Rights   143
   2 Group Rights in a Human Rights Framework   149
   3 Cultural Rights and Cultural Identity   154

PART IV   Human Rights and Development   161

9 Development-Rights Trade-offs: Needs and Equality   163
   1 The Conventional Wisdom   163
   2 Brazil: The Tragedy of "Success"   166
   3 Korea: A More Successful Success Story   170
   4 Implementing a Strategy of Equitable Growth   178
   5 Postscript: Brazil and South Korea in the 1980s   181

10 Development-Rights Trade-offs: Political Repression   184
   1 Inclusion, Exclusion, and Development Strategies   185
   2 Repression, Structural Transformation, and the State   187
   3 Repression and "Stages" of Development   191
   4 Legitimacy and the Breakdown of Authoritarian
      Regimes   194
   5 The Political Contingency of Repression   200

PART V   Human Rights and International Action   203

11 International Human Rights Regimes   205
   1 International Regimes   205

2 The Global Human Rights Regime   206
3 Regional Human Rights Regimes   213
4 Single-Issue Human Rights Regimes   218
5 The Evolution of Human Rights Regimes   223

12 Human Rights and Foreign Policy   229
1 Human Rights: A Legitimate Concern of Foreign
    Policy?   229
2 Dictatorships and Double Standards:
    Which Rights to Pursue?   237
3 What Means Should Be Used?   241
4 Integrating Human Rights into Foreign Policy   246

13 Implementing Human Rights: The Priority of
    National Action   250
1 The Limits of Multilateral Action   250
2 The Limits of Bilateral Action   259
3 The Limits of International Action   266

References   271
Index   293

Acknowledgments

Like most authors, I have accumulated numerous debts in writing this book. The community of scholars working in and around the field of human rights is particularly congenial and supportive, and I have taken advantage of the goodwill of many friends, colleagues, and acquaintances. I am especially grateful to Dave Forsythe for his careful critical comments on, and advice for revisions of, the penultimate draft of the complete manuscript. I also thank the following people, who have read or discussed parts of the manuscript with me at various points over the half-dozen years during which it took shape: Philip Alston, Paul Brietzke, Charlie Brockett, Herman Burgers, Shelly Feldman, Gary Gereffi, Ernie Haas, Glenn Hayslett, Ed Kent, Steve Leonard, Ted Lewellen, Alan McChesney, Craig Murphy, Hanna Pitkin, Addie Pollis, Cran Pratt, Jane Sweeney, John Vincent, and Claude Welch. This book is much better for their comments, criticisms, and advice—and probably would have been better still if I had listened more attentively.

I owe a special debt to Rhoda Howard. She is the co-author of Chapter 4, but her influence can be seen throughout the book. She has read every word of this book, often more than once, and her perceptive criticisms, unfailing support, and constant encouragement have saved me from numerous errors, forced me to be clearer and more concrete, and pushed me into new areas of research. For all that—and no less for her friendship—I am grateful.

Permission to reprint material of my own that appeared previously, usually in somewhat different form, has been granted by: the American Political Science Association, which gave permission to reprint here as Chapter 3 a revised version of ''Human Rights and Human Dignity: An Analytic Critique of Non-Western Human Rights Conceptions,'' *American Political Science Review* 76 (June 1982), and here as Chapter 4, Rhoda E.

Howard and Jack Donnelly, "Human Dignity, Human Rights, and Political Regimes," *American Political Science Review* 80 (September 1986); The Johns Hopkins University Press, which gave permission to reprint here as Chapter 6 a revised version of "Cultural Relativism and Universal Human Rights," *Human Rights Quarterly* 6 (November 1984); Princeton University Press, which gave permission to reprint here as Chapter 9 a revised version of "Human Rights and Development: Complementary or Competing Concerns?" *World Politics* 36 (January 1984), copyright © by Princeton University Press; the *Journal of International Affairs*, which gave permission to reprint as Chapter 13, section 2.B, and Chapter 12, section 3.C, a revised version of portions of "Human Rights, Humanitarian Intervention, and American Foreign Policy: Law, Morality, and Politics," *Journal of International Affairs* 37 (Winter 1984); MIT Press, which gave permission to reprint as Chapter 11 a much shortened version of "International Human Rights: A Regime Analysis," *International Organization* 40 (Summer 1986); and the Canadian Institute of International Affairs, which gave permission to reprint as Chapter 13 a revised version of "Human Rights: The Impact of International Action," *International Journal* 33 (Spring 1988).

  Acknowledgments always seem inadequate recognition and recompense, but this is particularly true in the case of those due my wife, Cathy. Without her, I simply could not have written this book.

JACK DONNELLY

Chapel Hill, N.C.

Universal Human Rights
in Theory and Practice

Introduction

The universality of human rights is the central theme of this volume. My principal aim is to explicate and defend an account of human rights as universal rights. I do not, however, argue that human rights are timeless, unchanging, or absolute; any list or conception of human rights—and the idea of human rights itself—is historically specific and contingent. Organized around the competing claims of the universality, particularity, and relativity of human rights, this book demonstrates that the historical contingency and particularity of human rights is completely compatible with a conception of human rights as universal moral rights and thus does not require us to accept strong claims of cultural relativism.

If human rights are the rights one has simply because one is a human being, as they usually are thought to be, then they are held "universally," by all human beings. They also hold "universally" against all other persons and institutions. As the highest moral rights, they regulate the fundamental structures and practices of political life, and in ordinary circumstances they take priority over other moral, legal, and political claims. These dimensions encompass what I call the *moral universality* of human rights.

Human rights in the contemporary world are universal in another sense: they are almost universally accepted—at least in word, or as ideal standards. All states regularly proclaim their acceptance of and adherence to international human rights norms,[1] and charges of human rights violations are among the strongest charges that can be made in international relations. Half the world's states have undertaken international legal obligations to

---

1. The most widely known international document, cited with almost universal approval by both states and human rights activists, is the Universal Declaration of Human Rights (1948).

implement these rights by becoming parties to the International Human Rights Covenants, and almost all other nations have either signed but not yet ratified the Covenants (the United States is most prominent in this group) or have otherwise expressed approval of and commitment to their content. I call this the *international normative universality* of human rights.

Part I of this book sketches an analytic theory of human rights that captures this universality but leaves room for their historical particularity. Chapter 1, "The Concept of Human Rights," examines the character of human rights, their source in human nature, and the ways they operate as a social practice. What kind of thing is a human right? How are human rights related to other kinds of rights? How can simply being human give rise to rights? The chapter concludes with a discussion of the particular human rights we have, explicitly linking the moral and international universality of human rights. Chapter 2, "The Interdependence and Indivisibility of Human Rights," looks at how internationally recognized human rights are related to one another, focusing on issues of categories and priorities of rights. I argue that both the conventional dichotomy between (1) civil and political rights and (2) economic, social, and cultural rights, and efforts to extract a short list of "basic" rights, are theoretically misguided and obscure the nature, function, and interrelationships of human rights.

Part II turns to the historical particularity of human rights, emphasizing the special connection between human rights and the rise and consolidation of "liberalism" in the modern West. Chapter 3, "Non-Western Conceptions of Human Rights," critically examines the common claim that all societies possess indigenous human rights conceptions. So-called non-Western conceptions of human rights are in fact not conceptions of human rights at all, but involve alternative conceptions of human *dignity* that seek to realize that dignity through devices other than human rights. All societies possess conceptions of human dignity, but the idea and practice of human rights—equal and inalienable rights held by all individuals against the state and society—emerged only in the modern West, principally in response to social changes associated with the rise of modern markets and modern states. However, similar social changes in virtually all areas of the world have given human rights a near universal contemporary applicability, despite their obvious historical contingency and particularity.

Chapter 4, "Human Dignity, Human Rights, and Political Regimes," which I wrote with Rhoda Howard, develops a parallel structural argument. Just as it is widely believed that all cultures have indigenous human rights conceptions, so it is regularly argued that a great variety of sociopolitical systems are compatible with the demands of international human rights. Clearly, though, if human rights are a particular kind of social practice based on a distinctive conception of human dignity, as argued in Chapter 1, they require a particular type of sociopolitical system or regime. We label the regime demanded by international human rights "liberal" (or "social democratic").

Chapter 5, "Human Rights and Western Liberalism," attempts to defend this attribution and to explore more fully the theoretical links between internationally recognized human rights and the Western liberal tradition. The chapter closely examines Locke's *Second Treatise of Government*, perhaps the single most important theoretical work in the liberal political tradition. I argue that although there are "possessive individualist" elements in Locke's theory, there is an alternative and more important strand that points not toward a minimal libertarian state but toward the social democratic welfare state that is required by international human rights standards and that has been implemented more or less successfully in most contemporary Western states.

Part I focuses on the universality of human rights. Part II stresses the historical particularity of universal human rights. Part III argues that this particularity does not require us to accept the cultural relativity of human rights. Human rights originated in the West. Cultural differences and diversity are an important, even desirable, social fact. But international human rights standards can be legitimately applied to non-Western societies.

Chapter 6, "Cultural Relativism and Universal Human Rights," addresses in general theoretical terms the problem of conflicts between universal human rights norms and indigenous social practices that rest on alternative conceptions of human dignity. Although the well-known dangers of cultural and political imperialism demand respect for cultural variety, I argue that we nonetheless ought to defend and seek to implement the universality of human rights norms, at least in their broad outlines. Variations in the details of implementation may be allowed, and even required, in order to accommodate valued cultural practices and different historical backgrounds—so long as these alternative practices are not fundamentally incompatible with universal human rights norms—but our emphasis needs to be on universality rather than on relativity.

Chapter 7, "Human Rights and Cultural Values: Caste in India," examines the particularly striking contrast between the demands of universal human rights and the long-established practices of the Indian caste system. The first half of the chapter sketches the nature of this conflict, presenting an extended illustration of the argument of Chapter 3. The second half applies the general argument of Chapter 6 to this case.

Chapter 8, "Human Rights, Group Rights, and Cultural Rights," considers a different version of the argument of cultural relativity. It is often argued that the inherent individualism of human rights, which reflects their modern Western origin, makes them fundamentally inappropriate for the more communal or collectivist societies of the Third World. In this chapter, however, I defend the idea of human rights as the rights of individuals only, extending arguments introduced in Chapters 1 and 5. This individualism, however, is quite compatible with recognizing individual persons as members of a variety of social groups, and even with the idea of rights—just not *human* rights—held by these groups.

Part IV considers a very different "relativist" challenge to the universality of human rights—the challenge not of culture but of development. It is often claimed that the paramount importance of development throughout the Third World requires "temporary" sacrifices (trade-offs) of many, even most, internationally recognized human rights. I reject these relativist arguments as well.

Chapter 9, "Development-Rights Trade-offs: Needs and Equality," examines arguments for the sacrifice of economic and social rights, comparing the development strategies (and their very different human rights consequences) of Brazil and South Korea in the 1960s and 1970s. Chapter 10, "Development-Rights Trade-offs: Political Repression," explores the alleged need to sacrifice civil and political rights. In both chapters I argue that human rights trade-offs reflect not general developmental imperatives but contingent sociopolitical forces and choices. Thus the struggle for development need not require substantial systematic sacrifices of human rights.

Parts I–IV focus on the "moral universality" of human rights, the fact that human rights are held by all human beings with respect to all persons and institutions. Part V explores the "international normative universality" of human rights, their universal (verbal) acceptance by virtually all states in the contemporary world, and the multilateral institutions and bilateral foreign policy practices devised to implement and enforce human rights.

Since the U.N. General Assembly adopted the Universal Declaration of Human Rights in 1948, a relatively strong normative consensus on the list of human rights set out in that document has been forged. Today, international norms provide the essential context even for national action. International action has helped to publicize numerous national human rights violations, and in some cases it has been an important support or stimulus to internal reforms and national struggles against repressive regimes. Thus, international political action can be and has been an important contributor to the struggle for human rights. It has often been an important impediment, as well. Furthermore, international action has been the focus of much of the recent discussion of human rights and of the bulk of the scholarly literature on human rights.

Chapter 11, "International Human Rights Regimes," reviews the considerable array of international and regional multilateral procedures developed over the past forty years. Chapter 12, "Human Rights and Foreign Policy," presents an overview of the possibilities and limits of bilateral foreign policy as an instrument in the struggle for human rights. Chapter 13, "Implementing Human Rights: The Priority of National Action," then attempts to assess the effects of these multilateral and bilateral practices. While noting the recent growth and important contributions of international action, these chapters emphasize the severe limits, and ultimately subordinate importance, of both multilateral and bilateral international institutions and practices. Implementing international human rights is largely a matter of *national*, not international, action. The volume thus closes on an appropriate note of particularity in the context of universality: the central importance of "particularistic" national action in the struggle to realize "universal" (international) human rights.

There are two other themes to which I want to draw attention. The first is methodological: the necessarily multidisciplinary character of the study of human rights. The second is more substantive: the interaction of theory and practice.

Consider the range of issues covered by the Universal Declaration of Human Rights, which recognizes personal rights to life, nationality, recognition before the law, protection against torture, and protection against discrimination on such bases as race and sex; legal rights to a fair trial, the presumption of innocence, and protections against ex post facto laws, arbitrary arrest, detention or exile, and arbitrary interference with one's family, home, or reputation; a comparable variety of civil liberties and political rights; subsistence rights to food and health care; economic rights to work, rest and leisure, and social security; social rights to education and protection of the family; and the right to participate in the cultural life of the community. A comprehensive account of these rights would require that we combine, at minimum, the perspectives of law, political science, economics, and sociology—plus philosophy, if we want to understand the conceptual foundations of human rights and the justifications for this particular list.

The study of human rights is an inherently multidisciplinary enterprise.[2]

2. The principal scholarly journal in the field, *Human Rights Quarterly* (which began its life as *Universal Human Rights*), bills itself as "A Comparative and International Journal of the Social Sciences, Humanities, and Law."

One of my principal aims is to take seriously this often stated but rarely heeded methodological dictum. To do justice to the scope and complexities of human rights, and to increase understanding of human rights, material and perspectives from various disciplines and subfields are offered. Within my own discipline of political science, I draw from the subfields of political theory, international relations, and comparative politics. I also draw on work in philosophy (especially in Part I), economics (particularly in Chapter 9), sociology (especially in Part III), and international law (particularly in Part V). The result, I hope, concretely illustrates the fruitfulness, even necessity, of approaching human rights issues without regard to conventional disciplinary boundaries.

The importance of the interaction of theory and practice is especially striking when we consider the practical implications of the theoretical arguments of relativism that are the subject of Parts III and IV. The way in which we think about a problem does not determine the way we act, but it may influence behavior. The way problems are conceptualized may also be important for justifying actions and policies. For example, if it can be established that the sacrifice of human rights is not an imperative of development, but merely a convenience for those who control development policy (or even simply a cover for their self-enrichment), then repressive regimes are deprived of one important defense of their human rights violations.

Clear thinking about human rights is not the key to the struggle to implement them, and it may not even be essential to successful political action on their behalf. In fact, such a utopian belief in the power of ideas is itself a dangerous impediment to effective political action. Nonetheless, conceptual clarity, the fruit of sound theory, can facilitate action. At the very least it can help to unmask the arguments of dictators and their allies.

This book thus aspires not merely to analyze the interaction of theory and practice but also to contribute in some small way to improving practice. This hope underlies, and perhaps even justifies, not only this book but much of the scholarly literature on human rights.

PART I

Toward a Theory of
Universal Human Rights

1

The Concept of Human Rights

Human rights are literally the rights one has simply because one is a human being—*droits de l'homme, Menschenrechte,* "the rights of man." This definition raises two central theoretical questions: what does it mean to have a right, and how does being human give rise to rights?

1. THE NATURE OF RIGHTS

"Right" in English, and equivalent words in several other languages, has two central moral and political senses: rectitude and entitlement. In the first sense, of rectitude, we talk of some*thing being right*; in this sense we say of an action that it *is* right. In the second sense, of entitlement, we talk of some*one having a right*. It is only in this latter sense that we typically talk of rights (in the plural). If we are to take human rights seriously as the rights one has simply because one is a human being, the first step is to understand what it means to have a right.[1]

Rights are titles that ground claims of a special force. To have a right to x is to be specially *entitled* to have and enjoy x. The right thus governs the relationship between right-holder and duty-bearer, insofar as that relationship rests on the right. In addition, and no less important, to have a right is to be empowered to press rights *claims*, which ordinarily "trump" utility,

1. The following account emphasizes the differences between (human) rights and other social practices and grounds for action, both because the first step in any analysis is to distinguish the object of analysis from similar or related objects and because many serious confusions result from inadequate attention to the special character of rights. However, the similarities between human rights and other grounds for action is an interesting and important topic that is perceptively discussed in Nickel 1987.

social policy, and other moral or political grounds for action (Dworkin 1977: xi, 90). This ascendancy places the right-holder in direct control of the relationship; the duties correlative to rights "belong to" the right-holder, who is largely free to dispose of those duties as he sees fit.

If it simply *is* right that A have *x*, but A does not *have* a right to *x*, A ordinarily will be in a weaker position in at least two important ways. Mere righteousness does not by its nature trump other considerations; in the absence of a right, A is not specially entitled to *x*. In addition, the protections afforded A are not under A's control; A is not able to advance rights claims and thus is especially dependent on the duty-bearer.

Claims of rectitude, claims that something *is* right—"That's wrong" ("That's not right"), "You really ought to do that"—are also an important part of moral and political discourse, but they are different in force and function from claims of rights. "That's wrong" is only a claim that there is a lack of conformity with established standards; it points out and appeals to, but does not really activate, someone else's obligation. However a rights claim ("I *have a right* to that") is more than a reminder or an appeal; it also involves a powerful *demand* for action. And this demand brings into play an array of special social practices that rest on the privileged position of right-holders. "Claiming a right makes things happen" (Feinberg 1980: 150).

"A has a right to *x* (with respect to B)" specifies a right-holder (A), an object of the right (*x*), and a duty-bearer (B). It also outlines the relationships in which they stand as a result of the right. A is entitled to *x* (with respect to B). B stands under correlative obligations to A (with respect to *x*). And should it be necessary, A may make special claims upon B to discharge these obligations.

Titles point from the right-holder toward the object of the right. Claims also point outward from the right-holder toward those obliged by the right. Rights thus create a field of rule-governed interactions centered on the right-holder. The key to understanding rights is to understand the nature of these interactions—that is, how rights "work."

Consider the following simple model. A right-holder *exercises* his right; he claims it and thus brings it into play. This activates the duty-bearer's obligation to *respect* that right. If it is respected, the right-holder will *enjoy* the right. The result of this process, as well as its ultimate aim, is to secure the right-holder's enjoyment of the *object* of the right.

We actually talk about rights, however, only when they are at issue. For example, if I walk into the supermarket and buy a loaf of bread, it would be silly to say that I had a right to my money, which I exchanged for a right to the bread, or that the clerk in the store and the people who did not steal my money or my bread were respecting my rights. Although it would not be exactly wrong to say this, it would be so much out of place that we might question the speaker's understanding of how rights work, or whether we heard what was said correctly. One's rights are important enough to talk about, and they have their real place and value, only when their enjoyment is in some way insecure. Rights are put to use, claimed, exercised only when they are threatened or denied.

We must therefore distinguish between three distinct forms of social interaction that involve rights:

1. *Assertive exercise of a right*, in which the right is exercised (claimed) and the duty-bearer responds by respecting (or violating) the right. As a result of "assertive exercise" we can say that the right is enjoyed (or not enjoyed) in the strongest sense of that term.

2. *Direct enjoyment of a right*, in which the duty-bearer takes the right actively into account in determining how he or she will behave, so that we can speak of the right being respected (or violated), and even enjoyed. In "direct enjoyment," there is no exercise (claim) of the right by the right-holder.

3. *Objective enjoyment of a right*, as in the example above of buying a loaf .of bread, in which we might say that the *object* of the right is "enjoyed" but the right is not exercised, and it would be stretching the term even to say that it was "respected."

Objective enjoyment of rights must be the norm. If social harmony is not to be excessively eroded, then the costs, inconveniences, discontent, or tension associated with even direct enjoyment of a right must be the exception rather than the rule. Assertive exercises, however, are both a defining feature of rights (as opposed to mere righteousness) and of unparalleled importance to the right-holder. Unless one can claim something as a "right (entitlement)"—that is, unless assertive exercises are ultimately available—one may *enjoy a benefit* but one does not *have a right* (compare Donnelly 1985a: 11–12, 47–51). The real value of a right is the special entitlement it gives one to press rights-claims if enjoyment of the object of the right is threatened or denied.

"Having" a right is therefore of most value precisely when one does not "have" the object of the right—that is, when one is denied direct or objective enjoyment of the right. I call this "the possession paradox" of rights: "having" and "not having" a right at the same time, the "having" being particularly important precisely when one *does not* "have" it. This possession paradox is characteristic of all rights, although we shall see below that it has special significance for human rights.

We must distinguish between *possession* of a right, the *respect* it receives, and the ease or frequency of *enforcement*. In a world of saints, rights would be widely respected and rarely enforced (except through the "self-enforcement" of saintly duty-bearers). In a Hobbesian state of nature, rights would be rarely respected (and then only out of the self-interest of the duty-bearer), and enforcement would be only through self-help. But such differing circumstances of respect and enforcement tell us nothing about the rights that anyone *has*. For example, I have the same right to my car whether it sits in my driveway; is borrowed without my permission, for good reason or bad; is stolen but later recovered; or is stolen, never to be seen again by me (whether or not the thief is ever sought, apprehended, charged, tried, or convicted).

To have a right to *x* is to be specially entitled to *x*. Legal rights arise from the law; contractual rights arise from special agreement; moral rights from principles of righteousness. But one has the right in question whether the law is violated or not, whether the bargain is kept or not, whether others comply with the demands of morality or not. The right-holder would prefer that the duty-bearer discharge his or her obligations directly, without the need to exercise the right; it is always preferable not to have to use (exercise, assert, claim) one's rights. Furthermore, it is preferable to be able to have one's rights effectively enforced, when necessary. But it is the ability to claim the right if necessary—the special force this gives to the demand and the special social practices it brings into play—that makes having rights so valuable and that distinguishes having a right from simply enjoying a benefit or being the (rights-less) beneficiary of someone else's obligation.

2. SPECIAL FEATURES OF HUMAN RIGHTS

Human rights are a special class of rights, the rights that one has simply because one is a human being. They are thus moral rights of the highest order. Usually, however, they are closely related to parallel "lower" rights, or the struggle to establish such rights.

Consider the right not to be discriminated against on the basis of race. In most countries, this human right can be claimed on several grounds. For example, in the United States it can always be claimed as a constitutional right. Depending on the circumstances, it may also be claimed as a federal statutory right (e.g., under the various Civil Rights Acts); a state or local statutory right; a right resting on an executive order (such as an affirmative action order) or a court order; a (customary) international legal right; or a contractual right (e.g., one based on a collective bargaining agreement). It can, of course, also be claimed as a moral right and as a human right, a particular class of moral rights.

Suppose an American is faced with racial discrimination on the job. How will he or she seek redress? In general, the "lowest" right to nondiscrimination available will be used. If one's employment contract explicitly covers racial discrimination, a grievance may be all that is required. If that fails, a legal action based on the contract may be brought. Barring that, one may be able to bring suit under a local human rights ordinance or a state nondiscrimination statute. At still a higher level, federal statutes and the Constitution may offer a remedy. If the particular form of racial discrimination is not covered by constitutional guarantees, one may have to resort to international human rights instruments, which may have a certain force in American law as part of customary international law.

What is striking is how far one can go before human rights arguments become necessary. For example, appeals may be made to moral human rights at "lower" levels in order to add moral force to the claim. Such appeals, or even their possibility, may have an impact on those who are in a position to respect or violate the right. But one typically has direct recourse to human rights claims only where legal or other remedies seem unlikely to work or have already failed. In fact, the special function of human rights virtually requires that they be claimed precisely when they are unenforceable by ordinary legal or political means.

As we saw above, one *claims* a right only when its enjoyment is threatened or denied. An appeal to human rights rather than "lower" rights usually testifies to the absence of enforceable positive rights. For example, homosexuals in the United States must claim a human right against discrimination on the basis of sexual preference because U.S. courts have held that constitutional and statutory prohibitions of discrimination do not apply to sexual preference (unless explicitly mentioned in the statute). In the Soviet Union, claims of a human right to free speech are required because the parallel legal right specified in the Soviet constitution is regularly violated. Even in Western Europe, where the European Convention on Human Rights has established a strong regional legal human rights regime (see Chapter 11), appeals to the European Commission of Human Rights represent a failure of lower-level national claims to satisfy the petitioner.

All rights claims are a sort of "last resort"; rights are claimed only when enjoyment of the object of the right is threatened or denied. Claims of *human* rights are the final resort in the realm of rights; no higher rights appeal is available. They are also likely to be a last resort in the sense that everything else has been tried and failed, so one is left with nothing else (except perhaps threats or violence).

By the same token, enforceable "lower-level" rights make higher rights temporarily superfluous. In particular, an enforceable legal right to the "same" thing leaves the parallel human right—which one of course continues to *have*—temporarily without a *use*. This is the ideal situation for a right-holder; rights are put to use only when things are not going well.

Human rights claims therefore aim to be self-liquidating. Systematically advanced human rights claims seek to establish or bring about more effective enforcement of a parallel "lower" right—which will eliminate the need to claim that human right. For example, the civil rights movement in the United States has tried to bring legal practice into accord with the constitutional requirements of equal protection and nondiscrimination. Likewise, claims of a human right to health care in the United States have as their principal political purpose the creation of a *legal* right to health care.

To the extent that human rights claims are politically effective, the need to make such claims is reduced or eliminated. One claims a human right in the hope of ultimately creating a society in such claims will no longer be necessary. Where human rights are effectively protected, we continue to *have* human rights, but there is no need or occasion to *use* them. This is simply another way of stating the centrality of the possession paradox to human rights.

Human rights claims thus are essentially extralegal; their principal aim is to challenge or change existing institutions, practices, or norms, especially legal institutions.[2] For example, Soviet dissidents press human rights claims in order to alter the standard practice of the Soviet state. Similarly, natural rights claims were literally revolutionary in the American Declaration of Independence and the French Declaration of the Rights of Man and the Citizen. If systematically unenforced rights are to be enforced and enjoyed, institutions must be changed. And the "higher" and more central the right, the greater the changes that will be required.

This is not to say that human rights cannot or should not be made justiciable in national, regional, or international law. Quite the contrary, giving effective legal force to these rights is the ultimate aim of the struggle for human rights. But when human rights are made effectively justiciable, those whose rights are violated will usually *claim* legal, not human, rights (although they continue to *have* all the same human rights).

Most broadly conceived, human rights are a standard of political legitimacy; to the extent that governments protect human rights, they and their practices are legitimate.[3] As the Universal Declaration of Human Rights

2. If one objects to this terminology (for example, on the ground that it makes "natural law" extralegal as well), a different word may be substituted; the point is that human rights claims aim to alter established positive law and practice.

3. Compare Paine (1945: I, 276–77), Locke (1967: par. 95), and Bay (1981: 5, 89). There has thus been a close link between the development of human rights ideas and social

puts it, human rights are a "standard of achievement for all peoples and all nations." But no less important, they empower citizens to act to vindicate these rights; to insist, through the exercise of their rights, that these standards be realized; to struggle to create a world in which they are realized in practice. Human rights express not merely aspirations, suggestions, requests, or laudable ideas, but rights-based *demands* for social change.[4] And these demands may be addressed even—in fact, especially—to one's own government.

We must therefore be careful that we do not fall into the trap of speaking of human rights simply as demands for rights—what Joel Feinberg calls rights in a "manifesto sense" (1980: 153). Human rights claims do imply a claim that one *ought* to have a *legal* right to the object in question. But in contrast to other grounds on which legal rights might be demanded—for example, justice, utility, self-interest, or beneficence—human rights-based demands for legal rights involve a moral *entitlement* to the right in question. Systematically unenforced human rights put one in a position to mount a particularly powerful moral attack on rights-abusive institutions. This is why having even an unenforced right is so important.

Human rights do imply a manifesto for political change, but this does not make them any less truly rights; it simply underscores that they are human rights, not legal rights. That one must claim human rights means that fundamental social changes are required, that one is not *enjoying* the human rights one has. But to claim a human right is to claim a (human) right one already has.

It is even misleading to say that this indicates an essential weakness of human rights (Martin 1980: 393). Most right-holders would prefer to have parallel legally enforceable rights as well, but the *moral* force of human rights will often be greater. And as we have already seen, the real strength and value of human rights is that they are available precisely when claims of legal and other lower rights fail.

Legal rights ground legal claims on the political system to protect already established legal entitlements. Human rights ground moral claims on the political system to strengthen or add to existing legal entitlements.

---

contract theory, for in standard contractarian accounts, Hobbes being the notable exception that proves the rule, legitimacy is a function of the sovereign's discharging his obligations under the contract, and those obligations can in large measure be summarized as ensuring the legal enforcement of the natural rights of the citizens.

4. Thus American conservatives, such as Jeane Kirkpatrick (1982: 7–9), go to great lengths to argue that economic and social rights are not really human *rights* (titles), but rather aspirations or dictates of justice or righteousness, in order to strip their special force as human rights. The theoretical issue of the status of economic and social rights is addressed in Chapter 2, section 1.B.

That does not make human rights stronger or weaker than legal rights, just different: it makes them human rights rather than legal rights. In fact, if they did not function differently there would be no need for both human rights and legal rights.

Thus, the familiar distinction between positive or legal rights and moral rights, of which human rights are a subset, simply specifies two different sources of rights and the two different sets of social institutions within which they are embedded. Neither is more truly or less truly a right than the other. Positive rights arise from legal enactment (or custom) and are backed by the force of the law. Moral rights arise from the principles of morality and are backed by the force of morality. In modern state societies it is usually easier to have legal rights enforced should they be threatened or violated. But this does not make positive rights more truly rights—unless one arbitrarily stipulates that the only true rights are legal rights.

A positivist account of rights that equates all rights with legally enforced rights—"if [the] corresponding duty be a creature of a law imperative, the right is a right properly so called" (Austin 1954: 158–59)—not only confuses possession of a right with enforcement, but further confuses enforcement with legal enforcement. One can have an unenforced right, even an unenforced legal right, as the example of successful theft clearly indicates. And one can have a right that is enforced by institutions other than the law—for example, by social pressure or conscience.

Whether a right is a moral right or a legal right, it is a right. Positive and moral rights are different kinds of rights, different varieties of the same species. Many of the practical differences do indeed rest on the fact that legal rights are legally enforceable. But this is hardly surprising: legal rights are legally enforceable, while other kinds of rights are not. Whatever the differences, they are both *rights*—titles that ground rights claims. Human rights are fully and completely rights.

3. THE SOURCE OF HUMAN RIGHTS

From where do we get human rights? The very term "human" rights points to a source: humanity, human nature, being a person or human being. Legal rights have the law as their source, contractual rights arise from contracts, and thus, apparently, human rights have humanity or human nature as their source.

But *how* does human nature—how *can* being a human being—give rise to rights? With law we can point to statute or custom. With contracts there is the act of contracting. How does being human give one rights?

Human needs are frequently held to define the human nature that gives rise to human rights: "needs establish human rights" (Bay 1982: 67). Unfortunately, "human needs" is almost as obscure a notion as "human nature." If we turn to science, we find an extraordinarily limited set of needs. Even Christian Bay, probably the best-known advocate of a needs theory of human rights, admits that "it is premature to speak of *any* empirically established needs beyond sustenance and safety" (1977: 17). If we turn elsewhere, though, "needs" takes on a metaphorical or moral sense, and we are back with philosophical wrangles over human nature. There is nothing wrong with philosophical theory, as long as it does not masquerade as science. In fact, to understand the source of human rights, we *must* turn to philosophy; the pseudo-scientific dodge of needs will not do.

The source of human rights is man's *moral* nature, which is only loosely linked to the "human nature" defined by scientifically ascertainable needs. Human rights are "needed" not for life but for a life of dignity; as the International Human Rights Covenants put it, human rights arise from "the inherent dignity of the human person." Violations of human rights deny one's *humanity*; they do not necessarily keep one from satisfying one's needs. We have human rights not to the requisites for health but to those things "needed" for a life of dignity, for a life *worthy* of a human being, a life that cannot be enjoyed without these rights.[5]

The human "nature" that grounds human rights is a moral posit, a moral account of human possibility. The scientist's human nature sets the "natural" outer limits of human possibility. The moral nature that grounds human rights is a social selection from these possibilities. The scientist's human nature says that beyond this we cannot go. The moral nature that grounds human rights says that beneath this we may not permit ourselves to fall.

Like other social practices, human rights arise from human action; they are not given to man by God, Nature, or the physical facts of life. Human rights represent a social choice of a particular moral vision of human potentiality, which rests on a particular substantive account of the minimum requirements of a life of dignity. Human potential is widely variable, and it includes both good and evil; there are probably at least as many potential rapists and murderers as there are potential saints. Society plays a crucial role in determining which potentials will be realized and how. Human rights specify in significant measure how that selection is to be made.

5. The particular things to which we have human rights is a problem addressed below in section 5 and in Chapter 2. I confine myself here to explicating this account of the source of human rights.

Although human rights theorists perhaps must deny Augustinian original sin and its secular analogues, they are able to recognize a full range of the less attractive elements in human nature. In fact, one of the central purposes of human rights is to single out such elements. Substantial political progress and moral development thus is promised but not guaranteed. Human rights point the way to such progressive development.

Human rights demand certain types of institutions and practices to realize the underlying moral vision of human possibility—namely, the implementation and protection of those rights. Human rights are a social practice that aims to realize a particular vision of human dignity and potential by institutionalizing basic rights. And when human rights claims have brought legal and political practice into line with their demands, they will have created the type of person posited in that moral vision.

Therefore, there is both a constructive interaction between moral vision and political reality and a constructive interaction between the individual and society (especially the state), which shape another through the practice of human rights. The limits and requirements of state action are set by human nature and the rights it grounds, but the state and society, guided by human rights, play a major role in creating (or realizing) that nature.

Human nature is thus a *social project* as much as it is a given. Just as an individual's "nature" or character emerges out of a wide range of given possibilities through the interaction of natural endowment, individual action, and social institutions, so the species (through the instrument of society) creates its essential nature out of itself. Human rights specify a structure of social practices to achieve a particular realization of human potential.[6]

Human rights point beyond actual conditions of existence; they are less about the way that people are, in the sense of what has already been realized, than about how people *might* live, a possibility that is viewed as a deeper moral reality. The Universal Declaration of Human Rights tells us little about what life is like in most countries, but it sets out minimum conditions for a *dignified* life, a life *worthy* of a *human* being, and it sets out these requirements in the form of *rights*, with all that implies. Even in wealthy and powerful countries, these minimum standards are met all too infrequently, but this is precisely when and perhaps even why having human rights is so important: they demand, as rights, the sort of social change required to realize the underlying moral vision of human nature.

6. Thus, "human nature" in the relevant sense is conventional, the result of social conventions (and individual actions). It is not arbitrary though, for it is limited by, among other things, the psychobiological bounds of human potential, the formative capabilities of social institutions, and morality.

Doctrines of human rights thus roughly equate having human rights and being human.[7] Without the enjoyment of (the objects of) human rights, one is almost certain to be alienated or estranged from one's moral nature. Thus human rights are regularly held to be inalienable, not in the sense that one cannot be denied the enjoyment of these rights, for every repressive regime daily alienates its people from their human rights, but in the sense that losing these rights is *morally* "impossible": one cannot lose these rights and live a life worthy of a human being.

At once a utopian ideal and a realistic practice for implementing that ideal, human rights say in effect, "Treat a person like a human being and you'll get a human being." That is their utopian side. But they also say, "Here's *how* you treat someone as a human being" and proceed to enumerate a list of human rights, which establishes the framework within which a legitimate government must act.

In this way, human rights are a sort of self-fulfilling moral prophecy: "Treat people like human beings—see attached list—and you will get truly *human* beings." The forward-looking moral vision of human nature that is the source of human rights provides the basis for the social changes implicit in claims of human rights. And the effective exercise of these rights will make this moral vision a reality, thus making claims of these rights unnecessary. The possession paradox, in the case of human rights, is simply another way of formulating this essential interaction of the real and the ideal, between moral vision and political practice.

The relationship between human nature, human rights, and political society is therefore "dialectical." Human rights shape political society, so as to shape human beings, so as to realize the possibilities of human nature, which provided the basis for these rights in the first place. The "human nature" underlying human rights combines "natural," social, historical, and moral elements; it is conditioned but not fully determined by objective historical processes.

4. The Subjects of Human Rights

Who has human rights? Do collective "persons," in particular, have human rights? I argue, briefly here and in more detail in Chapter 8, that only individuals have *human* rights.

7. This implies that not all societies have conceptions of human rights, because many do not even have a notion of "human beings" in the relevant sense. For example, many societies define persons not by their common humanity but by such ascriptive criteria as sex, age or birth. Similarly, it implies that human rights require a particular type of social structure. For detailed arguments on these points, see Chapters 3, 4, and 7.

If human rights are the rights that one has simply as a human being, then only human beings have human rights; if one is not a human being, then by definition one can not have a human right. Because only individual persons are human beings, it would seem obvious that only individuals can have human rights. And the Universal Declaration of Human Rights and the International Human Rights Covenants, with but one exception,[8] include only individual rights. Economic, social, and cultural rights, as well as civil and political rights, are the rights of individuals. It is individuals, not groups, that have rights to food, health care, work, social security, due process, freedom of the press, protection against discrimination, and the like.

In addition to being separate persons, individuals are members of communities. In fact, any plausible account of human dignity must include membership in society; people must be parts of social groups if they are to live lives worthy of human beings. It is also true that individuals have duties to society, and these duties may even correspond to rights of society. But from none of this does it follow that society, or any other social group, has human rights.

Individual human beings may hold human rights both as separate individuals and as members of a community. For example, cultural rights are held by the members of a particular cultural group, but such rights are held by individuals in their capacity as members of protected social groups. They are not rights *of* groups; in particular, they are not rights that the group can hold and exercise against the individual.

Families, for example, are protected by a number of internationally recognized human rights, but from a human rights perspective the family is only an intermediate social group whose intermediation protects individual family members. The human rights of families apply only against the broader society, and families may not exercise their rights in ways that infringe on the human rights of their members or on any other persons. For instance, families may not deny their members freedom of religion or the right to political participation, nor may they discriminate on the basis of sex.

Furthermore, *all* human rights are embedded in a social context and have important social dimensions. Due process and equal protection make no sense except in the context of a political community; speech, work, and politics take place only in communities; torture and social insurance alike occur only in a social context. The very ideas of respecting and violating human rights rest on the idea of the individual as part of a larger community

8. That exception is the right of peoples to self-determination, which is discussed below in Chapter 8, section 1.

and social enterprise (compare Ewin 1987). Even classic social contract theorists such as Locke held that the purpose of government and society was to protect natural rights, which were at best useless outside society. And a principal function of human rights is to shape social relations.

There is no special class of human rights that are rights of society or any other collectivity. Collectivities may indeed have rights. Society does have legitimate claims against individuals. Individuals do have important duties with respect to society.[9] But the rights of society are not human rights, and cannot be human rights, unless we are to redefine the term. We must not fall into the trap of calling everything good a human right, thus draining all meaning from the term.

5. WHAT HUMAN RIGHTS DO WE HAVE?

If the above account of the source of human rights is correct, a philosophically defensible list of human rights must be derived from a moral account of human nature, which in turn must be philosophically defended. Such a task is clearly well beyond our scope here: theories of human nature are notoriously controversial, and the disputes and problems they raise are seemingly intractable. We can, however, *indirectly* justify a list of human rights by taking a given list and showing that it rests on a plausible and attractive account of human nature. But let me first explain my refusal to launch a direct philosophical assault on the problem.

A. Human Rights and Theories of Human Nature

Doesn't my inability to defend, directly and in detail, a substantive theory of human nature, which would specify a precise and determinate source of human rights, leave the theory I have developed dangerously abstract, even empty (compare Morsink 1987: 131–33)? There is a certain force to this challenge, but it largely misses the point. The theory I have tried to sketch does not provide a comprehensive philosophical account of human rights, but it does provide an *analytic* theory of the *concept* of human rights.

The theory is analytic or descriptive, not normative or prescriptive. It seeks principally to describe and explain the way human rights actually

---

9. These duties, however, are *not* a condition for the possession or even the enjoyment of human rights (except in some very limited instances, such as restrictions on the enjoyment of personal liberty of those convicted of serious crimes). One *has* the same human rights whether or not one discharges one's duties to society, because one is a human being regardless of whether or not one is a good member of society. See Chapter 3, section 4, for further discussion of the relationship between duties and (human) rights.

work in contemporary social relations. My argument has been simply that human rights, as they are usually understood today, function in the way that I have indicated. I have not yet tried to argue that we *ought to* adopt the practice of human rights. Instead, I have given an account of the implications for social relations of taking human rights seriously.

My argument has been cast at the most abstract level of the concept of human rights—that is, I have described the character of any human right, whatever it substance may be. The first step in any theoretical inquiry must be to "define" the object of analysis. Before we can get down to specifying, let alone studying, particular instances of human rights (or any other set of things) we need to know what counts as an instance of the object under study. This preliminary definitional task has been one of the principal objectives of this chapter. The substantive "emptiness" of the theory is therefore in large measure intentional. The analytic conceptual theory I have sketched does tell us how a comprehensive philosophical justification of a list of human rights would have to be accomplished, but it provides little substantive guidance for carrying out such a justification. This is indeed a shortcoming of my theory, but it is almost unavoidable.

There probably is no topic in moral or political philosophy more controversial or intractable than philosophical anthropology, theories of the essential moral nature of human beings. We are all familiar with a number of well-developed and widely accepted theories—for example, Aristotle's account of man as a *zoon politikon*; Marx's account of man as a human natural being that distinguishes himself by producing his own means of subsistence and hence his material life; Mill's conception of man as a pleasure-seeking, progressive being; Kant's view of man as a rational being governed by an objective moral law expressed in the categorical imperative. Each of us probably has a favorite and up to a certain point would defend its plausibility, but there are few moral issues where discussion typically proves less conclusive.

Philosophical anthropologies are much more like axioms than theorems; they are starting-points that are more assumed, or at best indirectly defended, than the results of philosophical argument. Most philosophical discussions of human nature typically either rehash old arguments across theories or restrict themselves to controversies carried out within the safe confines of a particular theory. In neither case do we get much in the way of a persuasive justification. I therefore suggest that the attempt to provide a direct philosophical justification of any particular list of human rights is not likely to be of great interest—except perhaps to those who already accept it—or value. I doubt that there is anything new and significant to be said in defense of any particular substantive theory of human nature, and I am certain that I am unable to say anything new or decisive in defense of any particular philosophical anthropology.

If we were faced with an array of competing and contradictory lists of human rights clamoring for either philosophical or political attention, this inability to defend a particular theory of human nature might be a serious shortcoming, but there is a remarkable international normative consensus on the list of rights contained in the so-called International Bill of Human Rights, a list that is based on a plausible and attractive theory of human nature. Furthermore, in the philosophical literature on lists of human rights there is really only one major issue of controversy: the status of economic and social rights. This is a topic that I will address directly in the next chapter.

Taken together, these two features of contemporary discussions mean that my inability to defend a particular list with direct philosophical arguments is a far less serious problem than it first appears to be. And we can go a long way in dealing with most of the dominant contemporary theoretical and practical controversies connected with human rights before issues of philosophical anthropology intrude decisively. In fact, as shall become evident in several of the following chapters, many important theoretical controversies can be elucidated—and some even resolved—by the theory I have sketched here.

Finally, although it may sound perverse, let me suggest that the "emptiness" of a conceptual theory is not merely defensible but also one of its great attractions. Given that philosophical anthropologies are so controversial, there are great dangers in tying one's analysis of human rights to any particular theory of human nature. Because it is both analytic and conceptual, the account of human rights I have sketched above is compatible with many but not all theories of human nature (see, e.g., Chapter 7, section 1.D). It is thus available to provide "neutral" theoretical insight and guidance across a considerable range of important issues.

B. International Human Rights Standards

In contemporary circumstances, an indirect approach to justifying a list of human rights—taking a list and showing that it reflects a plausible and attractive theory of human nature—is especially appealing because the Universal Declaration of Human Rights and the International Human Rights Covenants, often referred to collectively as the International Bill of Human Rights, provide a widely accepted list of internationally recognized human rights. We can take this verbal acceptance by most states—what I called in the Introduction the "international normative universality" of human rights—as a prima facie indication of the attractiveness of the underlying moral vision.

The Universal Declaration of Human Rights (adopted December 10, 1948, by the U.N. General Assembly) and the International Human Rights Covenants (which were opened for signature in 1966 and came into force in 1976)[10] encompass a wide range of personal, legal, civil, political, subsistence, economic, social, and cultural rights. This list is further elaborated in a variety of single-issue treaties and declarations on such topics as genocide, political rights of women, racial discrimination, and torture. And it is generally agreed that these rights form an interdependent and interactive system of guarantees, rather than a menu from which one may freely pick and choose (see Chapter 2). The standard practice of states is to speak of, and thus in a limited sense treat, the norms of the Universal Declaration and the Covenants as binding. Although states refuse to allow much international enforcement, or even monitoring, of their performance in living up to these obligations (see Chapter 11), and although domestic practice regularly falls far short of international profession, these rights are widely accepted, even by states, as more or less binding international standards.

The list of rights in the International Bill of Human Rights can be seen as resting on a moral vision of human nature that views human beings as equal and autonomous individuals who are entitled to equal concern and respect (see also Chapter 4, section 1.B). Virtually the entire list of rights in the Universal Declaration can be easily and directly derived from such a conception.[11]

At minimum, people must be alive. This requires survival rights, such as the rights to life (Universal Declaration, Article 3) and to food (Article 22). And if this survival is to be more than brutish, it requires economic and social rights, such as the right to health care and social insurance (Article 25).

To be treated with concern and respect, a human being must first be recognized as a person and a member of society. The rights to protection against slavery and against torture and other inhuman or degrading treatment (Articles 4, 5) are minimum guarantees of full membership in society. Protection of the family, the fundamental social unit in almost all societies, is also required (Article 16). Rights to recognition before the law and nationality (Articles 6, 15) guarantee political membership. And to assure

10. U.N. resolutions 217A (III) and 2200 (XXI). They are widely reprinted, for example, in Sohn and Buergenthal 1973; Laquer and Rubin 1979; and Brownlie 1981.

11. The following four paragraphs draw heavily on Donnelly and Howard 1988.

that this membership is equal, rights to equal protection of the laws and protection against discrimination on such bases as race, color, sex, language, religion, opinion, origin, property, birth, or other status (Articles 2, 7) are required.

Freedoms of speech, conscience, religion, movement, and association (Articles 18, 19, 20) protect a sphere of personal autonomy, as does the right to education (Article 26). And if autonomy is to be a positive, active condition, it requires rights that permit participation and empower one to act in public so as to shape the conditions of one's life. Freedoms of the press, assembly, and association (Articles 19, 20) and the right to democratic political participation (Article 21) assure political participation. The rights to work and to free trade unions (Articles 23, 24) protect economic participation. The right to participate in the cultural life of the community (Article 27) guarantees cultural participation.

Finally, the special threat to both autonomy and equality presented by the coercive apparatus of the modern state requires a set of legal or protection rights, such as the presumption of innocence and rights to due process, an independent judiciary, privacy, and protection against arbitrary arrest, detention, or exile (Articles 8–12).[12]

Given the wide international acceptance, in word if not deed, of the rights contained in the Universal Declaration and the Covenants, and the ease with which they can be derived from a conception of human beings viewed as free, autonomous persons entitled to equal concern and respect, I henceforth take this list of rights to be authoritative. In the following chapter I explicitly and directly defend this list against its principal theoretical challengers, who deny the existence of economic, social, and cultural human rights.

C. The Evolution of Lists of Human Rights

Equality, autonomy, and equal concern and respect are very abstract values that can be realized in a great variety of ways. Nonetheless, an international consensus has formed around this particular list of human rights, not some other list. I suggest that this consensus can be largely

---

12. The two rights in the Universal Declaration that cannot be so simply derived from a conception of free, autonomous people entitled to equal concern and respect are the rights to property (Article 17) and to asylum (Article 14). (It is perhaps significant that they are not included in the International Human Rights Covenants.) A limited right to property, however, can be defended as a device to help secure the satisfaction of basic material needs and to provide a stable and dignified economic foundation from which to pursue personal values and objectives. The right to asylum can be seen as a device to assure that those who are subject to intolerable oppression by their government may find refuge in another state, so that political respect for their dignity is not completely tied to their nationality.

explained by the fact that the list responds to the major perceived threats to human dignity. Any particular list of human rights is a list of the principal "standard threats" to human dignity in a given era (Shue 1980: 29–34).

Consider a potential human right to excrete.[13] Why would such a right be so silly? Because it is never at issue, and therefore never would need to be claimed, and thus need not be recognized. If torturers should choose to supplement their field radios and cattle prods with preventing excretion, or if preventing excretion became a new a diabolical means of repressive social control, we might decide to recognize a human right to excrete. But unless this became a pervasive threat to human dignity, there would be no reason to recognize such a right.

Consider, in contrast, the internationally recognized right to periodic holidays with pay, which is often ridiculed by critics of economic and social rights (e.g., Cranston 1973: 67). Such a right is a completely appropriate response to an all-too-common threat to human dignity. The full right recognized in Article 24 of the Universal Declaration of Human Rights (and in Article 7(d) of the International Covenant on Economic, Social, and Cultural Rights) is a right to "rest, leisure and reasonable limitation of working hours and periodic holidays with pay." The denial of rest, leisure, reasonable working hours, and holidays is not the fantasy of a perverse imagination but a common assault on the dignity of workers, from nineteenth-century factories in Manchester, to twentieth-century sweatshops in New York, to textile and electronics factories in Seoul today.

Our list of human rights has evolved and expanded, and will continue to do so, in response to such factors as changing ideas of human dignity, the rise of new political forces, technological changes, new techniques of repression, and even past human rights successes, which allow attention and resources to be shifted to threats that previously were inadequately recognized or insufficiently addressed. Such evolution is particularly clear in the emergence of economic and social human rights.

Although John Locke's short list of life, liberty, and estates was in Jefferson's hands expanded to life, liberty, and the pursuit of happiness (see Locke 1967: pars. 85, 87, 123), it was only with the rise of the working class as an effective political force that the idea of economic and social rights began to make real headway. Such political changes were also associated with new ideas on the meaning of and conditions necessary for a life of dignity—new understandings provoked in large measure by the social and economic devastation of early industrialization—and with changing ideas of who the subjects of human rights were, particularly the

13. This right actually was advanced by Johan Galtung in a paper circulated in the mid-1970s, although I am no longer able to find the reference.

growing insistence that the propertyless were entitled to all the same rights as the propertied. As a result, by the middle of the twentieth century the right to property, the only economic right widely recognized in the seventeenth and eighteenth centuries, had been largely supplanted by an extensive set of economic, social, and cultural rights, fully co-equal with civil and political rights.

Our list of civil and political rights has also undergone dramatic changes. Today in the West we take the right to a free press largely for granted, but we must recall that less than two hundred years ago Paine was prosecuted for sedition because of his pamphleteering, and Jefferson as president made use of the notorious restrictions of the Alien and Sedition Acts. It has been scarcely more than a century (and in many countries much less) that the right to freedom of association has been held to extend to associations of workers. Article 11 of the International Covenant on Civil and Political Rights reads "No one shall be imprisoned merely on the ground of inability to fulfill a contractual obligation," outlawing the once familiar institution of debtors' prisons. Recently, "disappearances" have cast a new light on the rights to life and protection against arbitrary arrest and detention.

Lists of human rights emerge out of the political struggle for human dignity and indicate the principal directions of that struggle. This is but one more side of the interaction between moral ideal and political reality that lies at the heart of the practice of human rights. In the contemporary world, the rights enumerated in the International Bill of Human Rights represent a widely accepted consensus on the minimum necessary prerequisites for a life of dignity.

2

The Interdependence and Indivisibility of Human Rights

How are the human rights listed in authoritative international documents, such as the Universal Declaration and the Covenants, related to one another? Today it is commonly claimed that all human rights are "interdependent and indivisible," as it is regularly put in U.N. resolutions.[1] While I contend that this understanding is fundamentally correct, our standard categorizations suggest otherwise.

1. The Civil-Political, Economic-Social Dichotomy

In international discussions it has become almost a reflex to talk about "civil and political rights" and "economic, social, and cultural rights." Although I too occasionally use these categories in this book, the dichotomy is seriously misleading.

A. Evolution of the Dichotomy
A dichotomous division of any complex reality is inherently crude. It is also likely to suggest, or at least is easily misread to suggest, that the two categories are antithetical. This is especially true in the case of human rights, because the dichotomy itself was born of political controversy.

Human rights entered the mainstream of philosophical and political discussion in the seventeenth and eighteenth centuries under the terms "natural rights" and "the rights of man" (*droits de l'homme*), and they entered as a challenge to the reigning principles of political legitimacy: if

1. A long string of resolutions proclaims this, most notably U.N. General Assembly resolution 32/130, as well as an agenda item at the 41st General Assembly, "Indivisibility and Interdependence of Economic, Social, Cultural, Civil, and Political Rights."

all individuals (or at least all adult white males) had equal and inalienable natural rights, then virtually all seventeenth- and eighteenth-century governments stood condemned as radically unjust and illegitimate. The early proponents of natural rights occupied a relatively narrow place on the left of the political spectrum, and the issue of controversy was whether there were any natural rights at all. Therefore, discussions of categories of human rights were largely irrelevant. There certainly were differences between the lists of, say, Locke, Jefferson, and the French Declaration of the Rights of Man and the Citizen, but no major theorist (and to my knowledge no minor theorist either) paid serious attention to categorizing human rights. That came only with new political circumstances.

Crudely oversimplifying, the original and largely bourgeois proponents of natural rights gradually moved out of political opposition and into control. As a result, natural rights claims came increasingly from the political center and even the right, and arguments based on natural rights, especially the right to property, came to be used to impede further change, not as an instrument for political change. By the early decades of the nineteenth century, the language of natural rights was largely restricted to bourgeois political opposition movements, bourgeois ruling parties and classes, and liberal reformers (e.g., advocates of an extended franchise in Britain) who sought to spread the enjoyment of "bourgeois" natural (civil and political) rights to the masses. The radical left largely abandoned the language of human rights.[2]

Nonetheless, with the expansion of the franchise and the continued development of working-class politics, demands for economic and social justice were gradually incorporated into the political mainstream, especially in Europe. Furthermore, these demands came to be seen as demands for workers' *rights*. By the late nineteenth and early twentieth centuries, the struggle between capital and labor in the Western democracies was more and more seen as a struggle between the rights of property and the rights of the common man, especially the worker. This struggle in turn came to be represented as a struggle between civil and political rights and economic and social rights.

How did the defense of the right to unlimited accumulation of private property, a particularly extravagant economic right, come to be trans-

2. In particular, almost all socialists, from the early utopians through the Marxist International and the Bolsheviks, either ignored natural rights or dismissed them as bourgeois ideology. Marx himself occasionally recognized both tactical and fundamental value for bourgeois natural rights, but this was very much a minor strand in his thought—as it were, the exception that proves the rule. For a brief discussion of Marx's views on human rights, see Donnelly 1985a: 73–77.

formed into a defense of civil and political rights? Politics provides the only explanation for this bizarre situation. In a world of feudal and mercantilist economic constraints and the political dominance of a traditional aristocracy of birth, universal natural rights were a powerful weapon of the rising bourgeoisie. Initially, arguments based on natural liberty were used to free the process of capital accumulation from traditional restraints and to justify social and political mobility, but once bourgeois political power was established, arguments of natural liberty came to be used principally to prevent the rise, and even the protection, of lower classes—for example, U.S. courts used the right to freedom of contract to attack unions and strike down labor laws. The right to property was presented by its advocates as both a precondition for the enjoyment of the right to natural liberty and the most important consequence of the exercise of that natural liberty—"the" basic right, as it were. From this it was but a short step—politically, if not philosophically—to presenting the (economic) right to property as the paramount civil and political right.

Given such a partisan understanding of civil and political rights, it is not surprising that the economic and social rights championed by the left came to be seen by *both* sides as essentially antagonistic. But unlike 1688 or 1789, or even 1848, large portions of the political center and right no longer denied the idea of human rights, or at least no longer denied such political analogues as constitutional rights. Instead of attacking the idea of human rights, they attacked only one category or set of these rights—namely, economic and social human rights.[3] The left, in turn, often engaged in generalized attacks on civil and political rights, understood in this narrow, propertied reading.

The inherent implausibility of this adversarial dichotomy of human rights, however, has largely laid the issue to rest, except for reasons of partisan politics. If the right to property is seen as a basic human right in itself, conservatives face the insurmountable task of providing a plausible theoretical ground that yields only one, and precisely this one, economic right. If property instead is derived from the right to liberty, the door is opened for numerous other economic and social rights. For example, if property is defended because it provides needed resources and space for the effective exercise of liberty, the right to food serves such a function even more obviously. The conservative defense of the right to property thus either collapses in inconsistency or loses its political purpose (compare Chapter 4, section 1.C).

Political practice too has left the dichotomy behind. In the West the

3. Contemporary versions of such arguments are discussed and dismissed in the following subsection.

welfare state has largely ended controversy over the idea of economic and social rights. Today almost all ''bourgeois'' Western governments are strong defenders of economic and social rights, and in the Third World and the Soviet bloc economic and social rights have long been accepted as at least equal to civil and political rights.

Civil and political rights did have their initial social basis in the bourgeoisie, and the demand for economic and social rights did begin with the working class and socialist intellectuals. But questions of historical genesis must be kept separate from those of theoretical justification. We must not dismiss or disparage civil and political rights because of their bourgeois heritage or partisan abuses by industrial capitalist regimes, any more than the murderous excesses of Stalin, allegedly in the name of economic and social rights, should cause us to reject those rights.

Furthermore, because an idea or practice began in political controversy does not mean that it is forever tied to and restricted within the original boundaries of that controversy, as we can see in the effective use of civil and political rights by European workers and their allies to achieve the political recognition of economic and social rights. In fact, one of the principal reasons for abandoning the conventional dichotomy between civil and political and economic and social rights is to overcome the ideological biases of both the left and the right with which that dichotomy was so long associated and which too often lead to politically dangerous arguments for the priority of one set and the neglect or even suppression of the other.

B. The Status of Economic and Social Rights

A number of philosophers and a great many contemporary conservatives and libertarians have argued that economic and social rights are not really human rights, suggesting that the conventional dichotomy reflects not only the genesis of contemporary human rights norms but also an order of priority between these rights. Maurice Cranston offers the most widely cited version of the philosophical argument against economic and social rights. He argues that traditional civil and political rights to life, liberty, and property are ''universal, paramount, categorical moral rights'' (1964: 40). Economic and social rights,[4] however, are neither universal, practical, nor of paramount importance and ''belong to a different logical category'' (1964: 54)—that is, they are not truly *human* rights.

Cranston notes that many economic and social rights refer directly to a particular class of people, not to all human beings (1973: 67), but many

---

4. Like so many other critics of economic and social rights, Cranston simply ignores the fact that the right to property, which he enthusiastically defends, is an economic right.

civil and political rights also fail such a test of universality. For example, only citizens who have attained a certain age and completed any necessary formalities of registration have the right to vote. These rights—whether civil, political, economic, social, or cultural—are universal in the sense that they refer to anyone who should be in that class, and in the sense that the class is potentially open to all human beings, rather than defined by achievements or ascription.

As for paramountcy, Cranston singles out the right to paid holidays in attempting to eliminate economic and social rights. But is such a right really any less important than, say, the right of juveniles to separate prison facilities, a civil and political right recognized in the Covenants? Furthermore, the full right recognized is a right to "rest, leisure, and reasonable limitation of working hours and periodic holidays with pay." Denial of such a right would be a serious affront to human dignity; it was, for example, one of the most oppressive features of unregulated nineteenth-century capitalism. In any case, periodic holidays with pay is hardly the typical economic and social right. For example, the right to work is arguably as important as most basic civil and political rights; the psychological, physical, and moral effects of prolonged enforced unemployment may be as severe as those associated with denial of, say, freedom of speech. A right to education may be as essential to a life of dignity as freedom of speech or religion. Rights to food and health care may be as essential for protecting life as the civil and political right to life.

Cranston's argument of practicality is more complex. " 'Political rights' can be readily secured by legislation. The economic and social rights can rarely, if ever, be secured by legislation alone" (1964: 37).[5] "There is nothing especially difficult about transforming political and civil rights into positive rights,"[6] whereas realizing many economic and social rights is " 'utterly impossible' in most countries" (1973: 66–67). Because rights impose correlative duties and "ought" implies "can" (i.e., no one has an obligation to attempt what is impossible), Cranston argues that it is logically incoherent to hold that economic and social "rights" are anything more than utopian aspirations (1964: 41; 1973: 68). But the "can" in "ought implies can" refers to physical impossibility; unless it is physically impossible, one may still be obliged to try to do something that proves to be "impossible." The impediments to implementing most economic and social rights, however, are political rather than physical. For example,

5. No right, whether civil, political, economic, social, or cultural, can be realized through legislation *alone*. Unless legislation is backed by enforcement, no right is secure.

6. One is left to wonder how Cranston would avoid difficulties in establishing an effective positive right to, say, freedom of speech, press, and assembly in such countries as Bulgaria, Chile, South Africa, and Vietnam.

there is more than enough food in the world to feed everyone; widespread hunger and malnutrition exist not because of a physical shortage of food but because of political decisions about its distribution.

This leaves Cranston with little more than an argument that civil and political rights are relatively easy to implement. Bedau advances a similar "argument from indifference to economic contingencies" (1979: 36–37), but even granting the factual accuracy of these empirically dubious claims, it is not clear why ease or expense of implementation should have any conceptual or moral significance.

Underlying such arguments is the distinction between "negative" rights that require only forbearance on the part of others, and "positive" rights that require others to provide goods or services if they are to be implemented. Henry Shue, however, has shown that this distinction fails to correspond to the distinction between civil and political and economic and social rights and is in any case of little or no moral significance.[7]

The right to protection against torture is usually advanced as the archetypal negative right: it requires "nothing more" than that the state refrain from incursions on personal liberty and bodily integrity. But assuring that such incursions do not occur (i.e., *guaranteeing* this negative right as a practical political matter) will in almost all cases require major "positive" programs involving the training, supervision, and control of the police and security forces. In many countries this would be not only extremely expensive but politically impossible without changing the regime. In all circumstances, protecting people against torture requires significant positive endeavors by the state. Conversely, the very positive-sounding right to food in many circumstances can be realized simply by government restraint. Shue uses the example of government development programs that have encouraged producing cash crops for export rather than traditional food crops for local consumption (1980: 41–45). In such cases, the right to food would have been better realized if the government had done "nothing more" than refrain from interfering with agricultural incentives.

All human rights require *both* positive action and restraint on the part of the state. Furthermore, whether a right is *relatively* positive or negative usually depends on historically contingent circumstances. For example, the right to food is a fairly negative right in the wheatfields of Kansas but rather positive in Watts or East Los Angeles. The right to protection against torture is largely negative in Stockholm but somewhat more positive in the South Bronx; in Argentina it was very positive indeed in the late 1970s, but today it is much closer to a negative right.

---

7. The argument in this section has been strongly influenced by the work of Henry Shue (1979, 1980).

But even if civil and political rights were entirely negative, Shue shows that they would not therefore deserve priority. Here the key conceptual issue is the distinction between acts of omission and acts of commission. The thrust of the arguments of Cranston (1964: 38) and Bedau (1979: 38) is that "negative" civil and political rights deserve priority because their violation involves the direct infliction of injury, whereas the violation of "positive" economic and social rights usually involves only the failure to confer a benefit. Even accepting this (false) description of the rights, Shue shows that there is no significant moral difference. Imagine a man stranded on an out-of-the-way desert island with neither food nor water. A sailor from a passing ship comes ashore but leaves the man to die. This act of omission is as serious a violation of human rights as strangling him, an act of commission. It is killing him, plain and simple—indirectly through "inaction" but just as surely and perhaps even more cruelly (Shue 1979: 72–75). The moral difference lies not in the essential character of the acts per se but in contingent, empirical circumstances. Killing is killing whether it is achieved by directly inflicting injury or by failing to provide a benefit.

The categorical moral arguments against economic and social rights simply do not stand up to scrutiny. And with the rejection of such arguments, the conventional dichotomy also falls, for I am aware of no other positive arguments for it. There is no reason to view human rights as falling into these two categories—especially because the conventional dichotomy actually obscures our understanding of the range and diversity of human rights.

C. Transcending the Dichotomy

Consider the great variety of rights grouped into the conventional category of civil and political rights. A more useful and informative categorization would recognize at least four principal groups: personal rights, legal rights, civil rights, and political rights.

Personal rights provide minimal guarantees of individual bodily and moral integrity. The rights to life, protections against discrimination, prohibition of slavery, recognition before the law, protection against torture, and nationality (Universal Declaration of Human Rights, Articles 1, 2, 4, 5, 6, 15) fall into this category.

Legal rights provide procedural protections for individuals in their dealings with the legal and political system, especially the criminal law. The Universal Declaration (Articles 9–11) recognizes rights to habeas corpus, protection against arbitrary arrest and detention, as well as the presumption of innocence, and it prohibits ex post facto laws. These rights reflect the fact that the legal system is one of the principal mechanisms by which repressive states abuse human dignity.

Civil liberties protect selected areas of activity from interference by the state, combining "negative" restraints on the state with the idea that a life of dignity requires "positive" intellectual and associational freedoms to engage in public discourse and activity. Civil liberties define both a private sphere of conscience and belief and a public space in which these "private" issues, as well as public concerns, can be freely explored. In this category, the Universal Declaration (Articles 18–20) recognizes rights to freedom of thought, conscience, speech, press, association, and assembly.

Political rights empower citizens to participate in and ultimately control the state. The right to popular participation in government (Universal Declaration, Article 21), plus many public aspects of civil liberties, such as the freedoms of speech, press, and assembly, fall into this category.

Obviously, there are problems in sorting some rights. For example, I have classed protection against torture as a personal right, but it might also be treated as a legal right. More interesting is the dual (i.e., political) nature of many civil liberties. But breaking down the category "civil and political rights" alerts us to this important fact, which is actively obscured by the conventional dichotomy. And whatever the details, this or some other relatively fine categorization makes manifest the diversity of the human rights that ordinarily are lumped together. This is perhaps a minor, largely negative achievement, but it is nonetheless a conceptual advance.

"Economic, social, and cultural rights" are no less varied. Although the three basic categories seem serviceable, I suggest that a fourfold division here too would be more informative:

Subsistence rights guarantee the bare minimum resources for survival, principally the right to food and access to health care (Universal Declaration, Article 25).

Economic rights recognized in the Universal Declaration (Articles 22–24) include the rights to social security, to work, to rest and leisure, and to form trade unions. These rights reflect not only the material necessity of labor (or at least the products of labor) but also the fact that meaningful work is in itself highly satisfying and no less important to personal dignity and development than, say, civil liberties. For example, to be able to speak one's mind freely but not be able to work, and thus to be materially dependent on the state, is no less an intolerable affront than to be employed but unable to express one's true feelings and beliefs.

Social rights include the right to education, and certain elements of the right to found and maintain a family (Universal Declaration, Articles 12, 16, 26).

Cultural rights include principally the right to participate in the cultural life of the community (Universal Declaration, Article 27). One might also argue for classifying the right to education as a cultural right. The dividing line between the social and the cultural—as well as that between the economic and the social—is not especially clear, but the conventional division is perhaps useful and certainly not seriously misleading.

There are important affinities between rights that cross the conventional dichotomy. For example, I have already noted affinities between the right to work and many civil liberties. The right to work, however, is perhaps most closely related to political rights; it is a right to *economic* participation that is instrumentally and intrinsically valuable in ways very much like the right to political participation. Cultural rights are perhaps most closely related to individual civil liberties, given the integral place of religion, public speech and the mass media in the cultural life of most communities. The "social" or "cultural" right to education is intimately connected with the "civil" or "political" rights to freedom of speech, belief, and opinion. And so forth.

If forced to regroup these categories into some more coherent structure, I would suggest a fivefold division that completely confounds the conventional dichotomy: (1) subsistence and personal rights, which provide minimum personal protections but alone fall far short of protecting human dignity; (2) legal rights, which protect the individual in dealings with the state; (3) civil, social, and cultural rights, which ensure active membership in society; (4) economic rights, which give one power over the nature and circumstances of one's labor; and (5) political rights, which empower one to act to influence the fundamental rules and structures of society.

I do not, however, want to rest anything on this or any other particular categorization.[8] The point is that abandoning the conventional dichotomy can give us a clearer picture of the nature and range of human rights and allow us to see much more clearly their manifold interrelationships. Dispensing with the dichotomy, our categories are no longer at odds with the essential theoretical insight of the interdependence and indivisibility of all human rights.

Similarities and linkages across the categories of the standard dichotomy arise because our lives do not fall into largely autonomous political and socioeconomic spheres. Economic and social rights usually are violated by or with the collusion of elite-controlled political mechanisms of exclu-

---

8. I have tried to underscore this point by presenting both an eightfold and a fivefold categorization in this chapter, as well as an implicit fourfold categorization in Chapter 1, section 5.B—namely, survival rights, which guarantee minimum conditions of existence; membership rights, which assure full and equal membership in society; legal or protection rights, which insulate individuals from the power of the state and guarantee due process of law; and empowerment rights, which allow individuals and groups to act to shape the rules and structures of social life.

sion and domination. Poverty in the midst of plenty is a political phenomenon as much as it is an economic one, and civil and political rights are often violated to protect economic privilege. We must think about, and categorize, human rights in ways that highlight rather than obscure this social reality.

In particular, we must overcome the dangerous illusion shared by conservative critics of economic and social rights, radical critics of civil and political rights, and authoritarian regimes of various types that the state is or can become a neutral instrument of technocratic management and an impartial arbiter of politically neutral rules of social order. Political power cannot be neatly separated from economic power, and rarely is it exercised neutrally; those who wield political power do not rise above their personal, group, party, or class interests, merely because of their political position, nor do they exercise their power uninfluenced by such affiliations. Politics cannot be neatly insulated from the rest of social life. Therefore, to segregate civil and political rights from economic, social, and cultural rights is to distort reality. And where ruling elites are able to enforce such a dichotomization of human rights, the consequence is usually the systematic violation of the full range of human rights.

How one thinks about human rights does not and cannot determine political practice, but certain ways of thinking, such as the traditional dichotomy, can help to support widely prevalent patterns of human rights violations. No less important, well-conceived theory, even at the very basic level of classificatory schemes, can aid in the struggle for greater respect for human rights.

One might argue that my typology, or *any* such categorization, does not go far enough because it rests on no firm theoretical ground. Nonetheless, it—or any similar categorization that others find useful (the details are not the essential point)—is a step in the right direction. We need categories that are fine enough to capture the complexity of human rights, precise enough to reveal important practical relationships, and open enough to be compatible with a wide range of possible theories. Transcending the conventional dichotomy may help to free us from the weight of past political controversies, open our eyes to long-ignored theoretical issues, and begin to shift our attention to the central question of the mechanisms and social processes by which human rights are respected, protected, and violated.

2. BASIC RIGHTS

A very different scheme of classification has become prominent in the last decade, based on an effort to extract a short core of "basic" rights from the lengthy list in the Universal Declaration and the Covenants. Several such lists are summarized in Table 1.

A. Are There Any Basic Rights?

Henry Shue offers the most sophisticated and widely adopted[9] account of basic rights. Building on Rawls's notion of "primary goods" (1971: 92), Shue argues that a right is basic if its enjoyment "is essential to the enjoyment of all other rights" (1980: 19). The first half of Shue's very important book, *Basic Rights*, argues that there are at least three such rights: security, subsistence, and liberty.

Such "basic" rights, Shue argues, are not necessarily more valuable or more satisfying than other rights (1980: 20). Furthermore, Shue carefully and explicitly notes that his list is not necessarily complete (1980: 65). So long as we keep these two qualifications in mind, there is probably no reason to reject the notion. In fact, Shue puts the idea of basic rights to good and quite practical use by showing that subsistence is no less basic a right than security or liberty and that therefore the tendency in U.S. human rights policy to disparage subsistence, economic, social, and cultural rights is without theoretical basis. It is essential, however, to emphasize the limited and highly qualified nature of Shue's argument. He argues only that if any rights at all are basic, these three are, and that therefore they cannot be justifiably excluded as priority items in U.S. international human rights policy.

But if Shue (1980: 60–78, 92–93, 178 n. 13) is correct in his argument that all basic rights are mutually interdependent, so that failure to have even a single basic right means that no rights at all can be enjoyed, then any policy based on an incomplete list of basic rights is certain to fail. Coming up with a complete list, however, is an extraordinarily difficult theoretical problem that even Shue does not attempt to tackle. Or perhaps the problem really is trivial, for I would suggest that there probably are no basic rights at all in the sense in which Shue defines the term. Consider Shue's own list.

If one cannot *obtain* one's subsistence, one will die and thus be unable to enjoy any rights at all. But one can subsist without a *right* to subsistence. For example, mid-nineteenth-century workers enjoyed no such right: if they were starving they could not advance effective or even widely acknowledged subsistence rights claims against the state. Nonetheless, many of them subsisted and exercised a variety of (legal) rights. Without subsistence rights, subsistence may indeed be less secure. Should it be threatened or denied, one lacks arguments of entitlement to back one's struggle to

---

9. For example, Matthews and Pratt (1985) explicitly adopt Shue's definition, which is then picked up from them by Reiter, Zunzunegui, and Quiroga (1986: 640). See also Bedau 1979: 39, where a similar but apparently independent argument is developed.

Table 1. Selected lists of "basic" rights

Ajami 1978:

  Survival
  Protection against torture
  Protection against apartheid
  Food

Bedau 1979:

  Life
  Liberty
  Property
  Security
  Freedoms of speech, press, and assembly
  Protection against arbitrary arrest and detention

International Covenant on Civil and Political Rights, nonderogable rights:

  Life
  Protection against torture
  Protection against slavery
  Protection against ex post facto laws
  Protection against imprisonment for nonpayment of debts
  Recognition before the law
  Freedom of thought and religion

Matthews and Pratt 1985:

  Subsistence
  Protection against torture
  Protection against arbitrary arrest and detention
  Protection against extrajudicial execution

Reiter, Zunzenegui, and Quiroga 1986:

  Life
  Protection against disappearance
  Protection against torture
  Protection against arbitrary arrest and detention

Shue 1980:

  Security
  Subsistence
  Liberty

survive. That is why having a *right* to subsistence is so important. But literally millions of people have enjoyed (other) rights, do enjoy (other) rights, and will continue to enjoy (other) rights without enjoying a right to subsistence.

Much the same is true of the right to political liberty. Within this right Shue includes effective political participation ("genuine influence upon the fundamental choices among institutions and policies controlling security and subsistence'' [1980: 75]) and freedom of movement. But the typical Soviet citizen does not enjoy either of these rights and yet does enjoy a variety of economic, social, and legal rights, and although women in many traditional African societies lacked rights to political participation, they enjoyed rights to the use of land that generally secured their subsistence rights.

Some *goods* are prerequisites to the enjoyment of any other good or right, and subsistence and security are certainly among such goods, but there simply are no *rights* that must be enjoyed if other rights are to be enjoyed. One may enjoy basic (and other) goods without having a right to these goods.[10]

The rights Shue identifies may be ''basic'' in the narrower sense that if they are actively violated (that is, if enjoyment of the object or substance of the right is actively prevented or denied) no other rights can be enjoyed.[11] But whether a right is violated or respected is largely a matter contingent on history and politics. Therefore, it is difficult to see how such a notion of basic rights provides any theoretical guidance.

Perhaps, then, we need to redefine ''basic rights.'' Just about any other definition, however, is likely to violate Shue's second qualification—that basic rights are not necessarily more satisfying or more valuable than any other rights. Unless we define basic rights in functional terms, as Shue himself does, we are almost certain to make implicit or even explicit arguments that ''basic rights'' are more important than other rights. By distinguishing a core group of ''basic'' rights that are alleged to be more important than other rights, one almost unavoidably devalues the remaining human rights. For example, Narveson defines basic human rights as ''those which everybody may be required to observe with respect to everybody'' (1981: 196). This means either that all human rights are basic human rights—in which case ''basic'' is redundant—or that other (nonbasic) human rights need not be universally respected, which seems to do little more than open the door for repression.[12]

---

10. For a more detailed discussion of the difference between enjoying a good or benefit and having a right, see Donnelly 1985a: 11–12, 47–51. I am perplexed, however, that Shue explicitly recognizes a similar distinction between having a right and enjoying the *substance* of that right (1980: 15–16) but seems not to recognize its implications for his account of basic rights.

11. But even this does not seem to be the case for the right to liberty. For example, it is quite possible for slaves to have their liberty completely denied and yet still enjoy subsistence in some security.

12. Consider, for example, the claim made by the Polish foreign minister Stefan Olszowski, speaking to the U.N. General Assembly in justification of the declaration of martial law and the suppression of Solidarity: ''For the price of the provisional application of the extraordinary measures Poland avoided a civil war. We ourselves know how high a price it is

Consider some of the other lists from Table 1. Among those that do not cross the conventional dichotomy, Bedau (1979) restricts his list to set of personal rights and civil liberties. Reiter, Zunzunegui, and Quiroga (1986: 628, 651) restrict their list even further to protections against "killing, disappearances, physical and psychological torture, arbitrary arrest and exile," the purpose of which is to "protect the individual from physical and psychological torture." Among lists that do cut across the conventional dichotomy, Ajami argues for giving priority to "a certain 'core of rights,' a set of global common denominators": the rights to survive, to protection against torture, to protection against apartheid, and to food (1978: 28). In much the same fashion, Matthews and Pratt argue for a short list of basic rights to freedom from detention without trial, to freedom from torture, to freedom from extrajudicial execution, and to subsistence (1985: 160).[13]

These lists share a common and fatal problem. They could all be fully enjoyed, and still people could be left living anomic, degraded lives, unable to speak their minds, to choose their religion, to become involved in politics, to have a reasonable chance of finding a job, to get an education, to associate with whom they choose, and so forth. In other words, implementing such "basic rights" will not necessarily assure that life is anything more than "solitary, poor, nasty, brutish and short." Without other human rights, "basic human rights" are inadequate to protect human dignity in any plausible sense of that term. Human dignity, the realization of which is the aim of human rights, cannot be reduced to dimensions that can be encompassed by a short or narrow list of "basic" human rights. *All* human rights are "basic rights" in the fundamental sense that systematic violations of *any* human right preclude realizing a life of full human dignity— that is, prevent one from enjoying the minimum conditions necessary for a life worthy of a human being.

B. Basic Rights and International Action

How, then, can we explain the popularity of the idea of basic human rights? It is more than a coincidence that most uses have a direct foreign

---

but it is not the highest price, a mass scale loss of the basic human right—the right to live" (quoted in Miller 1988).

13. Compare also Nardin's suggestion that priority be given to rights "such as the right not to be tortured or enslaved, or subjected to arbitrary arrest, detention, or exile," above such rights as the right to vote and virtually all social and economic rights, which he considers to be "less fundamental" and "subordinate" because they make reference to particular forms of communities (Nardin 1983: 276–77). We can accept such a criterion of "basicness," however, only if we assume that all types of communities are fully capable of protecting human rights. This simply is not so (see Chapter 4). Human rights not only do, but must, exclude certain forms of community. And this is precisely what a right such as protection against slavery does.

policy application: the idea of basic rights offers a relatively narrow and manageable focus for international action on behalf of human rights.

This foreign policy emphasis is typically linked with ideas of the importance of international consensus. For example, Ajami suggests that his list of four core rights (survival, torture, apartheid, food) is "close to . . . the maximum feasible consensus at this time" (1978: 29). Matthews and Pratt likewise argue that beyond being basic in Shue's sense, their four rights (subsistence, arrest, torture, execution) "are basic in the . . . sense that they are now receiving near-universal acknowledgement" (1985: 160). But these two claims involve very different notions of international consensus.

Ajami has in mind what we can call de facto or practical consensus: virtually all governments typically refrain from violating these rights, but only these rights. Even granting that this is true, I suggest that little but disappointment at the extent of contemporary human rights violations follows. The sad fact is that in the contemporary world virtually all internationally recognized human rights are regularly and systematically violated.

Ajami, however, seems to believe that this practical international consensus implies that we ought to focus international efforts on these rights. Doing so may avoid arguments of unjustified intervention. But such a focus allows the forces of repression to define which rights should be our principal priority. It also implies that we should emphasize only rights that are *not* widely and systematically violated and that are *not* principal contemporary mechanisms of repression. This is completely unacceptable. Consensus is an important consideration in international politics, but practical or de facto consensus is too narrow a notion of consensus.

In the broad list of human rights in the Universal Declaration and the Covenants, there is a very different sort of consensus, reflecting what in the Introduction I called the international normative universality of human rights. We can call this de jure or theoretical consensus. Virtually all states have committed themselves, in word, to guarantee the rights recognized in these documents. This consensus is often very shallow—*merely* verbal, "theoretical" in a pejorative sense of that term. But states that have (theoretically) committed themselves to these rights certainly cannot legitimately complain when their own citizens, other states, or international governmental or nongovernmental organizations take them to task for failing to live up to these commitments. Such theoretical consensus thus may have real practical utility.[14]

14. The International Covenant on Civil and Political Rights distinguishes between rights with respect to which derogation in time of emergency is and is not permitted. The list of

Matthews and Pratt's list of rights must rest on such a notion of theoretical consensus,[15] for there is no de facto or practical international consensus on the right to freedom from detention without trial: preventive detention orders are regularly used by numerous repressive regimes, and even the United States, which has a generally good record on legal rights, has begun to experiment with preventive detention. But once we place freedom from detention without trial on our list of basic rights, it is difficult to exclude most of the rest of the rights in the Covenants. In any case, a short list of such basic rights would have to rest on an argument for the priority of the selected rights for which there is neither practical nor theoretical consensus.[16]

Nonetheless, the lengthy list of rights on which there is theoretical consensus—there are some thirty substantive articles in the two Covenants, encompassing perhaps twice as many separate human rights—probably is too extensive to provide adequate focus and direction for a country's international human rights policy. For the purposes of foreign policy, we may have to set ourselves relatively limited tasks and reserve what little influence we have for the "most important" human rights violations. Whatever the theoretical problems with current notions of basic rights, foreign policy may require something very much like a list of basic rights.

Deriving and defending such a list, however, itself requires the kind of comprehensive normative and empirical theory of human rights that, be-

---

nonderogable rights, specified in Article 4(2), might be advanced as a set of basic rights that rests on a consensus that is somewhat practical and somewhat theoretical. As a set of basic rights, however, it will work no better than any other, both because it excludes all economic and social rights and because even within the category of civil and political rights it results in an excessively narrow list (excluding, for example, rights to freedom of speech, press, religion, assembly, and association and the right to political participation).

15. They also rely heavily on a notion of practical consensus, which I believe is what leads them to draw the line at just four rights. To the extent that they do, however, they are vulnerable to the arguments made above against Ajami's list.

16. For example, Milne offers a list of seven "human rights properly so-called," or what we can call basic rights (1986: 124–39). These are rights to life, justice (fair treatment), aid, honorable treatment, civility, care (for children), and freedom from arbitrary interference. Whatever we may think of this list, any state that tries to base its policy on it is likely to be accused, with some justice, of imposing a list of rights to which no one else has agreed to be bound. Much the same problem faces Domínguez's (1979) effort to use the Lasswell-Kaplan schema of eight core human values (power, respect, rectitude, wealth, well-being, enlightenment, skill, and affection) or any other set of standards. Given that the list of rights in the Universal Declaration is a good one (both Milne's and Domínguez's list are in broad agreement with it), there is no reason to take on the considerable additional burden of justifying an alternative framework or to risk having that framework rejected because of relatively minor differences in the way in which it is presented.

cause of the immensity of the task, no one has seriously tried to provide. Yet without theoretical guidance, we may select our priority rights on dubious grounds. For example, the American emphasis on personal rights, civil liberties, and free elections probably can be best explained by the fact that the record in the United States with regard to those rights is generally good, while that of the Soviet Union and its allies is generally poor. The Soviet emphasis on the right to work and on other economic rights probably has a similar explanation.

Or consider the emphasis on freeing prisoners of conscience. This is an attractive policy priority because the personal dimension is appealing and its successes are clear, concrete, and easy to point to. But while freeing a small number of prisoners and halting or preventing the abuse of some others is an important and worthwhile policy objective, is it really the most that we can hope for? Is it even a reasonable item for high priority? I remain unconvinced that this is the best way to use scarce foreign policy resources, however much sense such a strategy may make for a nongovernmental organization like Amnesty International.

Without sound theoretical guidance, priority rights may be chosen on the basis of convenience and public relations as much as anything else. And unless we have sound theoretical guidance on how to realize particular rights and on how various human rights interact with one another, even a good list of priority rights is unlikely to lead to an effective policy. Therefore, even for the purposes of foreign policy, a sound empirical and normative theory of human rights is required. If we are to avoid distortion in our foreign policy, the list of priority rights must be narrowed without leaving out any major categories. It must also be narrowed in such a way that none of the principal mechanisms by which repressive regimes maintain themselves is ignored and with an eye to highlighting those human rights that in practice have proved most useful in the struggle against repressive regimes.

Our inability to defend any particular list of human rights except by indirect arguments (see Chapter 1, sections 5.A and 5.B), and the inadequate state of our empirical social scientific theories of the genesis and maintenance of rights-protective and rights-abusive regimes, leaves us at an impass.[17] We can sketch in very general terms what an adequate normative and empirical theory of human rights would look like, but we

17. Shue's list seems to be the best of those we have considered—it is short, *relatively* uncontroversial, and fairly wide-ranging—but I am not sure I could present much of a defense for this preference.

cannot produce such a theory. Nevertheless, we must continue to strive for greater theoretical rigor. At the very least, we must do our best to assure that our categories, typologies, and theories do not interfere with our understanding of the problems of human rights, for theoretical misunderstandings can easily lead to practical problems as well.

PART II

Human Rights, Liberalism, and the West

3

Non-Western Conceptions
of Human Rights

I have stressed, and will continue to stress, the universality of human rights. But we must be careful not to stretch the notion of universality too far. In fact, the principal purpose of the chapters in Part II is to demonstrate the historical particularity of the idea and practice of human rights—a particularity that is, however, fully compatible with both the moral and international universality of human rights.

The argument that "human rights are not a western discovery" (Manglapus 1978) is a common feature of contemporary discussions of human rights in non-Western settings. For example, Adamantia Pollis and Peter Schwab argue that "all societies have human rights notions," that "all societies cross-culturally and historically manifest conceptions of human rights" (1980: xiv, 15). Yogindra Khushalani goes so far as to argue that "the concept of human rights can be traced to the origin of the human race itself" and that "all the philosophies of our time" are committed to human rights (1983: 404). Such arguments, however, confuse human rights and human dignity, which many authors mistakenly treat as equivalent concepts (see, e.g., Pollis and Schwab 1980: 4, 8; Legesse 1980: 132; Harkin 1979: 15; Said 1978), and suggest a historical, cross-cultural universality of human rights that does not exist.

There are indeed close theoretical connections between the two concepts, but there are numerous conceptions of human dignity that do not imply human rights, as well as societies and institutions that aim to realize human dignity entirely independent of the idea or practice of human rights. Human rights are the rights one has simply because one is a human being (a person). As the Covenants put it, human rights "derive from the inherent dignity of the human person." The human rights approach is based on an understanding of human dignity that sees each person as an equal and valuable human being endowed with certain inalienable *rights* (in the strict sense of titles and claims) that may be claimed even against society as a whole.[1] Alternative conceptions of human dignity amount to challenges to the idea of human rights.

Human rights represent a distinctive set of social practices, tied to particular notions of human dignity, that initially arose in the modern West in response to the social and political changes produced by modern states and modern capitalist market economies. Most non-Western cultural and political traditions, like the premodern West, lacked not only the practice of human rights but also the very concept. As we look briefly at the ways in which several traditional cultures and one modern non-Western society have approached issues that we consider in terms of human rights, it will become apparent that these concerns have been handled almost entirely in terms of *duties* that are neither derivative from nor correlative to human rights. These societies recognize that certain social guarantees are essential to realizing human dignity, and they have elaborate systems of human duties designed to protect human dignity. But human rights are quite foreign to their approaches.

Nevertheless, although they are Western in origin and thus historically particular, I shall argue that human rights are of near universal contemporary relevance. Contemporary social conditions have given the idea and practice of human rights wide applicability.

1. "Human Rights" in Islam

"In almost all contemporary Arab literature on this subject [human rights], we find a listing of the basic rights established by modern conventions and declarations, and then a serious attempt to trace them back to Koranic texts" (Zakaria 1986: 228). The standard argument in this now extensive literature is that "Islam has laid down some universal fundamental rights for humanity as a whole, which are to be observed and respected

---

1. Recall the principal elements of the conceptual analysis presented in Chapter 1. Human rights are *rights*—not benefits, duties, privileges, or some other practice. And they are the special entitlements of *all persons*, simply because they are human. Having a right places a person in a specially protected position. Rights have prima facie priority over other action-justifying principles, such as utility. *Human* rights claims have prima facie priority even over the interests and rights of society and the state. Furthermore, human rights are conceived as naturally inhering in the human person; they are what Hart (1955) calls general rights, rights that arise from no special undertaking beyond membership in the human race. To have human rights one does not have to be anything other than a human being, and one need not do anything other than be born a human being.

under all circumstances . . . fundamental rights for every man by virtue of his status as a human being'' (Mawdudi 1976: 10). ''The basic concepts and principles of human rights [have] from the very beginning been embodied in Islamic law.''[2] Many authors, even argue that contemporary human rights doctrines merely replicate 1,400-year-old Islamic ideas (see Nadvi 1966: 14–15; Tabendeh 1970: 1, 8). But these claims prove to be almost entirely without basis.

Khalid M. Ishaque argues that ''Muslims are enjoined constantly to seek ways and means to assure to each other what in modern parlance we call 'human rights' '' (1974: 32). While he admits that ''human rights'' cannot be translated into the language of the Islamic holy works, he nevertheless claims that they lie at the core of Islamic doctrine. Ishaque even lists fourteen ''human rights'' that are recognized and established by Islam. These alleged human rights, however, prove to be only duties of rulers and individuals, not rights held by anyone. The scriptural passages cited as establishing a right to protection of life are in fact divine injunctions not to kill and to consider life as inviolable. The right to justice proves to be instead a duty of rulers to establish justice. The right to freedom is merely a duty not to enslave unjustly. Economic rights turn out to be duties to earn a living and to help provide for the needy. And the purported right to freedom of expression is actually an obligation to speak the truth—that is, the ''right'' is not even an obligation of others, but an obligation of the alleged right-holder. Muslims are regularly and forcefully enjoined to treat their fellow men with respect and dignity, but the bases for these injunctions are divine commands that establish only duties, not human rights.

In a similar fashion, Majid Khadduri lists five rights held by men according to Islam: rights to personal safety, respect of personal reputation, equality, brotherhood, and justice (1946: 77–78; compare Mawdudi 1976: 17–24; Tabandeh 1970). Again, the little evidence that is presented shows that Islam treated these subjects entirely in terms of right in the sense of what is right—that is, duties that are not correlative to rights. Khadduri claims that ''human rights in Islam are the privilege of Allah (God), because authority ultimately belongs to Him'' (1946: 78). This is quite literally incoherent: ''human rights'' that are not rights of human beings but privileges of God. He also claims: ''Human rights in Islam, as prescribed by the divine law, are the privilege only of persons of full legal status. A person with full legal capacity is a living human being of mature age, free, and of Moslem faith'' (1946: 79). This would make ''human rights'' the

2. Mr. Makki, representative of Oman to the Third Committee of the U.N. General Assembly, speech of October 25, 1979, in U.N. document A/C.3/34/SR.27.

privileges of free, male Muslims, not the rights of all human beings simply because they are human. Infidels receive only guarantees of life, property, and freedom of religion; slaves only a right to life; and women enjoy still another set of rights and duties.[3]

Similarly, Said claims that in Islam "human beings have certain God-granted rights" (1980: 92). But he fails to present a single piece of evidence in direct support of this claim, and the discussion he does offer demonstrates once more the absence of the concept of human rights in Islam. Said lists nine basic regulating precepts of an Islamic political system, which he apparently takes to be human rights (1979: 65–68). In every case, however, either there is merely a rights-less duty or the rights that exist are held not simply because one is a human being but because one has a certain legal or spiritual status. In fact, Said, much like Khadduri, implicitly admits this, without seeming to recognize its significance:

> The essential characteristic of human rights in Islam is that they constitute obligations connected with the Divine and derive their force from this connection.
> Human rights exist only in relation to human obligations. Individuals possess certain obligations towards God, fellow humans and nature, all of which are defined by Shariah. When individuals meet these obligations they acquire certain rights and freedoms which are again prescribed by the Shariah. (Said 1979: 63, 73–74)

In Islam, in the realm of human rights (read: human dignity) what matters is duty rather than rights. And whatever rights do exist are a consequence of one's status or actions, not the simple fact that one is a human being.

Islam does teach that "it is the state's duty to enhance human dignity and alleviate conditions that hinder individuals in their efforts to achieve happiness" (Said 1980: 87). One might even argue that "there is no aspect of human need but Islam, in its ethical, social and liturgical precepts, has made provision for it" (Tabandeh 1970: 10). The social and political precepts of Islam do reflect a strong concern for human good and human dignity. Such a concern is important in itself, and even a prerequisite for human rights notions. But it is in no way equivalent to a concern for, or a recognition of, human rights.

3. Tabendeh claims that the preferential treatment of Muslims in certain criminal cases is "quite free of difficulty" from a human rights perspective, because "people who have not put their reliance in conviction and faith, nor had that basic abiding-place nor believed in the one Invisible God, are reckoned as outside the pale of humanity" (1970: 17). Human rights thus are supposed to be based on a conception that sees the majority of the population of the world as "outside of the pale of humanity."

2. "HUMAN RIGHTS" IN TRADITIONAL AFRICA AND CHINA

"The African conception of human rights was an essential aspect of African humanism" (Asante 1969: 74). "It is not often remembered that traditional African societies supported and practiced human rights" (Wai 1980: 116). As in the case of similar claims about Islam, such assertions prove to be not only unsupported but actually undercut by the evidence presented on their behalf.

Dunstan Wai, author of the second passage quoted, continues: "Traditional African attitudes, beliefs, institutions, and experiences sustained the 'view that certain rights should be upheld against alleged necessities of state' " (1980: 116; compare Legesse 1980: 125–27). This statement confuses human rights with limited government. There are many bases on which a government might be limited—divine commandment, human rights, legal rights, and extralegal checks such as a balance of power, to name a few. Simply enjoying a limited government, even having a right to limited government, does not mean that one recognizes or has human rights. "There is no point in belaboring the concern for rights, democratic institutions, and rule of law in traditional African politics" (Wai 1980: 117). To this we can add only that it is particularly pointless in a discussion of human rights, given the form such concerns took. Even in the many cases where Africans had personal rights against their government, those rights were based not on one's humanity per se but on such criteria as age, sex, lineage, or achievement.

Asmarom Legesse argues along similar lines that "many studies . . . suggest that distributive justice, in the economic and political spheres, is the cardinal ethical principle that is shared by most Africans" (1980: 127). This is quite true, but once again irrelevant. Distributive justice and human rights are quite different concepts. One can base a theory of distributive justice on human rights, but one might as easily base it on some other principle. Plato, Burke, and Bentham all had theories of distributive justice, yet no one would ever think to suggest that they advocated human rights. Although giving to each his own—distributive justice—typically will involve respecting the rights of others, unless "one's own" is defined in terms of that to which one is entitled simply as a human being, the rights in question will not be human rights. In African societies, rights typically were assigned on the basis of communal membership, family, status, or achievement.

As with human rights in Islam, we see here an attempt to establish that the differences with the modern West lie only in the words used. "Different societies formulate their conception of human rights in diverse cultural idioms" (Legesse 1980: 124). In fact, though, the difference is not simply one of idiom, but also one of concept and practice. Although many of the same goals were valued, the ways in which they were valued and the practices established to implement those values are quite different. Recognition of human rights simply was not the way of traditional Africa, and this had obvious and important consequences for political practice (compare Howard 1986: chap. 2).

The available literature on China is similar. For example, Chung-Shu Lo, after noting that the Chinese language even lacked a term for rights until one was coined in the late nineteenth century to translate the Western concept, nonetheless insists that the absence of the language of rights "does not mean that the Chinese never claimed rights or enjoyed the basic rights of man" (1949: 186). One wonders how the Chinese managed to claim rights without having the language to make such claims. The assertion that basic human rights were enjoyed seems equally implausible. Did the Chinese have these rights, exercise them, assert them, or *only* "enjoy" them? One suspects that at most it was the latter, in which case Lo's claim collapses into the confusion between enjoying a benefit and having a right. Simply because acts that we would say involved violations of human rights were not permitted does not mean that people were viewed as having human rights.

Lo claims that "the idea of human rights developed very early in China," especially the right to revolt, which "was repeatedly expressed in Chinese history" (1949: 186–87), but the passages he quotes from the classic texts show only that the ruler "has a duty to heaven to take care of the interests of the people." Thus, the only particular human right he advances proves not to be a right at all, for a duty of the ruler to heaven is quite different from a right of the people vis-à-vis the ruler. Likewise Shao-Chuan Leng argues that "Chinese political theory sanctioned the people's revolts against oppressive rulers" (1980: 84), but he too fails to show that this sanction was based on human rights. Instead he simply assumes that democracy, in a very loose sense of the term, can be equated with human rights (1980: 82–85). For example, after outlining the elitist, hierarchical, and station-based character of traditional Chinese social relations and Confucian political and social philosophy, Leng adds, "There were also democratic traits in Chinese civilization," apparently taking this to demonstrate the existence of human rights (1980: 82).

Although elaborate duties were indeed imposed on rulers, obligation, is only one side of a rights-based relationship. Obligation does not in itself even suggest, let alone establish, the existence of rights on the part of those in whose interests one is obliged to act. Traditional Chinese doctrine is expressed almost entirely in terms of the duties of rulers, but Lo refers to this only as a "different approach to the problem of human rights" (1949: 188). In fact, it is actually an alternative approach to the problem of human dignity, an approach that does not involve human rights.[4]

3. RIGHTS AND DUTIES:
THE SOVIET UNION AND "HUMAN RIGHTS"

The conception of "human rights" reflected in official doctrine and practice in the Soviet Union is strikingly similar to the traditional, non-Western conceptions summarized above. Central to the Soviet approach is the fusion of rights and duties. The preamble of the 1977 Soviet constitution states that the Soviet Union "is a society of genuine democracy, whose political system ensures . . . the combination of real citizen's rights and liberties with their duties and responsibilities to society." Article 59 states: "The exercise of rights and liberties is inseparable from the performance by citizens of their duties." We see this same characterization in semi-official accounts. "The linkage of rights and duties [is] the special quality of socialist law" (Sawczuk 1979: 89). "The most important feature of the Soviet citizen's legal status is the organic unity between their rights and their obligations" (Chkhidvadze 1980: 18; compare Wieraszewski 1988: 28).

The correlation of rights and duties is a standard topic in the theory of rights. As ordinarily conceived, A's right to x with respect to B implies duties of B with respect to A's having or enjoying x—i.e., A's right entails B's obligation (compare Donnelly 1982). In Soviet doctrine, however, A's right is correlated with substantively parallel obligations on the part of A. For example, Article 40 of the Soviet constitution states that "USSR citizens have the right to labor . . . including the right to choice of occupation, type of employment and work," but in Article 60 labor is a citizen's duty: "Conscientious labor in one's chosen field of socially useful activity and the observance of labor discipline are the duty of, and a matter of honor for, every able-bodied USSR citizen." Soviet diplomats have been quite open and explicit in noting that "it [is] considered the individ-

---

4. There are striking similarities between traditional Chinese, African, and Islamic values and premodern Western ideas of natural law. For example, Aquinas's discussion of the problem of tyranny is virtually identical with the Chinese theory of the mandate of heaven. For a parallel argument that medieval notions of natural law do not involve a recognition of human rights, see Donnelly 1980. The differences we are concerned with here reflect differences in social structure—traditional versus modern societies—rather than essentially geographical factors (between East and West or North and South), a point underscored by the structural analysis of the next chapter.

ual's duty, as well as his right, to work for the benefit of society'' (U.N. Doc. E/1980/WG.1/SR.14). How, though, can rights and duties be conceptualized as coincident?

It is sometimes suggested, and not only by the Soviets, that this is just the way rights are, that it is part of the conceptual logic of rights:

> Rights and duties are two facets of the same picture. Whoever demands a right to liberty has to respect a similar right in others which circumscribes his right to personal liberty very considerably. If an individual thinks it his right to be fed and clothed and maintained in proper health and if he has a right to work, it is also his duty to work according to his energies and skill and accept the work which the welfare of the community demands from him. (Hakim 1955: 3)

But such duties, which we certainly do recognize, do not arise from the possession of rights—or rather, not from one's own rights. The duty to respect another person's liberty is imposed on me by *his* right to liberty, not by mine, and he may have such a right entirely independent of mine; he may have a right to liberty even if I do not. Likewise, I can have a right to work or a right to health care without having an obligation to work for, or to contribute to, the welfare of the community. It may be an unjust or immoral society that gives me such rights without these duties, but that is another matter altogether.

If the logic of rights does not render rights and duties coincident, the only way I can see to accomplish this is to treat all rights as social grants. If A (society), transfers x (e.g., jobs) to B (citizens), conditional on B accepting certain parallel or reciprocal duties (e.g., work), B's right to x would be simultaneously a duty. As a result of the transaction, the individual would have a right to a job, coupled with a non-rights-based duty to work, and the state would have a rights-based duty to provide jobs and a (contractual?) right to have citizens work in a socially productive field.

Such an analysis is particularly attractive because it reflects basic philosophical and ideological precepts of the Soviet system. The focus is unambiguously social, and the state is given a prominent place, with the individual conceptualized largely in terms of his social capacity. Furthermore, the emphasis is on objective and concrete rights, which the individual enjoys only through state agency, rather than subjective, abstract or formal rights inhering in the individual per se. A full system of such rights would indeed involve the organic unity of rights and duties, and such a system would be full of rights. *Human* rights, however, would be entirely absent, for human rights are not grants, either conditional or unconditional, of state or society, but are inherent to all human beings.

All (''human'') rights in the Soviet Union are contingent on the performance of duties. As we have seen, Article 59 of the Soviet constitution states: "The exercise of rights and liberties is inseparable from the performance by citizens of their duties." Article 50 grants civil rights "in accordance with the people's interests and for the purpose of strengthening and developing the socialist system." Even economic and social rights are treated as contingent and are forfeited when the duties that accompany them are not discharged. For example, despite the apparently unqualified character of the right to work mentioned in Article 40, jobs in their fields are regularly denied dissidents and Jewish activists, in accordance with Soviet law and administrative practice, on the grounds that these individuals have failed to discharge their social duties. As one Soviet commentator tellingly put it, "the significance and worth of each person are determined by the way he exercises his rights and performs his duties" (Egorov 1979: 36).

Any right, of course, has limits, which may be specified by law.[5] But the possession and exercise of human rights are not conditional on accepting either these limits or some parallel duty. A human right is inherent to the individual and independent of merit or the discharge of civic responsibilities. In contrast, the rights of Soviet citizens are contingent grants of the state. Men and women in the Soviet Union hold and enjoy numerous rights, but the rights are not held as "the rights of man." There are major substantive parallels between the rights of Soviet citizens and internationally recognized human rights. Nonetheless, Soviet citizens do not enjoy these rights as human rights, and this has important practical consequences for the way in which these rights work (see Chapter 4).

4. The Individual, Society, and Human Rights

One key difference between the modern (or "Western") and the traditional (or "non-Western") approaches to human dignity is the much greater individualism of the modern/Western/human-rights approach. We shall return to the issue of individualism and human rights in Chapters 5 and 8, but a few brief comments on the difference in emphasis are in order here because this difference is often stressed by non-Western authors. For example, Asmarom Legesse writes:

[A] critical difference between African and western traditions concerns the importance of the human individual. In the liberal democracies of the western

---

5. For example, the right to freedom of speech usually is limited by laws of slander and libel and by the general requirement that rights not be recklessly exercised so as to endanger others (such as by yelling "Fire!" in a crowded theater).

world the ultimate repository of rights is the human person. The individual is held in a virtually sacralized position. There is a perpetual, and in our view obsessive, concern with the dignity of the individual, his worth, personal autonomy and property. . . .

If Africans were the sole authors of the Universal Declaration of Human Rights, they might have ranked the rights of communities above those of individuals, and they might have used a cultural idiom fundamentally different from the language in which the ideas are now formulated. (1980: 124, 129)

Like many others, Legesse argues that ''any system of ideas that claims to be universal must contain critical elements in its fabric that are avowedly of African, Latin American or Asian derivation'' (1980: 123). But the issues at stake demand a substantive, rather than a geographical, argument. We certainly would not accept something as correct or useful simply because it is Western, so we must not make the parallel error of assuming that because something is non-Western that it is valuable, or that because it is distinctively Western it is somehow defective.

Human rights are held by individuals and exercised primarily in relation to society, usually in the person of the state. To accommodate the non-Western approaches we have considered above, we would have to establish an order in which an extensive set of social rights and duties takes priority over individual rights. In such circumstances, human rights will be, at best, largely a formality in practice. Even if one might be said to have or enjoy a ''human right'' in some new and very extended sense of the term, in those instances in which one would be inclined to assert or claim it (i.e., where the right is threatened, challenged, violated, or frustrated), the ''right'' would be largely useless because it would be easily overridden by the rights of society or associated individual duties. One would be able to enjoy the ''right'' only at the discretion of the state, but the state would not violate one's rights by denying that enjoyment.

This looks more like being granted a benefit than having a right. Having such a ''human right'' certainly would be very different from what we have heretofore understood by having a human right. In fact, the recommended syncretic approach seems to lead easily to the destruction of the very notion of human rights. To incorporate such non-Western understandings and practices with respect to ''human rights'' would come dangerously close to destroying or denying human rights as they have been understood, and certainly there would be major costs for human rights as those are or-dinarily understood. Such costs may or may not be justified. A society that regularly balanced individual human rights against the rights of society may or may not be preferable to a society that gives prima facie priority to individual human rights. But the issue must be addressed in substantive terms; it is not enough simply to demonstrate anthropological and historical differences.

This is especially true because such writers as Legesse appear to base their proposals on a wistful social vision of limited applicability to contemporary circumstances and aspirations. The social model they seem to have in mind is the small community based on groupings of extended families, the type of community so characteristic of traditional societies, both Western and non-Western. In particular, a relatively decentralized, nonbureaucratic, communitarian society seems to be the ideal (compare Howard 1986: chap. 2).

In such a society, the individual lacks many if not most of the rights that are so highly valued in the liberal democratic state. One does, however, have a place in society and a range of personal and social relationships that provide material and nonmaterial support. One also has available regularized social protections of many of the values and interests that in the West are protected through individual human and legal rights. It might even be argued that introducing individual human rights into such a society would actually diminish the prospects for achieving a dignified life. Such a society certainly is morally defensible, in many ways quite attractive, and can be said to protect basic human dignity.

One might even argue that in conditions of extreme scarcity *only* such a society is defensible (see, e.g., Keenan 1980: 90ff.). If extremely limited resources or environmental severity make survival precarious, the individual, in the absence of the close-knit community whose interests take priority, would be doomed to death, if only through accident or disease. Certainly our anthropological evidence suggests that such a communitarian solution appears to be "natural" to most peoples. But if we remove the pressures of necessity, and even more important, if we remove the social support and protection provided to the individual by the traditional community, things appear in a different light. It would then be difficult to justify the continued absence of individual human rights while still having a system that could be said to protect and give prominence to human dignity, in any plausible sense of that term.

Westernization, modernization, development, and underdevelopment— for better or worse, the dominant contemporary social and economic forces—have in most places significantly separated the individual from the small, supportive traditional community. Economic, social, and cultural changes in and disruptions of traditional communities have often removed the support and protection that would "justify" or "compensate for" the absence of individual human rights. Furthermore, in most places these communities have been penetrated and often radically transformed or disrupted by the modern state. Increasingly today in the Third World the individual is forced to "go it alone" against social, economic, and political forces that all too often appear to be aggressive and oppressive. Society, which once protected a person's dignity and provided a place in the world, now appears, in the form of the modern state, the modern economy, and the modern city, as an oppressive, alien power that assaults people's dignity and that of their families.

In such circumstances, human rights appear to be a "natural" response to changing conditions, a logical and necessary evolution of the means to realize human dignity. The individual *needs* individual rights—barring the implausible and often undesired reemergence of the traditional order. And given the power of modern institutions and the demonstrated inclinations of the individuals and groups that control them, not just any type of individual rights will do: individuals need rights with the moral force and range of universal human rights. In Marxist terms, the bourgeois economic revolution brings with it the bourgeois political revolution and bourgeois rights; capitalism and industrialization bring in their wake natural or human rights, which represent a major advance in the protection of human dignity in such circumstances.

The individualism of human rights is a response to objective conditions, so to rail against it in the absence of an alternative solution to the very real problems of protecting the individual and human dignity is at best utopian or shortsighted. Whatever the nature of traditional ideas and practices, the underlying concerns and needs in the area of human dignity are, for objective, historical reasons, largely the same today in the Third World as they were one, two, or three centuries ago in such countries as Belgium, England, France, or the United States. We must therefore put aside questions of the origin of concepts, practices, and institutions and focus instead on how they can be applied to the problems we face today in protecting and realizing human dignity.

5. THE RELEVANCE OF HUMAN RIGHTS

A recurrent theme in the contemporary literature is that human rights, because of their Western origin, are inappropriate or irrelevant to contemporary Third World problems and needs. For example, Adamantia Pollis and Peter Schwab contend that because in most countries "human rights as defined by the West are rejected or, more accurately, are meaningless," the Western concept is "inapplicable," "of limited validity," and "irrelevant" (1980: 13, 8, 9). These are strong claims. For the most part they are not justified.

"Inapplicable" and "irrelevant" have at least three important possible interpretations: that human rights objectively have no applicability, that their applicability is not recognized, or that the applicability of human rights is or would be rejected. All three raise serious problems.

Determining the objective relevance of human rights would be a difficult matter, but a simple demonstration that most people in a country have been and continue to be unaware of the concept, or that they have adopted alternative mechanisms to realize human dignity, will not establish that human rights are objectively irrelevant. A head count might be part of such a determination (although even that is not obvious), but it certainly would not be definitive. A positive, substantive, and probably even empirical argument would be necessary to establish objective inapplicability, but I am aware of no serious effort to make such an argument.

The two subjective senses of "irrelevant" raise different problems. For example, we are forced to ask what weight we should give such subjective decisions and preferences. We also need to determine who is to speak for the society and how, which is especially important given the basic political implications of such decisions. In answering such questions, we face at least partially competing intuitions. We want to recognize both the validity of claims of traditional values and institutions and the rights of modern nations and states to choose their own destiny. At the same time, though, we feel a need to keep these choices constrained within acceptable bounds and to reject an "anything goes" attitude. We shall return to this problem in greater detail in Chapter 6, but a few brief comments are in order here.

Certainly Louis XVI found the revolutionary rights of man to be inappropriate, and today's historians seem to be not altogether certain that the majority of his subjects, especially those outside of Paris, disagreed. More recently, "Emperor" Bokassa and Idi Amin found human rights concerns to be irrelevant, while Pol Pot and his successors alike determined that human rights are inappropriate to Cambodia's needs and interests. Although there is widespread agreement that these men were and are wrong in their judgments, elucidating the bases for such a conclusion and then applying the resulting principles to less extreme cases raises serious difficulties.

The practices of an Amin or Bokassa do not rest on an alternative conception of human dignity, but rather deny the very concept. For example, killing schoolchildren who protest school rules, as Bokassa did, simply is incompatible with any and all plausible conceptions of human dignity. Although claims of human rights would substantially increase the force of our condemnations of these regimes, we can both forcefully and appropriately condemn such practices on the basis of the concept of human dignity alone. Problems arise, though, when we are faced instead with competing conceptions of human dignity like those we have been considering here. In such cases, Pollis and Schwab and many others advocate extreme toleration for variations, coupled with an attempt to resolve differences through compromise or even a lowest-common-denominator solution (Pollis and Schwab 1980: 1, 14–17). However, lowest-common-denominator and compromise approaches seem to assume that human rights are not universal rights and that the human rights approach is not a better one and therefore does not deserve to be more widely or even universally applied. Neither of these assumptions seems obvious, or even correct.

In trying to assess whether human rights is a better way to approach human dignity and organize a society, we need to ask "Better for what?" This is a question of means, not of ends. Human rights are not ends in themselves. They are, among other things, means to realize human dignity. To the extent that they have instrumental value, we can in principle at least assess their merits largely empirically. I contend that for most of the goals of the developing countries, *as defined by these countries themselves*, human rights are as effective or more effective than either traditional approaches or modern nonhuman rights strategies.

If our concern is with the realization of human dignity, one could argue (along the lines suggested above) that the conditions created by modernization render the individual too vulnerable in the absence of human rights. If the concern is with development and social justice, a strong case might be made that recognizing and protecting human rights would increase participation and therefore popular support and productivity, open up lines of communication between people and government (thus providing greater efficiency and important checks against corruption and mismanagement), spur the provision of basic services through the recognition of economic and social rights, and provide dispossessed groups with regular and important channels for demanding redress. If one is concerned with stability, an argument might be advanced that a regime that systematically violates human rights engenders destabilizing opposition. We cannot simply assume that other strategies are as good or as valid merely because they are widely advocated or were once widely practiced. It is essential that we move beyond simply demonstrating differences in values (which is the level of most current discussions) to assessing the relative merits of competing approaches.

The case against the other assumption underlying lowest-common-denominator approaches—namely, that human rights are not universal rights—would have to be largely normative. The issue involved here is whether there are human rights, since nonuniversal human rights simply would not be human rights as they have been conceived even in such documents as the Universal Declaration of Human Rights. The compromise approach thus involves abandoning human rights as we have understood them, without even presenting arguments. But even granting that human rights are not universal, the most important result will be to increase the importance of the questions of relevance and instrumental value. Simply establishing that human rights are not universal does not show that an alternative or competing approach to human dignity is even defensible, let alone preferable. We would be left with several competing approaches that, unless we accept the crudest sort of value-relativism (e.g., emotivism), not only can but must be evaluated comparatively.

The differences between the so-called Western or human rights approach and other approaches to human dignity certainly are large. In fact, they are far greater than generally recognized in the contemporary literature. But these differences do not in themselves entail the necessity of a laissez-faire approach, nor do they establish the substantive merits of any particular approach, let alone the inferiority of the Western human rights approach.

If the alternative approaches to human dignity we have been discussing are accepted as legitimate conceptions of human rights, the practice of human rights is likely to suffer. For example, it would become easier for a repressive regime to cloak itself in the mantle of human rights while actually violating them, thereby turning "human rights" into an instrument of oppression rather than liberation. And in those countries with established human rights practices, the conceptual bases of human rights are likely to be eroded, thereby weakening the practice.

There is nothing in the concept of human rights that assures that it will not or even should not change or evolve. It might be desirable to reduce or minimize the place of human rights in political doctrine and practice, or even to replace human rights with entirely different organizing principles. But such arguments rarely are made today. Instead, human rights is used as roughly equivalent to "our approach to human dignity," and just about anything that is good or highly valued is labeled a human right. To the extent that we accept such ways of thinking and speaking, the distinctive and distinctly valuable aspects of a human rights approach are insidiously eroded. Human rights thus are attacked by practices bearing the label "human rights." And if we lose the concept through the corruption of the language, we stand in greater danger of losing the practice as well.

6. Postscript: The West and Human Rights

The human rights approach to human dignity has been referred to here as "Western" (or "modern") because it was first developed in Europe in the early modern period—more precisely, seventeenth-century England (see Chapter 5). It is important to stress, however, that the label "Western" does *not* imply that the West has necessarily made more progress in implementing internationally recognized human rights, that the West is not or has not been the source of many human rights problems and violations throughout the world, that cultural "Westernization" is essential or even necessarily helpful to realizing human rights, or that the West deserves special praise or should feel special pride for "discovering" (or inventing or creating) human rights.

At a recent conference on "Human Rights in Cross-Cultural Perspectives" at the Wilson Center, Robert Thurman suggested that arguments such as those made in this chapter were like proving that traditional African or Asian societies did not have seatbelts. Of course they didn't have seatbelts—they didn't have cars! But instead of undercutting my argument, this metaphor actually captures its essence. Why were there no human rights in traditional non-Western *and Western* societies? Because prior to the creation of capitalist market economies and modern nation states, the problems that human rights seek to address, the particular violations of human dignity that they seek to prevent, either did not exist or were not widely perceived to be central social problems.

The rise of a monetized market economy based on largely unlimited private property rights gradually destroyed the social bases of traditional communities and created separate and distinct individuals (in place of persons who are ascriptively defined by their position in a status hierarchy) who would become the bearers of human rights. Modern markets also created a whole new range of threats to human dignity and thus were one of the principal sources of the need and demand for human rights. And at roughly the same time, the modern state, both as an autonomous social actor and as an instrument of the newly ascendant bourgeoisie, was creating new institutions and practices that enabled it to invade the lives and threaten the dignity of a rapidly increasing number of people in new and increasingly ominous ways. In other words, the cars not only were on Western streets, they were running out of control and wreaking havoc on society. In response, Westerners began to invent and demand not only seatbelts but traffic safety laws, new car warranties, laws against "lemons," driver's licenses, driver training, better cars, better roads, and so on. Seatbelts—human rights—first emerged in the West because that is where the cars first were. But once cars began to run amok on the streets in other parts of the world, they brought with them the need for seatbelts and all the rest. This is in essence my argument above for the near universal contemporary relevance of human rights.

Modern states and markets may or may not be a good thing. To the extent that they are not, the West can perhaps be *blamed*, rather than praised, for inventing (or, rather, having been forced to invent) human rights.[6] Furthermore, although the contemporary state seems more powerful and more threatening than its predecessors of earlier generations, modern states and markets may not be an abiding feature of the lives of succeeding generations, in which case human rights may prove to be of only transitory value in the struggle for human dignity. But so long as such threats to human dignity persist, and wherever they exist, we are likely to need human rights. Human rights are the best—I would suggest the only effective—political device yet devised by human ingenuity to protect individual dignity against the standard threats of modern society.

6. Furthermore, to the extent that other countries were forced or coerced into participating in world markets, and to the extent that repressive states in the Third World are a legacy of Western colonialism and neocolonialism, the West can also be blamed for creating the conditions that required human rights in order to guarantee human dignity.

4

Human Dignity, Human Rights, and Political Regimes

by Rhoda E. Howard and Jack Donnelly

The particularity of human rights can be seen not only in conceptions of human dignity but also in the social systems and political regimes based on such conceptions. The international human rights elaborated in the Universal Declaration of Human Rights and the International Human Rights Covenants often are held to be compatible with a great variety of political regimes. For example, Graefrath argues that international human rights standards "can be adapted to any legal system" (1983: 6; compare Buultjens 1980; Gros Espiell 1979; Khushalani 1983; Marasinghe 1984; Mojekwu 1980; Pollis 1982; Ruffin 1982; Stackhouse 1984; Wiarda 1982). We argue, however, that international human rights standards are based on a distinctive substantive conception of human dignity. They therefore require a particular type of "liberal" regime, which may be institutionalized in various forms, but only within a relatively narrow range of variation. The authors cited above confuse human rights with human dignity.

"Human dignity" certainly figures prominently in international human rights documents—for example, the International Human Rights Covenants proclaim that human rights "derive from the inherent dignity of the human person" (1966). Furthermore, every form of political regime implicitly reflects a particular social conception of human dignity. Nonetheless, human rights and human dignity are quite distinct notions. Conceptions of human dignity, in their social and political aspects, express particular understandings of the inner (moral) nature and worth of the human person and his or her proper (political) relations with society. By contrast, human rights are the equal and inalienable rights (in the strong sense of entitlements that ground particularly powerful claims against the state) that each person has simply as a human being. Human rights are a particular social practice that aims to realize a distinctive substantive conception of human dignity. Conceptions of human dignity vary dramatically across societies, and most of these variations are incompatible with the values of equality and autonomy that underlie human rights. Most regimes, and their underlying social conceptions of human dignity, necessarily deny both the idea and the practice of human rights.

In examining the relations between human rights and conceptions of human dignity across a wide range of regimes, our analysis here relies heavily on the use of ideal types ("the construction of certain elements of reality into a logically precise conception" [Weber 1946: 59]) especially ideal-type conceptions of the human person and his or her obligations to and claims upon society and the state. We first show the philosophical and structural connections between the "liberal" conception of human dignity and the principle and practice of human rights, then we demonstrate how four major contemporary regime types, which we call "communitarian," necessarily repudiate human rights because of their commitment to alternative social conceptions of human dignity.

Although the interpretation of liberalism adopted here provides the philosophical and structural basis for international human rights norms, the focus is not on liberal theory (compare, however, Chapter 5). In another context we would argue for the authenticity of our interpretation, but here we claim only that it is a plausible, standard reading of the liberal tradition. The subject here is human rights, not liberalism. Therefore, even if our definition should prove to be stipulative, the substance of our argument, which focuses on the social and political requirements of human rights, would remain largely unaffected.

We should also note that we do not join arguments about the content of lists of human rights. Instead, as is common in the human rights literature, we accept the list in the Universal Declaration of Human Rights. In particular, we avoid rehashing old arguments about economic and social rights. Both on theoretical grounds (See Chapters 1 and 2) and in light of the nearly universal official acceptance of the Universal Declaration, we adopt the full list of rights it provides, with civil, political, economic, and social rights on an equal footing.

Although these two simplifying assumptions narrow our focus, our argument remains significant and controversial. Internationally recognized human rights require a liberal regime. Other types of regimes, and the conceptions of human dignity on which they rest, may be defensible on other moral or political grounds, but they will not stand up to scrutiny under the standard of human rights.

1. LIBERALISM AND HUMAN RIGHTS: A NECESSARY CONNECTION

A. Liberalism, Equality, and Personal Autonomy

Following Ronald Dworkin (1977: chap. 12; 1985: chap. 8), we contend that the heart of liberalism is expressed in the basic political right to equal concern and respect:

> Government must treat those whom it governs with concern, that is, as human beings who are capable of suffering and frustration, and with respect, that is, as human beings who are capable of forming and acting on intelligent conceptions of how their lives should be lived. Government must not only treat people with concern and respect, but with equal concern and respect. It must not distribute goods or opportunities unequally on the ground that some citizens are entitled to more because they are worthy of more concern. It must not constrain liberty on the ground that one citizen's conception of the good life . . . is nobler or superior to another's. (Dworkin 1977: 272–73)

The state must treat each person as a moral and political equal; it need not assure each person an equal share of social resources, but it must treat all with equal concern and respect. Inequalities in goods or opportunities that arise directly or indirectly from political decisions (and many such inequalities are easily justified within a liberal regime) must be compatible with the right to equal concern and respect.

Personal liberty, especially the liberty to choose and pursue one's own life, clearly is entailed in the principle of equal respect. If the state were to interfere in matters of personal morality, it would be treating the life plans and values of some as superior to others. A certain amount of economic liberty is also required, at least to the extent that decisions concerning consumption, investment, and risk reflect free decisions based on personal values that arise from autonomously chosen conceptions of the good life. But liberty alone cannot serve as the overriding value of social life, nor can it be the sole end of political association. Unless checked by a fairly expansive, positive conception of the persons in relation to whom it is exercised, individual liberty readily degenerates into license and social atomization. If liberty is to foster dignity, it must be exercised within the constraints of the principle of equal concern and respect.

In fact, autonomy and equality are less a pair of guiding principles than different manifestations of the central liberal commitment to the equal worth and dignity of each and every person. Each human being has an equal, irreducible moral worth, whatever his or her social utility. Regardless of who they are or where they stand, individuals have an inherent dignity and worth for which the state must demonstrate an active concern. Furthermore, everyone is *entitled* to this equal concern and respect. Minimum standards of political treatment are embodied in human rights; they are not merely desirable goals of social policy.

This implies a particular conception of the relation of the individual to the community and the state. Man is a social animal. Human potential, and even personal individuality, can be developed and expressed only in a social context. Society requires the discharge of certain political functions, and large-scale political organization requires the state. The state, however, also can present serious threats to human dignity and equal concern and respect if it seeks to enforce a particular vision of the good life or to entrench privileged inequality. Therefore, human rights have a special reference to the state in order to keep it an instrument to realize rather than undermine equal concern and respect.

In the inevitable conflicts between the individual and the state, the liberal gives prima facie priority, in the areas protected by human rights, to the individual. For the liberal, the individual is not merely separable from the community and social roles, but specially valued precisely as a distinctive, discrete individual—which is why each person must be treated with equal concern and respect. The state and society are conceived, in more or less contractarian terms, as associations for the fuller unfolding of human potential, through the exercise and enjoyment of human rights. Human dignity, for the liberal, is largely encompassed in the vision of a life in which each person is an equal and autonomous member of society enjoying the full range of human rights.

This view of man is rooted in structural changes that began to emerge in late medieval and early modern Europe, gained force in the eighteenth and nineteenth centuries, and today are increasingly the norm throughout the world. The "creation" of the private individual separate from society is closely linked to the rise of a new and more complex division of labor, the resulting changes in class structure (particularly the rise and then dominance of the bourgeoisie), and a new vision of the individual's relationship to God, society, and the state.

These developments are well known and need not be recounted here. The social changes of modernization—especially migration, urbanization, and technological development, in the context of capitalist market economies—replaced the all-encompassing moral whole of traditional or feudal society with a much more segmented social order. Politics was separated from religion, the economy, and law (which were likewise separated from one another). Individuals too were separated from society as a whole; no longer could they be reduced to their roles, to parts of the community. With the recognition of separate individuals possessing special worth and dignity precisely as individuals, the basis for human rights was established.

Occurring parallel to these changes in society was the equally well-known development of the modern state. The newly rising bourgeois class was initially a principal backer of the newly ascendant princes and kings, who also wanted to free themselves from the constraints of the old feudal order. As the state's power grew, however, it increasingly threatened the individual citizen. Bourgeois "freemen" thus began to demand that they indeed be free.

Such demands eventually took the form of arguments for the universal natural rights and equality of all people. In this new and socially mobile society in which entrance to and exit from the bourgeois class was relatively unpredictable, a new set of privileges could not readily be reserved for a new elite defined by birth or some similar characteristic. Therefore, in order for some (the bourgeoisie) to be able to enjoy these new rights, they had to be demanded and at least formally guaranteed for all. Thus human rights came to be articulated primarily as claims of any individual against the state. Human rights lay down the basic form of the relationship between the (new, modern) individual and the (new, modern) state, a relationship based on the prima facie priority of the individual over the state in those areas protected by human rights.

Human rights are morally prior to and superior to society and the state, and under the control of individuals, who hold them and may exercise them against the state in extreme cases. This reflects not only the equality of all individuals but also their autonomy, their right to have and pursue interests and goals different from those of the state or its rulers. In the areas and endeavors protected by human rights, the individual is "king"—or rather an equal and autonomous person entitled to equal concern and respect.

In practice, these values and structural changes remain incompletely realized even today, and for most of the modern era they have been restricted to a small segment of the population. Nevertheless, the ideal was established and its implementation begun. And even if the demand for human rights began as a tactic of the bourgeoisie to protect its own class interests, the logic of universal and inalienable personal rights has long since broken free of these origins.

Furthermore, although these processes of sociopolitical individuation and state-building were first played out in Europe, they are increasingly the rule throughout the world. The structural basis for a society of equal and autonomous individuals is thus being universalized despite its historically particular and contingent origin. Social structure today increasingly parallels the near universal diffusion of the idea of human rights and the philosophical claim that human rights are universal. Individual human rights therefore increasingly appear not merely as moral ideals but as both objectively and subjectively necessary to protect and realize human dignity.

B. Liberalism and International Human Rights

The standard list of human rights in the Universal Declaration of Human Rights can be easily derived from the liberal conception of the individual and the state (compare Chapter 1, section 4.B). Other lists have been and may be derived from these principles, but we contend that the near-perfect fit between liberalism and the Universal Declaration reflects a deep and essential theoretical connection.

In order to treat an individual with concern and respect, the individual must first be recognized as a moral and legal person. This in turn requires certain basic personal rights. Rights to recognition before the law and to nationality (Universal Declaration, Articles 6, 15) are prerequisites to political treatment as a person. In a different vein, the right to life, as well as rights to protection against slavery, torture, and other inhuman or degrading treatment (Articles 3, 4, 5), are essential to recognition and respect as a person.

Such rights as freedom of speech, conscience, religion, and association (Articles 18, 19) protect a sphere of personal autonomy. The right to privacy (Article 12) even more explicitly aims to guarantee the capacity to realize personal visions of a life worthy of a human being. Personal autonomy also requires economic and social rights, such as the right to education (Article 26), which makes available the intellectual resources for informed autonomous choices and the skills needed to act on them, and the right to participate in the cultural life of the community (Article 27), which recognizes the social and cultural dimensions of personal development. In its political dimension, equal respect also implies democratic control of the state and therefore rights to political participation and to freedoms of (political) speech, press, assembly, and association (Articles 19, 20, 21).

The principle of equal concern and respect also requires that the government intervene to reduce social and economic inequalities that deny equal personal worth. The state must protect those who, as a result of natural or voluntary membership in an unpopular group, are subject to social, political, or economic discrimination that limits their access to a fair share of social resources or opportunities. Such rights as equal protection of the laws and protection against discrimination on such bases as race, color, sex, language, religion, opinion, origin, property, birth, or status (Articles 2, 7) are essential to assure that all people are treated as fully and equally human.

In the economic sphere, the traditional liberal attachment to the market is not accidental. Quite aside from its economic efficiency, the market places minimal restraints on economic liberty and thus maximizes personal autonomy. Market distribution, however, tends to be grossly unequal. Inequality per se is not objectionable to the liberal, but the principle of equal concern and respect does imply a floor of basic economic welfare; degrading inequalities cannot be permitted (Shue 1980: 119–23). The state also has an appropriate interest in redressing market-generated inequalities, because a "free market" system of distributing resources is a creature of social and political action, actively backed by the state, which protects and enforces property rights.

Differential market rewards are not neutral; they reward morally equal individuals unequally. Market distributions may be substantially affected by such morally irrelevant factors as race, sex, class, or religion. Furthermore, many of the "talents" richly rewarded by the market are of dubious moral significance. Even "achieved" inequalities, should they threaten the (moral) equality or autonomy of other citizens, present at least a prima facie case for state intervention. The principle of equal concern and respect requires the state to act positively to cancel unjustifiable market inequalities, at least to the point that all are assured a minimum share of resources through the implementation of social and economic rights. In human rights terms this implies, for example, rights to food, health care, and social insurance (Articles 22, 25).

Efforts to alleviate degrading or disrespectful misery and deprivation do not exhaust the scope of the economic demands of the principle of equal concern and respect. The right to work (Article 23), which is essentially a right to economic participation, is of special importance. It has considerable intrinsic value (work is typically held to be essential to a life of dignity) as well as great instrumental value, both for the satisfaction of basic material needs and for providing a secure and dignified economic foundation from which to pursue personal values and objectives. A (limited) right to property (Article 17) can be justified in similar terms.

Finally, the special threat to personal autonomy and equality presented by the modern state requires a set of legal rights, such as the presumption of innocence and rights to due process, fair and public hearings before an independent tribunal, and protection from arbitrary arrest, detention, or exile (Articles 8–11). More broadly, the special threat to dignity posed by the state is reflected in the fact that all human rights are held particularly against the state. Moreover, they hold against all types of states, democratic as much as any other: if one's government treats one as less than fully human, it matters little how that government came to power. The individual does have social duties (Article 29), but the discharge of social obligations is not a precondition for having or exercising human rights.

We have thus moved from the liberal principle of equal concern and respect to the full list of human rights in the Universal Declaration. These rights, in turn, demand a liberal society and the ideal person envisioned by it, and if implemented these rights would play a crucial role in creating that society.

This conception of liberalism is very different from that held by many of its critics and defenders alike. The authenticity and appropriateness of this label will be discussed in detail in Chapter 5. In section C below, we explicitly distinguish it from the propertied libertarian "liberalism" of the minimal or nightwatchman state. Here, however, the empirical referent we have in mind is the social democratic welfare states of Europe, such as Norway and the Netherlands.[1] We are prepared to entertain with sympathy the hypothesis that a country such as the United States, even before President Ronald Reagan, is not an exemplar (in fact, falls far short) of this liberal ideal. For example, a society that has the material capacity to provide universal health care or universal maternal benefits but chooses not to does not appear to be a society based on equal concern and respect for all citizens. Racial issues point to another area of gross shortcomings in the record of the United States. The U.S. government's lack of respect for its own citizens can perhaps even help explain its support of such hideous client regimes as Pinochet's Chile, in sharp contrast to countries such as the European social democracies.

But the argument here should not be obscured by a dispute over labels. Suppose that we are wrong and this type of regime should not be called "liberal"—let us call it *x* instead. Our argument remains the same: international human rights standards require an *x* regime.

C. Liberalism versus the Minimal State

In practice, even the best of actual liberal regimes fall short of the ideal we have been discussing, and the human rights records of many self-professed liberal societies merit severe criticism. Furthermore, many avowed liberals view liberty and equality as largely antagonistic principles to be traded off against one another instead of as complementary dimensions of the single principle of equal concern and respect. One way to make this trade-off is to choose liberty and largely disregard equality, establishing a "minimal" or "nightwatchman" regime.[2]

1. Thus one might argue that "social democratic" is a better label than "liberal." We certainly would not object to such an argument.

2. In the contemporary world, minimalism is more a theoretical model than a practical model. In recent years, perhaps the only serious attempt to establish a minimal regime was the effort of the Pinochet regime and the "Chicago boys" in Chile in the late 1970s, an experiment that was an unmitigated disaster even by its own standards, let alone by international human rights standards.

Advocates of the minimal state (e.g., Nozick 1974) largely limit the state to protecting public order and private property. To assure the good behavior of the nightwatchman, "negative" civil and political rights are also required, especially civil liberties, narrowly conceived as rights to public noninterference in the private lives (very broadly understood) of individuals. But minimalism also explicitly protects property rights while rejecting all other economic and social human rights. Beyond minimalism's obvious incompatibility with international human rights standards (which minimalists readily allow), its deep commitment to protecting private property while denying all other economic and social rights borders on logical contradiction. We can see no way that precisely and only this one economic right can justifiably be allowed on the minimalist's list of human rights.

The standard rights-based (i.e., not merely utilitarian) arguments for the right to private property in such contexts rest on the importance of guaranteed private economic activity and resources for the enjoyment of personal autonomy. Clearly, however, such an argument does not justify a right to unlimited individual accumulation. At a certain point, additional economic resources contribute nothing at all to personal autonomy, and long before that point the marginal return becomes vanishingly small. Even more important, exactly the same argument can be made for other social and economic rights. In fact, a substantially stronger case can be made for rights to food, to work, and to health care.

In any case, the minimal state is almost certain to be self-destructing if it recognizes equal and universal civil *and* political rights. The denial of political participation usually rests on a desire to protect social and economic privilege, while those previously excluded from political participation tend to use their newly acquired power to obtain a fair or at least tolerable share of social resources (compare Goldstein 1983). The emergence of the Western welfare state and popular pressure throughout the Third World for social services clearly suggests that implementing equal and universal political rights will transform a minimal regime.

The only way to avoid this would be to entrench a right to private property against the exercise of all other human rights. This is obviously unjustifiable; no plausible theory of human nature or dignity yields this one right as superior to all other human rights. However, lesser entrenchment, allowing redistribution beyond a certain level of accumulation, would be ineffective. If the point beyond which redistribution would take place were set democratically, a minimal regime would almost certainly be democratically abolished, or at least dismantled over time. But any other way of setting the limit would deny the equality of political rights.

In other words, the minimal state, in its very essence, is a violator of human rights, even within the limits of its own terms of reference. Liberalism's dual pursuit of autonomy and equality is replaced in minimalism by a single-minded pursuit of autonomy understood largely as the social guarantee of the broadest possible sphere of private action, virtually irrespective of its social consequences. For the minimalist, human dignity is expressed principally in the unequal, achieved consequences of private and largely conflictual action. Thus, the minimal state is not the pure form of liberalism it is often represented to be by both minimalists and various leftist critics of liberalism. Rather, it is a perverse and internally inconsistent[3] narrowing of liberalism that is also inconsistent with international human rights standards.

2. Equality, Autonomy, and Communitarian Societies

Having shown that human rights and liberal regimes are closely matched, it remains to be shown that other types of regimes are incompatible with the demands of human rights, a task that we have begun with the discussion of the minimal state above. In this section we examine four major types of communitarian society, which together encompass the vast majority of contemporary nonliberal regimes.

We define *communitarian societies* as societies that give ideological and practical priority to the community (sometimes embodied in the state) over the individual. Such societies regard their members as worthy of concern and respect, but only as members of society performing prescribed roles. Their concepts of human dignity are therefore not rooted in the notion of human rights. Communitarian societies are antithetical to the implementation and maintenance of human rights because they deny the autonomy of the individual, the irreducible moral equality of all individuals, and the possibility of conflict between the community's interests and the legitimate interests of any individual.

A. Traditional Societies

Traditional societies are communal, status-based societies governed according to principles and practices held to be fixed by tradition.[4] They are usually ethnically homogeneous and agricultural, and frequently stateless.

3. We freely acknowledge that a regime can adhere quite comfortably to an inconsistent set of political principles. All other things being equal, however, fundamental theoretical inconsistency—especially inconsistency with a clear class bias—certainly should count against a regime.

4. Although there are few if any contemporary nation-states that could be described as traditional societies, the category remains of more than historical interest. Numerous remnants of such societies are found in most Third World states and many large rural enclaves still at least loosely approximate this model.

In the traditional society, one's worth, rights, and responsibilities arise from and remain tied to differential membership in a particular society, with unequal, status-based privileges and duties resting on age, sex, caste, or other ascriptive hierarchies. The idea that one is entitled to equal concern and respect and a wide range of inalienable personal rights simply because one is a human being is utterly foreign to traditional societies (see Chapter 3). Only certain kinds of people are defined as moral persons—that is, as human beings.

Most people in traditional societies have at least some rights and privileges. These rights are contingent on the proper fulfillment of social roles. Therefore they are neither held as basic personal rights valid against society and other individuals nor are they believed to be held by anyone outside the society. Even within the recognized social boundaries, some people may be defined as outsiders, as nonbelievers are defined in strict Islamic societies, or ethnic strangers are defined in traditional Africa.

The relationship between the individual (if he or she may be so called) and society is by definition nonconflictual; everyone's interests are incorporated into the higher value system represented by the political-religious-legal decision-makers. Man and society are assumed to be inseparable. The very idea of inalienable individual rights held equally by all against the community is, if comprehensible, likely to be viewed with horror (Legesse 1980: 124).

In traditional societies there is no notion of the autonomous individual. One's worth, even one's existence, is defined by one's place, one's role in the community; apart from the community, one does not exist, or at least such an existence is largely without moral value. One's dignity—which usually is conceived primarily as an attribute of one's kinship, age, sex, or occupational group—is obtained or validated by discharging the traditionally defined duties of one's station, rather than by autonomously creating or unfolding a unique individual existence. In traditional society, there are neither human beings, in the relevant moral sense, nor equal, inalienable, and universal rights.

Many traditional societies were slave or caste societies; few were subject to democratic control in even a very loose sense of that term. Individual deviations from communal norms usually were harshly repressed, and women and outsiders usually were treated as inferior beings. Nonetheless, in theory at least and often in practice as well, a certain sort of dignity, tied to the proper fulfillment of social roles, could be achieved by most people. Furthermore, social responsibilities usually were coupled with reciprocal social and economic protections. In traditional societies, most people had a defined, secure, and (within its own terms) dignified place in society.

One can therefore at least understand and perhaps even contextually justify traditional society's denial of human rights. One might even argue that the traditional conception of human dignity is superior to that of liberalism. For example, it might be argued that most people prefer regulated, secure social roles, with their concomitant sense of belonging, to autonomy and its attendant insecurities. Insider "individuals" may well have fared better in many ways as part of traditional society than as, say, a textile worker in mid-nineteenth-century England or in South Korea today.

Such arguments, however, are not human rights arguments. To defend traditional society is to reject a society based on equal, inalienable, universal personal rights in favor of a status-based society. To prefer traditional society to liberalism is to reject a society of equal and autonomous individuals with inalienable personal rights in favor of a society of unequal, regulated occupants of social roles, incorporated into the community. Traditional society and human rights cannot be combined without violence to both (compare Howard 1986: chap. 2).

B. Communism

By "communism" we mean an ideal type regime modeled on the structure and official ideology of contemporary Soviet bloc countries. The key feature of such societies is a communist party-state committed to total, revolutionary transformation of social and personal life. The connection between such regimes and the writings of Marx or the "authentic" Marxist tradition is an issue that cannot and need not be addressed here. Our concern instead is with the frequently encountered argument that existing communist regimes are entirely consistent with international human rights norms.

While there are striking similarities between traditional and communist societies, especially in the submergence of the individual to the community (state) and in the use of social (class) roles to define individual worth, there are no less striking differences. Traditional societies have at most a rudimentary state apparatus, whereas in communist societies the state is the central social institution, despite ideologically obligatory references to its withering away. Instead of the often more or less face-to-face relations of small traditional society, communist societies range in size from millions to more than a billion people. Instead of a relatively simple division of labor, they have a complex industrial division of labor, and instead of an ethnically homogeneous community often bound together by real or mythic kinship ties, most communist countries are multiethnic.

This alters the entire texture of social relations. The communist state simply cannot be the functional equivalent of the traditional community; it necessarily appears as a distant, separate institution incapable of providing the social and psychological support of close-knit traditional communities. Therefore, being subsumed into the "community" is quite a different process in communist societies.

In traditional society the individual is never fully differentiated from the group. In communist societies individuals have been thoroughly differentiated. The modern economy, with its complex division of labor and extensive role-segmentation, necessarily produces economically and therefore socially distinct individuals. Likewise, modern state bureaucracies are structured to deal (only) with (anonymous or interchangeable) individuals. The political task for communist regimes, therefore, is to *reabsorb* the individual into the (state) society. The primacy of the state/society therefore must be politically created, as is underscored by the very project of revolutionary social transformation. In communist societies, one must *be made* a part of the community. "No conflicts can exist between the individual and the state" (Wieruszewski 1988: 29).

The basic socioeconomic organization of life under communism, however, continues to (re)produce differentiated individuals. The process of (re)incorporation must therefore be constantly repeated. But undifferentiated economic reincorporation is impossible, and ideological reincorporation, no matter how hegemonic, is insufficient. Direct political coercion is therefore a feature of communist collectivism that generally is absent from traditional society (because of the effectiveness of other means of social control).

As the task of the state/party/proletariat is to transform all aspects of social existence, private life is not merely subject to public regulation, but must be made public and regulated by the state if the revolution is to succeed. Those who follow a "bourgeois" or otherwise reactionary road are entitled to neither respect nor concern: at best they are ignored, more often they are repressed. As one East German scholar states, "there is no freedom for enemies of the people" (Klenner 1984: 15), who are defined as social outsiders. Such a belief readily leads to the identification and repression of pariah social classes and in extreme cases to class-based "genocide" directed against kulaks or similar class enemies (Kuper 1981: 99–100).

The ethnic homogeneity of traditional society is replaced by enforced class homogenization. "Class position," however, means simply conformity to behavioral norms specified by the state. Equality, rather than a fundamental and inviolable moral fact, is reduced to mere social sameness. In communist societies one is equal not by birth or by nature but only to the extent that one is essentially indistinguishable from one's fellow communist citizens, an embodiment of the new communist man. Communist societies thus produce a distinctive sort of homogenized, deindividualized person.

It is clear that communist societies must violate a wide range of civil and political rights during the revolutionary transition—necessarily, not merely as a matter of unfortunate excesses in practice. Even after communism is achieved, the denial of civil and political rights remains necessary to preserve the achievements of the revolution. The permanent denial of civil and political rights is required by the commitment to build society according to a particular substantive vision, for the exercise of personal autonomy and civil and political rights is almost certain to undermine that vision.

Furthermore, for all their achievements in providing economic and social goods and services, communist regimes are fundamentally incompatible with economic and social *rights*. In communist societies the possession and enjoyment of all rights are contingent on the discharge of social duties. For example, Article 59 of the Soviet constitution of 1977 states: "The exercise of rights and liberties is inseparable from the performance by citizens of their duties" (compare Burlatsky 1982; Egorov 1979: 39). Thus, for example, access to higher education and desirable jobs is closely linked to political connections or behavior. Few rights of any sort are secure in such a regime, and no human rights, in the strong sense of equal and inalienable entitlements of all individuals, can be recognized.

It is important to stress the difference between having a human right and merely enjoying the substance of a right, between, for example, having food and having a right to food, or speaking freely and enjoying a right to free speech. In communist (and other communitarian) societies, one may be guaranteed the *substance* of certain human rights (Shue 1980: 75–76)— that is, goods, services, and opportunities may be enjoyed. They are not, however, enjoyed *as rights*; those who conform receive certain benefits, but the state may freely bestow or withdraw these as it sees fit. This is as true of economic and social rights as it is of civil and political rights. One is not entitled to these benefits simply as a human being, one does not have the special control provided by possession of a right, and one's claims to enjoy these benefits do not have the force of human rights.

In fact, in communist regimes even as a citizen one is entitled to nothing from—has no rights against—the state. "Human rights . . . do not exist outside the state or against the state. The state is their creator" (Lopatka 1979: 7; compare Weichelt 1979: 3). Rights are acquired only by the discharge of class obligations, as defined by the state (Lieberam 1979: 14). Social outsiders, such as landowners or the bourgeoisie, may lose not only their former property rights, but all other rights as well.

Communist society thus rests on a social utilitarianism fundamentally incompatible with human rights. The good of society, as determined by the state/party, always takes precedence over all else. Because individual "rights" must always yield to social purposes, as enunciated by the state, such "rights" are worthless. No matter what the state does, it cannot be held guilty of violating them. Whatever the benefits and opportunities citizens may (contingently) receive (and they are undeniably substantial in some communist regimes), communism represents a thorough denial of human rights.

C. Corporatism
Corporatism, a principal form of contemporary right-wing regimes, can be defined as

> a system of interest representation in which the constituent units are organized into a limited number of single, compulsory, noncompetitive, hierarchically ordered and functionally differentiated categories, recognized or licensed (if not created) by the state and granted a deliberate representational monopoly within their respective categories in exchange for observing certain controls on their selection of leaders and articulation of demands and support. (Schmitter 1974: 93–94)[5]

Corporatist regimes present themselves as neutral instruments to regulate and mediate the antithetical interests of labor and capital, with other groups, such as women and youth, often officially organized and incorporated into the political structure as well, further undercutting basic structural conflicts. In practice, however, class rule is unambiguously at the heart of corporatism. The essential purpose of its ideology and political structure is to prevent further class conflict and entrench the extant economic hierarchy.

The state proclaims the equal dignity of all segments of society. Meanwhile, unequal private power and property accumulate. Workers and peasants are not necessarily excluded from a share of social benefits—for example, state controlled trade unions may be allowed to pursue certain

5. We are thus using the term "corporatism" to refer only to what are sometimes called "state corporatist" regimes. The "corporatist" elements of so-called "social corporatist" or "neo-corporatist" regimes such as Austria represent a different phenomenon. Such regimes, in our framework, would be classified as liberal.

improvements in working conditions or living standards, so long as class conflicts are denied—but they benefit only inadvertently or as a side-payment to co-opt potential opponents of the ruling corporate coalition. Equal concern and respect is at best ignored.

One variant of corporatism, which can be called authoritarianism for want of a better term, preserves an important sphere of private autonomy and activity—for example, religion and education may be left as a private matter. But this privacy is only a realm of public indifference. It is quite different from positive respect for or protection of a right to privacy and related human rights. Privacy (of thought, religion, belief) is not so much protected in authoritarian regimes as it is ignored, and it is ignored only as long as it does not interfere with the basic corporatist bargain. Personal autonomy is at best not a right but a contingent benefit.

The fascist variant of corporatism is actively hostile to the private. In reaction to what it views as the unabated individualism of liberal society, fascism proclaims a romantic ideology of (mythic) consensus, homogeneity, and personal comfort in conforming to social roles. Human dignity is to be achieved through integration into an all-encompassing moral order, represented by the fascist state. Much as in communism, any challenge to this order, including deviation in personal values and beliefs, is treated as a threat to the entire social fabric.

This ideology of the primacy of the state readily leads to terror and scapegoating. Nonviolent denials of civil and political right are likely to be inadequate to prevent independent "political" activity, now redefined to include much of "private" personal life. Direct terror is likely to be necessary; so also is the creation and persecution of outsider or scapegoat groups, in extreme cases culminating in genocide. Such persecution not only allows the state to displace real social tensions arising from the corporatist character of society, but in the very denial of the rights of the scapegoat group it reaffirms the unity of the fascist individual, society, and state.

From a human rights perspective, however, fascism is merely the extreme form of corporatism; fascism may actively violate more rights, but authoritarian corporatism is unlikely to protect many more. One cannot even assuredly say that life is preferable for the average individual in authoritarian corporatism; for example, if public indifference results in anomie, the intense feeling of belonging espoused by fascism may seem preferable, at least for insiders. In any case, authoritarian corporatism's public indifference to the bulk of society is certainly a denial of equal concern, while its denial of independent political action is incompatible with equal respect. Whatever the form, corporatism denies inherent personal dignity and equal concern and respect in the very bargain that defines the regime.

D. Development Dictatorship

One further type of communitarian regime, which we call development dictatorship, should be briefly noted. In development dictatorships, the principal resource of the ruling elite is control of the means of coercion, which is justified in the name of the most rapid possible economic development.[6] Development, which has achieved an unprecedented ideological hegemony in the Third World, is easily presented as the moral equivalent of war, requiring the subordination of the individual to the state. Therefore, in the hands of repressive elites it nicely justifies a wide range of human rights violations, especially because the connection between particular violations and underlying development goals is likely to be at best very loosely defined.

Development dictatorship is distinguished from corporatism or communism in large measure by its class structure. In development dictatorships, economic class position is less the source of power than the result of control of the state. In nationalized economies, the organizational (Markovitz 1977: chap. 6) or bureaucratic (Shivji 1976: pt. 3) "bourgeoisie" is composed of occupants of high-level office in the military, the government, the bureaucracy, or the ruling party. A parasitic private bourgeoisie, essentially living off its economic relations with the state, may also exist. Controlled by members of these various elites, who have few resources other than coercion to maintain their power, development dictatorships frequently degenerate in cycles of coups and countercoups, or, once stabilized, evolve into some sort of corporatist regime. The regime rests lightly on top of society instead of being a political representation of deep underlying socioeconomic forces (compare Hyden 1983: chap. 2).

Even where the regime's commitment to development is genuine, rather than merely a cover for elite depredations (in which case there is likely to be an attempt to provide at least the substance of some economic and social rights), enshrining development as an overriding social objective assures that individuals and their rights will regularly be ignored. The value put on privacy tends to be low, because private goals might interfere with national development goals. The identification of "outsiders," economic saboteurs, or similar scapegoat groups is a common diversionary tactic when development plans fail. Full personal dignity is conceived largely as an

---

6. Part IV is devoted to a comprehensive critique of such justifications.

abstract future good, to be realized only after success in the struggle for development. In general, individual human rights, especially rights against the state, the essential agent of development, must wait until development has been achieved. Once more, we are faced with a choice between human rights and alternative social goals based on a radically different conception of human dignity.

E. Communitarianism and Human Rights

Whether communitarianism is forward-looking or backward-looking, it is structurally, ideologically, and philosophically incompatible with human rights. The view of human dignity found in all communitarian societies is that one realizes oneself as part of the group by unquestioningly filling his or her social role or being loyal to the state. This conception of human dignity is incompatible with human rights.

At the core of this incompatibility is the denial of social value to personal autonomy and privacy. In communitarian societies the state (or traditional authorities), as the representative of society, must control family life, religion, education, and all other potentially independent aspects of life. Any institution that might influence or challenge the reigning regime and its ideology must be eradicated or at least regulated. Often one's very beliefs, and certainly all aspects of one's behavior, are treated as legitimate matters for social regulation. When personal autonomy is thus denied, or even repressed as a threat to society, moral equality must also be denied. Some people, those who "fit in," are treated as more worthy of concern or respect than others. The full range of international human rights is thereby violated.

The rule of law and procedural due process are incompatible with such regimes; pursuit of the community's substantive goals overrides "mere procedures." Due process is also rejected because it suggests that political organs representative of the full community might treat citizens unfairly, a possibility denied by the communitarian premise of the regime. Equal protection of the laws and, more broadly, nondiscrimination also are incompatible with communitarian regimes. In fact, positive discrimination against social deviants is essential to the political pursuit of unity. Differences between individuals or groups (other than those that are officially sanctioned) are not to be protected, let alone valued as expressions of autonomy, but rather repressed or at best ignored. In communitarian regimes, one is entitled to the protection of the laws and a guaranteed share of social resources and opportunities only to the extent that one fits within certain substantive, ideologically defined categories.

Political participation is similarly restricted both in its substance and in its participants. Debate over fundamental social and political aims cannot be allowed, because these are already set by tradition or by the reigning ideology. Likewise, politics is dominated by a small elite chosen by ascription, restricted party membership, or other nondemocratic means— or where the forms of democratic politics are utilized (e.g., communism), real control lies elsewhere (e.g., a vanguard party).

Many communitarian societies, however, perform relatively well in providing the substance of economic rights. Many espouse and some achieve relative equality of material circumstances and a basic floor of material security. But such economic "rights" are mere benefits, contingent on approved membership in the political community and on the performance of social duties. Citizens are not entitled to these goods and services; at most they may petition for them, not claim them as rights. Material security certainly is valuable, whether it is a right or a privilege. Such "security," however, is precariously insecure in the absence of human rights held against the state, because it can be taken away as easily as it is granted.

In sum, communitarian regimes fall short of the standard of human rights in all major areas. Much as liberalism is necessarily committed to protecting, implementing, and fostering the enjoyment of the full range of internationally recognized human rights, communitarian regimes necessarily violate the full range of human rights.

3. HUMAN DIGNITY, HUMAN RIGHTS, AND POLITICAL REGIMES

We can pull together this discussion in a typology of social conceptions of human dignity. Table 2 lists the positions of our six types of regimes on the five sociopolitical variables shown in the discussion above to be important to the social definition of human dignity. It is immediately apparent from the first four columns that these regimes fall into two broad classes, *individualistic* (liberal and minimal) regimes and *communitarian* (traditional, communist, corporatist, and developmental) regimes.

It is not surprising that the first four variables—autonomy or role fulfillment, conflict or consensus, repression of outsiders, valuation of privacy— are closely related. Society's attitude toward autonomy is especially important. A commitment to personal autonomy requires accepting a certain degree of social conflict and largely precludes enforcing the substantive models of belief and behavior that are the basis for the repression of outsiders, leaving open a considerable realm of valued private activity. Likewise, a stress on role-fulfillment implies a consensual society: roles are

Table 2. Social conceptions of human dignity: A typology

Regime type	Autonomy vs. role-fulfillment	Conflict vs. consensus	Repression of outsiders	Valuation of privacy	Equality vs. hierarchy
Liberal	Autonomy	Conflict	No	High	Equality
Minimal	Autonomy	Conflict	No (?)	Very high	Hierarchy
Traditional	Roles	Consensus	Yes	Very low	Hierarchy
Communist	Roles	Consensus	Yes	Very low	Equality
Corporatist	Roles	Consensus	Yes	Low	Hierarchy
Developmental	Roles	Consensus	Yes (?)	Low	Equality

defined so as to produce consensus when properly performed, ''outsiders'' (those without approved or valued roles) are repressed, and privacy, which exists outside of predefined roles, is not socially valued.

There are, however, no less important differences within each of these two classes of regimes. Liberalism's commitment to autonomy is matched by a commitment to equality; for the liberal, human dignity requires the union of autonomy and equality. This commitment to equality further strengthens the tendency not to repress outsiders or even to define outsider groups other than noncitizens, who are ignored rather than repressed.

In contrast, those at the bottom of the minimal state's social hierarchy are denied economic and social rights as a result of the low value placed on equality and the extraordinarily high value placed on privacy, especially private economic activity. Thus, the lower classes may be seen as indirectly oppressed economic outsiders, and if they attempt to challenge this denial of economic and social rights, direct repression is likely. Furthermore, whereas liberalism merely accepts a certain amount of social conflict as an unavoidable consequence of personal autonomy, and even tempers conflict by the pursuit of social and economic equality, minimalists tend to view social and especially economic conflict in no worse than neutral terms, or even as desirable competition between unequal, atomistic individuals.

There are also important differences among communitarian regimes, for example, in the substantive bases used to define social membership and roles. The most important differences, though, concern the valuation of equality and belonging (the obverse of privacy), as we can see in Table 3, which correlates the major determinants of social conceptions of human dignity with the human rights performance of each type of regime.

All communitarian regimes reject civil and political rights, which can be recognized only when individual autonomy is valued over role-fulfillment. But traditional and communist regimes—one hierarchical, the other egali-

Table 3. Social conceptions of human dignity and human rights performance

Regime type	Equality or hierarchy	Valuation of belonging	Civil and political rights	Economic and social rights
Individualistic regimes				
Liberal	Equality	Moderate	Yes	Yes
Minimal	Hierarchy	Very low	Yes	No
Communitarian regimes				
Traditional	Hierarchy	Very high	No	Substance only
Communist	Equality	High	No	Substance only
Corporatist	Hierarchy	Varies	No	No (?)
Developmental	Equality	Moderate (?)	No	Substance (?)

tarian—do provide the substance of at least some economic and social rights, for insiders; that is, they provide goods, services, and opportunities, but without the power, control, or security that comes with enjoying these benefits as rights. The value placed on equality then largely determines the range and distribution of these benefits. Egalitarian communist regimes are committed to providing them equally and in great and ever-increasing quantity. Hierarchical traditional regimes, however, guarantee only a minimum floor for all (or at least all but chattel slaves, untouchables, and similar near-outsider groups).

Corporatist and developmental regimes—again, one hierarchical, the other egalitarian—do not generally offer even this much. The typical (authoritarian) corporatist regime protects only the interests of the ruling coalition (although fascist corporatism is likely to provide at least some economic and social benefits to all insiders—thus the questionable "no" in Table 3). Developmental regimes are ideologically committed to providing the substance of economic and social rights for all (insiders), at least in the long run, but because the social composition of such regimes usually belies and precludes the realization of this commitment, it remains of questionable practical significance.

This suggests that at least as important a variable as equality (or hierarchy) is the valuation of belonging. Traditional and communist regimes value belonging highly and thus provide the substance of many social and economic rights to all insiders. Corporatist and developmental regimes, which do not guarantee even the substance of economic and social rights, place lower value on a sense of belonging. Similarly, the absence of economic and social rights in minimal regimes is explained not only by the absence of a social commitment to equality but also by the very low value placed on belonging.

Only when autonomy, equality, and at least a moderately high value on belonging are combined, as in liberalism, do we find a commitment to economic and social *rights*, and not just their substance. Only with a commitment to personal autonomy will a regime actively protect civil and political rights. In other words, only in a liberal regime can there be a fundamental political commitment to the full range of internationally recognized human rights. Other social systems may claim to have competing views of human rights, but they do not. They rest on competing views of human dignity, all of which deny both the centrality of the individual in political society and the (human) rights of men and women to make and have enforced equal and inalienable civil, political, economic, and social claims on the state. Only liberalism, understood as a regime based on the political right to equal concern and respect, is a political system based on human rights.

5

Human Rights and
Western Liberalism

The use of the label "liberal" for the regime demanded by international human rights standards suggests an even more precise origin than the modern West for the idea and practice of human rights: the Western liberal tradition of political thought and practice. Nevertheless, this historical particularity is compatible with both the moral and the international normative universality of human rights. The widespread belief that the "Western" or "liberal" conception of human rights rests on a social vision of largely isolated individuals holding (only) property rights and "negative" civil and political liberties, if accurate, would mean that the liberal tradition is radically incompatible with the demands of internationally recognized human rights. I contend, however, that this belief is a partial and seriously distorted description of the liberal tradition.

1. LOCKE AND THE ROOTS OF LIBERALISM

This "conventional or minimalist" conception of liberalism is almost universal among liberalism's critics, from C. B. Macpherson (1962) on the left to Leo Strauss (1953) on the right. For example, Adamantia Pollis argues that the liberal conception of human rights rests on a definition of the person as "an isolated, autonomous individual . . . with inherent rights in the domain of the civil and political" and that, for the liberal, "individual self-aggrandizement, defined as power through the ownership of material things, (is) the essence of man (and) private property . . . a fundamental inalienable human right" (1982: 7, 5).[1] As Ian Shapiro recently put it, "the

1. For further statements of such a view in the human rights literature, see Somerville 1949: 152; Farer 1985; Renteln 1985: 518; Cobbah 1987: 311ff. Compare also Claude 1976: 43; Yamane 1987: 99.

negative libertarian view of the substance of rights has been an integral part of the liberal conception of individual rights since its inception'' (1986: 276),[2] and many self-professed liberals share this understanding.[3]

Although there is an element of truth in this conventional or minimalist conception, there is an alternative strand in the liberal tradition that rests on a broader, more subtle, more coherent, and much more defensible social vision. This "radical or social democratic" conception of liberalism is my focus here.

The roots of the liberal Western approach to human rights are conventionally and correctly traced back to the seventeenth century, particularly seventeenth-century England. By the time Locke's *Two Treatises of Government* were published in 1689, a fully developed liberal, natural rights conception of politics had become well established in the mainstream of English political debate. In order to simplify and focus the argument, this chapter is devoted to a careful reading of Locke's *Second Treatise*, which is not only a seminal and almost canonical work in the liberal tradition, but also one of the standard sources of the conventional conception. If we can make out the elements of the radical conception of liberalism even in Locke, we will have done so in a place that most critics consider to be particularly unpromising.

After a brief introduction, the *Second Treatise* begins by arguing that men naturally are in "a *State of perfect Freedom*" and "a *State* also *of Equality*" (4.1–8),[4] and each person has natural *rights* to freedom and equality.[5] But this state of nature is not a state of license: "The *State of Nature* has a Law of Nature to govern it, which obliges every one: And Reason, which is that law, teaches all Mankind . . . that being all equal and independent, no one ought to harm another in his Life, Health, Liberty or Possessions'' (6.6–10).

All men in the state of nature have a natural right to execute the natural law (secs. 7–11). This is in effect a right to protect one's natural rights through individual or collective self-help. But partiality, "ill nature, Pas-

---

2. Compare Bay 1981: chap. 1; Arblaster 1984: pt. 1, esp. chap. 4; and, in two different veins, Wolin 1960: chap. 9 and MacIntyre 1981.

3. Isaiah Berlin's "Two Concepts of Liberty" (1969) gives a classic contemporary exposition of the emphasis on "negative" rights and liberties. In the literature on human rights, this view is associated especially with the work of Maurice Cranston (1973), although A. I. Melden provides a far more subtle and nuanced defense (1977: chap. 6). The libertarian variant is represented by such writers as von Mises (1985), Hayek (1960), and Nozick (1974); compare also Lemos 1986 and Lomasky 1987. For a Straussian variant, see Mansfield 1978, e.g., p. 10: "There are two principal rights in a liberal democracy. . . . The first is the right of acquiring private property. . . . The other right is the right of free speech."

4. All otherwise unidentified references are to Locke's *Second Treatise* in Laslett's edition (Locke 1967) by section and line number.

5. See, e.g., 7.1–2; 54.10–12; 87.1–4ff.; 95.1–5; 123.1–8.

sion and Revenge'' lead to abuses in executing the natural law, such abuses produce ''Confusion and Disorder,'' and disorder engenders a desire to form civil society and government as a ''Remedy for the Inconveniences of the State of Nature'' (13.2–11).

This remedy requires that each person, in conjunction with his fellows, contractually transfers to a public authority his or her individual right to execute the law of nature, thus creating a common judge on earth to settle disputes (secs. 87–89). This transfer, however, is conditional: it is limited by the ends for which it was made—namely, to protect individual rights and freedoms from invasion and to secure their more effective guarantee.

To use a more twentieth-century vocabulary, all human beings are born with natural or human rights to freedom and equality, but in the state of nature the enjoyment of these rights is insecure. Society and the state are devices to guarantee a more secure enjoyment of human rights, and a government is legitimate (only) to the extent that it actually protects human rights through positive law and practice. This threefold commitment to equality, autonomy, and natural rights[6]—rather than the conventional conception's emphasis on radical individualism, private property, and negative civil and political rights—is, I will argue, the essence of the liberal approach to human rights, from Locke to our own day.

2. THE INDIVIDUAL AND SOCIETY

The very idea of human rights does entail a certain individualism. Each person, simply as an individual human being, is specially entitled to the treatment demanded by human rights. The fact that rights, and the claims they ground, are largely under the control of the right-holder implies a further element of individualism as well.

But in addition to being a individual, one is a member of a family, a society, and other communities and associations, as well as a citizen of a state (at least in the contemporary world). For many people the particularities of such communal memberships are at least as important to the shape and meaning of their lives as the universal individuality protected by human rights. A standard charge against liberalism, however, is that it cannot adequately encompass the communal aspect of human existence:

6. Compare Dworkin 1985: chap. 8. John Rawls's *A Theory of Justice* (1971) is the best-known contemporary theoretical defense of liberalism thus understood. With special reference to human rights, see Gewirth 1984 and Shue 1980, although both works are cast in self-consciously universalistic, rather than Western or liberal, terms. For the purposes of this chapter on the liberal Western theory of human rights, I stipulate that liberalism is a rights-based rather than a utility-based theory. A more complete account of liberalism would need to take utilitarian liberal theories into account.

The only reality liberalism perceives is the reality of the individual. (Horowitz and Horowitz 1988: 151)

The difficulties of modern liberal-democratic theory lie deeper than had been thought. . . . The original seventeenth-century individualism contains the central difficulty, which lay in its . . . conception of the individual as essentially the proprietor of his own person or capacities, owing nothing to society for them. The individual was seen neither as a moral whole, nor as part of a larger social whole, but as an owner of himself. (Macpherson 1962: 3)[7]

The extreme version of this charge is that liberal rights theory is largely a crude device to guarantee individual self-preservation: "The individual is consumed by a desire for self-preservation in a state of nature" (Cobbah 1987: 314). As Strauss puts it, for Locke "the individual, the ego, has become the center and origin of the moral world," and "the most fundamental of all rights is therefore the right to self-preservation" (1953: 224, 227). Locke does indeed argue that "men, being once born, have a right to their Preservation" (25.2), and he does speak of the "Fundamental, Sacred and unalterable Law of *Self-Preservation*, for which they enter'd into Society" (149.24–25), but individual self-preservation is hardly the central element of Locke's theory. In fact, *self*-preservation typically appears not alone but in conjunction with the right and duty to preserve *all mankind*.[8]

There are at least as many references in the *Second Treatise* to the preservation of *all* mankind as to individual self-preservation.[9] In fact, Locke argues that the preservation of all mankind (or society[10]) is *the* fundamental law of nature:

For *by the Fundamental Law of Nature, Man being to be preserved*, as much as possible, when all cannot be preserv'd, the safety of the Innocent is to be preferred. (16.9–11)

7. "The so-called *rights of man* . . . are nothing but . . . the rights of egoistic man, of man separated from other men and from the community" (Marx 1975: 3.162). "(The West) is so overzealous in its defense of the individual's freedom, rights and dignity, that it overlooks the acts of some individuals in exercising such rights in a way that jeopardizes the community" (Yamani 1968: 15). "There is a perpetual, and in our view obsessive concern with the dignity of the individual, his worth, personal autonomy and property" (Legesse 1980: 124). For a good selection of the some of the major arguments in the liberalism-communitarian debate in contemporary political theory in the United States, see Sandel 1984.

8. See 6.19–22; 11.11–16; sec. 128; 129.1–4; 135.10–12, 16–17; 143.1–3; 171.12–17.

9. For arguments based on the preservation of all without parallel references to self-preservation, see, e.g., 7.2–4; 8.17–18; 16.9–11; 134.5–8; 135.30–32; 159.17–19; 182.6–7; 220.5–6.

10. At 171.14–15 Locke explicitly equates these two formulations.

> The *first and fundamental natural Law*, which is to govern even the Legislative it self, is *the preservation of the Society*, and (as far as will consist with the publick good) of every person in it. (134.5–8)

> The *fundamental Law of Nature* being *the preservation of Mankind*, no Humane Sanction can be good, or valid against it. (135.30–32)

> The Fundamental Law of Nature being, that all, as much as may be, should be preserved, it follows, that if there be not enough fully to *satisfy* both viz. for the *Conqueror's Losses*, and Childrens Maintenance, he that hath, and to spare, must remit something of his full Satisfaction, and give way to the pressing and preferable Title of those, who are in danger to perish without it. (183.22–28)[11]

Notice further that in the first and last of these passages the preservation of all takes priority over egoistic claims. Egoistic self-preservation is at best one strand in Locke's argument.

In the *Second Treatise* there is also a recurrent, if secondary, theme of natural sociability, of "the love and want of society" (101.3). Locke speaks of men "sharing all in one Community of Nature" (6.15–16), and he argues that each person "and all the rest of *Mankind are one Community*" (128.5–6). In fact, the chapter "Of Political or Civil Society" begins with the claim that "God having made Man such a Creature, that, in his own Judgement, it was not good for him to be alone, put him under strong Obligations of Necessity, Convenience and Inclination to drive him into *Society*, as well as fitted him with Understanding and Language to continue and enjoy it" (77.1–5).

Certainly self-preservation is an important part of Locke's account of both human nature and the ends of society. Avoiding the state of war, which threatens the preservation of both self and others, is "one great reason of *Mens putting themselves into Society*" (21.4). But it is (only) *one* reason. Not only is the preservation of all given at least equal prominence but, as we shall see below, what is to be preserved is not merely life, but also liberty and property. Locke does see the individual as having interests separate from those of society, and in the areas protected by human rights he does give individual interests prima facie priority over those of society. But even for Locke the individual is *also* part of the natural community of mankind, and except in the state of nature he or she is a member of society, a citizen of a state, and a member of other social groups as well, especially the family. We may argue over whether Locke strikes the *proper* balance between individual and society, but it is obvious that he does not simply sacrifice society to the individual.

11. Compare 171.19–23. On special duties to preserve children, see also 56.10–11; 60.16–19.

3. Private Property and the State

Human rights do provide individuals with inalienable entitlements that hold even against state and society, but so long as the rights in question are not extravagant, there need be nothing socially corrosive about such rights. This brings us to the second element in the conventional conception: the claim that liberalism not merely recognizes but also privileges a right to largely unlimited individual accumulation. Liberalism, so this argument runs, is committed to a radical, property-based individualism that Macpherson (1962) aptly calls "possessive individualism."

"Locke's case for the limited constitutional state is largely designed to support his argument for an individual right to unlimited private property. Defenders of the modern liberal state see, or sense, that that right is at the heart of their state" (Macpherson 1980: vii–viii). Liberals, Macpherson argues, view human freedom simply as independence from the wills of others, as freedom even from social relations with others except insofar as those relations rest on mutual, voluntary consent (1962: esp. 263–64). Individuals are seen as proprietors of their persons and talents, with respect to which they owe nothing to society. Social relations are thus conceptualized as a series of voluntary market relations between individual proprietors. Political society is merely a device to protect individual property and maintain the minimal order required for successfully engaging in market relations.

Macpherson is correct that the principal aim, or at least the principal conclusion, of the property chapter of the *Second Treatise* is to justify largely unlimited individual accumulation (1962: 199ff.). Furthermore, Locke does argue at numerous points that the end of civil society is the preservation of property.[12] But possessive individualism is only one side of Locke's theory, and the possessive individualist defense of property succeeds only in contingent historical circumstances that no longer exist in most of the world.

A. Of Property and Accumulation

Locke begins his Chapter 7, "Of Property," by asking how private property can be justified if God has given the earth to man in common (sec. 25). His answer is that human beings have been given the earth to use for their comfort and support, and use clearly requires appropriation (secs. 26 and 35). And although the earth is given in common, one's person is one's own, to use as one sees fit (within the limits set by the law of nature). "Every man has a *Property* in his own *Person*. This no Body has any Right

12. See, e.g., 3.1–3; 85.15–16; 94.22–23; 124.1–3; 173.6–8.

to but himself'' (27.2–3). By laboring, one mixes the property one has in one's person with the common stock of nature, thus fixing a property in and excluding others from the resulting product (secs. 27–30).[13] Natural law sanctions such appropriation and is the basis for all positive property law (sec. 30). But it also limits appropriation.

One has a duty to labor productively (sec. 32), to use the common stock of nature for human betterment. There is also a parallel right to appropriate whatever one can put to use[14]—but no more. "*God has give us all things richly*, I Tim. vi. 17. is the Voice of Reason confirmed by Inspiration. But how far has he given it to us? *To enjoy*. As much as any one can make use of to any advantage of life before it spoils; so much he may by his labour fix a Property in'' (31.5–9).

One's right to take only as much as one can use I will call the "use limit" on appropriation. The "spoilage limit" in the passage just quoted is simply a corollary of the use limit: if something spoils, it cannot be used. Locke's third limit on accumulation is introduced in the initial discussion of labor fixing a property. "*Labour* being the unquestionable Property of the Labourer, no Man but he can have a right to what that is once joyned to, *at least where there is enough and as good left in common for others*" (27.10–13; emphasis added). This "sufficiency" limit—that "enough and as good" remain for others—recurs in at least five additional sections of the property chapter (secs. 33–37) and assures that no one can complain of injury as a result of another's appropriation (secs. 31, 33, and 36), because such use by some does not deny minimum equality for others.

Take only what you can use, and leave enough and as good for others—with such limits it is difficult to see how one can object to Lockean property rights. But "Locke's astonishing achievement was to base the property right on natural right and natural law, and then to remove all the natural law limits from the property right" (Macpherson 1962: 199). This transformation is brought about by the introduction of money. "Every one had a Right (as hath been said) to as much as he could use" (46.8–9). But barter can be no injury, and if one person will take a piece of gold in exchange for a useful item, no one is injured. That piece of gold, however—as opposed to, say, a measure of grain—will not spoil. And since it will not spoil, Locke argues, it can be accumulated without limit, "the *exceeding the bounds of his* just *Property* not lying in the largeness of his Possession, but the perishing of anything uselessly in it" (46.28–30). The tacit consent to the use of money implied by accepting it in exchange, Locke argues, effectively circumvents the natural law limits on individual accumulation.

---

13. And because labor gives nearly all the value to any product (secs. 40–43), individual appropriation actually increases the stock effectively available to mankind (secs. 37, 44).

14. Compare, e.g., sec. 37.39–41, 38.3–5, and 46.7–9 with 32.10–19 and 35.18.

Notice, though, that here Locke speaks only of the spoilage limit; the use and sufficiency limits are not taken into account. If there is an abundance of land (and other essential resources), such as existed in "the first Ages of the World" (36.11), then each may indeed take all that he can use while leaving enough and as good for others. This follows simply from the definition of abundance. Locke's frequent references to the abundance of America (e.g., 36.18; 41.1–3) and his argument that "there are still *great Tracts of Ground* to be found, which . . . *lie waste*" (45.19–22) suggest that he believed that abundance still prevailed,[15] at least on a global scale,[16] providing a contextual and empirical justification for his exclusive focus on the spoilage limit.

In our current world of scarcity, however, *we* must explicitly consider all three natural law limits on accumulation. And in conditions of material scarcity the defense of unlimited accumulation developed in the *Second Treatise* fails.

Consider once more the crucial conclusion: "*the exceeding the bounds of his just Property* not lying in the largeness of his Possession, but the perishing of anything uselessly in it." Mere size, it is true, is not evidence of unjust accumulation, but on Locke's own argument the absence of spoilage alone is not sufficient evidence of just accumulation. We must also ask whether the accumulated property is being put to use and whether enough and as good has been left for others.

"Use" is a slippery notion. For example, a very broad and elastic definition, such as one that counts the pure pleasure of possession as use, may make the use limit largely a formality. But once a certain stage of scarcity has been reached, private appropriation simply will not leave either as much or as good for the others. If justice in accumulation is to be secured in *all* circumstances, we must focus on the sufficiency limit, for only it guarantees minimum equality and assures that others are not injured by private appropriation. The spoilage limit focuses our attention on the process of accumulation and the person of the accumulator. Sufficiency

15. I take Locke's apparent belief in abundance at face value. His occasional use of the past tense when talking about abundance (e.g., 31.11–12; 36.33–39; 49.1–3), however, might suggest that he was beginning to see the specter of scarcity on the horizon, in which case the assumption of abundance in the property chapter might be a bit more problematic, even blameworthy, than my account suggests.

16. Locke did, however, recognize the existence of local scarcity, most clearly in his explicit argument against enclosing the English commons, because "the remainder, after such inclosure, would not be as good to the rest" (35.8–9). One might also ask whether a defense of property that requires others to make a wrenching, even dangerous, move to America in order to acquire their share of the "enough and as good" that is left really is as unproblematic as Locke seems to believe. Again, though, I have given Locke the benefit of the doubt here, because my principal argument does not require a less sympathetic reading.

shifts our attention to the resulting distributional pattern and the consequences of individual accumulation *for others*. It thus requires us to ask not whether the accumulator acquired his wealth "fair and square," but whether his holding such wealth is just or fair to others.

When unlimited private accumulation threatens the very life of others— as it did in early industrial England, as it would do again today even in the wealthy West without state intervention, and as it certainly did for the very poorest in seventeenth-century England—Locke seems committed not merely to allowing but actually to *requiring* remedial political action (that is, limits on accumulation), even if that accumulation has satisfied the use and spoilage limits. Such arguments, as I will suggest below, point toward a Lockean defense of economic and social human rights.

But what of the "tacit and voluntary consent" (50.6) to money? Locke is quite insistent that "the *Invention of Money*, and the tacit Agreement of Men to put a value on it, introduced (by Consent) larger Possession and a Right to them" (36.37–39). Consent, however, cannot cancel natural law limits. "The *fundamental Law of Nature* being *the preservation of Mankind*, no Humane Sanction can be good or valid against it" (135.30–32; compare 12.16–19; 135.23–27). In conditions of scarcity, unlimited accumulation simply will not leave enough and as good for others, as the natural law requires. Therefore, to the extent that positive law allows such accumulation in circumstances of scarcity, it is unjust, and not to be obeyed.

This leaves us with an interpretative problem. Must liberals, to the extent that they are Lockean, defend a right to unlimited accumulation? Critics, such as Macpherson, clearly believe that they must, and many self-professed liberals, over not merely generations but centuries, have indeed defended a largely unlimited right to property. But the use of "Lockean" arguments by Locke and some other defenders of private property is no more decisive than, say, an attack on or defense of socialism based on Soviet practice backed by selective quotations from Marx.

We cannot ignore the use to which a theory has been put, especially when that use can be plausibly traced back to (at least part of) the original theoretical source. Locke did argue for unlimited accumulation, and contemporary libertarians can situate themselves within a tradition of thought and practice that goes back at least to Locke. But, as we have seen, there is also a very different strand in Locke's argument. Furthermore, this radical strand informs another, quite different, "Lockean" tradition, which runs through Paine, to contemporary theorists such as Rawls and Dworkin, and has been embodied in the contemporary social democratic welfare state.

If our interest were purely historical or hermeneutical, we might stop here, with the demonstration of two competing strands in the liberal tradition that flow out of Locke's *Second Treatise*. But because our interest in Locke here is as a representative and source of the liberal tradition, we must move beyond descriptive or historical questions to deeper analytical or interpretative, and perhaps even moral, issues and ask whether there are grounds for choosing one of these strands over the other. If we can show that one strand of a theory is substantially more compatible with its central theoretical premises, that strand deserves interpretative priority. By such a test, the "best" interpretation of Locke (and liberalism) will give priority to the limits on accumulation.

Recall the starting point of Locke's theory: the natural freedom and equality of all men, within the limits of the law of nature (which enjoins respect for that freedom and equality). Recall also Locke's conception of a legitimate society: a society that secures enjoyment of the rights and privileges of nature (which cannot be securely enjoyed in the state of nature). Restrictions on the right of individual accumulation clearly are required by these fundamental theoretical presuppositions. In many cases, unlimited accumulation would violate Locke's natural law and threaten not merely the freedom and equality but the very existence of the propertyless.

The argument for unlimited accumulation is valid, on Locke's own terms, only in conditions of abundance. Scarcity, however, is the rule. Locke's defense of unlimited accumulation thus is at best an argument applicable only to a bygone era. The property chapter of the *Second Treatise* simply does not justify a *universal* right to unlimited accumulation. Therefore, on even Lockean grounds liberals today are under no obligation to defend such a right. In fact, they would seem instead to be obliged to deny claims to a right to unlimited accumulation.

B. Property and the Ends of Government

Although Locke does not privilege a right to *unlimited* accumulation, he does repeatedly claim that the purpose of society and government is to preserve property. Such passages do suggest that he gives priority to a more limited right to property and thus may be a possessive individualist in a somewhat more limited sense of that term. But Locke repeatedly states that by "property" in such contexts he means men's lives, liberties, and estates, not merely their possessions:

He seeks out, and is willing to joyn in Society with others who are already united, or have a mind to unite for the mutual *Preservation* of the Lives, Liberties and Estates, which I call by the general Name, *Property*. (123.14–17)

. . . to preserve his Property, that is, his Life, Liberty and Estates. (87.5)

By *Property* I must be understood here, as in other places, to mean that Property which Men have in their Persons as well as Goods. (173.4–6)[17]

It is true that Locke often uses "property" in the sense of estates only, including in one discussion of the ends of government (secs. 138, 139), but Macpherson is simply wrong in his claim that "in his crucial arguments on the limitation of the power of governments he (Locke) is clearly using property in the more usual sense of lands and goods" (1962: 198).

Locke begins chapter 11, his principal discussion of the limits on state power, by arguing that the great end of entering society is the peaceful and secure enjoyment of property. The great means and instrument of achieving that end is government through settled laws. Therefore, establishing the legislative power is "the *first and fundamental positive law* of all commonwealths . . . as the *first and fundamental* natural law, which is to govern even the Legislative itself, is *the preservation of the Society*, and (as far as is consistent with the publick good) of every person in it" (134.4–8). (We have already seen above how this line of argument undercuts the charge of atomistic individualism.) He then begins to list the limits of the legislative power implied by this end of preserving property:

First, It is *not*, nor can possibly be absolutely *Arbitrary* over the Lives and Fortunes of the People. . . . (The legislative) Power in the utmost Bounds of it, is *limited to the publick good* of the Society. It is a Power, that hath no other end but preservation, and therefore can never have a right to destroy, enslave, or designedly to impoverish the Subjects. (135.4–5, 19–23)

Notice the clear presence here of the triple definition of lives (destroy), liberties (enslave), and estates (impoverish). And in this section as well, the fundamental natural law of the preservation of all Mankind is prominently featured.

Locke's second limit requires the legislative power to rule "by *promulgated standing Laws, and known Authoris'd Judges*" (136.4) in order to assure that it will fulfill its charge "to determine the Rights, and fence the Properties of those that live under it" (136.9–10). Otherwise "their Peace, Quiet and Property will still be at the same uncertainty, as it was in the state of Nature" (136.23–24). Property here includes estates only, but it is explicitly linked, through the reference to peace and quiet, to the other elements of the broader definition. Locke here also explicitly states that the

17. See also 85.12–15; 171.15–17; 221.4–8; 222.14–21.

purpose of government is to determine (*all*) the rights of the citizens, not just to fence their estates. And in the following section he repeats the central claim that the reason men enter society is "to preserve their Lives, Liberties and Fortunes; and by *stated Rules* of Right and Property to secure their Peace and Quiet."[18] Without such protections "their Persons and Estates" would be subject to arbitrary power (137.4–6, 9).

Only after all of this, as a third limit on the legislative, do we come to the passages that Macpherson emphasizes almost exclusively (1962: 198 n. 6). "*Thirdly*, The *Supream Power cannot take* from any Man any part of his *Property* without his own consent" (138.1–2). Locke is indeed speaking only about the preservation of estates here, but Macpherson is simply wrong in his claim that these are the crucial passages on the ends of government; they are quite explicitly subsidiary. In all the crucial passages—and even in most of the minor passages—lives, liberties, and estates is the meaning Locke clearly attaches to "property" when he specifies it to be the end of government.[19]

Furthermore, because property in the sense of estates only is part of the broader definition, it seems most appropriate to read the rare passages that reflect the estates only sense as partial accounts of the ends of government. Occasionally Locke does refer to estates only, but sometimes he talks of lives only (e.g., 149.24–25) and sometimes he talks of lives and liberties together without reference to estates (e.g., 66.23). Because Locke at a number of points talks about the parts separately does not alter the fact that they are, quite explicitly, only parts of the broader whole. Estates are only one part of the "property" that government is created, and obliged, to protect.

Locke also offers several alternative formulations of the ends of politics

18. Notice again that Locke says rules of right *and property*. Here, as in most other places where Locke uses "property" in the narrow sense of estates when discussing the ends of government, he speaks of rights (or right) generally *and* property, not just property alone.

19. Compare also 123.13–17 and 173.1–8. We should also note that the terminology of lives, liberties, and estates occurs at a number of points throughout the work (e.g. 57.25; 59.30; 65.30–32; 69.14; 209.5–6), along with various similar or equivalent formulations, such as "Peace, Liberties, and Fortunes" (75.16–17), "Life, Liberty, or Possessions" (135.15), "Life, Health, Liberty or Possessions" (6.9–10), "the Life, the Liberty, Health, Limb or Goods" (6.24–25), "comfortable, safe and peaceable living" (95.7), "Person and Possessions" (120.15; 123.2), "Lives and Fortunes" (171.18–19), and "Property or Actions" (74.10). Furthermore, there are a number of passages (e.g., 3.1–3; 87.10; 94.22–23; 127.5–9; and sec. 199) linking society and the preservation of property where "property" is not defined. In almost all of these passages, the broad definition of property makes at least as much sense as the narrow definition. Compare also the discussion of the slave as one incapable of having property (secs. 173–174), which makes little sense except on the broad definition.

that make sense only on a broad interpretation of property as roughly equivalent to *all* natural rights. The very last words of the chapter on the ends of political society are "and all this to be directed to no other *end*, but the *Peace, Safety* and *publick good* of the People" (131.20–21). As we saw above, Locke argues in a number of passages that "the *end of Government* (is) the *preservation of all*" (159.26–27). And in the discussion of the dissolution of government, Locke argues: "Where there is no longer the administration of Justice, for the securing of Mens Rights . . . there certainly is *no Government left*" (219.10–14).

I therefore suggest that a reading in line with the radical conception is to be preferred to Macpherson's minimalist reading. John Locke, and many self-professed liberals, have indeed attempted to give a special, higher status to the right to property. The historical record of the liberal democratic West, especially prior to the twentieth century and in its relations with the Third World in particular, has indeed given inordinate emphasis to individual property rights. But even in Locke's *Second Treatise* there is another strand to the argument that is *at least* as important. The liberal tradition, even in its seventeenth-century roots, possesses theoretical resources that allow—actually, require—a broader and more humane approach to human rights.

4. "Positive" Rights

The third element in the conventional conception is the argument that the liberal tradition recognizes only "negative" (especially civil and political) rights. As we saw in Chapter 2, Henry Shue has shown that the distinction between "negative" and "positive" rights is artificial and incorrect, that virtually all rights have both "positive" and "negative" correlative duties (Shue 1979; 1980: 41–46; compare Taylor 1979 and MacCallum 1973). Let us grant, though, that in many standard circumstances many rights entail *primarily* positive or *primarily* negative correlative duties.

The liberal tradition has indeed given considerable, and often preponderant, emphasis to primarily negative rights. Even today, it is primarily defenders of liberal democratic rule who emphasize "negative" civil and political rights; most other theoretical perspectives and social systems devote the bulk of their attention to duties and to "positive" rights and protections. Locke in particular emphasizes that protecting the lives, liberties, and estates of citizens requires restraint—"negative" action—on the part of the government; the government may not destroy, enslave, or impoverish its citizens (171.22–23), and it must not *interfere* with their lives, liberties, or estates except in very limited circumstances. He often even defines liberty as absence of dependence on the wills of others (e.g., 4.3–6). But Locke also has a much more "positive" conception of liberty:

> *Freedom* then is not what Sir R[obert] F[ilmer] tells us . . . *A Liberty for every one to do what he lists, to live as he pleases, and not to be tyed by any Laws*: But *Freedom of Men under Government*, is, to have a standing Rule to live by, common to every one of that Society, and made by the Legislative Power erected in it . . . As *Freedom of Nature* is to be under no other restraint by the Law of Nature. (22.8–16)

> *Law*, in its true Notion, is not so much the Limitation as *the direction of a free and intelligent Agent* to his proper Interest, . . . *the end of Law* is not to abolish or restrain, but to *preserve and enlarge Freedom.* (57.10–13, 17–18)

Unlike Hobbes, who defines liberty in almost entirely negative terms, as absence of constraint (*Leviathan*, chaps. 14, 21), Locke's account includes the limits of natural and civil law as *part* of, not a restriction on, liberty (compare 6.1–2ff.).

The liberal commitment to personal autonomy does imply a considerable degree of freedom from external determination. The practice of rights does put considerable power in the hand of the individual right-holder, power that is often used to prevent external interference with individual choices. But to the extent that the core values of equality and autonomy require positive rights for their realization—for example, to protect the basic moral equality of despised and long oppressed minorities—liberalism is not only free, but also *committed*, to embrace them. Both liberty and equality can be plausibly interpreted in primarily negative, primarily positive, and mixed terms. Natural rights to freedom and equality simply do not demand a negative interpretation. And even Locke gave a prominent place to the principally positive, not negative, rights to political participation and private property.

5. ECONOMIC AND SOCIAL RIGHTS

The related argument that liberalism does (or can consistently) recognize only civil and political rights is clearly without basis; the right to private property is manifestly an economic or social, not a civil or political, right. One might respond, though, that the point of the conventional conception's argument is that liberalism recognizes *only one* economic and social right, the right to property. This is at least an accurate description of Locke's *Second Treatise*, and of most liberals until at least well into the nineteenth century. But this is a contingent historical fact, not an essential feature of liberalism.

The fundamental natural law of the preservation of *all* mankind clearly allows the recognition of additional economic and social rights. In fact, rights to food and health care would serve this end better than a right to private property (especially a right to unlimited accumulation). Furthermore, if we recognize that liberty has a significant positive component—that is, that liberty is not merely the absence of restraint, but the genuine opportunity to choose a way of life—then economic and social rights are likely to be essential for establishing the material prerequisites for true freedom, especially for the propertyless. Likewise, if equality is interpreted as having a substantial positive component, economic and social rights are likely to follow as well.

More generally, there is no theoretical reason why liberals ought to—let alone must—restrict their understanding of either liberty or equality to civil and political relations, to the exclusion of the economic and social dimensions that are so important to both individual and social life. Not even Locke did that, as the triad of life, liberty, and estates indicates. And, as we saw in the critique of minimalism in Chapter 4, once one lets in the right to property, it is impossible to (consistently) keep other economic and social rights out.

The commitment to private property, which has been an important part of the liberal tradition, probably does rest in large measure on a Lockean entitlement argument: one is the proprietor of one's labor, and thus the rightful owner of its products (insofar as natural law allows). It also reflects a recognition of the important sphere of autonomy that property can provide. The related preference for market mechanisms rests on the minimal (direct) interference with personal liberty entailed by market systems of production and distribution, along with considerations of efficiency (which became a central part of the tradition with Adam Smith).

But these liberal preferences are just that—prima facie preferences, which must give way to the basic rights and values of liberty and equality. Unless property is balanced by other human rights and the market gives way when it infringes human rights, we have not a liberal theory of human rights but a partisan and quite crude defense of class privilege.[20] If government is to preserve the "property" of all, it should do precisely that: guarantee the life and liberty, as well as the justly held estates, of all

20. This is in many ways the broader theoretical point and the essential insight of the theory of possessive individualism: to give priority to the right to private property *is* to reduce human relations to market relations and to erode social bonds in favor of a clutching, competitive individualism.

individuals. Locke emphasizes that this should be accomplished through protecting citizens against arbitrary political power. This is certainly an important task, but there is no theoretical reason to preclude requiring the government to protect life and liberty from other threats, including the threats of economic scarcity and deprivation.

In human rights terms, this implies recognizing at least rights to food and to health care. In fact, life and liberty can probably be best protected from economic threats by a right to work. The right to work also has the special advantage, from a liberal perspective, of guaranteeing life and providing the material bases for liberty in a way that assures at least some minimum economic autonomy and equality.

I am well aware that I am taking liberal principles well beyond where Locke would have been comfortable going, but my point is simply that John Locke's failure to pursue this particular development of his principles no more binds liberals to repeat his secondary theoretical choices or even errors than, say, contemporary Aristotleans are bound to believe that some men are naturally slaves and all women are rationally deficient, or contemporary utilitarians are bound to accept Bentham's particular catalog of pleasures and pains and Mill's low opinion of "barbarian" races. Liberalism is not a matter of a fixed set of canonical details set out in Locke or anywhere else; there is neither Koran nor Sharia in this tradition. Its essence is found instead in its fundamental principles—that is, in its commitments to equality and autonomy and to protecting these values through human rights.

Theoretical traditions do have founders and seminal figures, but as long as a tradition is alive, and not merely a ritual formality or a matter of antiquarian interest, it will evolve in response to the challenges and opportunities of new ideas and new circumstances, criticism from within and from without, past errors, the unintended consequences of previous actions, and so forth. The only traditions that are static are dead, dying, or dogmatic. To insist on restricting liberalism to what Locke wrote, and nothing more (or less), would be not an exercise in defense, fidelity, or even rational thinking, but to write the epitaph for the liberal tradition or to participate in an unreflective, ritual affirmation of dogmatic faith.

The core values and fundamental principles of a tradition are, of course, "contestable"; their precise meaning, content, and implications are matters over which reasonable and thoughtful people not only may but also are likely to disagree (compare Gallie 1968). In fact, political debate within a tradition is largely a matter of controversy over the proper understanding of the core values—in the liberal case, of equality, autonomy, and human rights. As a living political tradition, liberalism (like all other traditions) is characterized by an evolving self-understanding of the meaning and implications of its central theoretical commitments.

6. LOCKE, LIBERALISM, AND THE BOURGEOIS POLITICAL REVOLUTION

In discussing Locke and liberalism, we have yet to give more than glancing attention to the revolutionary character of liberal natural rights ideas. The *Second Treatise* was largely written before 1688, but it was in an important sense "produced"—in the way that a play is produced, brought before the public—by the Glorious Revolution, and it concludes with a defense of the right to revolution. That defense may not be all that rousing. Locke's right to revolution turns out to be restricted to a right of "society," which in effect means the majority of those qualified to vote. The Glorious Revolution may not even have been all that "revolutionary," at least by today's standards, but it was a crucial step in the consolidation of the bourgeois political revolution in England, which was indeed a radical change from the Elizabethan political system of the beginning of the century.

Locke's *Second Treatise*, however sedate and "moderate" we may find it today, was a revolutionary document when it appeared in 1689. Like most revolutionary tracts, it is strongest in its negative arguments—arguments against arbitrary rule, against absolute power, against unlimited royal prerogative, an unconditional duty to obey, the right of conquest, tyranny, usurpation, and so forth. Natural rights are used by Locke principally for criticizing inequality, privilege, and oppression under Stuart rule; they provide Locke with only a very vague and general positive model of what society ought to look like. The *Second Treatise* is much more about how society and government should not act than how they should.

The specific revolutionary character of the *Second Treatise* also points to the particular historical limits of Locke's project, limits that arise largely from the limited aims of the bourgeois political revolution. For all the shortcomings of the conventional conception as a general theory of liberalism, it does at least accurately highlight the fact that liberalism in the seventeenth and eighteenth centuries was indeed principally about overthrowing traditional aristocratic rule and replacing it with bourgeois rule. The bourgeoisie, who provided the principal support for early liberalism, did demand equality, simply as human beings, against the traditional inequalities of birth. Whatever the philosophical merits or shortcomings of this claim, it was undeniably in their interest to make it. The bourgeoisie demanded both political and economic liberty, against royal prerogative, aristocratic privilege and both traditional and mercantilist economic regulations. This too was in their interest. They emphasized their rights, in contrast to the traditional emphasis on duty; their individuality, based on an allegedly universal human nature, in contrast to traditional ascriptive and communitarian definitions of persons; and labor, accumulation, and property, rather than leisure, display, consumption, and status. They also emphasized the limits on the state and the civil and political rights of the citizenry. And Locke did give one of the richest and most compelling defenses of these arguments in the entire liberal corpus.

It is therefore both fair and informative to say that *in the beginning* liberalism was the bourgeois revolution of the seventeenth and eighteenth centuries. It is also fair, and informative, to say that in the eighteenth and nineteenth centuries the *main* stream of liberalism, both in theory and in practice, tended to lose its initially revolutionary character and to solidify into a new form of privilege, inequality, and oppression based on property rather than on birth. But liberalism is not *merely* the bourgeois revolution or its fossilized remains. We must avoid the genetic fallacy in interpreting a theoretical tradition: its origins simply do not necessarily define its ultimate development, however much they may condition, constrain, or limit it. The original underlying principles of equality, autonomy, and natural rights could be, and indeed were, used by more radical liberal theorists, activists, and politicians to attack precisely this new form of class rule and inequality.

This implies that liberalism, or at least the radical strand of liberalism stressed here, is essentially and inherently ''revolutionary.'' Locke was only one of many liberals, for more than three centuries now, who have used and continue to use human rights arguments to rebel against injustice and oppression. It is therefore not coincidental that today we contrast liberals with conservatives; liberals, from Locke to today, have been champions of rights-based political change. Human rights for liberals are thus primarily ''negative'' rights in a very different sense of that term: their principal use is to demand that old ways, however convenient or time-honored, give way to the legitimate demands of the equal and inalienable rights of all human beings.

This ''negative'' or ''extralegal'' character of human rights is essential to their nature as human rights (see Chapter 1). While we *have* human rights simply as human beings, human rights, like other rights, are *claimed*—put to use, actively advanced against duty-bearers—principally when they are violated or at risk. The principal use of human rights is to bring about political change, and the very idea of human rights commits their defenders to a politics of change, for which human rights provide the model.

Having demonstrated the existence, perhaps even the primacy, of the radical conception of liberalism even in Locke, I think there can be little quarrel with my broader claims that Western liberalism is the source of the contemporary idea of human rights and that a (radical or social democratic) liberal regime is demanded by international human rights standards. But this radical or social democratic strand of liberalism is not merely a theoretical ideal; it has been embodied in practice in most Western liberal democratic states. Whether we are concerned with economic and social rights or with civil and political rights, and especially if we are concerned with both sets of interdependent and indivisible human rights, it is in the liberal democratic regimes of Western Europe that human rights have been most fully realized in practice.

Furthermore, the social democratic strand of liberalism was a fairly well developed theoretical tradition backing the emerging working-class struggle against capitalism at least half a century before Marx. For example, Paine, in *Rights of Man, Part Two*, advocated a state-funded system of social security, and in *Agrarian Justice* developed a strong argument for a variety of economic and social rights.[21] It would be another century or more until positive economic and social rights became firmly established within the dominant mainstream of liberal practice, but the struggle for these rights was part of the radical strand of liberalism well before the emergence of revolutionary socialist parties in the mid-nineteenth century.

Horrors have indeed been committed in the name of liberalism (understood as the political complement to an economic system of unlimited capitalist accumulation), both in the West and in the Third World, but all doctrines have been abused by dictators and tyrants. Consider, for example, the fate of socialism in the hands of Stalin, or traditional African values in the hands of Macias Nguema of Equatorial Guinea. In the case of liberalism we have a long tradition of both theory *and practice*, culminating in the social democratic welfare state of our era, which suggests that it is not only the source of contemporary human rights ideas but also the type of political system that is best able to realize those rights in practice.

21. For an excellent discussion of the crucial role of Paine in the emergence of the English working-class movement at the end of the eighteenth century, see Thompson 1963: 86–113.

PART III

Human Rights and Cultural Relativism

6
Cultural Relativism and Universal Human Rights

Cultural relativity is an undeniable fact; moral rules and social institutions evidence an astonishing cultural and historical variability. The doctrine of cultural relativism holds that at least some such variations cannot be legitimately criticized by outsiders. But if human rights are literally the rights everyone has simply as a human being, they would seem to be universal by definition. How should the competing claims of cultural relativism and universal human rights be reconciled? I defend an approach that maintains the fundamental universality of human rights while accommodating the historical and cultural particularity of human rights discussed above.

1. DEFINING "CULTURAL RELATIVISM"

In its most extreme form, what we can call *radical cultural relativism* would hold that culture is the sole source of the validity of a moral right or rule. *Radical universalism* would hold that culture is irrelevant to the validity of moral rights and rules, which are universally valid. The body of the continuum defined by these ideal typical end-points—that is, those positions involving varying mixes of relativism and universalism—can be roughly divided into what we can call strong cultural realism and weak cultural relativism.

Strong cultural relativism holds that culture is the *principal* source of the validity of a moral right or rule. Universal human rights standards, however, serve as a check on potential excesses of relativism. At its furthest extreme, just short of radical relativism, strong cultural relativism would accept a few basic rights with virtually universal application, but allow such a wide range of variation for most rights that two entirely justifiable sets might overlap only slightly.[1]

Weak cultural relativism holds that culture may be an *important* source of the validity of a moral right or rule. Universality is initially presumed, but the relativity of human nature, communities, and rights serves as a check on potential excesses of universalism. At its furthest extreme, just short of radical universalism, weak cultural relativism would recognize a comprehensive set of prima facie universal human rights, but allow occasional and strictly limited local variations and exceptions.

We must be careful not to use merely quantitative measures of relativism; qualitative judgments of the significance of different cultural variations must also be incorporated. In a rough way, three hierarchical levels of variation can be distinguished, involving cultural relativity in the *substance* of lists of human rights, in the *interpretation* of individual rights, and in the *form* in which particular rights are implemented. As we move "down" the hierarchy, we are in effect further specifying and interpreting (in the ordinary sense of that term) the higher level, and the range of permissible variation at a given level is set by the next higher level. For example, "interpretations" of a right are logically limited by the substance of a right; even the range of variation in substance is set by the notions of human nature and dignity from which the list of rights derives. I shall ultimately defend a weak cultural relativist position that permits deviations from universal human rights standards[2] primarily at the level of form.

2. RELATIVITY AND UNIVERSALITY: A NECESSARY TENSION

The dangers of the moral imperialism implied by radical universalism hardly need be emphasized. Radical universalism is subject to other moral objections as well. Moral rules, including human rights, function within a moral community. Radical universalism requires a rigid hierarchical ordering of the multiple moral communities to which individuals and groups belong. In order to preserve complete universality for human rights, the radical universalist must give absolute priority to the demands of the cosmopolitan moral community over all other ("lower") moral communities.

---

1. This is very similar to the argument from practical consensus for basic rights that was discussed and rejected in Chapter 2, section 2.A.

2. Henceforth, I shall be concerned only with cultural relativist views as they apply to human rights, although my argument probably has broader applicability to other types of relativistic arguments as well.

This complete denial of national and subnational ethical autonomy and self-determination is not acceptable. Even if the nation should prove to be a doomed, transitory stage in the development of human moral community, there is no inescapable logical or moral reason why peoples cannot accept or choose it as their principal form of social organization and the locus of important extrafamilial moral and political commitments. Similar arguments might be made for other communities that do not encompass the entire human race.

Once we allow the moral validity of such commitments, we are bound to accept at least certain types of substantive moral variability, including variability in human rights practices. Such moral "nationalism" may be based on political reasons, such as an inability to agree on the structure of a supranational organization, or a fear of creating an instrument of universal tyranny. More directly moral reasons might also be advanced—for example, the advantages of international diversity provided by a strong commitment to national or local customs. Most important, it rests on the notion of self-determination. But however it is justified, at least certain choices of such moral communities demand respect from outsiders—not necessarily uncritical acceptance, let alone emulation, but, in some cases at least, tolerance.

If radical universalism cannot be justifiably maintained—at least with respect to any robust substantive list of human rights, such as that provided in the Universal Declaration and the Covenants—even a weak cultural relativist account of human rights seems on its face guilty of logical contradiction. If human rights are based in human nature, on the simple fact that one is a human being, then how can human rights be relative in any fundamental way?

The simple answer is that human nature is itself in some measure culturally relative (compare Chapter I, section 3). There is a sense in which this is true even biologically—for example, if marriage partners are chosen on the basis of cultural preferences concerning height, weight, hair color, skin tone, or other physical attributes, the gene pool in a community may be altered in ways that are equivalent to "natural" mechanisms of selection. More important, culture can significantly influence the presence and expression of many less easily quantified aspects of human nature—for example, by encouraging or discouraging the development or perpetuation of certain personality traits and types.

The effects of culture in shaping individuals are systematic and may lead to the predominance of distinctive social types in different cultures. For example, there are important, structurally determined differences between the modal "natures" of women in modern Western and traditional Islamic societies. In any particular case, "human nature"—the realized nature of real human beings—is a social as well as a "natural" product.

Whether we conceive of this process as involving cultural variation around an unalterable core or as cultural variation largely within a physiologically fixed range, there is a social side to human nature that cannot be denied, at least insofar as that nature is expressed. "Human nature" is a range of possibilities varying, in part in response to culture, within certain psychobiological limits; it is as much a project and an individual and social discovery as it is a given. Even if all behavior should prove to be ultimately genetic, the expression of that genetic endowment in human behavior— which also merits being called "human nature"—is in considerable measure culturally determined.

The cultural variability of human nature not only permits but requires significant allowance for cross-cultural variations in human rights (see Chapter 1).[3] But if all rights rested *solely* on culturally determined social rules, as radical cultural relativism holds, there could be no human rights, no rights one has simply as a human being. This denial of human rights is perfectly coherent and has been widely practiced. Nevertheless, it is morally indefensible today (compare Chapters 3 and 4).

The strongest form of radical cultural relativism would hold that the concept "human being" is of no moral significance, that the mere fact that one is a human being is irrelevant to one's moral status. Many premodern societies have not even recognized "human being" as a descriptive category, but instead defined persons by social status or by group membership. For example, the very names of many cultures mean simply "the people" (e.g., Hopi, Arapahoe), and their origin myths may define them as separate from outsiders, who are somehow "not-human." Similarly, the ancient Greeks divided the world into Hellenes and barbarians.

This view, however, is almost universally rejected in the contemporary world. For example, chattel slavery and caste systems, which implicitly deny the existence of a morally significant common humanity, are almost universally condemned, even in the most rigid class societies. Likewise, moral distinctions between insiders and outsiders has been seriously eroded by greatly increased individual mobility and by an at least aspirational commitment to the idea of a universal human moral community. Even more striking is the apparent cross-cultural consensus on a few practices that cannot be justified by even the hoariest of traditions, and certainly not by any new custom. For example, the prohibition of torture and the requirement of procedural due process in imposing and executing legal

3. I am arguing not that *all* such variations are morally justifiable but, quite the contrary, only that *some* variations *may* be justifiable.

punishments seem to be accepted as binding by virtually all cultures, despite profound differences in specifying the practical and substantive meanings of these notions. There is also a striking cross-cultural consensus on many of the values that today we seek to protect through human rights, especially when those values are expressed in relatively general terms. Life, social order, the family, protection from arbitrary rule, prohibition of inhuman and degrading treatment, the guarantee of a place in the life of the community, and access to an equitable share of the means of subsistence are central moral aspirations in nearly all cultures.

The radical relativist might respond that such consensus is irrelevant. Logically, this is correct; cross-cultural consensus does not necessarily entail any additional force for a moral rule. But most people do believe that such consensus adds force to the rule, so this kind of radical relativism, although logically impeccable, is in an important sense morally defective. In effect, a moral analogue to customary international law seems to operate. If a practice is nearly universal and generally perceived as obligatory, that practice is required of all members of the community. And if there is at least a weak cosmopolitan moral community, it would impose certain substantive limitations on the range of permissible cultural moral variation.

Notice, however, that I contend only that there are at least a few cross-culturally valid moral *values*. This still leaves open the possibility of a radical cultural relativist denial of human *rights*. Such an argument would hold that while there may be universal moral rules or values, human rights in the strict and strong sense of the term (inalienable entitlements held equally by all, grounding particularly strong claims that may be made against the state and society) are but one of several defensible mechanisms to protect human dignity, which in any case is largely a culturally determined notion.

Plausible arguments can be advanced to justify alternative mechanisms to guarantee human dignity—for example, natural *law*, which imposes transcultural moral obligations that are not correlative to rights (compare Donnelly 1980). Few if any states, however, actually advance such arguments. In the First, Second, and Third Worlds alike, a strong commitment to human *rights* is almost universally proclaimed, even where practice throws that commitment into question. And even if such proclamations are mere rhetorical fashion, such a widespread international moral "fashion" must have some substantive basis.

That basis is the moral hazard presented by the modern state. Traditional rulers usually faced substantial moral limits on their political power, customary limits that were entirely independent of human rights, and the relative technological and administrative weakness of traditional states and nonstate political institutions further restrained arbitrary abuses of power. In such a world, inalienable entitlements of individuals held against state and society might plausibly be held to be superfluous (because basic dignity was being guaranteed by alternative mechanisms), if not positively dangerous to well-established practices that realized a cultural conception of human dignity.

Such a world exists today only in a relatively small number of isolated areas. And the modern state, particularly in the Third World, not only operates relatively free of the moral constraints of custom but also has far greater administrative and technological reach. It thus represents a serious threat to basic human dignity, whether that dignity is defined in "traditional" terms or in "modern" terms. In such circumstances, at least certain human rights seem necessary rather than optional. In contemporary circumstances, then, radical or unrestricted relativism is as inappropriate as unrestricted universalism. Some kind of intermediate position is required.[4]

3. VARIETIES OF CULTURAL RELATIVISM

A. *Internal versus External Judgments*
What we can call an *internal judgment* asks whether the practice is defensible within the fundamental value framework of that society. An *external judgment* applies the standards of the evaluator (modified, as appropriate, by relativistic arguments). Practices that are internally defensible but unacceptable by external standards are the practices that are of interest in the discussion of cultural relativism and human rights.

This distinction between internal and external evaluations roughly corresponds to, and further elaborates, the distinction between strong and weak cultural relativism; the stronger one's relativism, the greater one's reliance on internal evaluations. It also helps to elucidate the dilemma we face in judging culturally specific practices, torn between the demands of relativism and universalism.

Respect for autonomous moral communities would seem to demand internal evaluations, but to rely on internal judgments alone abrogates one's moral responsibilities as a member of the cosmopolitan moral community. Membership in one's own national or local moral community might also demand (a different type of) external judgments. Furthermore, moral judgments (at least as they are typically understood in the West) are

---

4. This argument is quite self-consciously empirical and functional. Others may want to construct a more ambitious argument for the universality of human rights, but in this volume I restrict myself to a more limited historical horizon (without abandoning the normative notion of the universality of human rights).

Figure 1. Types of conflicts over culturally relative practices

Internal judgment of practice

		Morally unimportant	Morally very important
External judgment of practice	Morally unimportant	Case 1	Case 2
	Morally very important	Case 3	Case 4

by their nature universal, or at least universalizable, even though we know that moral values and particular judgments are at least in part historically specific and contingent.

The choice between internal and external evaluations thus is itself a moral choice. Should we abandon an external judgment because a practice has a long and well-established place within another cultural tradition? Our answer to that question should depend in large measure on the moral importance of the practice, from both the external and the internal perspectives, and on the nature of the internal judgment.

We can identify four ideal types of evaluative controversies, as indicated in Figure 1. Case 1 (morally unimportant both externally and internally) is uninteresting; whether or not one maintains one's initial external condemnation is relatively unimportant to anyone. Case 2 (externally unimportant, internally very important) is probably best handled by a refusal to press the negative external judgment; given the sensitivity of external judgments and the dangers of cultural arrogance, to press a negative external judgment that one feels is relatively unimportant when the issue is of great importance internally is at best insensitive. By the same token, Case 3 presents the best occasion to press an external judgment even in the face of internal opposition. Because the issue is of great moral significance to the external evaluator and of little importance internally, external pressure is most likely to be effective and least likely to be resented, so long as the argument against the practice is made with some tact and cultural awareness.

Case 4, in which the practice is of great moral importance to both sides, is the most difficult to handle. But even here we may have good reasons to press a negative external judgment. Consider, for example, slavery. Most people today would agree that no matter how ancient and well established the practice of slavery may be, to turn one's back on the enslavement of human beings in the name of cultural relativity would reflect not moral sensitivity but moral obtuseness. Human sacrifice, trial by ordeal, and female infanticide are other practices sanctioned by some cultures that are rightly condemned by almost all external observers.

Underlying such judgments is the inherent universality of basic moral precepts, at least as we understand morality in the West. We simply do not believe that our moral precepts are for us and us alone. This is most evident in Kantian and other deontological moral theories, but it is no less true of utilitarianism; the principle of utility is explicitly advanced by Bentham and Mill as a universal moral principle. And, of course, natural or human rights theories are also inherently universal. For most of us, morality is inherently universalistic and egalitarian.

Furthermore, our moral precepts are *our* moral precepts. As such, they demand obedience of us. To refuse to act on our own precepts simply because others reject them is to fail to give proper weight to our own moral beliefs, at least in the case of central moral precepts, such as the equality of all human beings and the protection of innocents. And no matter how firmly someone else, or even a whole culture, believes differently, at some point we simply must say that those contrary beliefs are wrong. Negative external judgments may be problematic, but in some cases at least they seem not only permissible but also demanded.

B. Relativism in Implementing Human Rights

The distinction drawn above between variations in substance, interpretation, and form is another important consideration in evaluating arguments of cultural relativism. Even very weak cultural relativists—that is, relatively strong universalists—are likely to allow considerable variation in the form in which most rights are implemented. For example, whether free legal assistance is required by the right to equal protection of the laws is best viewed as largely beyond the legitimate reach of universal standards. Important differences between strong and weak relativists are likely to arise, however, when we move to the levels of interpretation and substance.

The distinction between variations in form and in interpretation may be difficult to draw with precision, but it is fairly clear and important. Consider a particular right, such as the right to political participation. In further specifying the right to political participation, we can begin by distinguishing electoral from nonelectoral forms of participation. Within the realm of electoral participation, we can distinguish elections based on universal adult suffrage from those based on a suffrage limited by sex, income, or some other such criterion; elections where voting is a right from those where it is a privilege or even a duty; elections intended to determine the will of the people from elections that serve principally to mobilize popular support for government policy; and so forth. These variations in "interpretation" clearly are qualitatively different from questions of "form," such as how often elections, town meetings, plebiscites, or gatherings of village elders will be held or how they shall be called.

Particular human rights are like "essentially contested concepts," in which there is a substantial but rather general consensus of meaning, coupled with a no less important and apparently unresolvable conflict of interpretations (Gallie 1968). In such circumstances, culture provides one plausible and defensible mechanism for selecting interpretations (and forms). Nonetheless, there are strong limits on the acceptable range of variation. Not all "interpretations," however, are equally plausible or defensible. They are *interpretations*, not free associations or arbitrary stipulations. The meaning of "the right to political participation," for example, is controversial, but the range of controversy is limited by the substance of the concept: an election in which a people were allowed to choose an absolute dictator for life ("one man, one vote, once," as a West African quip put it) is simply an indefensible interpretation. Furthermore, even logically valid interpretations are more subject to external criticism than variations in form.

Variations in form and interpretation may also be required by considerations of scarcity. The effective political implementation of virtually all human rights consumes resources. For example, there are significant direct costs, as well as indirect costs, such as the diversion of resources, in running an election, operating a legal system in accord with principles of due process, providing universal education or health care, and protecting citizens against arbitrary or inhumane and degrading treatment by officials of the state. Fiscal constraints may also require difficult decisions concerning priorities, decisions that are in part tied to culture.

When such priorities are set, an especially extreme emphasis or deemphasis of a right (or set of rights) brings us to the edge of the third type of relativity—namely, variations in substance. Such substantive differences in lists of human rights should rarely be accepted.

Rights that vary in form and interpretation still may be "universal" in an important sense if the substantive list of rights can be said to have considerable international normative universality. There may also be a weaker universality even in the midst of considerable substantive diversity—for example, if there is a large common core with relatively few differences "around the edges," or if there are strong statistical regularities and the outliers are few and are clearly overshadowed by the central tendency. I am somewhat uncomfortable with the degree of relativity implied by even such an extended notion of "universality," but some such variations are perhaps defensible.

Another important consideration is the extent to which the listed rights are aggregated. At the level of such broad categories as civil, political, economic, and social rights, there is widespread agreement that "universality" is required; any defensible list must include rights from all these categories. As we disaggregate, however, the permissible range of relativity expands, in part because disaggregation is largely a process of interpretation, in a broad sense of that term.

Consider, for example, the right to work, which is almost universally recognized when economic rights are disaggregated. This right might be interpreted as a right to seek employment, to be compensated for unemployment, or to be employed, or even a right to employment appropriate to one's interests and talents. Certain rights specified at this level, however, will be missing from some defensible lists of human rights, including many lists that recognize a right to work. Further disaggregation—for example, specifying the length and amount of unemployment benefits, or the extent of vocational training or retraining made available—is likely to bring us into the realm of variations in form, where a demand for universality usually is inappropriate.

Thus we see once more and in greater detail that we do not face an either-or choice between cultural relativism and universal human rights. Rather, we need to combine the universality of human rights and their particularity, and thus accept a certain limited relativity for even universal human rights.

4. Culture and Relativism

The cultural basis of cultural relativism must be considered too, especially because numerous contemporary arguments against universal human rights standards strive for the cachet of cultural relativism but actually are entirely without cultural basis.

Standard arguments for cultural relativism rely on such examples as the precolonial African village, Native American tribes, and traditional Islamic social systems, but we have seen that human rights are foreign to such communities, which employed other mechanisms to protect and realize human dignity. I argued in Chapters 3 and 4 that where there is a thriving indigenous cultural tradition and community, arguments of cultural relativism offer a strong defense against outside interference—including disruptions that might be caused by introducing "universal" human rights.

Such communities, however, are increasingly the exception rather than the rule. They are not, for example, the communities of the teeming slums that hold an ever-growing proportion of the population of most Third World states.[5] Even most rural areas of the Third World have been substantially penetrated, and the local culture "corrupted," by foreign practices and institutions, including the modern state, the money economy, and "Western" values, products, and practices. In the Third World today we see most often not the persistence of traditional culture in the face of modern intrusions, or even the development of syncretic cultures and values, but rather a disruptive "Westernization," cultural confusion, or the enthusiastic embrace of "modern" practices and values (compare Howard 1986: chap. 2). In other words, the traditional culture advanced to justify cultural relativism far too often no longer exists. But communitarian defenses of traditional practices usually cannot be extended to modern nation-states and contemporary nationalist regimes.

Therefore, while recognizing the legitimate claims of self-determination and cultural relativism, we must be alert to cynical manipulations of a dying, lost, or even mythical cultural past. We must not be misled by complaints of the inappropriateness of "Western" human rights made by repressive regimes whose practices have at best only the most tenuous connection to the indigenous culture; communitarian rhetoric too often cloaks the depredations of corrupt and often Westernized or deracinated elites.

Arguments of cultural relativism are far too often made by economic and political elites that have long since left traditional culture behind. While this may represent a fundamentally admirable effort to retain or recapture cherished traditional values, it is at least ironic to see largely Westernized elites warning against the values and practices they have adopted. At their best, such arguments tend to be dangerously paternalistic. For example, "villagization," which was supposed to reflect traditional African conceptions, was accomplished in Tanzania only by force, against the vocal and occasionally even violent opposition of much of the population. And even such a troubling sincerity is unfortunately rare.

Arguments of cultural relativism regularly involve urban elites eloquently praising the glories of village life—a life that they or their parents or grandparents struggled hard to escape and to which they have not the slightest intention of returning. Government officials denounce the corrosive individualism of Western values—while they line their pockets with

5. In what follows, I restrict myself to relativistic arguments made on behalf of practices in the Third World because these are the practices for which relativistic justifications for deviations from international human rights standards are most frequently made.

the proceeds of massive corruption, drive imported luxury automobiles, and plan European or American vacations. Leaders sing the praises of traditional communities—while they wield arbitrary power antithetical to traditional values, pursue development policies that systematically undermine traditional communities, and replace traditional leaders with corrupt cronies and party hacks. Such cynical manipulation of tradition occurs everywhere. Let me cite, however, a few examples from Africa, where "some leaders have even resorted to picking out certain elements of traditional African culture to anesthetize the masses. Despite what is said, this frequently has little to do with a return to the positive, authentic dimensions of African tradition" (All Africa Council 1976: 45).

In Malawi, President Hastings Kamuzu Banda utilizes "traditional courts" to deal with political opponents outside the regular legal system. For example, Orton and Vera Chirwa, after being kidnapped from Zambia, were brought before a "traditional court" made up of five judges and three tribal chiefs, all appointed directly by Banda. While there was a prosecutor, no defense attorney was allowed, and the only possible appeal was to Banda personally. Such procedures have not the slightest connection with authentic traditional practices. In Zaire, President Mobutu has created the practice of *salongo*, a form of communal labor with a supposedly traditional basis. In fact, it is essentially a revival of the colonial practice of corvée labor (Callaghy 1980: 490). In Niger, *samarias*, traditional youth organizations, have been "revived," but not so much out of a respect for traditional culture as "to replace party organizations so as to channel youthful energies away from politics" (*Africa Contemporary Record* 14 (1981–82): B490–91). And Macias Nguema of Equatorial Guinea, probably the most vicious ruler independent black Africa has seen, called himself "Grand Master of Popular Education, Science, and Traditional Culture," a title that might be comical were the situation not so tragic.

The cynicism of many claims of cultural relativism can also be seen in the fact that far too often they are for foreign consumption only. The same elites that raise culture as a defense against external criticisms based on universal human rights often ruthlessly suppress inconvenient local customs, whether of the majority or of a minority. National unification certainly will require substantial sacrifices of local customs, but the lack of *local* cultural sensitivity shown by many national elites that strongly advocate an international cultural relativism suggests a very high degree of self-interest.

Furthermore, a number of regrettably common practices, such as disappearances, arbitrary arrest and detention, or torture, are entirely without cultural basis. Idi Amin, Pol Pot, and the death squads of El Salvador cannot be attributed to local culture; while these names have become justly synonymous with modern barbarism, such practices are not an expression of established cultural traditions. Rigged elections, military dictatorships, and malnutrition caused by government incentives to produce cash crops rather than food are just a few of the widespread abuses of internationally recognized human rights that do not express, but rather actually infringe, indigenous cultural values.

In traditional cultures—at least the kinds of traditional cultures that might justify deviations from international human rights standards—people are not victims of the arbitrary decisions of rulers whose principal claim to power is their control of modern instruments of force and administration. In traditional cultures, communal customs and practices usually provide each person with a place in society and a certain amount of dignity and protection. Furthermore, there usually are reciprocal bonds between rulers and ruled and between rich and poor. The human rights violations of most Third World regimes are as antithetical to such cultural traditions as they are to "Western" human rights conceptions. In fact, authentic traditional cultural practices and values can be an important check on abuses of arbitrary power. Traditional African cultures, for example, usually were strongly constitutional, with major customary limits on rulers; as a Basotho maxim says, "A chief is a chief by the people." Not only are these traditional checks a resource that human rights advocates may be able to tap, but it has even been argued that transgressions of traditional limits have figured in the collapse of some recent regimes (Le Vine 1980: 672).

Finally, there are substantive human rights limits on even well-established cultural practices, however difficult it may be to specify and defend a particular account of what those practices are. For example, sexual, racial, ethnic, and religious discrimination have been widely practiced but are indefensible today. Likewise, the depth of the tradition of anti-Semitism in the West is no defense for the maintenance of the practice. This is not to say that certain cultural differences cannot justify even fundamental deviations from "universal" human rights standards, but if cultural relativism is to guarantee local self-determination, rather than cloak despotism, we must insist on a strong, authentic cultural basis, as well as on the presence of alternative mechanisms to guarantee basic human dignity, before we justify cultural derogations from universal human rights.

5. ASSESSING CLAIMS OF CULTURAL RELATIVISM

The international normative consensus on human rights presents a strong prima facie case for a relatively strong universalism—that is, for weak cultural relativism. Even if this "consensus" is largely the compliment of vice to virtue, it does reveal widely shared notions of "virtue," an underlying "universal" moral position that compels at least the appearance of assent from even the cynical and corrupt. Furthermore, as I have argued above, in the conditions of modern society human rights are a particularly appropriate mechanism to protect human dignity. The modern state, the modern economy, and associated "modern" values tend to create communities of relatively autonomous individuals who lack the place and protections provided by traditional society. And regardless of the relative degree of individual autonomy, people today face the particularly threatening modern state and the especially fierce buffeting of the ever-changing modern economy. Rights held equally by all against the state—rights that both limit its legitimate range of actions and require positive protections against certain predictable economic, social, and political contingencies—are a seemingly natural and necessary response to typically modern threats to human dignity and basic human values, traditional and modern alike.

If these arguments are correct, and the Universal Declaration of Human Rights represents a minimal response to the convergence of cross-cultural human values and the special threats to human dignity posed by modern institutions, then this set of rights has a strong claim to relative universality. In other words, we can presume that these rights apply universally, although that presumption can be overcome in particular circumstances by specific cultural arguments. This is the position I have called weak cultural relativism.

Rights are formulated with certain basic violations, or standard threats to human dignity, in mind (Chapter 1). Therefore, the easiest way to overcome the presumption of universality is to demonstrate that the anticipated violation is not standard in that society, that the value is justifiably not considered basic in that society, or that the object of the right is guaranteed by an alternative mechanism. To overcome the presumption of universality, one would have to show that the underlying cultural vision of human nature or society is both morally defensible and incompatible with the implementation of the "universal" human right in question.

Such a test can be met only rarely today. For example, it is difficult to imagine cultural arguments against recognizing the personal rights of Articles 3–11, which recognize rights to life, liberty, and security of the person; the guarantee of legal personality; and protections against slavery, arbitrary arrest, detention, or exile, and inhuman or degrading treatment. These are so clearly connected to basic cross-cultural requirements of human dignity, and are stated in sufficiently general terms, that any morally defensible contemporary form of social organization must recognize them (although perhaps not necessarily as inalienable rights). I am even tempted to say that conceptions of human nature or society that are incompatible with such rights would be indefensible almost by definition.

Such civil rights as freedom of conscience, speech, and association may be a bit more relative. Because they assume the existence and positive evaluation of relatively autonomous individuals, they may be of questionable applicability in strong, thriving traditional communities. In such communities, however, they would rarely be at issue. If traditional practices truly are based on and protect culturally accepted conceptions of human dignity, then members of such a community simply will not have the desire or need to claim such civil rights. In the more typical contemporary case, however, in which the relatively autonomous individual faces the modern state, they too would seem to be universally demanded; it is hard for me to imagine a defensible modern conception of human dignity that did not include at least most of these rights. A similar argument can be made for the economic and social rights of the Universal Declaration.

The Declaration does list some rights that are best viewed as "interpretations," subject to much greater cultural relativity. For example, the right of free and full consent of intending spouses reflects a specific cultural interpretation of marriage that is of relatively recent origin and by no means universal today, even in the West. Notice, however, that the right (as Section 2 of Article 16) is subordinate to the right to marry and to found a family, for which there is a strong cross-cultural consensus. Furthermore, some traditional customs, such as bride-price, provide alternative protections for women and a type of indirect conditionality to marriage that addresses at least some of the underlying concerns of Article 16(2).

When we consider the much more detailed International Human Rights Covenants, a number of listed rights approach specifications at the level of form. For example, Article 10(2)(b) of the International Covenant on Civil and Political Rights requires the segregation of juvenile defendants. In many cultures the very notion of a juvenile criminal defendant does not exist. Similarly, penitentiary systems, mentioned in Article 10(3), are culturally specific institutions.

Finally, we should note that even the strongest cultural relativist faces a particularly serious problem where cultures clash or are undergoing substantial transformation, as is the case in much of the Third World. In evaluating customary practices that involve otherwise justifiable deviations from or interpretations of prima facie universal human rights, we often face the problem of "modern" individuals or groups who reject traditional practices. Should we give priority to the idea of community self-determination and permit the enforcement of customary practices against modern "deviants," even if this violates "universal" human rights? Or should individual self-determination prevail, thus sanctioning claims of universal human rights against traditional society? We return to this issue in Chapter 8, but a few brief comments are in order here.

In a recent discussion of women's rights in Africa, Rhoda Howard suggests an attractive and widely applicable compromise strategy (1984b: 66–68). On a combination of practical and moral grounds, Howard argues against an outright ban on such practices as child betrothal and widow inheritance, but she also argues strongly for national legislation that permits women (and the families of female children) to "opt out" of traditional practices. Where practical, guaranteeing a right to "opt out" of traditional practices in favor of "universal" human rights or alternative human rights interpretations seems ideal, for it permits an individual in effect to choose his or her culture, or the terms on which he or she will participate in the traditional culture.

Conflicting practices, however, may sometimes be irreconcilable. For example, a right to private ownership of the means of production is incompatible with the maintenance of a village society in which families hold only rights of use to communally owned land; allowing individuals to opt out and fully own their land would destroy the traditional system. Less dramatic, full freedom of religion, including a right to apostasy, is incompatible with certain well-established traditional Islamic views. But even such conflicts may sometimes be resolved, or at least minimized, by the physical or legal separation of adherents of old and new values. Although separation may be difficult—given the interpenetration of rural and urban sectors, for example—it may be possible, particularly with practices that are not material to the maintenance or essential integrity of either culture.

Nevertheless, a choice must sometimes be made, at least by default, between competing practices or conceptions of human rights. Such cases take us out of the realm in which useful general guidelines are possible. Fortunately, though, they are the exception rather than the rule. I believe that we can justifiably insist on some form of weak cultural relativism— that is, a fairly strong universalism. It may be necessary to allow limited cultural variations in the form and interpretation of particular human rights, but we must insist on their fundamental moral universality. Human rights are, to use an appropriately paradoxical phrase, relatively universal.

7

Human Rights and Cultural Values:
Caste in India

The caste system in India is an especially striking example of the contrast between indigenous practices and universal human rights. This chapter uses the example of India's caste system to bring together, further illustrate, and extend both the argument of Chapter 3 that human rights are foreign to all traditional societies and the proposed general approach to dealing with conflicts between universal human rights standards and local cultural practices set out in Chapter 6.

One-seventh of the world's people are Indian. India's population is larger than that of the United States and Western Europe, or Latin America and Africa, combined, and the diversity of the Indian people is perhaps even more striking than their numbers. India is the birthplace of two major world religions (Hinduism and Buddhism), has more Muslims than any country in the Middle East or North Africa, and has many other religions of local or regional importance (e.g., Sikhs in the Punjab). Differences between city and countryside (where almost three-fourths of all Indians still live) are striking, and a relatively prosperous modern industrial economy sits loosely and uncomfortably on a largely traditional agricultural economy. Furthermore, this contemporary diversity is matched by a long, complex, rich, and varied history, as invaders, from the Aryans to the British, periodically injected major new elements into and then were gradually absorbed by an increasingly complex culture.

To talk of "India," therefore, requires reducing this complex diversity to manageable proportions, typically by selecting a single place or a single part to stand, however imperfectly, for the whole. I follow the second course, taking Hinduism as the locus of traditional Indian values.

1. "HUMAN RIGHTS" AND TRADITIONAL INDIAN SOCIETY

The dominant tendency in the literature is to argue that human rights ideas have been present in all societies at all times, but India is a partial exception to this tendency. For example, in two of the best-known articles on Hinduism and human rights, Kana Mitra (1982) and Romila Thapar (1966) deny that the concept of human rights exists in Hindu India (compare Puntambekar 1949: 196; Coomaraswamy 1982: 50), but a surprising number of authors argue that human rights ideas are present in traditional Indian (Hindu) ideas and practice. Yougindra Khushalani claims that "Hindu civilization had a well-developed system which guaranteed both civil and political as well as the economic, social and cultural rights of the human being" (1983: 408). Ralph Buultjens speaks of India's "traditional, multidimensional views of human rights" (1980: 113). Max Stackhouse devotes two chapters of *Creeds, Society, and Human Rights* (1984) to Hinduism, taking it for granted that there is a Hindu concept of human rights. And S. K. Saksena, although not explicitly using the language of human rights, speaks of "Hinduism, with its basic principle of equality of opportunity" and argues that prefeudal Indian society was based on "standards of equality and of the freedom of the individual as an individual" (1967: 367, 360–61).

In fact, though, social structures and the underlying social visions of human dignity in traditional India, as in other traditional societies, rest not on human rights but on social duties and status hierarchies: "Indians . . . base their social structure on duties and obligations rather than on rights."[1] Persons are seen first and by nature as bearers of duties, not rights, and whatever rights one does have rest on the discharge of duties or one's status.[2] And in traditional Indian (Hindu) society, "people's duties and rights are specified not in terms of their humanity but in terms of specific caste, age and sex" (Mitra 1982: 79), while the caste system made the ascriptive hierarchy so rigid that for all intents and purposes one's duties and rights were almost completely defined by birth.[3]

1. Saksena 1967: 372. Compare Pandeya 1986: 271; Gautam 1982: 175–76; Mitra 1982: 78–79; Thapar 1966: 35.

2. Recall that a focus on duties is not a roundabout equivalent to a focus on rights. For example, Mitra with particular reference to India, argues that "it is possible to formulate ideas about rights from ideas about duties" (1982: 79). Such views misconstrue the nature of the correlation of rights and obligations (see Chapter 3, section 3).

3. Birth, of course, includes sex, and differences between castes discussed below interact with a sexual division of rights and duties that is no less oppressive. The basic situation is nicely summarized in the *Laws of Manu* (5.147–48): "By a girl, by a young

2. CASTE, STATUS, AND PURITY

Caste is the fundamental institution of traditional Indian society.

> Caste may be defined as a small and named group of persons characterized by endogamy, hereditary membership, and a specific .style of life which sometimes includes the pursuit by tradition of a particular occupation and is usually associated with a more or less distinct ritual status in a hierarchical system. (Beteille 1965: 46)

> The caste system divides the whole society into a large number of hereditary groups, distinguished from one another and connected by three characteristics: *separation* in matters of marriage and contact, whether direct or indirect (food); *division* of labor, each group having, in theory or by tradition, a profession from which their members can depart only within certain limits; and finally *hierarchy*, which ranks the groups as relatively superior or inferior to one another. (Dumont 1980: 21, summarizing Bouglé)

Individual elements of the caste system are common elsewhere: all societies have social hierarchies, with a tendency of different groups to separate from one another, and hereditary occupational specialization has usually been the norm, even in the West until very recently. But the combination of these three of separation, division, and hierarchy in the intensity characteristic of India makes the caste system largely unique to South Asia (Hutton 1963: 46; Dumont 1980: 215–16; Bouglé 1971: 11ff.), and the division of society into an extremely large number of endogamous groups kept separate by extraordinarily powerful and detailed rules of ritual purity is particularly characteristic of Hindu India.

The most ancient Indian formulas recognize four castes, or *varnas* (colors): Brahman, Kshatriya, Vaishya, and Shudra (symbolized by the colors white, red, yellow, and black), which roughly correspond to priests, warriors/rulers, the landed and mercantile classes, and the servile classes. Below these four *varnas* were Chandalas, "untouchables." It is unclear whether this fourfold (or rather fivefold) division ever accurately described Indian society,[4] but by the third or fourth century A.D. a much more

---

woman, or even by an aged one, nothing must be done independently, even in her own house. In childhood a female must be subject to her father, in youth to her husband, when her lord is dead to her sons; a woman must never be independent." This topic is far beyond my scope, but for an introduction to some of the issues, see, e.g., Srinivas 1977, Richman and Fisher 1980, and Sharma 1985.

   4. Compare Bouglé 1971: 25–26, 124; Chakravarti 1985; Gupta 1980: 256; Houtart and Lemercinier 1980: 39–45; Senart 1975: 115ff. See also Chakravarti 1983: 131; Chethimattam 1971: 35–36; Organ 1974: 195; Saksena 1967: 362.

complex system of caste segmentation existed, based on the *jati*, an endo-gamous descent group traditionally linked to a particular occupation. To-day "there are so many (castes) that it is virtually impossible to determine their exact number."[5]

The boundaries between castes are maintained by exquisitely detailed rules of ritual purity: contact with, in some instances even sight of, lower castes is viewed as polluting; intimate contact, especially in marriage or at meals, is especially defiling. "Scruples concerning purity are the keystone, or better the foundation stone, of all Hindu construction, and . . . the parts are only ordered and kept in place by sentiments of pious respect and sacred horror" (Bouglé 1971: 125). The fear of pollution is so intense that it not merely separates, but actually repels, castes from one another (Dumont 1980: 46ff.; Bouglé 1971: 22).

None of this is intended to suggest that questions of power and class can be ignored, let alone that purity is causally prior (compare Greenwold 1975; Borgstrom 1977; Dumont 1980: app. B). Traditionally, however, purity, wealth, and power have largely coincided. Purity offers the clearest entry into the philosophical and cultural logic of the caste system and allows us to treat the practice of caste according to its own terms of self-justification. Furthermore, whether we adopt the Weberian notion of legit-imacy or the Gramscian idea of hegemony, the ideological structure of justification must be a central part of the analysis of such a long-lived and deeply ingrained social structure. Nevertheless, I do try to link ideas of purity directly to issues of power by considering traditional values as they were embedded and embodied in the actual practice of Hindu-dominated India.

3. THE ONTOLOGY OF CASTE

In the traditional Hindu world, all reality is one: Brahma, the Absolute. "Hinduism is a monistic religion which . . . believes in one ultimate spiritual reality or existence which reveals itself as this and many other worlds, and is present everywhere in the universe and beyond it, and which dwells in every living being" (Chatterjee 1950: 7). Physical existence, however, clouds one's recognition of this reality. Hinduism is "a unique

5. Beteille 1969: 230. Hutton gives a rough estimate of more than three thousand (1963: 67). In one Tamilnad village, Beteille found 12 distinct endogamous divisions within a Brahman community of 92 households, plus 24 major and many more minor subdivisions among 168 non-Brahman caste-Hindu households (1965: 73, 80ff., and table 3). Sharma found 16 separate castes in a village of only 144 households (1985: 68 and table 7).

life style concerned primarily with developing . . . the paradigmatic self-aware man'' (Organ 1975: 75) and, having achieved such awareness, attaining ultimate and complete reunion with divine reality.

Everything is made of three basic *gunas*, three radical ''substances'': *sattva*, *rajas*, and *tamas*. Very roughly, *sattva*, the substance of purity, resides in the mind, provides true knowledge of all reality as simply manifestations of Brahma, and is symbolized by the color white; *rajas*, the substance of virility, resides in life itself, is associated with egoism, selfishness, and virulence, and is symbolized by the color red; and *tamas*, the substance of dullness, resides in the body, gives rise to ignorance, and is symbolized by the color black. Everything—deities, human beings, demons, animals, plants, objects—is composed of these three substances, but in different proportions: *sattva* predominates in deities, *rajas* predominates in demons and animals, and *tamas* predominates in plants and objects.[6] This cosmic hierarchy is replicated at the level of human society, creating a fundamental ''parallelism'' between cosmic and social orders (Hiebert 1982: 291). As described by Davis (1976: 6, 11):

> Hindus regard the natural and the cultural as non-dualistic features. Each is immanent in the other; each is inseparable from the other; each is a reflection of and realization of the other. . . .
>
> The entire . . . cosmos is ordered by a premise of ranked inequalities; all life forms within the cosmos are defined by the same radical material substances (*gun*) and the behavioral code or *dharma* appropriate to those *gun*. The same is also true, significantly . . . of human society. All persons are viewed as belonging to a number of birth-groups (*jati*) arranged in a series of ordered ranks. And these birth-groups are defined according to the internal physical nature and the behavioral code held appropriate to that nature, which are viewed as a duplex criterion of rank.

Placement in this social hierarchy, or caste system, is by birth, which according to the Hindu theory of reincarnation is not an accident or an arbitrary fact of nature, but a reflection of moral justice and order. ''One is born where one belongs by reason of his actions over many incarnations'' (Organ 1974: 194). ''The body or family in which a person is born, the society in which he lives, and the position or station in life which he occupies, are all determined by his past conduct and behaviour'' (Chatter-

---

6. Davis 1976: 8–9; Zimmer 1951: 295–97; Mahadevan 1967: 162; Manu 12.24–50; *Bhagavadgita* 14.5–20.

jee 1950: 78). Rebirth is an essential mechanism in the law of *karma*, or punishment and reward for one's deeds.[7]

Caste hierarchy thus "is the expression of a secret justice" (Bouglé 1971: 76). "In a just and stable society a correspondence was presumed between a person's qualities and his social position" (Beteille 1983: 10). Caste divisions and hierarchy are seen not as a matter of social convention but as part of the fabric of the universe. Caste rests on natural distinctions, not on social action; its justification is ontological and metaphysical, not functional. Both the hierarchical structure itself and the placement of each person within that structure rest on a divinely ordained natural order.

Thus, the very ideas of human nature are radically different in traditional Indian and in modern Western thought. In traditional India, human nature is not viewed as a common possession of all people. Rather, "human nature," if we can even use that term without gross anachronism, differs from person to person—or rather, from group to group. "In Indian thought, the caste is a *species* of mankind" (Kolenda 1978: 150; compare Zimmer 1951: 152).

This helps explain the central role of endogamy (compare Dumont 1980: chap. 5; Mandelbaum 1970: chap. 6). Intermarriages between castes appear as unnatural, almost literally "unholy," alliances. It is believed that miscegenation can only lead to miscreants, or at best offspring less pure than their fathers.[8] For example, Chandalas (untouchables) are traditionally believed to have begun as the offspring of Brahman women and Shudra men. It may therefore be only a slight exaggeration to say that the dominance of the Brahmans can be attributed "solely to the prestige of their blood" (Bouglé 1971: 56; compare Manu 1886: 11.85).

Birth and blood set only the upper limits of purity, however. Even for those born (relatively) pure, pollution can easily come from one's own acts; even the most pure remain subject to the temptations of selfishness and physical desire, and even the most scrupulous remain vulnerable to viola-

---

7. O'Flaherty 1980; Herman 1976: 251ff.; Dasgupta 1969: 53ff.; Manu 12.52–82; Sinari 1970: 14ff. Keyes and Daniel (1983) present a series of contemporary anthropological studies of the continuing relevance of such ideas in the popular culture of South Asia.

8. Just how much lower depended on whether the marriage was hypergamous (*anuloma*; higher-caste male with lower-caste female) or hypogamous (*pratiloma*; higher-caste woman with a lower-caste male). Roughly, hypergamy raised the offspring to a status intermediate between the parents, while hypogamy placed the offspring below the lower (male) caste of the parents (Davis 1976:18–19 and tables 4, 5; Dumont 1980: 116–18, 126–28, 301; compare Manu 10.6–73). Hypergamy has a sociological basis in such practices as female infanticide, suttee, and the prohibition of widow remarriage, which restricted the supply of available female marriage partners. This is but one example of the importance of questions of sexual status and roles mentioned in note 3 above.

tions by others. Even mere contact with those less pure is polluting; impurity is, as it were, contagious.

Caste and purity also serve as the basis of a functionally specialized division of labor, as seen in the frequent correspondence of caste and profession names. Anything connected with the body, especially with its wastes, is polluting; thus the low ranking of washers, sweepers, and scavengers. In fact, manual labor in any form is considered an inferior form of activity, and thus artisans and agricultural laborers are ranked below those, such as Brahmans, who do not depend on labor. Occupation, lifestyle, and birth are therefore mutually reinforcing parts of a hierarchic social order of purity.

With a passion for the most subtle distinctions, traditional India elaborated an incredibly varied and complex structure of castes and subcastes. For example, we find intricate gradations among crafts: some artisans have relatively high status (e.g., goldsmiths claim to be Brahmans in some places [Beteille 1965: 88]), while others lie at or near the bottom of the social hierarchy (particularly leatherworkers, who are untouchables because of the special religious significance of cattle). In agriculture as well, tasks have differential ritual status or purity; plowing is especially degrading, in part because it is likely to involve killing insects and other lower life-forms, which have religio-moral value as bodily forms into which souls are born.

The "secret justice" of caste, the intimate link between and mutual reinforcement of the type of life one leads and one's natural worth, gives social inequality a special moral significance. One's station has its duties (*dharma*), which are held to be perfectly suited to one's nature, and the discharge of those duties, whatever they may be, gives one a place in society and a certain personal dignity. Both the *Bhagavadgita* (3.35) and the *Laws of Manu* (10.97) emphasize that it is better to perform one's own duties poorly, even to die doing so, than to perform another's well. And the proper discharge of the duties of one's station will be rewarded in the next life.

In practice, the "inherited defilement" (Kolenda 1978: 65) of membership in the lower castes has been the central social fact, but caste theoretically assures that each person is treated according to his or her desert and therefore can achieve a sort of contextual dignity. Therefore, the inequality and group repulsion of the social and ritual hierarchy may be partially mitigated by the fact that all are bound together into an intricately articulated social and natural order. Each group is in part defined in relation to the others and requires them. Brahmans, for example, could not even survive without the services of other castes.

The caste system in India represents an extreme form of Durkheimian organic solidarity, a social solidarity based on bringing together qualitatively different social groups. Brahma, the divine unity of all existence, provides an ontological and metaphysical point of reference toward which all reality aspires (to the extent that it is self-aware). Likewise, the Brahman caste provides not merely a social point of reference—purity in its broad outlines is perhaps most easily measured by the nature and extent of a caste's permissible contact with Brahmans—but the point toward which all social structures are directed and ultimately converge.

4. FLEXIBILITY, MOBILITY, AND EQUALITY

The caste system of traditional India was an extraordinarily rigid social structure, but it was by no means static. The proliferation of castes, which occurred principally through the fission of existing castes, involved considerable change. Regional variations, not only in particular details (see, e.g., Hutton 1963: 52, 55–63, 71–72; Marriott 1960; Davis 1976: 24) but even in fairly substantial ways, such as the paucity of intermediate castes between Brahman and Shudra in southern India (Dumont 1980: 73), also suggest an openness to evolutionary change.

Because purity rests on a combination of birth and act, downward mobility is a very real possibility; there are even *jatis* of "degraded Brahmans" who are shunned by most other castes (Mandelbaum 1970: 438). Upward mobility is more problematic, however. Special individual merit, through particularly dedicated performance of the duties of one's station or by becoming a religious ascetic, would be rewarded by a higher rebirth, but there was almost no way an individual could move to a higher caste in a single lifetime.[9] Individual upward mobility, with the partial exception of hypergamous marriages, was virtually impossible.[10]

Upward group mobility was also theoretically impossible, but in practice upward caste mobility, especially the local rise of a wealthy or powerful

9. The closest approach was the special respect, occasionally even veneration, accorded gurus and ascetics, who might be of humble birth. But although one could thus effectively place oneself outside the mundane manifestations of the caste system, one could not, in a single life, rise to a higher caste even by special spiritual merit.

10. One might try to "pass" by moving to a new village, but even if the initial suspicion of outsiders could be overcome, one would likely be found out when it came time to arrange the marriage of one's children, because the necessary genealogical information that would be required to be accepted as a marriage partner probably could not be successfully manufactured. The difficulty of passing, even in recent years, is illustrated by the story Beteille (1965) recounts of a Palla (untouchable) who in the early 1950s passed for three or four years as a Padayachi (a higher caste) but was found out. "Needless to say, he was beaten . . . and had to flee the village, leaving most of his belongings there" (p. 81).

jati, has been a rare but real phenomenon throughout Indian history. "The reigning, ideal principle is that of social immutability, while the ruling, actual principle is that of social competition among those close to each other in rank."[11]

David Mandelbaum presents a particularly thorough analytical account of the process of upward *jati* mobility (1970: chaps. 23–25). The *jati* origin myth is typically revised, usually to claim membership in a higher *varna*. This also provides a new behavioral model for the group. Srinivas refers to this process of lifestyle change as "Sanskritization" (1966: 1– 45). In addition, social contacts are revised to reflect the new, aspired-to status. On its own, a *jati* can try to cut its contacts with groups that it now considers beneath itself. Much more important, though, is acceptance into the new reference group: ultimately, one's children will have to be acceptable as marriage partners or the "mobility drive" will fail.

Building alliances and patron-client linkages—for example, by lending money or purchasing services over an extended period—can also be important. Securing the services, and thus tacit recognition, of Brahmans or even lower superior castes is often a crucial step. For the mobility drive to succeed, wealth is necessary, but "wealth alone . . . is no guarantee of higher rank. *Jati* members must use it properly so that the *jati*'s rank may be elevated for their children" (Mandelbaum 1970: 473). In effect, a materially successful *jati* can attempt to achieve "closer parity between a *jati*'s secular powers and material resources" (1970: 444). With some luck and considerable political skill, the *jati* can raise its status over the course of a few generations.[12]

Such changes, however, involve only relatively minor and local rearrangements of the parts; they leave the caste *system* untouched. The rising caste typically couches its claims almost entirely in reference to the traditional ideology (Bouglé 1971: 88–89), and once it has successfully risen it adopts the way of life of its new station and defends the immutability of caste divisions (Mandelbaum 1970: 480). This is a classic example of system maintenance by selective co-optation. Traditional Indian society could be remarkably flexible about particulars, but it was exceedingly unyielding about basic structures.

Even religious movements that began as hostile to Hinduism, either in general or in its "standard" Brahmanic versions, typically have fallen

11. Mandelbaum 1970: 430. Compare Bouglé 1971: 18–19; Beteille 1969: 57–58; Hutton 1963: 50–52, 122.

12. Similar results have been achieved by occupational separation, migration, alliance with a new ruling group, trade, and direct political action, as well as by participation in religious reform movements and new religions. See, e.g., Mandelbaum 1970: 480–84, 488–93, chap. 28ff.; Kolenda 1978: 95–104; Srinivas 1977: 227.

victim to reabsorption. Mandelbaum discusses one common pattern: a charismatic leader teaching ideas of personal purity largely distinct from notions of caste and ritual becomes the leader of a social movement, which then is reabsorbed into the dominant society as a new caste (Mandelbaum 1970: chap. 28; compare Hutton 1963: 117–18). This pattern is so common that a standard complaint about such *bhakti* (devotional) movements is that "in historical retrospect, their function appears to have been to reinforce the existing social order by channeling discontent into a negative form, rather than bring about structural change" because no matter how spiritually egalitarian they are "they tend to get organized and function within the existing socio-cultural order" and accept the existing hierarchy in secular contexts (Ishwaran 1980: 74–75).

The absorptive power of Hindu caste society can also be seen in the penetration of caste ideas and practices into introduced religions, such as Islam and Christianity (Mandelbaum 1970: chaps. 29, 30; Dumont 1980: 202–8). Even more striking is the fact that Buddhism, a radically egalitarian religion that began in India, largely died out there and never seriously challenged the caste system. In fact, in some areas of southern Nepal there is even a Buddhist caste system (Greenwold 1975: 50–52).

Nonetheless, religious opposition to caste inequality, and the underlying social discontent on which it must have flourished, should not be denigrated. "The burden of caste, with its oppressive gradations, generated its own antithesis on the ideological plane, and the question of equality was insistently raised in a succession of religious movements that go back to the beginnings of recorded history" (Beteille 1979: 534). There would even seem to be at least some religious resources for reform within traditional Indian Hinduism (compare Mitra 1982: 80–81; Gautam 1982: 170). For example, the doctrine of reincarnation implies a divine essence in each person, a doctrine that might be transformed in ways that are compatible with the idea of human rights. Organ suggests that the notion of *varnas* should be read simply as an appropriate recognition of moral differences and that efforts at reform should focus on making it possible to move through the entire circuit and become a Brahman in a single life (1975: 101–2). Many reformers, including Gandhi, have seen the fourfold *varna* scheme as a remedy for the *jati*-based caste system. Swami Nikhilanandra (1958), among many others, has presented Hindu spiritualism as a remedy for many of the ills of modernity. And more examples could be added.

In other words, in the contemporary struggle for human rights there may be important traditional cultural resources on which India can draw, but these resources lie at the fringes of a tradition dominated by the remarkably resilient caste system. If the practice of human rights is to be realized in India, a radical break with tradition is required.

5. CASTE AND CULTURAL RELATIVISM

The radical incompatibility between caste and human rights is obvious. We have already noted the social primacy of duties over rights in India. India also shares with other traditional societies a group orientation that is in contrast to the inherent individualism of viewing each person as possessing natural and inalienable rights that ordinarily take precedence even over the claims of society and the state. "Hindu society is organized around the concept of *dharma* (the duties of one's station) in a way roughly similar to modern society around that of the Individual" (Dumont 1970: 140).

Perhaps even more important is the difference between the egalitarianism of human rights and the status orientation of the caste system, that reflects a fundamentally different understanding of the moral significance of being human. Human rights "derive from the inherent dignity of the human person," to quote the International Human Rights Covenants once again. Each person has an inherent dignity and worth that arise simply from being human, and thus each person has the *same* basic dignity; human rights are held equally by all. No less important, human worth and dignity is radically distinguished from the worth and dignity of the rest of creation; human rights are radically different from the rights of all other beings.

The caste system, by contrast, denies the equal worth of all human beings. It draws sharp, qualitative moral distinctions between human beings in different castes, and it does not sharply distinguish human beings from other parts of creation. The human soul is not qualitatively different from that of beasts and even plants; it is only a somewhat more evolved (self-aware) incarnation. In fact, in many ways the distance between high castes and low castes is greater than that between lower castes and animals. For example, the *Law of Manu* prescribes the same penance whether a Brahman kills a cat, a mongoose, a blue jay, a frog, dog, iguana, owl, crow, or Shudra (11.132), and considerably more attention is devoted to the crime of killing a cow (11.109–117) than to killing a Shudra (11.127, 131). "Dying, without the expectation of a reward, for the sake of Brahmans and of cows" will secure beatitude for Chandalas (10.62; 11.80). In a following life, "the slayer of a Brahman enters the womb of a dog, a pig, an ass, a camel, a cow, a goat, a sheep, a deer, a bird, a chandala . . ." (12.55). And, to take a modern example, Beteille reports that in the village he studied Brahmans do not even include those of other castes in their count of the village's population, and non-Brahman caste-Hindus likewise do not count untouchables (1965: 25).

Given the traditional Hindu understanding of what it means to be a human being, the idea of human rights is a moral outrage, an affront to and attack on natural order and justice. Caste, the principal social expression of this understanding of human nature, must be forever antithetical to human rights.

A defender of caste could point out that I have yet to show why we should not resolve the conflict by dismissing human rights as an alien incursion. Although human rights purport to be universal, the simple claim of universality provides no reason for those in another culture to accept it. Therefore, we must pause to consider the counterclaims of cultural relativism, applying the general argument of Chapter 6 to the case of caste.

All Indian governments since independence have rejected the caste system. Untouchability—which presents the most serious human rights problems that arise from the caste system, those involving the grossest exploitation of roughly the bottom fifth of Indian society, the poorest of the poor in a very poor country—is explicitly outlawed by the Indian constitution. Furthermore, both the central government and the separate states have long pursued a variety of relatively aggressive remedial legal, social, and economic programs. Such official government policies, however, might be held to represent only the efforts of a largely Westernized elite. In fact, the persistence of caste endogamy and caste-based patterns of social deference—especially in the countryside, where most Indians live—might suggest that the traditional caste system better reflects popular "human rights" values. But even if we were to grant that this is true, there are good reasons for pressing universal human rights arguments against caste.

Chapter 6 distinguishes between "internal" judgments, which rest on the standards of the society in question, and "external" judgments, which rest on the standards of an outside evaluator. We have already seen that the external human rights judgment of caste is in all respects negative. Should we abandon this external judgment just because caste has a long history and is deeply ingrained in Indian society? If the rights violations inherent in the practice are of great external importance, it may be appropriate to press a negative external evaluation of even a very important and long-established culture practice. We should, of course, be wary of external moral judgments that contradict very important internal moral precepts, but when a large group of people are classified and treated as less than fully human, as they are in the caste system, we have crossed the boundaries of appropriate respect for diversity and self-determination.

In the case of India, the dangers of moral imperialism that may seem to lurk beneath pressing such an external evaluation are greatly reduced by the strong cross-cultural international consensus on the indefensibility of the caste system; the external judgment is not simply a "Western" judgment, but one widely shared throughout the Third World as well. Furthermore, caste stands externally condemned not on the basis of a controversial interpretation of human rights or even the violation of just a few rights; the Indian caste system violates virtually the full range of internationally recognized human rights, under all plausible interpretations of those rights.[13] And this international consensus has considerable internal support, not only in the policies of Indian governments but also in the political activity of the victims of caste.

Caste is no longer "hegemonic," no longer accepted as legitimate, especially by those at the bottom of the system, who increasingly see themselves as victims of oppression and exploitation. In such circumstances, cultural relativist arguments against international human rights standards must be decisively rejected as misguided at best and as little more than upper caste/class ideological subterfuge at worst. It may be necessary and even desirable to take persisting caste attitudes and practices into account when implementing internationally recognized human rights in India, but we must insist that the caste system and caste-based domination give way to the demands of human rights, as the victims of caste are themselves increasingly demanding in contemporary India.

6. CASTE AND THE CONTEMPORARY STRUGGLE FOR HUMAN RIGHTS

The preceding account of traditional Indian values is not merely of historical interest; attitudes and practices rooted in the ideas and institutions of the caste system remain of central importance in the struggle for human rights in contemporary India, especially in the countryside. But the caste *system*, the hegemonic complex of caste ideas and practices, has eroded significantly.

Although caste still has great social, economic, and political relevance, especially for rural untouchables, the traditional coincidence of caste, class, and power is increasingly under attack, both indirectly through the processes of economic modernization and political democracy, and directly through political action by and on behalf of untouchables and other "backward" or "depressed" communities. In fact, the struggle for the human rights of lower caste Indians can in many ways be seen as a struggle against the increasingly violent efforts of dominant castes, classes, and political elites to maintain the traditional correlation of caste, class, and power.

The principal challenge to the caste system has been and will continue to

13. Caste thus is an "easy" case for those who argue for a relatively universalistic account of human rights. For arguments dealing with more difficult cases, in the context of Africa, see Howard 1984a and 1984b.

be economic change. In the countryside, the development of a money economy—and with it, increased opportunities for upward mobility by delinking wealth and traditional status—has weakened the relative power of Brahman castes and radically altered traditional patron-client relations.[14] In the cities, new jobs (filled in significant measure on the basis of merit, or at least on qualifications), new residential patterns, greater educational opportunities, and the mixing of largely anonymous people on the streets, in buses, and in government offices have created important opportunities for at least some individuals to escape many of the burdens of caste.

Such tendencies have often been supported and strengthened by direct interventions by central and state governments. Untouchability is outlawed by Article 17 of the constitution, and the Protection of Civil Rights Act (the 1976 successor to the Untouchability (Offenses) Act of 1955) gives special legal backing and enforcement to this prohibition. Bonded labor is similarly prohibited both by the constitution and by subsequent laws. Furthermore, there are relatively aggressive programs of what in the United States would be called "affirmative action," reserving places in educational institutions, jobs in the public sector, and even legislative seats for Untouchables, other Scheduled Castes, Scheduled Tribes, and other Backward Classes.[15] Special measures intended to benefit these depressed groups are also a regular feature of economic development and social service programs. Land reform and minimum-wage measures as well have often been intended to benefit the lower castes. The efficacy of such political interventions and the vigor of state functionaries in applying the law are frequently open to question, but the general tendency has been to hasten the erosion of the caste system.

The institutions and practices of political democracy, which probably are as deeply rooted in India as in any other country in Asia, Africa, Latin America, or southern Europe, also have helped to weaken the caste system. In the gram panchayats (village councils) and other local political bodies,

14. The principal beneficiaries of these changes usually have been Shudra and Vaishya castes. Untouchables often end up brutally victimized by modern, monetized agricultural production and the practices required to enforce these new economic relations.

15. "Scheduled Castes" are officially recognized lower-caste Hindu groups eligible for reservation and other affirmative action programs. "Scheduled Tribes" are similarly recognized "tribal" groups located principally in mountainous areas in the northern parts of the country. "Backward Classes" are other officially recognized and protected groups. The most comprehensive account of such legal and political measures is Galanter 1984. Perhaps most striking is the reservation of legislative seats. In the 1980 parliamentary election, 79 of 542 Lok Sabha (lower house) seats (15 percent) were reserved for scheduled castes, and 38 additional seats (7 percent) were reserved for Scheduled Tribes. In state elections in 1980, some 542 and 315 (of 3,821) seats were reserved (Commissioner for Scheduled Castes 1981: 38–39).

non-Brahman caste-Hindus usually have predominant power because of their economic, numerical, and political power. Representatives of the untouchables usually do not exercise substantial power, but simply their presence is often of social and psychological significance. The electoral power of non-Brahman groups at both the state level and the federal level has also been an important source of power and social change, especially as government grants and services play an ever-larger role in the economic and social life of both rural and urban communities. And electoral and local political activity has provided political skills, knowledge, and models for organizing and strengthening caste associations and grassroots political pressure groups.

But while the caste *system* is on the decline, caste retains central significance in economic, political, and social relations. Consider the following assessments, drawn arbitrarily from literally dozens of others:

> The comparative breakdown of certain features of the caste system does not mean that caste identities have been lost. (Channa 1979: 1)

> The descent-group structure has persisted although its functions have differed . . . the persistent feature of Indian society, its basic building block, is the endogamous descent-group (caste). (Kolenda 1978: 151)

> The horizontal cleavage among castes that are competing for power and valued resources in the village has many of the characteristics of class conflict but has thus far not become separate from caste status. . . . To an overwhelming extent, caste and class overlap and remain congruent with one another for rural India. (Sharma 1985: 70)

> In both villages endogamous units are identified as separate castes and are reference groups for purposes of interaction. (Atal 1968: 246)

> Caste is denounced almost universally, but its actual impact on the society at large has been well manifested. (Gupta 1984: 175)

> I have avoided the hotly debated questions of whether caste is disappearing or whether it is finding new bases and justifications. It is possible to say yes to both questions, depending on one's perspective. (Bhatt 1975: 199)

> Political conflicts seem to have followed more closely the cleavages of caste than those of class. (Beteille 1965: 207)

It might be argued that in rural areas untouchables and other lower castes have to date been harmed at least as much as they have benefited from changes in both rural relations of production and the forms of elite political domination. Michie (1981) argues that the breakdown of traditional patron-client relations in India has been associated with an *increasing* concentration of resources and the denial of the benefits of traditional clientage, without the slack having been taken up by either the state or the market. As a result, the landless in particular tend to end up even more excluded and more oppressed.

This is particularly true given the widespread and flagrant disregard for such protective programs as rural minimum wages. In traveling with a government labor officer in South Gujarat, Breman was not able to find a single worker earning the statutory minimum wage; he computes the typical underpayment as equivalent to between one-fourth and one-third of the laborer's annual income. But in 1983 and 1984, out of more than 27,000 inspections (virtually all of which must have turned up violations of the law) only 82 cases (0.003 percent) were investigated and prosecuted to a conclusion (Breman 1985: 1047). When Breman questioned the responsible officials, it became clear that they had little interest in acting against offending employers. In fact, the chief of the local office plausibly claimed in his own defense that he was powerless to act because tough enforcement would be met by landlord violence against his officers (Breman 1985: 1048).

The rise of private rural violence, often with the acquiescence, collusion, or active support of the police, is a chilling and relatively recent development. Traditional forms of rural social control, especially the caste system, are losing their efficacy. Feeling challenged and threatened by economic change, government policies, and the growing assertiveness of depressed groups, rural elites have increasingly tended to work to overcome traditional (caste) divisions among themselves in the interest of maintaining a united front against the lower castes and classes, especially the landless (among whom untouchables are disproportionately represented). And superordinate groups have increasingly turned to direct overt violence against depressed groups in order to maintain their control: "The landowners control the landless with intimidation and, when this fails, with outright terrorisation" (Breman 1985: 1055; compare Prachand 1979: 17).

In Bihar, terror campaigns have been carried out against peasants who have attempted to organize to protect their rights and interests. Three major caste-based "*senas*" (private armies)—Bhumi Sena (used by Kurmi landlords), Bramharsi Sena (Bhumihars), and Lorik Sena (Jadavs)—in collaboration with local *dacoits* (bandit gangs), have been used by landlords, often with the collusion of local authorities. Gujarat has an analogous problem with *zim rakhas*, "field guards," usually hired by local landowners from urban gangs to keep the lower castes/classes in line. Other areas have similar organizations, and even where the violence is less organized, it is a regular feature of rural economic and political relations.[16] And, of course, such caste/class violence is only the most visible and dramatic evidence of an intense and multifaceted human rights struggle.

In the short run and medium run, this new combination of more class-like economic and political oppression probably leaves most of the traditional victims of the caste system little or no better off.[17] Economic, demographic, legal, and political changes have dramatically increased the social and economic opportunities available to some individual members of traditionally low status groups. These changes have also opened new opportunities for them to act politically to better their condition. But caste identification remains a central social reality; the struggle of traditionally oppressed groups for equality is being met by strong opposition from both old and new elites, and the groups traditionally at the bottom of the social hierarchy still remain, for the most part, at the bottom.

The struggle against caste and its legacies remains at the center of the struggle for human rights in India, but we must be careful not to equate the two, particularly to the extent that caste, class, and political power have become separate bases of domination. Difficult and momentous as it is, the struggle against caste will not be the end of the struggle for human rights in India. It may not even be the decisive phase. To free landless untouchable agricultural laborers, for example, from the stigma of untouchability—to truly, not just legally, free them, so that neither they nor others would identify them as untouchables—would be a major victory, a decisive break with a grossly oppressive traditional practice. But unless these laborers are able to obtain ownership of land, a fair wage and good working conditions, or access to a decent urban or industrial job; unless they are able to organize, economically and politically, without fear of official and unofficial violence and harassment; and unless their children can have a real hope for a better future, their human rights will continue to be violated—in a new form, but no less surely. Class oppression is different from caste oppression, but it is no less oppression.

16. See, e.g., Anon. 1986a; Anon. 1986b; Commissioner 1981: 148–57; Das 1986; Dutta 1986; Joshi 1982; "K.B." 1985; Shatrunga 1985; Sinha 1985. Urban violence too is a regular feature of politics. It is also more likely to have a "communal" (religious) component—another related subject, along with the rise of Hindu fundamentalism and social chauvinism, that is beyond my scope here.

17. These burdens fall especially hard on low-caste women, who in addition are victims of sexual exploitation and a disturbing trend of growing official and unofficial sexual assault. Sharma, for example, details the triple exploitation of low-caste rural Indian women: oppressed by their husbands and sexually abused by their employers, exploited through their landlessness by landowners and moneylenders, and exploited as laborers by capitalist agricultural production (1985:83–84).

The real human rights question is not *whether* caste domination is to be replaced, but *what* is to replace it. Although still powerful, the caste system, in its traditional form, is on the decline. This significant advance must be pursued further with all possible speed and energy, but overthrowing the caste system is not enough, any more than overthrowing imperialism sufficed. The struggle against caste in India must be evaluated both by how far India has moved away from the caste system and by how close it has moved toward implementing human rights—two important and perhaps even related, but quite distinct, directions of social change.

8

Human Rights, Group Rights, and Cultural Rights

Cultural relativists often argue that the group orientation of non-Western societies requires subordinating individual human rights to the rights, interests, or needs of society, that the prima facie priority of rights over other grounds for action does not hold in the case of human rights in group-oriented societies. For this reason, it is argued, non-Western societies cannot, ought not, or at least need not give a central place to individual human rights. In view of my contentions that the processes of state-building and economic "modernization" have created individuals who are in need of human rights and that the individualism of human rights need not be possessive or atomistic—in fact, cannot be possessive or atomistic if human rights are to be realized—it should come as no surprise that I reject this relativist argument as well.

1. HUMAN RIGHTS AND PEOPLES' RIGHTS

Before discussing the relationship between individual human rights and the rights of society and other social groups, which is far less antagonistic than often presumed, I want to address an especially troubling attack on human rights: recent arguments that certain rights of society *are* human rights.

A. A Third Generation of Collective Human Rights?
These collective rights of society or "peoples" are often presented as a "third generation" of human rights (Vasak 1984). Just as the "first generation" of civil and political rights (based on the idea of "liberty" and providing protection against state violations of the person) was supple-

mented by a "second generation" of economic and social rights (based on "equality" and guaranteeing positive access to essential social and economic goods, services, and opportunities), so now, the argument runs, a "third generation" of human rights (based on "fraternity" and requiring new forms of international cooperation) is required in order to overcome the international inequality that has frustrated the realization of the first two generations of rights, particularly in the Third World. A human right to development has been codified in a 1986 U.N. General Assembly Declaration.[1] Other third-generation rights prominently mentioned by their proponents include the rights to peace, to a healthy environment, to share in the exploitation of the common heritage of mankind, to communicate, and to humanitarian assistance (compare Marks 1981: 441–51).

The metaphor of generations, however, is troubling. Biological generations beget and therefore must precede one another, suggesting that first-generation civil and political rights must be established before economic and social rights, which themselves must precede solidarity rights. An analogy with the metaphor of technological "generations" is even more disturbing: a new generation of technology replaces and renders obsolete the preceding generation. This suggests that solidarity rights ought to *replace* already established civil, political, economic, and social rights. And both readings fly in the face of the widely accepted notion of the interdependence of all human rights discussed in Chapter 2.

The source of these alleged human rights also raises serious problems. "The notion of solidarity . . . (is) the key feature of the rights of the third generation" (Marks 1981: 441; compare International Dimensions 1979: par. 42). But solidarity simply cannot serve as a source of *human* rights, at least as they have ordinarily been understood. Human rights, to quote the Covenants once more, "derive from the inherent dignity of the human person." Civil, political, economic, social, and cultural rights all clearly arise from the idea of innate personal dignity. To have a human right, one need be nothing other than a human being, nor do anything other than be born human. To be human is to have human rights.

But solidarity is a *relationship among* persons or groups and confers benefits on the basis of membership in a particular community. Any rights that might arise from solidarity would not be *human* rights. If these are a "third generation" of human rights, they cannot arise from solidarity

1. General Assembly resolution 41/128. The most thorough discussion of the sources and dimensions of this (alleged) human rights is still the report of the U.N. secretary-general (International Dimensions 1979). See also Alston 1988. For an extended legal, moral, and political argument against the right to development, see Donnelly 1985b. The following discussion draws heavily on arguments developed in greater detail there.

unless "human rights" is to be radically redefined. If they are "solidarity rights," they cannot be human rights. We have in these alleged new rights not merely a difference in substance, analogous to the difference between civil and political and economic and social rights, but a radical qualitative difference in types of rights.

Additional problems arise from the fact that these are held to be rights of groups, especially peoples and states (e.g., Abi-Saab 1980: 163–64; Sanson 1980: 195), or at least of individuals *and* groups (e.g., M'Baye 1980: 74–75; Alston 1981: 108). This is simply incoherent—unless, again, we are to redefine the very idea of human rights. Human rights, as they have heretofore been understood, rest on a view of the individual person as separate from and endowed with inalienable rights held primarily in relation to society, and especially the state. Within the area defined by these rights, the individual has prima facie priority over social goals or interests.

The idea of *collective human* rights represents a major and at best confusing conceptual deviation. Groups, including nations, can and do hold a variety of rights. But these are not *human* rights. Whatever their relative importance, (individual) human rights and (collective) peoples' rights are very different kinds of rights and should be kept distinct. There are legitimate social limits on the exercise of all individual rights. Society does have certain rights, or at least responsibilities, that legitimately constrain the exercise of many human rights; a properly ordered society must balance individual rights (against society) with individual duties (to society). Thus the Universal Declaration, after concluding its enumeration of rights, explicitly notes the existence and importance of individual duties (Article 29).

Human rights, however, refer to but one side of this balance between rights and duties. Human rights do have to be weighed against social needs, but they should not be confused or conflated with them. It makes no more sense to try to conceive of individual duties to society as collective human rights than it does to try to reduce all social duties to obligations correlative to individual human rights. Both rights and duties are important. They are often even correlated. But they are quite different.

In any case, the real danger in most places today is not an overemphasis on individual human rights. In most countries, individual human rights are only tenuously protected. The conceptual obfuscation inherent in the idea of collective human rights can only lead to a further overemphasis on social duties. Appeals to the rights of the people collectively are most often used by oppressive, paternalistic regimes to ignore or repress the desires, or to deny the rights of, real, concrete people. The rhetoric of the rights of peoples or the masses too often seems to have little purpose other than to justify the denial of most specific (human and other) rights of most people. The dangers of political abuse are especially strong when the collective body held to possess these third generation human rights is the state. For example, the state is regularly alleged to have a human right to development not only by the Soviet bloc states, who as we saw in Chapters 3 and 4 tend to see all "human rights" as contingent grants of the state, but also by a variety of Third World states, the former director of the Division of Human Rights of the United Nations, and a number of academic commentators.[2]

There are insurmountable conceptual problems in the claim that states have human rights. Even if we allow the existence of collective human rights of peoples, societies, and families, we must draw the line at states, which are artificial legal and territorial entities. And we must draw the line here because of the very real threat that the so-called human rights of states will be set against the human rights of individual citizens, transforming human rights from an instrument of human liberation into a new and particularly cruel cloak for repression and domination. To recognize a *human* right of *states* to peace, development, and the like will merely undercut the ability of the victims of repression to advance effective human rights claims against their governments.

Furthermore, the duty-bearers of these new rights are obscure. Traditional human rights, both civil and political and economic and social, are held primarily against one's own state, but third-generation rights, such as the right to development, are allegedly held against everyone and all groups (International Dimensions 1979: pars. 94–114). On the one hand, this suggests that they are held against no one in particular, but on the other hand, being held against the world at large, they provide a convenient basis for repressive regimes to shift the blame for their failures onto the shoulders of others.

In addition, the grand and amorphous character of the goals of peace, development, and the other third-generation rights can be used to cover a multitude of official sins. For example, "development" is the standard excuse of repressive regimes throughout the Third World for even the most brutal systematic violations of human rights. Even a right of *peoples* to peace or development presents similar dangers, because of the near universal role of the state as the legally recognized representative of a people in the contemporary world.

Peoples' rights are especially dangerous when they are presented as

2. See, e.g., U.N. documents E/CN.4/1984/SR.16 par. 83; C/CN.4/AC.39/5; E/CN.4/1984/SR.18 par. 64; E/CN.4/1983/SR.17 par. 65; E/CN.4/1983/SR.18 par. 46; E/CN.4/1983/SR.19 par. 76; E/CN.4/SR.1483 par. 58; E/CN.4/AC.34/WP.12 par. 5, 21, 24; Graefrath 1982; Haquani 1980: 31; Sanson 1980: 195. Compare also Brietzke 1985: 565.

prerequisites for other human rights. For example, Abi-Saab argues that in general "the satisfaction of the collective right is a necessary condition, a condition-precedent for the materialization of the individual rights" and that the right to development in particular is "a necessary precondition for the satisfaction of the social and economic rights of individuals" (1980: 171, 172). Such arguments can be easily used by repressive regimes to justify the "temporary" denial of most internationally recognized human rights in order to pursue policies allegedly aimed at realizing collective "human" rights. Once more, this turns "human rights" into an instrument of repression rather than liberation.

B. Peoples' Rights and Individual Rights

The International Human Rights Covenants, however, do recognize a right of *peoples* to self-determination:

> Article 1. (1) All peoples have the right to self-determination. By virtue of the right they freely determine their political status and freely pursue their economic, social and cultural development.
> (2) All peoples may, for their own ends, freely dispose of their natural wealth and resources. . . . In no case may a people be deprived of its own means of subsistence.

Furthermore, the right to development is proceeding steadily through the process of international legal codification and is already held to be an internationally recognized human right by a number of states and publicists. Therefore, whatever the merits of the arguments against collective human rights above, it is clear that the language of peoples' rights is here to stay.

But if we must speak of such collective third generation, solidarity, or peoples' rights *as human rights*, they should be interpreted merely as the rights of individuals acting as members of social groups. For the purposes of illustration, let us consider the right to self-determination, the one unambiguously well established peoples' right. In line with my argument concerning the evolution of lists of human rights in response to new threats to human dignity, we can see this right as an appropriate response to imperialism, which usually denied it victims the full range of human rights. The threat to human dignity posed by imperialism is foreign in origin and affects the human rights of entire peoples. Therefore, the emphasis is on the collective dimension of the right to self-determination, and that right is formulated as a right of peoples.

This collective dimension, however, is closely linked to some well-established individual human rights. For example, the right of a people to determine its political status and path of development can be seen as a collective expression of the right to political participation, which under imperial rule was systematically denied to entire peoples. Likewise, the right of a people to its natural wealth and resources can be seen as a guarantee that the material means to satisfy a wide range of rights will not be subject to continued plunder by foreign states or corporations. In fact, I suggest that the right to self-determination, even in its collective dimensions, is essentially a right of individuals acting collectively.

What does respecting the right to self-determination involve? Roughly, it involves respecting all other human rights, and in particular rights to political participation and freedom of speech, press, assembly, and association. If these rights are fully respected, it is difficult to see how the right to self-determination could be denied. Conversely, denial of the right to self-determination takes place principally through the denial of these individual human rights (and is likely to have further deleterious consequences for most other individual rights). There is little or nothing that can be done with the right to self-determination that cannot be accomplished by the exercise of other human rights.

Redundancy, however, is the least of the problems raised by the right to self-determination as it is ordinarily conceived today. Peoples obviously can be denied self-determination by fellow nationals as well as by foreigners. Furthermore, peoples within or spread across established national boundaries (e.g., Ibos in Nigeria, and Somalis in the Horn of Africa) would seem to have the same right. But contemporary political practice restricts the right to self-determination largely to peoples who have been or are subject to Western imperial domination (Pomerance 1982; Buchheit 1978). For example, Kurds in Iraq and Iran, Tamils in Sri Lanka, and Eritreans in Ethiopia have been almost universally held not to be entitled to self-determination.

In practice, then, the internationally recognized right to self-determination, despite its seeming breadth, has been treated as an extremely narrow right. States' fears of secession and governments' fears of revolution have combined to restrict the right to self-determination to little more than a right to sovereignty for those states (and colonies) that currently exist. Given that the right to self-determination emerged as part of the struggle against Western imperialism, this is not surprising, but as we saw above, linking human rights with the rights of states is extremely dangerous.[3]

3. For recent official statements holding the right to self-determination to be a human right of states, see U.N. documents number E/CN.4/1987/SR.10, pp. 7 (Ukraine) and 10 (Cuba); ibid., SR.11, pp. 13 (U.S.S.R.) and 14 (Morocco); and ibid., SR.14, p. 5 (Argentina).

Other peoples' rights as well, to the extent that they are conceptualized in human rights terms, should be seen in a similar light. At best they summarize the collective dimensions of the struggle against widespread and systematic violations of, or impediments to the realization of, already recognized individual human rights, and they are thus at best conceptually redundant. They are also probably politically redundant. For example, I find it difficult to conceive of individuals, states, or organizations that are unmoved by rights to food, health care, social security, education, or work being moved by an appeal to the abstract and disembodied idea of a collective right to development. Collective human rights provide little new leverage in the struggle for human dignity,[4] but they do provide additional intellectual, or at least ideological, ammunition for the forces of repression. When we combine such practical dangers with the conceptual difficulties posed by the very idea of collective human rights, the only reasonable course seems to be to reject them.

For all the talk of excessive individualism, the problem in the world today is not too many individual rights but that individual human rights are not sufficiently respected. States and societies have a variety of claims on individuals, and modern states have awesome powers to bring individuals to their knees—if necessary, to break their minds as well as their bodies. Human rights, and parallel legal rights, are among the few resources of individuals in the face of the modern state. The balance is already (always?) tilted against the individual. The only likely result of advocating collective human rights, let alone the so-called human rights of states, is a further strengthening of the forces of repression.

Every day we see individuals crushed by society. Rarely, if ever, do we see society torn apart by the exercise of individual human rights. Social disorder and decay are instead usually associated with the *violation* of individual human rights by the state or some other organized segment of society. Human rights are a rare and valuable intellectual and moral resource in the struggle to right the balance between society (and the state) and the individual. Unless we preserve their distinctive character, and stand firm on their character as individual rights, their positive role in the struggle for human dignity may be compromised.

2. GROUP RIGHTS IN A HUMAN RIGHTS FRAMEWORK

Having argued against collective human rights in the strongest of terms, I must insist that there *are* collective rights, just not collective

4. Even the struggle for decolonization could have been, and in considerable measure actually was, carried out using arguments that the rights of individuals were being denied,

human rights, and that a number of human rights are exercised by individuals *as members of a collective group.*

A. Individuals as Group Members

The range of collective groups that hold rights is extremely wide—for example, families, private clubs, professional associations, charitable organizations, business corporations, racial minorities, ethnic groups, religious communities, peoples, and states. In a discussion of human rights, the group rights of families, racial and ethnic minorities, religious communities, and "peoples" are likely to be especially important. Individual human beings today often see their personal identity as defined in significant measure by membership in these groups, and thus a life of meaning and dignity for such individuals will be closely associated with their membership and participation in these groups.

Even in the modern West, where individualism seems to have reached the pinnacle of its historical development, few people define themselves *entirely* as individuals; the isolated, atomized individual is the exception rather than the rule. Most Westerners still define themselves as part of a family; for many, in fact, the family is their most important locus of personal identity. Many individuals define themselves in significant measure by their religion. This has long been the case in European Catholic communities, and in the United States today we have recently seen the rise of aggressively evangelical Protestants, who strongly emphasize the link between their religion and their personal identity. Most blacks see their race as an important facet of both their self-definition and their definition by others in society. The same is true of many other ethnic minorities. Gender functions similarly for many women who, though a numerical majority of the population, are a discriminated against minority in positions of power. Most Westerners also have at least a weak sense of "national" pride that is in some cases a significant element of their self-definition. And so forth. Outside the West, such group self-identifications are widely held to be predominant for many, if not most, people.

To the extent that individuals define themselves and live their lives as part of such collective groups, they will tend to exercise their individual human rights less as a separate individual and more as group members. In fact, far from being inherently hostile to the rights of groups, many human rights explicitly protect individuals in their capacity as group members, especially in the case of families, or protect them from discrimination on

---

especially the rights to democratic political participation and freedoms of speech, press, assembly, and association.

the basis of that membership. Even more important, many human rights can be used by those with strong group affiliations to defend or even strengthen those groups. For example, rights to freedom of speech, association, and religion have been essential to the flourishing of minority religious communities, such as the Mormons and Amish in the United States.

This is not to suggest that group rights and individual human rights are never at odds. Conflicts typically arise from efforts to enforce the primacy of group identity over individual identity against those who would dissent or defect from the group. For example, many societies have denied women an existence and an identity outside the (male-dominated) family. A number of religious sects, ranging in the United States from the Amish and Hasidic Jews to the Nation of Islam and the Unification Church, strictly limit and regulate contacts with those outside the community. The Indian caste system presents perhaps the most extreme example of coercively defining personal identity through group membership. In such cases we do face a dilemma. The exercise of many individual human rights may indeed erode, transform, or even destroy the group. Therefore, we must in some sense choose between individual and group rights.

Human rights define persons as individuals and give prima facie priority to the claims of individuals over society and other social groups. To the extent that individuals exercise their human rights in ways that are incompatible with social practices that rest on a definition of persons as group members, the integrity of the group is likely to be threatened. To protect individual rights in such cases is to threaten the very existence of the group.

Even in such cases, individual human rights ordinarily ought to be given priority. So long as the group is eroded or transformed by the free exercise of the human rights of its members, such an outcome is likely to be morally and politically acceptable, and often even desirable. For example, if the Amish choose to retain their distinctive style of life, their socioreligious communities are likely to be preserved. If not, they will go the way of the Shakers, who are now on the verge of extinction because of the failure to renew their numbers. There is a real loss when a community dies out, but if its members freely choose another way of life, that is a loss that we must be prepared to accept. The only real alternative is to force group membership on those who see that membership not as a creative self-fulfillment but as an oppressive limitation of their existence and identity.[5]

5. Actually, there is an alternative, or at least a way to do something other than merely stand by while a community dies. Some communities can be actively protected against incursions by the dominant culture, or state-sponsored social programs that encourage (without forcing) members to remain in the community can be devised.

When the enforcement of group membership comes largely from outside the group—for example, in the Indian caste system or South African apartheid—the argument for the priority of equal and inalienable individual human rights is relatively easy to make. When the enforcement of group membership comes from within the group, the case may be somewhat more problematic, but here too the prima facie priority of individual rights should be recognized. The case for this priority is most clear if we conceive of this as a matter of protecting dissidents from externally imposed coercive pressures to conform. For example, the Unification Church and other religious groups have been known to use extreme psychological pressure, and sometimes even physical force, against those who attempt to leave the church. The Soviet Union and numerous other countries harass, arrest, imprison, and torture dissidents simply for holding or publicly advocating beliefs contrary to those that are officially sanctioned, and in many instances will not even allow dissidents to leave the country. Such repression of nonviolent dissidence, even by a group against its own members, is what internationally recognized human rights preclude.

Even granting that individual human rights to, say, freedom of speech, press, religion, and association would destroy or radically transform the group, the human rights perspective I defend here would say so much the worse for the group: if the group can persist only through the systematic denial of the human rights of its members, it has no claim to our respect.

B. Aboriginal Rights and Human Rights

Special difficulties are presented by the group rights of aboriginal peoples, where the principal threat to the survival of the group comes not from internal defection or dissidence but from external pressure or assault. It may be an oversimplification to say that in traditional societies individuals do not exist, but in traditional societies persons are not typically defined *principally* as individuals. We must be careful not to assume that traditional societies exist where in fact they have given way to modern or syncretic successors, but where they do exist, human rights raise serious moral and political problems.

Even the exercise of human and other individual rights by outsiders who come into contact with traditional or aboriginal groups can have dramatic, even devastating, consequences. Religious missionaries, itinerant traders, outside educators, public health workers, and a host of other modern individuals have transformed the way of life of most traditional societies in the world. But so long as such outside forces have simply come and offered, rather than imposed, new goods, ideas, and technologies, the resulting changes represent the free choices of group members that must command our respect, if not always our concurrence.

Such choices will change, and have changed, these societies. Most of these changes have costs, and some of the costs may even appear to outweigh the benefits. Nonetheless, they are costs and choices that we must accept, because those who bear the costs have freely chosen to bear them.[6] The alternative is a frightening paternalism, where we deny to others rights that we take for granted on the ground that these rights are not good for them.

The most serious assaults on native peoples and traditional societies have typically come not through the exercise of human rights by either insiders or outsiders but through the destruction of the material basis of the community's way of life by external actors. Particularly important has been the introduction of private property rights in land, especially by the expropriation of native community lands by outsiders (as occurred on a massive scale in nineteenth-century North America and as is occurring today in the Brazilian Amazon), often in conjunction with the forceful imposition of alien rule. It is the modern state and its economic counterpart of fully alienable property rights in land, not human rights, that typically poses the most serious threat to traditional communities and to the collective rights of aboriginal peoples.

However different the details of their problems, aboriginal peoples and modern individuals face the same enemy—the modern state. Human rights provide the best hope of protecting aboriginal peoples and their rights, both as individuals and as groups, against this threat. Human rights, however uncomfortably they fit with the traditional social structures of such communities, offer powerful protections for the rights and interests of aboriginal groups and traditional communities.

Individual human rights guarantee the autonomy of individuals to choose a way of life. In the case of persons who define themselves not principally as individuals but as members of a traditional community, *that* choice of a way of life must be guaranteed. And it can be plausibly guaranteed in the name of individual human rights. The genuine self-determination of native peoples is possible within a broader social context of internationally recognized individual human rights, so long as such peoples are allowed the opportunities to shape, maintain, and influence the evolution of community institutions. This is precisely what internationally recognized human rights attempt to guarantee.

By focusing on rather small minority groups within societies that have a more or less coherent dominant culture, I have avoided dealing with the most difficult cases. Lebanon presents a particularly tragic example. The

6. More precisely, they have made choices that will result in bearing the costs. To the extent that they are unaware of the costs, certain educational or other efforts might be justified by an "informed consent" argument.

group rights demands of even much smaller minorities, such as French-speakers in Canada and Basques in Spain, can cause extremely difficult political problems. And Sub-Saharan Africa is replete with examples of extremely serious political problems caused by competing groups. Even in such cases, however, the strategy of tolerance, even protection, of diversity and respect for autonomy outlined above would seem to offer one of the few avenues for peaceful solutions of competing demands.

Sometimes the harmonious resolution of individual and group rights may be politically impossible.[7] Nevertheless, in theory and often in practice, such a resolution may be possible, especially if individuals really do continue to see their identity as fundamentally tied to the group and choose to shape their own lives with their compatriots according to their shared understandings and desires. In such cases, the human rights approach is at least a plausible—and I would argue the best—way to protect not only individual but group rights as well.

3. CULTURAL RIGHTS AND CULTURAL IDENTITY

The discussion of group rights above has made implicit reference to cultural rights. Cultural rights, however, usually receive far less attention than the other principal categories of internationally recognized human rights, perhaps most strikingly in the common tendency to elide "and cultural" in discussions of the conventional dichotomy between civil and political rights and economic, social, and cultural rights. However, a full account of group rights in the context of individual human rights requires explicit attention to the question of cultural human rights.

A. Defining Cultural Rights

There would seem to be a political basis to the relatively scanty attention paid to cultural rights. Relatively few regimes attempt to control participation in the cultural life of the community, except as part of a broader program of "totalitarian" control of social life or in connection with essentially political attacks on civil liberties and political rights. Therefore, cultural rights per se are rarely a matter of intense political controversy and thus usually are not given the consideration of more controversial rights. And when they are a subject of controversy, those

7. I am at a loss to say anything in general theoretical terms about how we should proceed in such cases. My inclination would be to continue to give prima facie priority to individual rights, but if this strategy would create such political turmoil that all human rights were threatened, certain *limited* infringements on the exercise of *some* individual human rights *might* be justifiable.

whose cultural rights are under attack usually tend to be politically weak, and thus less able to insist on the importance of their rights. In addition, unlike most economic and social rights, in most countries it is not held to be the state's duty to undertake strenuous positive efforts on behalf of cultural rights.[8]

Part of the problem may also be the term "culture" itself. In a broad anthropological sense, all of our human rights might be called "cultural," for they rest on our culture and make reference to culturally defined entities, such as courts, prisons, the press, religion, education, and even the individuals who are bearers of rights. It is too narrow, though, to think of culture in the sense of "art," even if we add popular or mass culture to elite culture or high art, or in the sense in which we speak of someone being "cultured." In fact, many of the things connected with the arts and being cultured simply are not ordinarily thought of in human rights terms at all.

Cultural rights refer to a community's "way of life," but not those aspects of the way of life regulated by other classes of human rights. "Cultural rights" is thus in many ways a residual category. It is, nonetheless, an essential category, because a community's distinctive way of life typically possesses an important value, at least for its members, and we do see participation in "culture" as essential to a life of dignity.

The Universal Declaration and the Covenants enumerate a number of cultural rights. Article 27 of the Declaration recognizes "the right freely to participate in the cultural life of the community." Article 15 of the International Covenant on Economic, Social, and Cultural Rights recognizes the right of everyone "to take part in cultural life" and the duty of state parties to take those steps "necessary for the conservation, the development and the diffusion of science and culture." Furthermore, Article 13 provides for the liberty of parents to send their children to schools other than those established by the state; this can be an important device for minority cultures and other groups to preserve the cultural identity. Article 27 of the International Covenant on Civil and Political Rights assures members of minority groups "the right, in community with other members of their group, to enjoy their own culture, to profess and practice their own religion, or to use their own language." Furthermore, as we saw above, many other human rights, especially the rights to freedom of speech, press, assembly, religion, and political participation, and the rights to nondis-

8. The principal exception to this rule of relative political quiescence with respect to cultural rights is the case of minority cultures, such as French-speakers in Canada or English-speakers in Cameroon, and most especially traditional minority cultures embedded in modern or modernizing societies. Societies in which there is no clear majority culture, such as Lebanon and Belgium, also tend to be an exception.

crimination and equal protection of the laws, can be effectively used to protect the cultural rights of minorities, and even majority groups.

In what follows, "cultural rights" refers to the rights of members of communities, especially minority communities, to preserve their distinctive culture. In this sense, cultural rights are a surprisingly widespread issue. Most Third World countries have minority and even previously dominant cultures that are threatened. The issue is significant as well in a number of First World and Second World countries—for example, Indians, Inuit, and Métis in Canada; Native Americans, Chicanos, and Cubans in the United States; Bretons in France; the Welch in Britain; and Armenians, Estonians, Khazaks, and Uzbeks in the Soviet Union. In extreme cases, such as the Amazonian Indians, cultural rights may be literally a matter of life and death.

B. Culture, Individuals, and Groups

The subjects of all human rights are individuals and individuals are members of communities. They may hold human rights both as separate individuals and as individual members of a community. The very ideas of respecting and violating human rights rest on the idea of the individual as part of a larger community and social enterprise. But it is nonetheless true that most human rights do refer *principally* to the individual considered separate from the community, and they are valued primarily as claims against the community. Cultural rights, however, refer principally to individuals as members of a community. Furthermore, while the community referred to by most other human rights is the *political* community—in particular, the political community as expressed in the state—cultural rights refer to cultural communities, which typically are smaller than and exist within the confines of a state (from which both individuals and the cultural community are seen as separate). Cultural rights are especially important because they protect individuals in cultural communities against the state and the majority community. All human rights provide protections against incursions of the state in areas that are essential to a life of full human dignity. Cultural rights protect those essential aspects of personal dignity that are based on membership in a cultural community, much as political and economic rights protect those aspects that rest on membership in political and economic communities.

All human rights protect individuals in their choice of a way of life and, within certain limits, in their pursuit of a way of life. Some human rights focus on minimum standards that are required for the pursuit of any autonomous way of life. Others emphasize the idea that the state cannot be allowed to impose a particular substantive conception of the good life.

Civil liberties represent this emphasis most clearly. Cultural rights as well seek to protect—or, rather, to allow those in a community to seek to defend—a way of life against the incursions of other communities, and especially the state. But cultural rights may require more than just non-discrimination, or at least a very active and affirmative policy of non-discrimination. Protecting a way of life may require not simply the guarantee of formal equality, but special policies of support. In fact, the social homogenization of formal equality may be the most serious threat to cultural rights.

Consider a relatively simple case, such as Hispanic minorities in the United States. Language is an important feature of their culture, and thus bilingual education can be seen, and often has been seen, as an issue of cultural rights. Protecting these rights has required considerable positive efforts on the part of school districts, often in the face of resistant majority communities. In other generations and for other groups, the public schools were a principal mechanism by which the children of immigrants lost their cultural, and especially linguistic, distinctiveness. Bilingual education makes the schools an instrument for preserving, rather than overcoming, cultural differences, and the idea of cultural rights not only sanctions but requires this change in the socializing function of American public schools.

Many have argued that bilingual education "disadvantages" Hispanic children. Even if this were true, it would do little to reduce the force of cultural rights arguments. The issue is one of cultural choice, not external judgments of what would be better for others. Culture has a value that is not easily quantified, but that value is no less real than the alleged economic and social costs of bilingual education. So long as Hispanic communities are willing to pay the costs of preserving their distinctive cultural identity, cultural rights require that their choice be protected.

This process of choosing a way of life with social or economic disadvantages is much more widespread than it might appear to be at first sight, extending well beyond the domain of cultural rights. Religion provides a number of familiar examples in which individuals have chosen to define their lives in large measure in terms of membership in a religious community, with significant apparent economic disadvantages. Fringe political groups, especially radical leftists, have frequently moved in economically disadvantaged communities defined largely by political affinities. And in most major cities today there are thriving homosexual communities; in a city such as San Francisco, if one chooses to, one rarely need ever leave the gay community.

Many people do see certain natural or acquired characteristics as essential to their definition of their lives and persons. Such defining choices often place a person in a distinctive community. Cultural rights protect the choices of those who see themselves as in an important way part of communities of shared culture, and as human rights they protect those choices in distinctive ways.

For example, freedom of religion may be exercised in ways that emphasize the group. It is usually seen, however, as being at least as much concerned with protecting individual religious liberty from all religious groups. Thus, Article 18 of the Universal Declaration includes the right to "freedom to change his religion or belief." In contrast, cultural rights give greater emphasis to the group aspect. In addition, religion is a relatively precise notion, and membership in other communities of affinity as well usually is defined in relatively narrow terms. By contrast, culture is much broader and more amorphous. It is therefore not just an important and different basis by which group membership may be defined; it differs in significant and theoretically important ways.

C. A Right to Cultural Identity?

This special character of culture, along with the value we place on human (and thus cultural) diversity, might suggest the desirability of recognizing a right to cultural identity. Such an idea is currently circulating in UNESCO circles.[9] But even if we ignore the collective human rights dimensions of a purported right to cultural identity, I contend that recognizing such a right is a bad idea.

What would a right to cultural identity look like and imply? In a very strong and positive sense, it would be a right to *have* a cultural identity. In this sense, it is clearly a silly right, or even worse. People simply do not have a right to cultural identity in the same way that they have, for example, a right to nationality or to social insurance. Cultural identity is not something that can be provided to individuals by the state or by any other group; it is not a good, service, or status that can be given to people. Cultural identity, at least insofar as it has special value, is something that individuals acquire in living their life. In fact, where the state provides individuals with a cultural identity, it is done usually in order to discriminate against them, as in South Africa's homelands policies.[10]

Cultural identity certainly is something that can be attacked by the state

9. For example, it was a central topic of a conference held on the occasion of the fortieth anniversary of the Universal Declaration of Human Rights by the Netherlands Commission for UNESCO in Middleburg in June 1988.

10. Here again we see the dangers of externally imposed definitions of group membership, which once more underscores the importance of allowing group membership to reflect the free choice of individuals.

or other groups or institutions, resulting in serious affronts to human dignity. To protect autonomously chosen cultural identity from such attacks is an admirable aim, but it is not something that requires recognizing a new human right to cultural identity.

How will such attacks be carried out? Almost always they will involve discrimination on the basis of the already prohibited grounds of "race, color, sex, language, religion, political or other opinion, national or social origin, property, birth or other status." They are also likely to involve denials of equal protection of the law, and infringements of rights to freedom of thought, conscience, religion, speech, press, assembly, and association, as well as violations of the cultural rights explicitly recognized in the Universal Declaration and the Covenants. The way to protect cultural identity is to protect already established civil, political, and cultural rights. In particular, cultural identity will be best protected when members of culturally distinctive groups are allowed to participate in their culture, both in public and in private, and to transmit it to their children without fear of discrimination, retaliation, or attack by the state or other groups. Cultural identity, in other words, is already protected by internationally recognized human rights.

In response one might argue that, rather than being redundant, a right to cultural identity is implicit in already recognized rights and that it now deserves to be made explicit. But nothing can be done with a right to cultural identity that cannot now be done with already recognized rights. One already has a right to participate in cultural life and to choose freely one's beliefs and opinions. Minority cultures, whose cultural identity is most likely to be subject to attack, are already specially protected. Other civil and political rights allow public action on behalf of distinctive cultural practices. And states already have obligations to conserve and develop culture.[11] A right to cultural identity might add a new layer of rhetoric, but that is hardly a major benefit.

There are, however, a variety of costs, beginning with the costs of the proliferation of human rights. The Covenants contain more than thirty substantive articles containing at least two or three times that many separate rights. If human rights are to continue to be conceived of as paramount moral rights, we need to keep their number as small as possible. Certainly as circumstances change—as standard threats to human dignity evolve— we will need to recognized new rights. But the needless proliferation of

---

11. This is strictly speaking true only of parties to the International Covenant on Economic, Social, and Cultural Rights, but a new convention on the right to cultural identity would probably have few parties that are not already parties to the Covenant.

human rights only risks devaluing the very idea of human rights, and thus subtly weakening all human rights (compare Alston 1984). By itself, recognizing a human right to cultural identity will have little or no impact, but we ought to remain vigilant to the potential dangers of recognizing new human rights for which there is no clear and pressing need.

We must also ask how states are likely to use such a right to cultural identity. In South Africa it could be used, not entirely implausibly, to justify apartheid. In the Soviet Union it could be used, again with some plausibility, to justify continuing to identify Jews on their identity cards and official records, an identification that is often used in a discriminatory fashion. And in a large number of states it is certain to be used as a justification for infringement of other human rights. I do not want to suggest that the proponents of a human right to cultural identity have such uses in mind, but such uses are easy to anticipate. In the absence of readily apparent positive uses, this would seem more than enough to preclude recognizing such a right.

To repeat, protecting cultural identity, so long as that identity is more or less freely chosen by the individual, is a valuable goal. It is also a goal closely connected with both the protection and the exercise of human rights. But not everything good—not even everything connected with human rights—is itself a human right. We do not need a human right to cultural identity.

The problem we face is not that our lists of human rights are defective, but rather that states regularly and systematically violate internationally recognized human rights. Therefore, our attention and effort ought to be focused on implementing and protecting already recognized human rights, not conjuring up new ones of dubious utility. If we want to protect cultural identity, we need to do a better job of protecting the cultural, civil, political, and other rights recognized in the Universal Declaration and the Covenants, just as we need not a new right to development but effective action to implement rights to food, health care, work, and so forth. Contemporary human rights problems do not lie in defects in authoritative international human rights norms or in the cultural insensitivity of such norms, but rather arise from deviations from these norms.

PART IV

Human Rights and Development

9

Development-Rights Trade-offs:
Needs and Equality

1. The Conventional Wisdom

Conventional wisdom holds that short-run and medium-run sacrifices of human rights are required to achieve rapid development. In the 1960s, the necessity of temporarily sacrificing both civil and political rights and economic and social rights was the reigning orthodoxy.[1] In the 1970s, authoritarian repression was still widely viewed as useful or even essential for development,[2] although a growing concern in development economics for issues of distribution and basic needs blunted some of the enthusiasm for trade-off arguments. Furthermore, leading theoretical paradigms, such as dependency/world systems theory (Frank 1969; Wallerstein 1974) and the bureaucratic-authoritarian model (O'Donnell 1973; Collier 1979), despite their explicit opposition to modernization theory, still argued for the developmental necessity of massive human rights trade-offs, at least for capitalist development in the contemporary Third World. This conventional wisdom has recently come under increasing criticism,[3] but even today developmental defenses of repression are common:

> What is preeminent in Cuba and in other areas of the third world is the necessity of development that supersedes all other legitimate claims and prior rights. (Ruffin 1982: 122)

1. See, e.g., Almond 1970: 230–32; Apter 1965: 452; Gerschenkron 1962; LaPalombara 1963: 27; Moore 1966; Organski 1965; Riggs 1963: 135; deSchweinitz 1964: 269.
2. See, e.g., Huntington and Nelson 1976: 168–69; Kim 1981: 12; Overholt 1978: 17; Feitcher 1975: 207.
3. See, e.g., Goodin 1979; Alston 1981; Howard 1983; Hicks 1984. Compare also Beitz 1981; Horowitz 1982: 171ff., 261–62; Soedjatmoko 1985.

The fact of the matter is that industrial takeoff in the mid-twentieth century has some supremely painful human consequences . . . impressive economic performance . . . in the modern period has depended upon massive poverty and political repression, and it would not have been possible under democratic governments pursuing egalitarian economic policies. (Hewlett 1980: 4)

The tough political systems associated with successes (in satisfying basic needs) of the socialist and capitalist types have not so far had a good record in terms of liberal virtues. This may not be accidental: a more liberal political system may be incapable of producing and sustaining the reorientation in the economy necessary for these types of success. (Stewart 1985: 212)

The best one can ask for then, I suppose, is a set of institutions or attitudes that permit a country or a government to back off after it has scored its initial gains or goals. (Jansen 1984: 229)

Three trade-offs have been widely advocated: the needs trade-off, the equality trade-off, and the liberty trade-off.

The needs trade-off.[4] Rather than devote scarce resources to social programs in order to satisfy basic human needs (and associated human rights to, for example, food and health care), relatively high levels of absolute poverty (need deprivation) must be accepted in order to maximize investment. This forgone consumption, however, will be returned with interest in the additional production thus purchased, thereby minimizing the total economic *and human* cost of overcoming mass poverty. What may be called a ''strong'' needs trade-off would attempt to constrain and control consumption in order to capture the largest possible share of total resources for investment. A ''weak'' needs trade-off would simply exclude considerations of consumption-oriented human rights from development planning.

The equality trade-off.[5] A ''weak'' equality trade-off is based on the so-called Kuznets (1955) or (inverted) U hypothesis. Both average incomes and income inequality tend to be lower in the ''traditional'' sector than in the ''modern'' sector. Therefore, during the transition to a modern econ-

---

4. ''An autonomous reduction in consumption . . . is the human price that must be paid for a rapidly growing domestic national product'' (Enke 1963: 181). ''A conscious effort must be made to increase savings, either from existing incomes or by capturing a major share of the rising incomes that result from inducing greater effort and productivity'' (Morris 1967: 306).

5. ''Equality, in other words, is a luxury of rich countries. If a poor society is to achieve anything at all it must develop a high degree of inequality—the small economic surplus must be concentrated in a few hands if *any* high-level achievements are to be made'' (Boulding 1958: 94). ''There is likely to be a conflict between rapid growth and an equitable distribution of income; and a poor country anxious to develop would probably be well advised not to worry too much about the distribution of income'' (Johnson 1962: 153).

omy, inequality in the size distribution of income will first increase, then be maintained at a high level, and finally recede at moderately high levels of national income, thus producing a U-shaped curve when inequality is plotted against the per capita gross national product (GNP).

A "strong" equality trade-off sees inequality as a contributor to, not just an unavoidable consequence of, development. Because only the relatively well-to-do can afford to save and invest, and investment is the key to rapid growth, inequality is often held to be in the long-run best interest of the poor. Inequality is also often justified as an incentive and a reward for superior economic performance and therefore desirable, at least as long as the resulting distribution satisfies some principle of equity, such as Pareto-optimality (that is, no one can be made better off without someone else being made worse off) or the Rawlsian difference principle (that is, the resulting inequality benefits the least advantaged in society).

The liberty trade-off.[6] The exercise of civil and political rights may disrupt or threaten to destroy even the best-laid development plan. Elected officials may feel pressured to select policies based on short-run political expediency rather than insist on economically essential but politically unpopular sacrifices; freedoms of speech, press, and assembly may be exercised so as to create or inflame social division, which an already fragile polity may be unable to endure; free trade unions may merely seek additional special benefits for a labor aristocracy; elaborate and punctilious legal systems on the Western model may seem to be extravagant anachronisms; and so forth. Civil and political liberties therefore must be temporarily suspended.

All three trade-offs have been widely held to be not only *necessary* but also *temporary* and *self-correcting*. The trickle-down theory of growth is a theory of eventual automatic returns to the poor. The U hypothesis envisions an automatic return to greater equality. And, as was evident in programs such as the Alliance for Progress, growth and development have been widely held to be crucial to establishing, maintaining, and expanding liberty in the Third World. So long as rapid growth was achieved—and development was regularly equated with growth, a confusion that further encouraged such trade-off arguments—it was expected that everything else, even the deep absolute and relative poverty of the masses, would take care of itself. Each of these trade-offs thus implies what we can call "growth first" development strategies.

This conventional wisdom has been tragically misguided. Some sacri-

---

6. See, e.g., Lipset 1959; Heilbroner 1963; Bayley 1964; Apter 1965; Bhagwati 1966; Huntington 1968.

fices of human rights may be unavoidable in the struggle for development, but the *categorical* trade-offs of the conventional wisdom are almost always unnecessary and often positively harmful to both development and human rights. Human rights trade-offs, except perhaps at the very early stages of the move from a "traditional" to a "modern" economy (compare Chapter 10, sections 2 and 3), are not development imperatives. They are contingent political choices undertaken for largely political, not technical economic, reasons.

This chapter considers the needs and equality trade-offs (the liberty trade-off will be reserved for the following chapter) primarily through comparison of the development experiences of Brazil and South Korea in the 1960s and 1970s.[7] Both countries pursued state capitalist strategies of dependent development, and both "succeeded" by the standard measure of growth of per capita GNP. The consequences for social and economic rights, however, have been dramatically different.

2. BRAZIL: THE TRAGEDY OF "SUCCESS"

During the 1960s and 1970s, growth in Brazil was rapid, with an average increase in per capita GNP of 5.1 percent per year from 1960 through 1980; during the peak years of the Brazilian economic "miracle" (1968–73), real gross domestic product (GDP) grew at a remarkable 11.5 percent per year. By 1980, Brazil's per capita GNP of $2,050 was among the highest in the Third World (World Bank 1982: table 1; Hewlett 1980: table 2). This growth resulted in increased average real incomes for rich and poor alike—absolute poverty was reduced—but "Brazilian policy was characterized by inattention to the short-run poverty problem" (Fields 1981: 218). Brazil's strategy, in other words, involved at least a weak needs trade-off.

Urban wages and standards of living in Brazil were stagnant throughout the 1960s and 1970s; during the 1960s the urban standard of living actually appears to have declined (Hewlett 1980: 166ff. and tables 15 and 16), and social services were woefully inadequate: "Brazil has the second highest rate of illiteracy in South America and one of the worst infant mortality records in the region" (Hewlett 1980: 122). The 1978 infant mortality rate of 92 per 1,000 live births was more than triple that of Costa Rica, which had virtually the same per capita income and more than one-third higher

7. In this period, the strategic contrast between the two countries was strongest, the needed data is much more readily available, and we can abstract from the impacts of the global recession following the second oil shock. A brief discussion of the 1980s, which underscores almost all the differences, is appended at the end of the chapter.

than in Thailand and the Philippines, both of which had per capita incomes one-third that of Brazil. In fact, urban infant mortality *increased* steadily in the 1960s and early 1970s; in 1978 it was about 20 percent higher than in the early 1950s (World Bank 1981: table 21; Taylor et al. 1980: tables 10–11). This rise is in part attributable to significant levels of malnutrition—for example, in the first half of 1975 more than one-seventh of total urban hospitalizations involved children suffering from malnourishment (Hewlett 1980: 127).

Although the 1981 daily per capita caloric supply was 107 percent of the requirement (World Bank 1984: table 24), this average figure ignores the gross economic inequality that pervades Brazil, where the destructive consequences of the Brazilian strategy are most evident. Figures on income distribution in the Third World are notoriously unreliable,[8] but there is general agreement that the Brazilian situation is particularly appalling. Hewlett places the share of national income of the bottom fifth of the population at just over 3 percent in 1976 (down from almost 4 percent in 1960); the bottom three-fifths received less than 19 percent, down from almost 25 percent in 1960 (1980: table 13). In contrast, over half of the total national income went to the top tenth of the population (up from under 40 percent in 1960) and the one percent at the top alone received more than 17 percent (12 percent in 1960), which was more than the total income of the entire bottom half of the population.[9] Growth thus has made the poor significantly worse off in relative terms.

According to the conventional wisdom, Brazil by the 1970s had grown to the point at which benefits should have been not merely trickling but cascading down to the poor. They were not, and they still are not. According to the conventional wisdom, income inequality should have been declining. It still is not.

One common explanation for this state of affairs stresses Brazil's position as a late-developing state on the periphery of the world capitalist system:[10] a colonial export economy based on mining and a commercial agricultural enclave dissipating the proceeds of its production on the purchase of foreign manufactures and luxury good; the replication of a sharply

8. See, e.g., Rajaraman 1976; Rogers 1978; White 1979; Fields 1980: chap. 2; Nugent and Walther 1982.

9. World Bank figures show an even more lugubrious state of affairs: in 1972, a scant 2.0 percent of total income is estimated to have been received by the poorest fifth of the population, while the top fifth received 66.6 percent, twice the income of the bottom four-fifths combined (World Bank 1981: table 25). Compare also Fishlow 1972; Fields 1977; Taylor et al. 1980: chap. 10.

10. See, e.g., Furtado 1963; Frank 1969; Martins 1976; Cardoso and Faletto 1979; Hewlett 1980: chap. 3.

dualistic economy during the initial period of industrialization through the encouragement of inefficient, oligopolistic, protected, import-substituting manufacturing; the distortions induced by the special problems of "late development"; the role of foreign capital and the stunted development of the national bourgeoisie; and so on. The role of internal factors and political decisions, however, must also be stressed. There is nothing natural or inevitable in the Brazilian pattern of development. In principle, all the structural constraints on balanced and equitable growth could have been overcome by concerted governmental action, at an acceptable *economic* cost. For example, redistributing wealth or income would have stimulated demand for wage goods and industrial products and thus encouraged growth. But for rather obvious political, not economic, reasons, such a course was rejected in favor of strategies compatible with defending inequality. "The specifics of the industrialization strategy and the particular policies of modernizing regimes have served to aggravate the structural components," and "the cumulative effect of these policies was to rigidify and exacerbate" structural inequities (Hewlett 1980: 97, 40).

From 1930 to 1964, when Brazil was making its first major push for industrialization, import substitution was the chosen "engine of growth." Because of the distorted pattern of economic demand resulting from Brazil's skewed income distribution, industrialization was focused on the inefficient, protected (re)production of luxury goods and consumer durables. The mass of the population was thus largely excluded from the benefits of industrial growth in the form of either jobs (production was not only inefficient but relatively capital-intensive) or wage goods. The system was held together by a semi-populist government that assured its survival by buying off the industrial, landowning, and labor elites with the benefits of growth, thereby further exacerbating inequality—and inflation. When inflation became unbearable and the military took over in 1964, the poor, who had been hit especially hard both by inflation and by the policies that produced it, were forced to bear the burden of stabilization, now in the company of the previously favored urban working class (Hewlett 1980: table 13; Foxley 1981).

"Readjustment" did set the stage for the Brazilian "miracle," but its benefits went principally to the rich—those who had prospered all along— rather than those whose consumption had been "deferred." Thus, the Brazilian strategy amounted to a trickle-*up* strategy of growth. And the Brazilian elite did not even save and invest with any special vigor: gross domestic savings and investment in Brazil were only marginally above the average for middle-income, oil-importing countries in 1960, and slightly below the average in 1979 (World Bank 1981: table 5).

The political components of inequitable growth are stressed here because the orthodox trade-off theses, which have been used to justify the Brazilian strategy, are blindly apolitical. All three trade-offs aim to remove the political and moral constraints of human rights in order to free the state to direct a maximally efficient development strategy. The assumption seems to be that this liberated state apparatus will act as a neutral, even beneficent, instrument of technocratic management. In fact, though, the removal of the moral and political constraints of human rights only protects the power of established elites. The trade-offs exclude the mass of the population, but not the traditional elites, who with their new allies in the bureaucracies and public enterprises are given a free hand. The exclusion of the masses is thus perpetuated, even reinforced, and the poor receive few benefits in return for their sacrifices.

Economic growth per se simply will not assure increased enjoyment of economic and social rights. That is a contingent *political* consequence of the *distribution* of power and benefits. The benefits of growth do not automatically trickle down to the poor in defensibly large quantities, and decreasing income inequality is not a natural consequence of relatively high levels of per capita GNP—especially if, during the period of growth, an economic, bureaucratic, and political elite becomes firmly entrenched and convinced of its right to act without political constraints from below. In Brazil, poverty, inequality, and repression have systematically reinforced one another. The culprit, however, has not been rapid growth per se, but rather the particular strategy chosen by the Brazilian elite. Even a late-developing dualistic economy on the periphery of the world capitalist system is, at most, predisposed to inequitable growth. The social consequences of Brazilian-style growth are "necessary" only to the maintenance of elite political domination and gross inequality.

We should not disparage the *absolute* improvement in the real average incomes of the Brazilian poor; many countries have accomplished even less. But this relatively minor trickle-back-down seems to rest on Brazil's unusually high growth rate rather than on its development strategy: unless the elite is virtually awash in new money, little is likely to spill over and trickle down. In the absence of "miracle growth," the Brazilian strategy probably would have been a complete disaster for all but the privileged few who were its direct beneficiaries. A growth-first strategy encompassing the needs and equality trade-offs is not necessarily incompatible with ultimate improvements in at least absolute needs satisfaction for the masses. Nothing in the Brazilian case, however, suggests that massive human rights sacrifices are *necessary* for either rapid growth or needs satisfaction, and the example of South Korea strongly suggests that rapid growth, needs satisfaction, and a high level of income equality can be achieved simultaneously.

3. KOREA: A MORE SUCCESSFUL SUCCESS STORY

A. *Growth with Equity*

If Brazil's growth was a miracle, South Korea's defies description. Between 1960 and 1980, the real per capita GNP of South Korea grew at an average rate of 7.0 percent a year—that is, 40 percent per year (compounded over twenty years) better than Brazil's. In 1965, South Korea's per capita GNP was about half that of Brazil; by 1986, Korea's per capita GNP of $2,370 was more than 30 percent greater than Brazil's (World Bank 1982: table 1; ibid., 1988: table 1). The structural transformation of the South Korean economy has also been remarkable. During the 1960s and 1970s, manufacturing registered a 17 percent average annual rate of real growth, a figure matched by no other country, developed or developing (World Bank 1981: table 2). The share of industry in GDP rose from 20 percent in 1960 to 41 percent in 1980, while the share of agriculture declined from 37 percent to 16 percent (World Bank 1982: table 3). Moreover, all this was quite unexpected. Twenty-five years ago South Korea was widely viewed as an economic disaster saved from complete collapse only by massive and seemingly endless infusions of American aid, which amounted to half the national budget.

Despite these changes, South Korea has maintained an income distribution that by international standards is very egalitarian. The income share of the bottom 40 percent of South Korea's population is comparable to that of Yugoslavia and the United States, and the relative gap between the top and bottom quintiles in Korea is less than one-third that of Brazil (see Table 4).[11] The case of Brazil shows that the equality trade-off is easily derailed. South Korea's example suggests that there is no need to get on the track in the first place. And the Korean experience merits close examination because Taiwan, Israel, Japan, Yugoslavia, and China have achieved similar results through similar means.[12]

11. Although the data in Table 4 are not suited to intertemporal comparisons, the apparent rise in inequality in the 1970s would seem to be real, resulting from output and value added growing four times as fast in manufacturing as in agriculture (Hasan and Rao 1979: 3–4, 20). But this change suggests only a minor weak equality trade-off: uneven sectoral growth in no way implies that absolutely high levels of inequality are required; less equal does not necessarily mean, and in the case of South Korea has not meant, grossly unequal.

12. The general contours of the following argument are most closely associated with the work of Irma Adelman and her colleagues. See Adelman and Morris 1973; Adelman 1975, 1980; Adelman, Morris, and Robinson 1976.

Table 4. Size distribution of income in South Korea, Brazil, and selected countries

Country (year)	Income share					Ratios	
	1st quintile (bottom)	2nd quintile	3rd quintile	4th quintile	5th quintile	5/1	5/(1 + 2)
South Korea							
(1970–71)[a]	7.2	11.4	15.5	22.3	43.8	6.0	2.4
(1976)[b]	5.7	11.2	15.4	22.4	45.3	8.0	2.7
Brazil (1970–72)[c]	2.8	6.2	10.4	17.1	63.6	22.7	7.1
U.S. (1980)[b]	5.3	11.9	17.9	25.0	39.9	7.5	2.4
Yugoslavia (1978)[b]	6.6	12.1	18.7	23.9	38.7	5.7	2.3
Sweden (1981)[b]	7.4	13.1	16.8	21.0	41.7	5.6	2.0

SOURCES:
[a] Average of four estimates in Hasan and Rao 1979: table D.46; Ahluwalia 1976: table 8.
[b] World Bank 1986: table 24.
[c] Average of three estimates in Hewlett 1980: table 13; World Bank 1981: table 25; and Ahluwalia 1976: table 8.

Politics is central to a country's income distribution at *all* levels of development. For example, Ahluwalia, Carter, and Chenery find that on the upswing of the U, distributional policies are at least as important as growth per se in determining the incidence of poverty and inequality, and any turnaround as well is largely a political product (1979: 322–23). Cline goes so far as to dismiss all economic theoretical explanations of income inequality (1975: 369–74). On *economic* grounds it thus appears that, in at least some important cases, substantial income equality need not be sacrificed for rapid growth.

South Korea also suggests that the needs trade-off can be avoided. Between 1961 and 1975, real income rose for all rural and urban groups in South Korea, and real total consumption of the bottom two-fifths of the population increased by 75 percent. Per capita food production grew by almost 1.5 percent per year from 1961 to 1976, and in light of South Korea's income distribution the per capita calorie supply in 1981 of 126 percent of the requirement indicates a relatively good basic nutrition situation.[13] Adult literacy in 1977 was 93 percent, primary school enrollment in 1979 was virtually universal, and secondary school enrollment was over 75 percent. Infant mortality and child death rates were about average in the 1970s for a country at South Korea's level of development, but by 1985 these too were substantially better than the average for upper-middle-income countries. The 1980 ratio of nurses to population of 1 to 350 was

13. Hasan and Rao 1979: 4, 23; World Bank 1984: table 24; Lee 1979: 501–5; Ghose and Griffin 1980; Khil and Bark 1981; Rao 1978: 389.

excellent by Third World standards (comparable to that of Switzerland and the United States in 1960) and indicative of an emphasis on primary health care (although there still is room for low-cost improvements). There is a shortage of doctors, especially outside the main cities, but it is not acute. In general, rural access to services is relatively good.[14]

The human rights consequences of growth and development rest on the interaction of political and economic structures and strategies. At the risk of gross oversimplification, three elements of the South Korean strategy should be highlighted: egalitarian rural development; export-led, labor-intensive industrial development; and education.

B. Egalitarian Rural Development

Throughout the Third World the poor dwell primarily in rural areas, so any strategy for equality and needs satisfaction must rest on a sound rural basis. Because Brazil focused its agricultural efforts on commercial crops, such as coffee, benefits were concentrated in the hands of larger farmers. In contrast, South Korea focused on food and directly attacked the basis of rural inequality: inequitable land tenure and ownership. Half of the country's agricultural land was redistributed in the late 1940s and early 1950s in a massive land-to-the-tiller program: the percentage of full owners rose from less than 15 percent to 70 percent, tenancy was reduced from almost 50 percent to about 7 percent, individual holdings were limited to about 3 hectares, and the average post-reform holding was less than one hectare. These transfers, combined with very low repayment burdens, resulted in a 20 to 30 percent increase in income for the bottom four-fifths of the population and an 80 percent decrease for the top 4 percent.[15] Land reform thus provided the basis for mass rural self-sufficiency during the extended transition to a "modern" economy. It also laid the foundation for a rural mass market, which spurred and supported growth in manufacturing, and radically restructured agricultural incentives.

If basic needs are to be satisfied in rural areas, land must remain productive enough to support its owners. Furthermore, rural life must remain attractive enough to prevent an uncontrolled and unabsorbable migration to the cities that would at best relocate poverty rather than reduce it. In South Korea, agricultural value added grew by 4 percent a year from 1961 to 1975, and real rural income and agricultural wages increased by one-half between 1963 and 1975 (Hasan and Rao 1979: 3–4, 207, and tables 1.12

14. World Bank 1981: tables 21, 22; 1982: tables 1, 23; 1984: table 24; 1988: table 33; Hasan and Rao 1979: 73–74, table 5.5; Rao 1978: 384, 389.

15. Lee 1979: 493–94, 507–8; Ban, Moon, and Perkins 1980: chap. 10; Mason et al. 1980: chap. 7; Tolley, Thomas, and Wong 1982: chap. 2.

and D.45). This growth appears to have been sufficient to permit the structural transformation of the South Korean economy to proceed in an orderly and relatively equitable fashion.

Inequality is a strong *dis*incentive for those at the bottom of the ladder, especially in traditional tenancy agriculture: landlords reap most of the benefits of increased production; peasants, especially tenants, are frequently unable to put away a surplus to invest and are generally too vulnerable to take risks in order to increase production; credit and marketing discriminate against the peasant; and so on. In the absence of very large economies of scale (which do not exist in Korean agriculture) rural inequality would seem to be unjustified on economic grounds, and it is even less justifiable when the human and social costs of needs deprivation are added to the account.

Market forces, however, tend to reestablish inequality by squeezing out the smallest farmers and increasing the relative rewards of the large or efficient. Small farmers are especially vulnerable to natural disasters and family calamities; they also face significant disadvantages in marketing, credit, and access to agricultural services and improved technologies. Inequality is also fostered by natural population increases, which create surplus agricultural labor. The reestablishment of inequality, however, can be (and in the Korean case largely has been) modified or corrected by vigorous state action. For example, enforcing the 3 hectare limit on holdings has prevented the development of a free market in land. In 1975 only 1.5 percent of all holdings (1.2 percent in 1965), covering only 7.0 percent of the total cultivated area, exceeded the limit, and fewer than 8.0 percent of rural households were tenants (Lee 1979: 508–9; Hasan and Rao 1979: 205). The South Korean government, through its fertilizer monopoly and its dominant role in marketing (maintained by a policy of forced sales), has exercised considerable control over the course and consequences of agricultural development (Lee 1979: 496; Ban, Moon, and Perkins 1980: tables 112, 115). Although it used this dominant position in the 1950s and 1960s to extract an agricultural surplus to finance industrial development, in the late 1960s and early 1970s (the period of most rapid industrial growth, when the urban-rural gap would have ''naturally'' increased quite dramatically) government intervention actually restored agricultural terms of trade to levels above those of the early 1960s.[16]

16. Hasan and Rao 1979: 39–40, tables 1.13, D.44; Lee 1979: 510–12; Rao 1978: 387; Ban, Moon, and Perkins 1980: tables 108–10; Kim and Roemer 1979: table 37; Hasan 1976: 22, 45–46, table 12. After considerable backsliding in the later 1970s, agriculture seems to have again been favored in the 1980s, as indicated by an average annual growth rate of 5.6 percent per year for the period 1980–86 (World Bank 1988: table 2).

C. Export-Led, Labor-Intensive Industrialization

Equitable rural development, however, is not likely to do more than prevent a serious deterioration in living conditions. For example, while the South Korean labor force grew at the unexceptional rate of 3.4 percent a year in the 1960s and 1970s, agricultural employment increased by only one percent a year, despite the fine performance of the agricultural sector and the very low use of agricultural machinery (Hasan and Rao 1979: 223–24, 229–29). Major industrial growth thus was necessary simply to avoid the accumulation of an impoverished labor reserve army. Yet South Korea not only absorbed these new entrants into the labor force, but absorbed them with steadily rising real wages (Hasan and Rao 1979: 173, table D.38; World Bank 1988: table 9).

The South Korean strategy of industrial development was no less exceptional than its agricultural strategy. It emphasized exports and domestic demand rather than import substitution. From 1955 to 1968, import substitution produced only about 2 percent of the growth in manufacturing; between 1968 and 1973, import substitution in manufacturing was actually negative. Exports accounted for about one-fourth of the growth, and increased domestic demand picked up the remainder. Despite an average annual real increase in exports of 34 percent a year between 1965 and 1975 (so that exports constituted 36 percent of GNP in 1976), only 15 percent of total manufactures were exported in 1970, and 25 percent in 1976 (Hasan and Rao 1979: 4–6, 242–43, and tables 8.3 and 8.4). Despite the general export orientation of the Korean development strategy, industrialization has largely satisfied mass domestic demand, thereby spreading the benefits of growth.

Exporters, rather than sell to a protected domestic market, must compete against the whole world. This fosters productive efficiency, from which domestic consumers benefit in the form of low world-market prices for goods that are also produced for export, lower prices for imports (because the need for protection is greatly reduced), and more jobs. One-third of all new employment in the 1960s came from export production (Hasan and Rao 1979: 250). Exports also generate foreign exchange, a shortage of which often presents a major development bottleneck. And because South Korea exports manufactured goods rather than primary products, exporting has fostered the structural transformation of the economy. Export promotion, however, is no more natural or automatic than import substitution. Resources, especially credit, must be mobilized and channeled, and the South Korean government has done this effectively (Hasan and Rao 1979: 365ff., 387). Support and subsidies, at a level at least sufficient to assure that there is no disincentive to exports, are essential. In South Korea they have been forthcoming. In particular, the temptation of an overvalued currency has generally been resisted.[17]

But while export promotion was necessary for rapid growth, concentration on labor- and skill-intensive industrial production has been essential to distributing its benefits equitably. Relatively highly-paid industrial employment has been maximized, diffusing the benefits of growth as widely as possible and preventing urban unemployment attributable to capital-intensive production. South Korea's advantage in labor-intensive and skill-intensive manufacturing, however, is also a product of social and political decisions, including public and private investment in education.

D. Education and Equitable Development

Whether because of its socializing effects or its impact on cognitive development, primary education and basic literacy are strongly associated with greater productivity (Colclough 1982). The percentage of Korean workers with no education dropped from 45.5 percent in 1959 to 23.8 percent in 1970; for production workers, the drop was from 22.9 percent to 9.0 percent (Hasan and Rao 1979: table 5.8). By 1980, adult literacy was well over 90 percent. Employers thus can draw on a rapidly growing pool of relatively well prepared workers, a fact that helps to explain the more than 90 percent increase in real value added per worker, despite an essentially constant ratio of capital to labor, as well as the 10 percent average annual increase in employee earnings in the 1970s (Hasan and Rao 1979: 19, table D.38; World Bank 1987: table 8).

The benefits of education were then magnified by labor- and skill-intensive industrialization, which education made feasible in the first place. Once more we see the interaction and reinforcement of the various elements of the South Korean strategy. Primary education also improves access to agricultural extension services and to new technologies and greatly simplifies disseminating information concerning nutrition, health, and family planning. It provides rural migrants with an entry into the better-paying urban-industrial sector. And since education is an important productive asset, universal primary education and very high secondary enrollments amount to a relatively egalitarian distribution of this key industrial resource, laying a foundation for further equitable growth.

E. Assessing the South Korean Strategy

Whereas Brazil pursued rapid growth that excluded the mass of the population, the basic thrust of the South Korean strategy, in industry as

17. Hasan and Rao 1979: 236–39, 266–69, table D.43. For a brilliant case study, see Morawetz 1981; see also Krueger 1979: 92–99, 172–98.

well as agriculture, has been to incorporate as much of the population as possible into the process of growth and the sharing of its benefits. (The exception has been political participation, a topic that will be addressed in the following chapter.) Although economic inclusion and exclusion would both seem to be compatible with rapid growth, the consequences for needs and equality are very different. Growth *can*, in at least certain circumstances, be made to serve equality and the satisfaction of basic human needs, but only through a conscious and comprehensive political effort.

South Korea should not be romanticized. It has been an oppressive and often ruthless military dictatorship. A growing gap between city and countryside is a serious problem; housing and industrial working conditions are often poor; access to pure water is inadequate; women still face serious economic and social discrimination; and so forth. To many observers, an especially troubling aspect of the South Korean development strategy has been its dependence on foreign capital and markets. This dependence is high, however, only in comparison to "self-reliant" strategies; compared with more orthodox state capitalist *and socialist* strategies, it is not extreme. For example, throughout the 1980s South Korea's debt service as a percentage of exports has actually been below the average for (upper) middle income economies (see, e.g., World Bank 1982: table 13; 1986: table 18; 1988: table 19). And, as China under Mao suggests, self-reliance too has major costs, even for a country with a relatively high objective potential for self-sufficiency, which South Korea and most Third World countries simply do not have.

Where dependence does not lead to poverty, inequality, unemployment, the adoption of inappropriate technologies, commodity concentration, declining terms of trade, and the host of other problems highlighted by dependency theory and the agenda of the new international economic order, one must at least pause before condemning dependence too strongly. Self-reliant poverty may have its attractions, but if the alternative is a relatively prosperous dependence—and that may indeed be the choice facing many Third World countries—dependence too has its attractions, or at least its compensations, especially if it is managed, as in South Korea, to minimize its costs.

In generalizing from the South Korean experience, we must guard against several possible misreadings. There is no single element to the South Korean strategy, and no single part can be implemented in isolation with any hope of similar success. Only the interconnection of multiple policy goals and instruments explains South Korea's success at combining rapid growth and structural transformation of the economy, substantial alleviation of absolute poverty, and a relatively egalitarian income distribution. South Korean growth and development have rested on export-oriented industrialization—more precisely, labor-intensive industrialization pursued in a context of egalitarian rural development. Simply exporting more is not enough. In fact, exporting cash crops that disrupt traditional agriculture is likely to sacrifice both needs satisfaction and equality.

In addition, South Korea's success in alleviating absolute poverty, as in Brazil, can in significant measure be attributed to unusually high rates of growth. It is much easier for a dominant elite to share new wealth with the masses when there is a veritable flood of new wealth available. Therefore, even if a comprehensive strategy of growth with equity is implemented, we may not be able to expect comparable improvements in needs satisfaction, or similar success at maintaining income equality, unless extremely rapid growth is achieved.

The role of the state also needs to be emphasized (compare Haggard and Moon 1983: esp. 141–52). South Korea may use market mechanisms more than the typical Third World country, but it is by no stretch of the imagination a free market economy, even if we take the contemporary United States to define a free market system. For example, entrepreneurial freedom exists in Korea only within limits set by the government, which has played the central role in determining the direction and priorities of investment and of development in general. Likewise, "restraint" in the workers' demands for higher wages and improved working conditions—a restraint that has contributed substantially to Korea's comparative advantage—is largely the result of government control and even repression.

South Korea has prospered by finding and aggressively exploiting a niche in the evolving world economy and "the new international division of labor" based on the comparative advantage provided by its abundant, cheap, and disciplined labor force. Such a comparative advantage simply does not exist, for example, in most of Africa. Thus, although South Korea and similar cases refute simple dependency theory core-periphery models of the global economy, they also undermine equally simplistic arguments for unrestrained and virtually unthinking integration into the reigning international economic order.

Finally, we must give due weight to special circumstances. Cultural homogeneity and a traditional emphasis on family and education have contributed to South Korea's achievements. Japanese colonialism, followed by World War II, occupation, and civil war, undermined the established indigenous elites and repressive social hierarchies. Korea was even "fortunate" in its colonial past: Japan wanted food (rice rather than coffee, cocoa, copper, sugar, or tin) and thus built up an agricultural system that was relatively easily converted to needs-oriented rural development. The process of land reform was eased by the presence of large Japanese land-holdings that were relatively easy to expropriate. A terrain that largely precludes mechanized agriculture has helped to keep holdings small. Massive amounts of American aid permitted industrial investment despite an extremely low level of domestic savings in the 1950s and early 1960s. In addition, the security threat from the north increased social discipline; high population density facilitated the delivery of social services; and the scarcity of natural resources prevented South Korea from falling into the trap of commodity dependence.

Most of these "advantages," however, had parallel drawbacks: the debilitating effects of colonialism need not be enumerated; partition, occupation, and civil war were economically, socially, and psychologically traumatic; aid in many countries has been squandered or has sapped initiative; the military threat required massive military spending, which largely dissipated American aid on unproductive investments; population density puts pressure on land, housing, and social services; and shortages of resources have held back more than one country.

South Korea is undeniably a special case, but its background is not radically different from that of many other much less successful Third World countries. At least part of its uniqueness lies in its success, not in its starting point. At the very least, we must recall that thirty years ago the only people who emphasized Korea's uniqueness did so to apologize for its failures.

4. IMPLEMENTING A STRATEGY OF EQUITABLE GROWTH

"It is the initial distribution of assets which sets the pattern for growth. If asset distribution is unequal, it is probable that the additions to income from growth will be distributed unequally" (Griffin and James 1981: 7). All other things being equal, more assets yield greater income—and where all other things are not equal, those with fewer assets usually are at a disadvantage, especially in a market system. The market rewards those who are best able to cope with its demands, and the ability to cope is again in considerable measure a function of one's economic assets: in a market economy, the rich tend to get richer faster than the poor get less poor. But markets are a social product; neither they nor the inequalities they engender are "natural." The distribution of income and wealth in a country rests on structural features of the state, society, and economy that are in large measure susceptible to political control.

The case of South Korea shows that gross income inequality is not a necessary condition for rapid growth. Therefore, let us assume here that a relatively egalitarian income distribution should be a major medium-run objective of any defensible development strategy; a strong equality trade-off is unnecessary, and considerations of justice and human rights make it undesirable. The policy question, then, is whether "redistribution" should precede growth or follow growth. The conventional wisdom advocates "growth first." The preceding discussion of South Korea, however, suggests many of the benefits of a strategy of "redistribution first" or "equity first"—or at the very least equitable redistribution during even the early stages of growth.

"Growth first" implies a capacity for redistributing afterward, but such a strategy ignores the extremely strong and probably overwhelming resistance to ex post facto income redistribution.[18] Even nominally progressive direct taxes often prove to be neutral or regressive in practice, and indirect taxes, which for administrative and political reasons are widely used in the Third World, tend to reinforce inequality. Social services are also unlikely to be effective instruments of redistribution because of the serious disadvantages the poor typically face in obtaining access to services. In fact, public services are usually concentrated in the cities and rarely penetrate the countryside below the level of the relatively well-to-do, thus actually increasing inequality. Benefits tend to trickle *up* in structurally unequal environments.

"Equity first" not only goes to the root of the problem, it also enhances the value and efficacy of other measures (Griffin and James 1981: 39–42). Furthermore, it requires that future interventions merely hold the line; starting from relative equality at least reduces much of the structural resistance that plagues incremental and after-the-fact approaches. "Redistribution first" may also ameliorate economically based rural powerlessness by weakening the hold of traditional landowning elites. And, beyond all speculative arguments, it has worked in several of the cases in which it has been tried *and* where the redistributed assets have been vigorously supported by later state policy.

Redistributing first also minimizes the need for the speculative and questionable trade-offs underlying the conventional wisdom. Trade-off arguments demonstrate a serious general problem in the policy sciences. Our "best" theories tell us that if A does x, y, and z, then he will suffer costs a, b, and c, and receive benefits q, r, and s. But there usually is only a loose connection between theory and current (let alone future) "reality."

18. See esp. Adelman and Robinson 1978. Compare Adelman et al. 1976 and the studies cited in Cline 1975: 378–87.

For example, scholars and planners with a statistical bent are likely to be quite willing to plunge ahead with an r^2 that means that they literally do not have half an idea of what is going on. Such theories are the best we have, so they probably should be used, at least if the costs of error are relatively low. But the needs and equality trade-offs imply major sacrifices by literally hundreds of millions of people. The conventional wisdom thus seems to border on culpable social science malpractice.

We should be particularly wary of trade-off arguments in environments of despotism and oligarchy, for under such conditions "trade-offs" tend to involve people *being* sacrificed rather than *making* sacrifices. But even if our theories are sound and the people are willing to shoulder the burden of implementing them, the standard procedure for justifying these trade-offs is open to serious question. For example, there is a widespread failure to discount for uncertainty. The inability of most Third World countries to meet even modest goals for growth suggests that trade-offs may not be justifiable once we take into account the (un)likelihood that present sacrifices will achieve the predicted future benefits—whether because of poor planning, inept or corrupt administration, insufficient information, or just plain bad luck.

A more serious problem is the standard assumption that *who* receives a benefit (or bears a cost) and *when* are not relevant issues—that is, that all costs and benefits are equal, regardless of recipient or time frame. This is quite implausible in the cases with which we are concerned here. It may make all the difference in the world to a marginal peasant family whether they get an extra hundred calories per person a day now, or in five, ten, or twenty years. To such a family, it may well be an issue of life or death, and it certainly will at least be an issue of basic health. To another family, though, the extra calories may mean a full stomach rather than just barely enough to survive; meat instead of rice to a third family; and overweight to a fourth. Who receives what and when, and who sacrifices what and when, can radically alter our calculations. The standard arguments for economic trade-offs require magnified sacrifices from those least able to sacrifice. "Short-run" suffering therefore may quickly come to outweigh any plausible long-run succor, or else we are likely to be faced with particularly problematic decisions that resemble sacrificing a generation or two for the future good of later generations.

Political opposition to redistributing first is of course sure to be great, but incremental or after-the-fact redistributions are not obviously preferable even on such pragmatic grounds. For example, incrementalism leaves established elites relatively free to wage a sustained and quite possibly effective rearguard struggle to reassert their privileged position. The Machiavellian strategy of disposing of all one's enemies in one quick initial strike has much to be said for it. Redistributing first also poses serious problems of planning and administration, but those problems seem no more daunting than the problems faced by more traditional strategies.

The cases of South Korea and Brazil, and reflection on the models they represent, suggest that there is a complex and variable relationship between human rights and development. No aspect of the relationship is automatic, fixed, or given. Much more work is needed before we can say how much of the East Asian model can be generalized. The example of South Korea does, however, shatter the conventional orthodoxy that has held that, except in the very long run, development and human rights are competing concerns—at least in the case of the needs and equality trade-offs.

5. POSTSCRIPT: BRAZIL AND SOUTH KOREA IN THE 1980s

The preceding discussion has focused on the 1960s and 1970s, but the South Korean strategy looks even better in the 1980s. Despite the export orientation of the Korean economy, or perhaps because of it, South Korea has much more successfully weathered the second oil shock and the global recession of the early 1980s. Brazil's per capita GNP has actually declined from $2,050 in 1980 to $1,810 in 1986, while South Korea's has climbed from $1,520 to $2,370. For the period 1980–86, Brazilian manufacturing grew by an average annual rate of 1.2 percent, compared with 9.8 percent for South Korea; Brazilian exports increased by 4.3 percent per year, compared with 13.1 percent for South Korea; Brazil's imports declined by 5.1 percent per year, while South Korea's rose by 9.3 percent; the average annual inflation rate in Brazil was 157.1 percent, compared with 5.4 percent for South Korea; and even Korean agriculture grew faster than Brazil's, at 5.6 percent per year, compared with 2.0 percent.[19] South Korea also continued to outperform the average upper-middle income country in the period 1980–86 by a substantial margin, with an average annual growth in GDP of 8.2 percent, compared with 2.5 percent for the group as a whole; a 5.5 percent annual increase in private consumption, compared with a 1.8 average; and a 9.6 percent increase in gross domestic investment, in contrast to the average annual *decline* of 1.9 percent (World Bank 1982: tables 1–3; 1988: tables 1–4, 11).

19. For an overview of Brazil's problems in the 1980s and their relationship to earlier development decisions, see Frieden 1987.

The structural transformation of the South Korean economy also is continuing. By 1986, industry accounted for 42 percent of South Korea's GDP. Textiles still accounted for 17 percent of value added in manufacturing in 1985, but this figure is identical to that for 1970, while the percentage attributable to machinery and transport equipment had grown to 23 percent, up from 11 percent in 1970. Earnings per employee grew by 4.4 percent per year for the period 1980–85 (they declined by 2.1 percent annually in Brazil) and gross output per employee grew by 39 percent (it declined by 26 percent in Brazil). And while 60 percent of Brazil's exports in 1986 were primary commodities and only 15 percent were machinery and transport equipment, 33 percent of South Korea's exports were machinery and transport equipment, a figure slightly above that for Japan in 1965 (World Bank 1988: tables 3, 8, 9, 12).

South Korea has also sustained its relatively good record on a variety of standard social indicators. While in Brazil life expectancy at birth increased from 63 years in 1980 to 65 years in 1986, in South Korea it jumped from 65 to 69 years. South Korea cut its population growth rate from an already low annual average of 1.9 percent for the period 1965–80 to 1.4 percent for 1980–86; the comparable figures for Brazil are 2.4 and 2.2 percent. The daily calorie supply per capita in Brazil went from 2,405 in 1965 to 2,562 in 1977 to 2,657 in 1985; the comparable figures for South Korea are 2,255, 2,785, and 2,806. Brazil and South Korea have comparable ratios of population to physician (1,300 and 1,390), but in 1981 there were 1,140 people per nurse in Brazil, compared with 350 in South Korea. In South Korea in 1979, 76 percent of the relevant age-group was enrolled in secondary school, a figure that had increased to 94 percent in 1985; in Brazil, the increase was from 32 percent to an equally dismal 35 percent. Brazil did cut its infant mortality rate significantly, from 77 in 1980 to 65 in 1986, but the figure for South Korea dropped much more dramatically, from 34 to 25. And all these figures for South Korea (except that for calories) are at least equal to and usually substantially better than the group average for upper-middle income countries (World Bank 1982: tables 1, 21–23; 1988: tables 1, 27, 29, 30, 33).

South Korea has even managed to achieve all of this without acquiring a crushing debt burden. In fact, its export orientation has left South Korea better able than most to service its debt. External public debt service consumed only 16.7 percent of South Korean exports in 1986 (down from 19.5 percent in 1970), compared with a 19.7 percent average for upper-middle-income countries and 33.2 percent for Brazil. And South Korea's current account deficit was better than average for the 1980s; in 1986 South

Korea even turned a surplus of $4.6 billion (World Bank 1987: table 20; 1988: tables 15, 19, 20).

Perhaps the most encouraging aspect of South Korea's performance in the 1980s, however, has been the reduction in political repression, especially in 1987 and 1988, but this brings us to the third of the conventional trade-offs, the liberty trade-off.

10

Development-Rights Trade-offs: Political Repression

South Korea may give us reason to hope for a constructive relationship between development and economic and social rights, but its record on civil and political rights has been dismal. In addition to abrogating political freedoms and civil liberties, the military regimes that until very recently ruled Korea for over a quarter of a century regularly engaged in such practices as mysterious deaths, kidnapping, political imprisonment, and torture.[1] Other countries that have pursued a similar strategy of development, such as Taiwan, Yugoslavia, and prewar Japan, also offer little encouragement to those who would defend protecting civil and political rights at all stages of development.

Repression—direct state action that systematically violates basic civil and political rights—is the norm in developing countries, largely irrespective of development strategy or social system. State socialist strategies clearly rest on the elimination or at least forcible neutralization of "reactionary" elements and "class enemies." Most accounts of successful capitalist growth give no less central a role to repression, whether it be to manage and protect capital accumulation (locally or on a world scale), to defend class rule and privilege, to manage the crises of peripheral development, to assure consistency, direction, and purpose in development planning, to guarantee labor discipline, or to force savings and investment. And the fate of civil and political rights in states pursuing intermediate or mixed

---

1. See, e.g., Cohen 1979; Amnesty International 1981; Asia Watch 1985. For preliminary accounts of the 1987 liberalization, see Han 1988 and West and Baker 1988. I am writing this in August 1988, when the implications of liberalization are unclear. Therefore, in what follows, when discussing South Korea I will largely ignore the 1987 reforms, other than to speculate (especially in section 4) on the popular pressures that helped bring them about.

strategies has not been much better. We can point to countries that have developed with some success without widespread resort to systematic political exclusion, such as Costa Rica, but they appear more as difficult-to-explain anomalies than possible models for emulation. Nonetheless, I argue that the liberty trade-off—the sacrifice of civil and political rights to economic development—is no less a matter of contingent political choice than the needs and equality trade-offs.

Third World regimes that have respected a wide range of civil and political rights for an extended time are decidedly a rarity, and neither the Western nor the Soviet experience can be applied in any straightforward way to most contemporary developing countries. In fact, we lack even the relatively crude indicators available for economic and social rights, such as health, nutrition, and literacy statistics. For example, the Freedom House map is far too crude, Amnesty International reports are too restricted, and such national sources as U.S. State Department reports are incomplete and subject to political bias. There are also special empirical problems in evaluating arguments for the liberty trade-off. Human rights objectives that are associated with needs satisfaction or income equality can be roughly translated into monetary terms. Consider, for example, the right to food: raising the caloric intake of group A to point x might be viewed as requiring y additional income per group member, at total cost z, which would have a roughly calculable effect on GNP. At least the broad outlines of an empirical cost-benefit evaluation thus are clear. By contrast, it is extremely difficult, if not impossible, to state the costs of the liberty trade-off in monetary terms. We thus seem to be required to make a "trade-off" between incommensurable items. As a result, the discussion in this chapter will be somewhat more abstract than that of the preceding chapter, but it may provide some useful general observations and demonstrate the political contingency of repression and the liberty trade-off.

1. Inclusion, Exclusion, and Development Strategies

For our purposes here, regimes and their associated development strategies can be characterized as exclusionary or inclusionary, both economically and politically (see Figure 2). Economic exclusion usually must be enforced by political exclusion. It is extraordinarily rare for a politically included population to choose continued economic exclusion, because the maintenance of massive economic exclusion usually rests on repression. In Figure 2 I call this familiar pattern of a growth-first economic strategy coupled with the systematic denial of civil and political rights an *exclusion-*

Figure 2. Regime types and associated development strategies

	Politically exclusive	Politically inclusive
Economically exclusive	Exclusionary regime/strategy	
Economically inclusive	Paternalistic regime/strategy	Participatory regime/strategy

ary regime or development strategy. For greater clarity and emphasis, it can be called a "doubly exclusionary" regime or strategy.

The need to maintain economic exclusion is a standard explanation for repression and the breakdown of democratic regimes, especially in Latin America (O'Donnell 1973; Linz and Stepan 1978; Collier 1979). Bureaucratic-authoritarian rule requires repression to demobilize, and if necessary to eliminate, populist and radical forces and to protect economic inequality and elite privilege, thus excluding major segments of the population from participating in and enjoying the benefits of development. Such repression, however, clearly is "required" not by "development" per se but rather in order to establish, sustain, or cope with the contradictions of a particular (exclusionary) *style* of development.

By a similar logic, the upper-right-hand corner of Figure 2 is likely to have few if any empirical referents. Political inclusion seems to lead unavoidably to greater economic inclusion, as civil and political rights are exercised to further popular economic and social interests. In fact, it is often precisely the fear of such an exercise of civil and political rights that triggers repression. Political exclusion, however, is compatible with both economic inclusion and economic exclusion. South Korea illustrates that a highly repressive military dictatorship can pursue an economically inclusionary strategy; China and Cuba represent a different version of such a *paternalistic strategy* or regime.

The particular victims of repression are also politically contingent. Who is to be repressed and how are not determined by transhistorical forces or morally neutral technical economic imperatives, but by political decisions: the victims of repression are *chosen* by those who control the repressive apparatus of the state. In a doubly exclusionary strategy, such as Brazil's, the victims usually have been peasants, workers, slum-dwellers, and leftists. In paternalistic strategies, political exclusion is largely to enforce a particular style of economic inclusion. In the Marxist-Leninist variant, "capitalists," "kulaks," and freethinkers (dissidents) of various types have been the principal victims. In the state capitalist variant of a paternalistic strategy, as practiced in South Korea and Taiwan, the principal victims have been labor, particularly those who have tried to organize, and autonomous political organizations, especially of the left and liberal center.

Not all repression is developmental. Some regimes, such as Mobutu's Zaire, are pursuing no plausible development strategy of any sort. In many personalist dictatorships, so-called development strategies are largely a cover for official theft. In many other instances, repression is little more than a reflection of or spillover from intra-elite struggles. Much repression in the contemporary Third World is ideologically justified. And most repression, whatever else it does and whatever other purposes it may (claim to) serve, protects (or is part of the process of acquiring) class or elite privilege.

Much repression in a number of countries, however, can be called developmental. In addition, successful development has always been accompanied by substantial repression. Therefore, whatever the abuses of the language of developmental repression, there is a real issue that must be explored further.

2. REPRESSION, STRUCTURAL TRANSFORMATION, AND THE STATE

Although the contingency of human rights trade-offs must be emphasized, some repression is likely to be "required" (or at least extraordinarily difficult to avoid) in pursuit of what can be called *the structural task* of removing institutional and sociocultural barriers to development and *the policy task* of assuring conformity to development plans.

Whether the chosen strategy is "capitalist" or "socialist," or a difficult-to-classify mixture of market and nonmarket approaches; whether it involves political inclusion or exclusion; and whether the principal immediate goal is growth or equity or a combination of the two, all development strategies and political regimes face the structural task of radical social transformation to remove established institutions that are incompatible with modernization and development. Capitalist strategies require that precapitalist institutions, practices, and ways of thinking be eliminated or at least subordinated. Socialist strategies require subordinating capitalism in addition.

Such radical social transformations rarely occur peacefully. They usually have involved considerable violence and widespread violations of most civil and political rights. Whether in the core or the periphery, capitalist development has in all notably successful cases involved massive violence and repression directed against established precapitalist institutions. Much the same structural tasks face even Marxist-Leninist regimes, given that most (all those not directly imposed by the Red Army?) arose in precapitalist countries (e.g. China, Angola) or at best in countries in the very early stages of capitalism (e.g., Russia). In addition, socialist regimes face the further structural tasks of overcoming whatever capitalist or proto-capitalist institutions and practices have been established.

No matter how it is defined, development has rarely if ever been achieved without considerable resort to repression. The reasons for this are not difficult to discern: the central role of the state in the process of economic development in the modern world. As the repression of labor in nineteenth-century Europe and North America clearly indicates, even the nightwatchman state was more than willing to become directly involved in the economy and to smash heads in order to further a particular style of development. And, as the example of nineteenth-century labor again indicates, when the state becomes involved it tends to act in favor of certain classes or social groups and against others, even when (as is *not* always the case) it is also acting in some plausible sense to further "the national interest." All states pursue development policies with a (greater or lesser) class bias, which almost always will involve a certain amount of repression, and rulers are likely to be strongly tempted to resort to allegedly developmental repression for reasons that in fact rest on class, group, or personal interests. Given these political realities, repression is likely to be at least temporarily unavoidable, especially given the high priority assigned to development by virtually all states.

The distinction between repression being politically *unavoidable*, as opposed to the conventional argument that it is economically *necessary*, is subtle but crucial. If they chose to do so, moderate, humane, and enlightened ruling elites could avoid much—probably most, perhaps even nearly all—developmental repression. But we have little or no historical experience of such elite rule, so that one might argue that repression is "necessary" regardless of development strategy. But this necessity is rooted in "human nature," or the character of ruling elites, not in the technical economic imperatives of development. The "necessity" of developmental repression lies largely in the realm of politics, not economics.

The abstract theoretical question that is usually asked—"Is nonrepressive development possible?"—simply is *not* the central issue. Instead we must ask, "Is development possible *here* while avoiding *these* kinds of repression?" "Does development in country *x* at time *y* require repression of type *z*?" Some repression may be unavoidable in any development strategy, but that does not make any particular repressive act or policy justifiable, let alone necessary or unavoidable. Even if repression of some sort is unavoidable, any particular act or strategy of repression is politically contingent. Both the intensity and the targets of repression are largely matters of political "choice."

Because civil and political rights have important inherent and instrumental value, governments stand under a strong (moral and political) obligation to minimize developmental repression. All repressive acts must be evaluated in terms of both their necessity and their benefits. This forces the discussion back to the question of trade-offs, which must be instrumentally justified according to the familiar canons of cost-benefit analysis, in contrast to the almost always overly general, abstract, and at best vaguely justified assertions of the need to sacrifice human rights that tend to pass for "trade-off arguments."

The contingency of human rights trade-offs is especially important because so much of what passes for developmental repression reflects instead regime maintenance, or even the personal interests of officials, and has only the most tenuous connection to a development strategy. Development strategies do in large measure reflect political regimes and the interests that underlie them, but not everything done to maintain a regime—let alone everything done to maintain political incumbents—is connected with the development strategy in question. For example, the extensive use of particularly brutal forms of torture in Park's last years in South Korea had nothing to do with development; if anything, excessive repression in the late 1970s became economically dysfunctional. Similarly, much of the repression in Brazil and the Southern Cone countries in the 1970s was justified on political and ideological, not economic, grounds.

One might argue that even economically "superfluous" or dysfunctional repression is a tolerable, if not exactly unavoidable, side-effect or cost of consciously chosen policies. For example, it might be argued that given the need for state direction of the economy, the benefits of even repressive direction, if economically successful, are sufficient to outweigh the costs— that is, that the positive role of the state in development planning and direction outweighs the costs of a relatively strong state resorting to excessive repression. Such arguments are most plausible in repressive countries, such as South Korea, where the chosen development path (equitable growth) has involved relatively low needs and equality trade-offs. They are perhaps even plausible in economically successful exclusionary regimes. But in far too many instances repression is without significant economic rewards, except for a tiny predatory elite, and thus is capable of no plausible developmental justification.

This is clearest in extreme cases of negative growth combined with massive repression, such as Zaire, which has suffered through a 2.2 percent per year *decline* in per capita GNP for the period 1965–86 (which corresponds with the period of Mobutu's rule); or Guatemala, which suffered a 1.2 percent annual decline in total (not merely per capita) GDP for the period 1980–86 (which roughly corresponds to the height of repression there) (World Bank 1988: tables 1, 2). In the more typical case of relative stagnation, such as Nicaragua under Somoza or Chile under Pinochet, the problem is less dramatic but only slightly less serious. Where there has been below-average growth, little structural transformation of the economy, and no redistribution of wealth or income (or, even worse, where inequality has increased), we have, if not outright pillage, at least a bankrupt policy or regime in which repression is exercised out of self-interest instead of any plausible conception of the national interest. Such abuses of allegedly developmental repression only underscore the central point of the political basis and contingency of most repression.

This contingency is equally true of both capitalist and socialist regimes. Some capitalist regimes are more exploitive than others, some use more repression than others, some produce greater growth than others. In a few cases, such as Mexico or Costa Rica, (direct) repression may even be infrequent or rare. All, however, resort to repression primarily to assure *capitalist* development, rather than development per se. Repression is no less essential to socialist development strategies, and the results have not been notably better. The unsurpassed repression of revolutionary Cambodia or Ethiopia has purchased no apparent developmental benefits, no matter how development is defined; in fact, it has produced little but social and economic disaster. Mozambique, Angola, and Guinea-Bissau have used repression more moderately, but their economic performance has been as disappointing as that of most of the rest of Africa. In Cuba, extensive repression over more than two decades has brought undoubted improvements, but even here recent performance has been disappointingly mixed (Packenham 1986; Rabkin 1987). And the bulk of the repression, both in the revolutionary phase and after the government has been firmly established, is to assure *socialist* development.

At this point, though, to throw up our hands and say that in the pursuit of development repression is unavoidable would be both unjustifiably fatalistic and irresponsible. Although you can't make an omelette without breaking eggs, just breaking eggs does not an omelette make. There is also a great difference whether one has to break three, four, five, or a dozen eggs to end up with a three-egg omelette. The omelette can be burned, runny, or properly cooked. Once the omelettes have been made and we sit down to eat, there may or may not be enough to feed everyone. And even if there is enough for all, some still may get a disproportionately large share while others go hungry. In other words, even if we grant that some repression probably is politically unavoidable, the real issue remains "*What* repression for *what* development?"

3. Repression and "Stages" of Development

When or where in the development process we are—how much progress has been made toward the goals of growth and equity—should influence both the "need" for and the nature of developmental repression. Repression is likely to be linked not only with strategic choices based on power and politics but also with the "stage" or "phase" of development already achieved.

Stage theories of development are justly notorious. In the mechanistic way they have often been advanced, they represent a gross and distorting oversimplification. Nonetheless, in considering the relationship between repression and development it is useful to distinguish between three "stages" or phases of development in virtually all successful strategies:

Modernization: Creation of the institutions of capitalist (or socialist or mixed) development, such as private (or state or mixed) ownership of the means of production, commodity production, market (or administered) exchange, and national economic integration.

Industrialization: The rise of the modern urban industrial sector to a position of economic predominance, including at least some significant heavy industrial development.

Graduation: Further relative decline of agriculture, emerging predominance of heavy industry over light industry, further industrial deepening in many sectors, and the beginnings of the development of indigenous advanced technological capacity—roughly, the transition ("graduation") from a developing economy to a developed economy.

There is nothing inevitable about movement through these particular phases, and success at one does not necessarily guarantee success at, or even a move to, the next higher stage. But all countries that have achieved sustained successful development in any plausible sense of that term (the United States, Western Europe, Japan, East Germany, and the Soviet Union, and now such countries as South Korea and Taiwan) have followed this rough pattern. And this pattern of phases has important implications for assessing the relationship between repression and development.

The repression characteristic of modernization was discussed above as being associated with the structural task of removing established structures and practices that impede development. Resistance, which usually will be met by repression, is certain to come from the dominant groups that the modernizers are seeking to displace, such as large landowners, aristocrats, chiefs, priests, and mullahs. Such opponents might be co-opted, which seems to have occurred with traditional chiefs in Ghana (Howard 1978) and priests (marabouts) in Senegal (Klein 1987), and they may even voluntarily acquiesce in the rise of new elites and sources of power. But repression at this stage seems to be extremely difficult to avoid, especially if traditional leaders resist modernization.

Clearly the details of this process of modernization will differ from country to country depending on such factors as the nature of the traditional social system, colonial history, and resource base, not to mention even more variable and contingent factors, such as leadership personalities and political ideology. Nevertheless, modernization, and the apparent unavoidability of repression in its pursuit, would seem to be essential to any successful development strategy. This is why arguments about the necessity of repression in development will never leave us: there is a certain (limited) truth to them.

Repression, however, is at best a means to a desired end; it is obviously *un*desirable in itself. Therefore, even modernizing repression must be evaluated according to its contributions to the end of modernization, and the human and economic costs of repression must never be overlooked. Furthermore, we must not allow arguments for modernizing repression to be used at later stages. This is especially important because often the repression we are concerned with (for example, the practices of dictators such as Park, Pinochet, Geisel, or Castro) is undertaken to assure conformity to a particular plan long after the stage of modernization has been passed.

In pursuit of industrialization, repression should be less necessary, if only because of the foundation for change laid during modernization. In contrast to the essentially revolutionary struggle between old and new that dominates the phase of modernization, industrializing repression is characteristically associated with disputes over the intermediate ends sought and the means used in a particular development strategy. Thus, the structural task recedes and the policy task (and repression), with its obviously greater contingency, comes to the fore. Repression is likely to be used during industrialization principally to enforce a particular distribution of the benefits and burdens of development. ''As tensions and conflicts over economic growth become aggravated, the different social groups change from defense of a *rate* of economic growth to a defense of a *pattern* of economic growth'' (Fernandes 1966: 191). And even the way that similar patterns are defended may differ markedly, as a comparison between Brazil and Mexico makes clear (Collier 1982; Baloyra 1986: 48–50). With traditional forces subordinated and modern economic institutions established, the need for state intervention is less generic and more focused on a relatively small set of strategic sectors, bottlenecks, or opportunities. This need not imply less of a need for repression—consider the Brazilian or Argentine justification for repression in the need for targeted intervention to produce industrial deepening—but such repression is clearly tied to the demands of a particular strategy.

The newly industrializing countries (NICs) in Asia and Latin America raise the most interesting questions with respect to repression, for they are now at or near the stage of graduation, where we begin to see clearly the transition from developing country to developed country (whether or not the transformation is in the end successfully achieved). Developmental arguments for repression are likely to be particularly weak at this stage.

By this stage, human capital and economic infrastructure should be developed to such a point that heroic efforts to mobilize resources should no longer be necessary. For example, administrators should be sufficiently experienced to be able to manage state participation in the economy without relying heavily on coercion and violence. Most markets, to the extent that they are central to the economy, should be fairly well established and capable of functioning with only modest levels of coercive state involvement, and entrepreneurs should be sufficiently skilled to operate successfully within the confines of a reasonably regulated market. And in a nonmarket strategy, administration should be replacing political coercion.

Although government intervention may be inherently inefficient in a strict economic theoretical sense, when we compare state economic intervention not with the perfect markets of economic theory but with real Third World markets, it may turn out to be the least inefficient alternative, especially during the phases of modernization and industrialization. As the stage of graduation is reached, however, a strong interventionist state should be increasingly unnecessary, especially in capitalist strategies. Repression too should therefore be less "necessary"—that is, both more easily avoided and even more obviously contingent on political choices.

Even in a fundamentally capitalist strategy, we cannot expect the state to remove itself from the economy altogether. As we saw above, South Korea's success in achieving both growth and equity can be attributed in significant measure to the economic direction provided by the state. Furthermore, the need to prevent backsliding, and the legitimate demand to maintain the most rapid possible pace of development, *may* in certain circumstances justify *certain types* of repression. But prior developmental successes should have greatly reduced the need for further repression in the name of central economic direction. The persistence of such arguments for repression once the stage of graduation has been reached may even be evidence of the failure of previous efforts or strategies.

Creating the capability to generate future growth and development is an important element of virtually all definitions of development. In the early stages of the process, development may not be self-perpetuating—for example, until some critical mass is reached, or simply because of the structural incompleteness inherent in the early phases of anything. At some point, however, such arguments must fail. If development has not become relatively self-generating and self-sustaining by the graduation phase, then it is difficult to see when it will. By the stage of graduation, allegedly developmental repression is almost certain to be based not on the demands of development, but on the need to maintain an unpopular development strategy—or, to be more precise, on an increasingly unpopular and politically intolerable distribution of economic and political benefits, burdens, and opportunities.

4. LEGITIMACY AND THE BREAKDOWN OF AUTHORITARIAN REGIMES

Reference to unpopularity raises the issue of legitimacy. So far we have focused almost entirely on the perspective of those at the top who are deciding to "trade off"—sacrifice someone else's—rights. The other side of the picture—how these sacrifices are perceived and responded to by those whose rights are infringed; roughly whether they see themselves as *making* sacrifices of *being* sacrificed—is no less important in evaluating developmental repression.

A. The Demand for Liberty

By the stage of graduation the population is likely to be significantly less willing to accept repression—political exclusion—whether the strategy pursued is economically inclusionary (e.g., Korea, Cuba, Taiwan) or exclusionary (e.g., Brazil, Chile). At lower levels of development the lure of material gain may adequately compensate for repression. The bulk of the population may be willing to tolerate the liberty trade-off at early stages of development if the promised material benefits are delivered in a reasonable time.

In *some* circumstances the mass of the population *may* be willing to trade off civil and political rights for more rapid development, although such acquiescence is certainly much rarer than dictators would like us to believe, as the electoral defeat of even the extremely popular Indira Gandhi after the Emergency indicates. But one paradox of developmental repression is that the claim of popular acquiescence is virtually impossible to confirm. This alone should render such claims extremely suspect. Arguments of popular acquiescence to repression are also morally suspect. Just as the popularity of, say, racial or sexual discrimination is usually held to be irrelevant (discrimination is wrong no matter how popular it is), so the popularity of beating, arresting, torturing, or killing "radicals" or "counterrevolutionaries" should be morally irrelevant. In fact, if we take human rights seriously, they are *most* important precisely when there is popular support for their violation (see Chapter 1, section 2).

Let us, however, lay aside such concerns. Civil and political rights may be more or less willingly sacrificed for material gain by poor people, or at least I am unable to conclusively refute this common claim, but rarely are they willingly sacrificed for incremental material gain by those who have modest means or more. Even in an (economically) inclusionary authoritarian regime, material progress is increasingly unlikely to remain sufficient once the economy has grown to the point where the material needs of most citizens are regularly being satisfied. The old saying that man does not live by bread alone is still true. Most people want to have a say in the political direction of their lives, and an opportunity to pursue personal or group interests free of the coercive guidance of the state. Once such interests and desires have come to the fore, willingness to sacrifice civil and political rights—that is, willingness to tolerate repression and political exclusion—for further increments of material progress is likely to erode. South Korea may be an example of such a process in action. And even if earlier acquiescence to repression simply reflected fear, fear too would seem to be less of a reason to tolerate repression once a certain amount of material comfort has been achieved.

In exclusionary regimes, such as that in Brazil under military rule, popular opposition is likely to be especially strong. In particular, the masses of the population, who have not shared in the benefits of growth, are likely to be reaching the point at which they are no longer willing to be excluded, no longer willing to wait for the benefits to trickle down, no longer willing to entrust their interests to a government in which they have no say. Even in an economically inclusionary regime, excluded or repressed elements (e.g., labor in Korea) are likely to come to similar conclusions, with similar consequences for the development of more active resistance to repression. And in both kinds of regimes, even favored elements are likely to find restrictions on civil and political rights increasingly irksome.

The upshot is likely to be a crisis of legitimacy: either growth continues, but is rejected as no longer enough, or growth slows or even stops, in which case a central underlying economic rationale for repression is removed.

Faced with such a crisis, a regime is likely to be forced to choose between democratization, or at least liberalization, and further repression. This presents a dilemma for repressive regimes: repression simply cannot reach the causes of the crisis, even if it should alleviate the symptoms, but substantial liberalization may alter the fundamental character of the regime.[2] Political exclusion thus is likely, in the end, to back the ruling elite into a corner in which none of the available options is acceptable to it. A debilitating and perhaps even deadly legitimation crisis would seem to lay at the end of the road for exclusionary and paternalistic development strategies and regimes.

B. Repression and the Legitimation Crisis

For simplicity, let us assume that such legitimation crises are essentially a matter of economic performance. Although such an assumption is somewhat unrealistic (and therefore will be relaxed in the following section), it focuses our attention on the link between repression and development and on what is probably the most persuasive justification for repression: economic success.

To restate the problem, popular acceptance of repression is likely to decline as development comes closer to a society's reach, which in turn is likely to lead to a serious legitimation crisis in countries at the level of development achieved by the Latin American and East Asian newly industrializing countries. Striking examples are the continuing *abertura* in Brazil and the rise of the opposition in South Korea (in the legislature, on campuses, and in union activity) since the assassination of Park. The return of civilian governments to Argentina and Uruguay, renewed opposition to Pinochet culminating in his defeat in the 1988 plebiscite, and electoral problems for the ruling party in Mexico, point to the seeming generality of such a crisis.

This may be part of a more general phenomenon of limited long-run popular tolerance for repression (consider also the fall of Marcos and Somoza, continued opposition to Suharto in Indonesia, and the general long-term instability of most military regimes in Africa and Latin America), rather than a process particularly linked to the phase of graduation. But even this suggests problems for maintaining traditional levels of repres-

---

2. The international illegitimacy of repressive regimes further intensifies the dilemma, especially for Western-oriented regimes that aspire to full membership in the "club" of Western developed *and* liberal-democratic countries. This apparently was an important, if secondary, factor in the democratization of Spain, and it may be a constraint on reexclusion in such countries as Argentina and Brazil. It may also help to explain the liberalization now under way in South Korea.

sion in the NICs. Furthermore, the theoretical argument that the legitimacy of repression declines with development success suggests that any such general problems should be especially serious in the NICs.

Although the newly industrializing countries have available to them relatively substantial institutional, administrative, and technical resources that might be turned to repression, repressive responses may simply intensify the crisis. Especially in an exclusionary regime, further repression will make it increasingly obvious that elite privilege rather than development is the reason for mass deprivation and political exclusion. Such a strategy is unlikely to be stable (compare Canak 1984: 24). Paternalist (especially Leninist) regimes may be better able to assure stability by further repression, particularly where the apparatus of the state is highly developed, but sluggish economic performance, as in Cuba, is the likely cost of such repressive stability. And here too such a strategy is likely to underscore the fact that repression is for particular social and political purposes, for a particular style of development—and one that is not very popular with its alleged beneficiaries.

Democratization offers a solution that might prove compatible with future growth and development at a rapid pace. Having served its avowed purpose of bringing the country to the point of graduation, repression probably can be *relatively* easily relaxed at this point, with the past record of economic inclusion providing a base for a move toward political inclusion. The ruling class or elites, however, must be "willing" (or must have come to feel forced by popular resistance) to allow liberalization leading to democratization. Such "enlightened self-interest" cannot always, or even often, be counted on.

Democratization is not without its pitfalls, including reactionary efforts to convert the (economically) inclusionary regime into an exclusionary regime. Problems in a transition to democracy are likely to be exacerbated by a lack of political experience among those to whom the government will pass as political inclusion proceeds. If the newly ascendant political groups mismanage the economy, or pose what is perceived to be an excessive and intolerable threat to the prior political and economic elite, a return to authoritarianism (or at least a coup attempt) is a real possibility. In the worst of all case, this might initiate a cycle of liberalization and repression that saps the economic and political strength of the country (compare Richards 1986: 451–61).

Authoritarian failure may provide a honeymoon for a new democratic regime, but it hardly guarantees success. Ultimately, political legitimacy must be earned by positive action, which will usually involve a degree of economic success. Unless the new regime can restore growth and development, it is likely to face its own crisis of economic legitimacy and the threat of authoritarian overthrow. Economic success or failure, however, may not be entirely under the control of the government. If an exclusionary regime has been forced to democratize as a result of its own failures—for example, by economic mismanagement or failed political repression—a new democratic regime, by selecting and successfully implementing appropriate policies, may be able to establish a record of achievement that will legitimate democracy. But to the extent that the economic crisis that undermined the old regime was due to factors largely beyond its control, a new democratic regime will be unlikely to be able to turn the economy around and thus will be subject to the same sort of delegitimizing failure that brought it into power.[3] Likewise, if authoritarian failure arose from the refusal of economic or political elites to allow the government to implement a successful development strategy, a new democratic regime will face the specter of a disaffected former ruling class waiting in the wings to step back in and reassert (authoritarian) control.

C. Brazil: An Illustration

Who controls the state, and their relationships with and degree of control over (or by) major social classes, elites, factions, or coalitions, will be crucial to the way a state responds to crisis. In the newly industrializing countries, state-society relations tend to be fairly complex. In most cases, we need to consider the place of at least eight major groups: local capital, international capital, the military, the (nonmilitary) bureaucracy, landowners, urban workers, the urban masses, and the rural masses. The relationship between these groups and the state goes a long way toward determining the nature and direction of repression. A very quick and crude example may help illustrate this point.

From 1930 to 1964, with the acquiescence of the military and the bureaucracy, Brazil was ruled by a loose populist coalition of land, (organized) labor, and capital that largely ignored the rural and urban masses (Roett 1984, chaps. 2–5). Economic crisis in the early 1960s led to the rise of the military—which had been a decisive but usually behind-the-scenes actor, at least since the collapse of the empire in 1889—as the senior party, joined by the "triple alliance" of local, international, and state capital (Evans 1979), in a new ruling coalition. Labor, now, was also excluded. This required considerable repression both in the short run, in order to establish the new regime, and in the longer run, in order to defend its

---

3. One might plausibly argue that the recent wave of redemocratization in South America fits this pattern.

(inequitable) policies (Alves 1985). Furthermore, the increasing role of civilian and military bureaucracies in both the economy and in politics had a direct influence on several key elements of development planning and probably an indirect impact as well on the nature of repression.

By the late 1970s and early 1980s, political relations had been fundamentally reshaped (Remmer 1985: 270). Furthermore, Brazil came to be faced with serious and persistent economic problems, an especially important consideration in a regime that based much of its legitimacy on economic success (Lafer 1984: 182). Repression was largely discredited, both by its success in (literally) eliminating serious radical opposition, which rendered further repression largely superfluous, and by widespread opposition to, or at least second thoughts about, the excesses of the early 1970s (Lamounier 1984: 172). Popular opposition to military rule continued to increase, especially after the serious recession combined with the return of runaway inflation beginning in 1981. And in the 1980s this opposition increasingly came to include significant numbers of businessmen, professionals, and even some military officers, key elements of the ruling coalition, calling for a return to democracy (Epstein 1984: 45–46; Cardoso 1986). Industrialization also made mass poverty particularly evident, while "successful" growth under military rule made it especially difficult to ignore.

The new regime is substantially less authoritarian but even more bureaucratic (Moreira 1984: 162). The military is thus again receding into the background, having largely been replaced by the bureaucracy as the key element in holding together the ruling coalition. And the strategy being pursued seems to include greater economic inclusion, "a broadening of the basis of political legitimacy which is helping to overcome economic distress" (Moreira 1984: 165).

Even this brief survey shows that the contingency of both repression and decompression in Brazil is striking. The exclusion of the working class and the brutal repression of opponents was a policy choice, not an unavoidable necessity, and the worst of the repression under Médici had little or no connection to any development strategy, but was instead justified by arguments of state security (Alves 1985; McDonough 1981). The politically dominant groups in Brazilian society in the mid-1960s certainly were strongly inclined to make this particular choice, but there were alternatives. Furthermore, the choice was "imposed," if at all, only to protect and extend a particular style of inegalitarian development. Similarly, there was nothing inevitable about the return to electoral politics: the military *could* have responded to its crisis of legitimacy with a new round of repression, but at least haltingly chose to withdraw from direct control, a gradual process that was by no means fully completed with the ascension of a civilian president in 1985. And there is nothing inevitable about the military either staying out of or returning to power.

We can go from country to country and see the same sort of contingency in the presence or absence and particular character of repression. Such choices certainly are conditioned by history, politics, personality, fortune, and so forth. Nonetheless, they are political *choices*. Repression is an instrument of a particular policy much more than a general requisite of development, especially once the stage of modernization has been passed.

5. THE POLITICAL CONTINGENCY OF REPRESSION

So far, we have largely excluded nondevelopmental sources of repression in order to simplify the analysis and focus it on the strongest form of the argument for the liberty trade-off. Reintroducing the other bases of repression complicates the account, but it also underscores the essential contingency of repression.

Repression for the self-aggrandizement of the ruling elites further underscores the contingent character of repression in the struggle for development. The billions acquired by dictators like Mobutu, Marcos, Duvalier, and Somoza and their retainers and cronies, and the repression required to protect the pillaging of the public coffers, have no plausible economic or moral justification. Such policies are purely political choices of predatory elites. Unfortunately, those who wield repressive power far too often (and almost certainly more often than not) use it at least indirectly for self-enrichment.

National security arguments and other noneconomic sources of legitimacy complicate the picture in a very different way. For example, the threat from the north in South Korea has given the military a rationale for continued control that was largely absent in Brazil, Uruguay, or Argentina, where now there is not even an internal communist threat to which to appeal. Likewise, the 1986 state of siege in Chile may have been made to appear more palatable to some elements of the center and the right by what the government presented as a major resurgence of urban terrorism. "Charismatic" legitimacy adds similar complications, although the inability of Perón to pass this on illustrates the long-run fragility of such power. The special legitimacy of the military as an apolitical source of order, vision, and technical-bureaucratic expertise, also can be an important factor, and clearly has been in such countries as Brazil and South Korea. Electoral legitimacy should not be overlooked either, not only because such countries as Mexico underscore its significance throughout the development process, but also because it is likely to be crucial to successful and sustained transitions to democracy. For example, Lamounier suggests that the relatively strong roots of electoral politics (although not particular parties) in Brazil have been crucial to political decompression there (1984: 171).

Multiple sources of legitimacy greatly complicate the simple scenarios presented above, but again the complications underscore my central theme of the contingency of repression in the process of development. Some repression almost certainly is unavoidable. Much repression is undoubtedly functional for a *particular* ''development'' strategy. But the familiar general claim that development requires repression is at best grossly misleading.[4]

In addition, there may be significant economic *benefits* to the exercise of many civil and political rights. For example, obtaining an adequate and timely flow of information is a major practical problem of economic management, especially in the Third World, where even simple official statistical information tends to be of doubtful reliability. Freedom of speech, press, association, and assembly, and the right to petition for redress of grievances, can be important channels of information for the government. Electoral campaigns can also provide important information for planners, but only if there is true competition in relatively free, fair, and open elections (even if only one-party elections). More generally, imposed social discipline usually will engender inefficiency that at least partially cancels any gains derived from suspending civil and political rights. Civil and political rights may also help turn a country toward equitable development, and in many cases they are likely to be the only way, short of revolution, to bring about the transition. And even if bread does come first, civil and political rights may be the best and usually the most peaceful way to obtain bread, because poverty is in large measure a social and political rather than a natural phenomenon.

In addition, it is clear that a blanket trade-off of civil and political rights, whatever its economic effects, unjustifiably ignores the manifest diversity of these rights. For example, torture, disappearances, and arbitrary execu-

4. If repression is a contingent political response to particular opportunities, problems, and challenges, what is really needed is not a general theoretical argument of the type developed here, but case-study analysis, particularly if we want to understand the *causes* of repression. My principal response to this fair and telling criticism is that the continued prevalence of the belief in the developmental necessity of repression, which I documented in some detail in the opening section of Chapter 9, suggests that the essentially negative argument of the contingency of repression still needs to be made. Given the current state of the discussion, the first step in understanding the causes of repression and the links between repression and development is to recognize that these causes simply do not lie in any general developmental imperative.

tions can almost always be eliminated with no costs to development; rights to nationality and to equality before the law would also seem to have very low development costs; due process is likely to be a bit more costly, but not wildly so; and even such rights as freedom of speech, press, and assembly, and the right to vote, which have relatively high development costs, need to be assessed in light of particular empirical circumstances. In other words, any potentially justifiable trade-off of civil and political rights must be selective, flexible, and specific; there can be absolutely no justification for a blanket trade-off of civil and political rights.

Finally, whatever the analytical and practical difficulties, it is necessary to keep civil and political rights always in the picture. The ultimate purpose of development is to lay the basis for realizing human dignity. Whatever its other attractions, a strategy that assures material progress at the cost of political participation, the enjoyment of civil rights, and the unfolding of the higher nature of human beings is radically incomplete. On moral grounds, at least, we must insist that development strategies strive to minimize any shortfall, rather than justify or even increase it.

Development strategies and repression are political actions resting on moral and political choices. Like all such choices, they are subject to both instrumental and moral evaluation and criticisms. And they are *choices* from among a variety of alternatives. Some development alternatives involve little repression; all involve repression only contingently.

PART V

Human Rights and International Action

11

International Human Rights Regimes

Human rights have hardly replaced considerations of power, security, ideology, and economic interest, but they have become a significant concern in international relations in recent years—a standard topic of talk and occasionally even action—in a variety of bilateral and multilateral contexts. These final chapters explore briefly the dimensions of this "international normative universality." In this chapter, the multilateral machinery that has been developed over the last several decades to implement internationally recognized human rights is reviewed. The following chapter considers human rights in bilateral foreign policy, and the final chapter assesses the overall impact of international action.

1. INTERNATIONAL REGIMES

In recent years it has become common for students of international relations to speak of "international regimes," systems of norms and decision-making procedures accepted by states as binding in a particular issue area.[1] Regime norms, standards, or rules (I use the terms interchangeably here) may run from fully international to entirely national. International human rights norms, especially as expressed in the Universal Declaration and the Covenants, are relatively strong; they border on being authoritative international norms. Roughly half the states of the world are parties to the International Human Rights Covenants, and virtually all the rest (including most prominently, the United States) have either signed but

1. The standard discussion is Krasner 1983. See also Donnelly 1986; Haas 1980: 358; Keohane and Nye 1977: 19; Young 1980 and 1986. For a good review of the state of current theoretical work on international regimes, see Haggard and Simmons 1987.

not ratified the Covenants or otherwise expressed their acceptance of and commitment to these norms. Furthermore, as we saw in Chapters 1, 2, and 4, these norms are comprehensive and coherent and rest on a plausible and attractive philosophical anthropology. As we shall soon see, however, international implementation is neither as well developed nor as widely accepted.

Regime decision-making procedures also may run the gamut from purely national to fully international. They can be roughly grouped into enforcement, implementation, and promotional activities. International enforcement involves binding international decision-making and perhaps very strong forms of international monitoring of national compliance with international norms. International implementation includes weaker monitoring procedures and policy coordination, in which states make regular use of an international forum to coordinate policies that ultimately remain entirely under national control. International promotion may involve the international exchange of information and efforts to promote or assist the national implementation of international norms.

These types of activities provide a convenient scheme for classifying regimes as *promotional*, *implementation*, and *enforcement regimes*, each of which can be further classified as relatively strong or weak. To this, we can add the class of *declaratory regimes*, which involve international norms but no international decision-making (except in the creation of norms). Figure 3 provides a rough general typology of regime types.

2. The Global Human Rights Regime

The Universal Declaration and the Covenants provide the norms of what we can call "the global human rights regime," a system of rules and implementation procedures centered on the United Nations. The principal organs of this regime are the U.N. Commission on Human Rights and the Human Rights Committee.

A. The U.N. Commission on Human Rights
The most important body in the global human rights regime is the United Nations Commission on Human Rights, which has served as the principal forum for negotiating international human rights norms (including the Universal Declaration and the Covenants) and in recent years has even acquired some modest monitoring powers. The commission's strongest powers rest on Economic and Social Council (ECOSOC) resolution 1503 (1970), which authorizes the commission to investigate communications (complaints) that "appear to reveal a consistent pattern of gross and reliably attested violations of human rights."

Figure 3. Types of international regimes

	National decisions	Promotion or assistance	Information exchange	Policy coordination	International monitoring	International decisions
International norms	Strong declaratory		Strong promotional	Strong implementation		Strong enforcement
International standards with national exemptions						
		Weak promotional		Weak implementation	Weak enforcement	
International guidelines	Weak declaratory					
National standards	No regime					
	Declaratory regime	Promotional regime		Implementation regime	Enforcement regime	

Stringent criteria of admissibility[2] limit the cases considered, and only *situations* of gross and systematic violations are covered; particular violations cannot be investigated. Furthermore, the entire procedure is confidential until it has been concluded.[3] Although confidentiality may encourage cooperation by states, it dramatically slows the process.[4] In practice, the 1503 procedure is largely a promotional device involving only sporadic and limited monitoring. Given the sensitivity of human rights questions, even this may be of real practical value. Nevertheless, its weakness is evident.

Much the same is true of the commission's other activities. For example, the Sub-Commission on the Prevention of Discrimination and Protection of Minorities' annual public discussions, and the commission's own public proceedings, under the authority of ECOSOC resolution 1235 (XLII) and a variety of ad hoc procedures, have increased general awareness of human rights issues. The commission's work has also helped to focus international public opinion on violations in at least a few countries (e.g., South Africa and Chile) and on a few types of pervasive and particularly reprehensible violations, such as torture and disappearances (Weissbrodt 1986, Tolley 1987: 104–10). In addition, the commission, along with the U.N. Secretariat, coordinates and encourages the use of advisory services in the field of human rights. Nonetheless, virtually nothing has been achieved in the areas of international implementation and enforcement.

The commission's one real advantage is that it may look into situations, insofar as it is able to look anywhere, in all countries, not only those party to a particular treaty. Therefore, it is in many ways the procedural core of the global human rights regime.

B. The Human Rights Committee

The other principal body of the global human rights regime is the Human Rights Committee, a body of eighteen independent experts established to monitor compliance with the International Covenant on Civil and

2. See Cassese 1972; Zuijdwijk 1982: 30–39; Tolley 1987.

3. Even when consideration of an issue has been completed, the commission has typically done nothing more than pass an extraordinarily mild resolution that attempts to avoid any hint of criticism. The commission may also, with the consent and cooperation of the state in question, appoint a committee to investigate a situation, but there has been no such investigation.

4. The commission has circumvented some of the strictures of confidentiality by publicly announcing a "black list" of countries being studied. (Since 1978, the practices of more than thirty countries have been examined.) Given the procedural hurdles involved in reaching this stage of the procedure, it "is often interpreted as at least demonstrating that the allegations in a communication have some merit" (Shelton 1984: 65).

Political Rights. The parties to the Covenant "undertake to submit reports on the measures they have adopted which give effect to the rights recognized herein and on the progress made in the enjoyment of those rights" (Article 40 (1)). The principal function of the committee is to review these periodic reports, which must be submitted every two years.[5]

Formal evaluations of or even comments on the compliance or noncompliance of individual states have not been made. But public questioning of state representatives is relatively free of ideological posturing, often penetrating, and by diplomatic standards at least, neither excessively deferential nor merely pro forma, and state representatives often are fairly responsive. The procedure has even provoked occasional minor changes in national law, and at least a few parties (e.g., Canada; see Nolan 1988) use their dealings with the committee to review and reexamine national laws, policies, and practices. The reporting procedure thus has provided a fairly widely accepted promotional mechanism, but it involves only information exchange and the weakest monitoring. And even the information exchange is flawed. The reports of many countries are thorough and revealing, but others are farces,[6] and some are not even submitted (as illustrated by the extreme case of the report of Zaire, due in 1978 but still not submitted in 1986, despite ten reminders). Furthermore, only parties to the Covenant (87 as of March 1, 1988) must report; half the countries of the world are exempt from even this minimal international scrutiny.

The one area where guarded optimism may be appropriate is the committee's consideration of individual petitions under the Optional Protocol of the Covenant.[7] In its first nine years of operation, through mid-1986, the committee received 211 communications and expressed its views—that is,

5. The International Covenant on Economic, Social, and Cultural Rights also requires periodic reports. Until recently, these reports were reviewed by a Sessional Working Group of ECOSOC (Fischer 1984: 173–76). A committee of experts (the Committee on Economic, Social, and Cultural Rights), roughly analogous to the Human Rights Committee, was created in 1986 (see Alston 1987).

6. For example, many Soviet bloc countries have reported that all the enumerated rights were fully implemented before the Covenants were ratified; many reports consist principally of extracts from national constitutions and statutes, and a significant number are simply evasive. To cite just a few instances, Guinea has claimed that "citizens of Guinea felt no need to invoke the Covenant because national legislation was at a more advanced stage" (A/39/40 par. 139), Bulgaria has reported that "all the rights and freedoms stipulated in the Covenant were covered in the appropriate national laws" before ratification (A/34/40 par. 112), and the Mongolian representative, in response to a question by a member of the committee, proudly claimed that there had never been a complaint about torture or cruel or inhuman treatment made in his country (A/35/40 par. 108).

7. The Covenant also contains optional provisions (Articles 41–42) for interstate complaints, but these have not been and are not likely to be used.

made a substantive determination on the merits of the case—on 72 of these communications. Although the majority of these decisions involved a single country (Uruguay), the procedure does seem to be relatively open and highly independent, providing genuine if limited international monitoring, which in at least a few cases has altered state practice. But by mid-1986 only thirty-seven countries had accepted the Optional Protocol, so less than one-quarter of the countries of the world are covered. It is not surprising that almost none of those covered are major human rights violators. As a result, relatively strong procedures apply primarily where they are least needed. Unfortunately, this is only to be expected, given that participation is entirely voluntary.

C. Political Foundations of the Global Regime

The global human rights regime is a relatively strong promotional regime composed of widely accepted substantive norms, largely internationalized standard-setting procedures, and some general promotional activity, but very limited international implementation, which rarely goes beyond information exchange and voluntarily accepted international assistance for the national implementation of international norms. There is no international enforcement. Such normative strength and procedural weakness is not accidental; it is the result of conscious political decisions.

Regimes are political creations set up to overcome perceived problems arising from inadequately regulated or insufficiently coordinated national action. Keohane (1982) offers a useful market analogy: regimes arise when sufficient international "demand" is met by a state or group of states willing and able to "supply" international norms and decision-making procedures. As Krasner (1978: 52) puts it, in each issue area there are makers, breakers, and takers of (potential) international regimes; understanding the structure of a regime (or its absence) requires that we know who has played which roles, when and why, and what agreements they reached.

Even fifty years ago, human rights were almost universally viewed as the exclusive preserve of the state; despite occasional references to minimum standards of civilized behavior, there was not even a weak declaratory international human rights regime.[8] World War II marks a decisive break; the defeat of Germany ushered in the contemporary international human

---

8. In the interwar period, the International Labor Organization (ILO) undertook some minor efforts in the area of workers' rights, and the League of Nations' Minorities System, the only other significant international human rights activity in this period, not only was restricted to a single class of rights but for the most part covered only those states defeated during or created in the aftermath of World War I.

rights regime. Revulsion at the array of human rights abuses that came to be summarized in the term "Nazi" engendered a brief period of enthusiastic international action. Although Hitler's actions shocked the conscience of the international community, they did not clearly contravene well-established explicit international norms. It was therefore *relatively* easy to reach general agreement on a set of international principles against gross and persistent systematic violations of basic rights—namely, the Universal Declaration (followed the next year by the Convention on Genocide, which was even more clearly a direct legacy of Hitler).

It is perhaps surprising that this moral "demand" should have produced even this much in a world in which more material national interests usually prevail. In the years immediately following World War II, however, there were willing and able makers, numerous takers, and no significant breakers of an international human rights regime. The moral and emotional demands for an international human rights regime ran both wide and deep, while in this pre–Cold War era no countervailing concerns or interests had yet emerged. A cynic might suggest that these postwar "achievements" simply reflect the minimal international constraints and very low costs of a declaratory regime: decision-making under the Universal Declaration remained entirely national, and it would be more than twenty years until resolution 1503 and nearly thirty years before even the rudimentary promotion and monitoring procedures of the Covenants came into effect. Yet prior to the war, even a declaratory regime had rarely been contemplated. In the late 1940s human rights became a recognized international issue area for the first time.

Moving much beyond a declaratory regime, however, has proved difficult. It is in this relative constancy of the regime (critics and frustrated optimists are likely to say "stagnation") that the weakness of the demand is most evident. A strong international human rights regime simply does not rest on any perceived material interest of a state or coalition willing and able to supply it; the necessary makers for a substantially stronger global human rights regime do not exist. Barring extraordinary circumstances, states typically participate in an international regime only to achieve *national* objectives in an environment of perceived international interdependence. Even then they typically participate only when independent national action has failed and only when participation appears "safe," all things considered—a very serious constraint, given states' notorious jealousy of their sovereign prerogatives.

A stronger global human rights regime simply does not present a safe prospect of obtaining otherwise unattainable national benefits. Moral interests such as human rights are no less "real" than material interests. They are, however, less tangible, and national policy, for better or worse, tends to be made in response to relatively tangible national objectives. In addition, the extreme sensitivity of human rights practices makes the very subject intensely threatening to most states. National human rights practices often would be a matter for considerable embarrassment should they be subject to full international scrutiny. In fact, compliance with international human rights standards would in numerous countries mean the removal of those in power. Finally, human rights are ultimately a profoundly *national*, not international, issue, both from the point of view of international legal jurisdiction and with respect to effective action to establish a rights respecting government (see Chapter 13). International action usually can be at best an impetus toward and support for national action on behalf of human rights.

But if international regimes arise primarily because of international interdependence—the inability to achieve important national objectives by independent national action—how can we account for the creation, and even modest growth, of the global human rights regime? First and foremost, by the persisting relevance of the "moral" concerns that brought it into being in the first place. Butchers such as Pol Pot and Idi Amin still shock the consciences of all people and provoke a desire to reject them as not merely reprehensible but prohibited by clear and public, authoritative international norms; even governments with dismal human rights records of their own seem to feel compelled to join in condemning the abuses of such rulers, and those of lesser despots as well.

Although cynics might interpret such condemnations as craven abuse of the rhetoric of human rights, they are just as easily seen as implicit, submerged, or deflected expressions of a sense of *moral* interdependence. States—not only governments, but frequently citizens as well—often are unwilling to translate this perceived moral interdependence into action, let alone an international regime with strong decision-making powers. But they also are unwilling (or at least politically unable) to return to treating national human rights practices as properly beyond all international norms and procedures.

A weak global human rights regime also may contribute, in a way acceptable to states, to improved national practice. For example, new governments with a commitment to human rights may find it helpful to be able to draw on and point to the constraints of authoritative international standards; we can see this, perhaps, in the case of the Alfonsin government in Argentina. Likewise, established regimes may find the additional check provided by an international regime a salutary supplement to national efforts, as seems to be the case for many smaller Western powers. And most states, even if only for considerations of image and prestige, are likely to be willing to accept regime norms and procedures, especially norms, that do not appear immediately threatening.

An international regime reflects states' collective vision of a problem and its solution, and their willingness to "fund" that solution. In the area of human rights, this vision seems to extend not much beyond a politically weak moral interdependence, and states are willing to "pay" very little in the way of diminished national sovereignty in order to realize the benefits of cooperation. Because it rests on a politically weak sense of *moral* interdependence, there is no powerful demand for a stronger regime. The result is a regime with extensive, coherent, and widely accepted norms, but extremely limited international decision-making powers—that is, a strong promotional regime.

3. REGIONAL HUMAN RIGHTS REGIMES

Adopting a metaphor from Vinod Aggarwal, Keohane notes that international regimes "are 'nested' within more comprehensive agreements . . . that constitute a complex and interlinked pattern of relations" (1982: 334). Although "nesting" may imply an arrangement that is too neat and too hierarchical, there are regional and single-issue human rights regimes that might be considered largely autonomous but relatively coherently "nested" international human rights (sub-)regimes. After looking at regional regimes in this section we shall take up single-issue human rights regimes in section 4.

A. The European Regime

A strong regional regime exists among the (primarily Western European) members of the Council of Europe. Personal, legal, civil, and political rights are guaranteed by the (European) Convention for the Protection of Human Rights and Fundamental Freedoms (1950) and its Protocols, while economic and social rights are laid down in the European Social Charter (1961).[9] The lists of rights in these documents are very similar to those of the Universal Declaration and the Covenants. The decision-making procedures of the European regime, however, are of special interest, especially the very strong monitoring powers of the European Commission of Human Rights and the authoritative decision-making powers of the European Court of Human Rights.

9. I shall restrict the term "European human rights regime" to the norms and procedures established in these documents. For a good brief introduction see Higgins 1984 and Vasak 1982.

The principal function of the European Commission of Human Rights, an independent body of experts (one from each member state), is to review "applications" (complaints) from persons, groups of individuals, non-governmental organizations (NGOs), and states alleging violations of the rights guaranteed by the Convention in the seventeen (of twenty-one) parties that have authorized the commission to receive applications. If friendly settlement cannot be reached, the commission may formally report its opinion on the state's compliance with the Convention. Although these reports are not legally binding, they are usually accepted as authoritative by states, and within three months of the commission's report, either the commission or the state in question may refer the case to the European Court of Human Rights for binding enforcement action. These procedures, which are implemented with scrupulous impartiality, are not only of unprecedented formal strength and completeness, but also almost completely accepted in practice.

Economic and social rights are supervised through separate and significantly weaker procedures. Implementation is entirely through biennial reports, which along with comments from national organizations of employers and workers are reviewed by a Committee of Experts. Individual communications are not permitted, nor are interstate complaints, and there is no machinery for authoritative enforcement. In practice, however, reporting has yielded some policy coordination and rather strong monitoring: the genuine commitment of the parties to the regime's norms often makes the give-and-take discussion of reports adequate incentive for policy changes, especially given the official participation of workers' and employers' organizations and the national political pressure they and other private groups can exert "from below."

The real strength of the European regime lies in voluntary acceptance of the regime by its participating states. Formal procedures may support and strengthen national resolve, but in the final analysis they largely supplement national commitment and state acceptance; strong procedures are less a cause than a reflection of the regime's strength. In any international regime, strong procedures serve primarily to check backsliding, to apply pressure for further progress, to remedy occasional deviations, and to provide authoritative interpretations in controversial cases. These are hardly negligible functions; they are precisely what is lacking in the international regime. But strong international procedures rest ultimately on national commitment, which is both wide and deep in Europe.

A regime's shape and strength usually can be explained largely by perceptions of interdependence, by the benefits states expect to receive or the burdens they hope to avoid, and by the risks they expect to incur in turning over authority to an international agency. The strong national commitment of the European states to human rights greatly increases the perceived value of the "moral" benefits states can expect to achieve, suggesting that moral interdependence can indeed rival material interdependence in political force when national commitment to moral goals is particularly strong. Furthermore, relatively good national human rights records reduce the political risks of strong international procedures. The European regime is also "safe" because it operates within a relatively homogeneous and close sociocultural community, which greatly reduces the likelihood of radical differences in interpreting regime norms and dramatically decreases the risk of partisan abuse or manipulation of the regime. Perceived community also helps to increase the perception of moral interdependence.

National compliance is the key. If this is achieved voluntarily, as it is for the most part in Europe, so much the better; the relatively infrequent use of authoritative regional decision-making procedures is, if anything, desirable rather than regrettable. But we should belittle neither the strength nor the significance of the European regime's enforcement measures. Not only is completely voluntary compliance a utopian ideal, but the European case suggests a process of mutual reinforcement between national commitment and international procedures. A strong regime is a device to increase the chances that states will enjoy the best that they "deserve" in that issue area—that is, the best to which they will commit themselves to aspire, and then struggle to achieve.

B. The Inter-American Regime

(1)   The American Declaration of the Rights and Duties of Man (1948) presents a list of human rights very similar to that of the Universal Declaration. (2) tion. The American Convention on Human Rights (1969), like its European counterpart, is limited to personal, legal, civil, and political rights, plus the right to property. There is no American equivalent to the European Social Charter Charter or to the International Covenant on Economic, Social, and Cultural Rights Rights. As in the European case, though, the procedures rather than the norms are of most interest.

The Inter-American Court of Human Rights, established in 1979 and sitting in San José, Costa Rica, may take binding enforcement action, although (as in the European regime) its adjudicatory jurisdiction is optional. By mid-1985, eight states had accepted its jurisdiction, and in 1988 it decided its first substantive case (against Honduras). As in the European regime, individuals have no direct access to the court, although the commission may bring cases involving individuals to the court. The court may also issue advisory opinions requested by members of the Organization of American States (OAS); through early 1987 it had issued seven advisory opinions.

The Inter-American Commission of Human Rights, however, is the procedural heart of the regime. It is empowered to develop awareness of human rights, to make recommendations to governments, to respond to inquiries of states, to prepare studies and reports, to request information from and make recommendations to governments, and to conduct on-site investigations (with the consent of the government). The commission also may receive communications (complaints) from individuals and groups concerning the practice of *any* member of the OAS, whether a party to the Convention or not. An "autonomous entity" within the Organization of American States, established twenty years before the Inter-American Court, the commission has vigorously exploited this autonomy. It has adopted decisions and resolutions arising from individual communications from more than twenty countries in the region, including the United States. Country Reports documenting particularly serious human rights situations in more than a dozen countries have been issued, usually to be followed up by renewed and intensified monitoring. And the commission has adopted special resolutions on major regional problems, such as states of siege.

The wide-ranging nonpartisan activism of the commission can be attributed largely to the fact that its members serve in their personal capacity; it is more a technical, quasi-judicial body than a political body. But how are we to explain the fact that the American states, many of which are not notably solicitous toward human rights, allow the commission to be so powerful and so active? Part of the explanation lies in the dominant power of the United States. In the literature on international economic regimes, it is often argued that the power of a single hegemonic state is crucial to the establishment (although not necessarily to the maintenance) of strong, stable regimes.[10] Although such hegemonic power had virtually nothing to do with the European regime, it does help to explain the genesis and operation of the Inter-American regime. The United States, for whatever reasons, has often used its hegemonic power to support the Inter-American regime, which has also been strongly supported by some of the more democratic regimes of the region. There is always a U.S. member of the commission, and even a U.S. judge on the Inter-American Court, even though the United States is not a party to the Convention. And the United States has often helped to persuade reluctant, even recalcitrant, governments of the wisdom of cooperating with the investigations of the commission.

10. The most subtle version of the theory is Keohane 1984. For representative critiques, see McKeown 1983, Stein 1984, and Snidal 1985.

Consensual commitment and hegemonic power are to a certain extent functional equivalents for establishing state acceptance. Voluntary compliance is, of course, the ideal, both for its own sake and because of the limited ability of even hegemonic power to overcome persistent national resistance. But coercion may produce a certain level of limited participation from states that otherwise would not accept a regime. This has been essential to the grudging participation of a number of Latin American dictatorships, including Chile and Argentina during the 1970s.

Nevertheless, the relative mix of coercion and consensus does influence the nature and functioning of a regime. Coerced participation is sure to be marked by constant and often effective national resistance, and regime procedures are likely to be more adversarial. Hegemony may ensure a certain degree of international monitoring, but even a hegemon can impose only a limited range of changes. The result is something of a paradox: the Inter-American Commission is relatively active and effective in the worst cases, which by their very extremity may mobilize relatively strong pressure or support from the United States, but it is relatively less active in less serious situations, which therefore are in many ways not easier but harder to ameliorate through international action.

C. Africa, Asia, and the Middle East

The African Charter on Human and Peoples' Rights, drafted in Banjul, Gambia, was adopted by the Organization of African Unity (OAU) in Nairobi in June 1981.[11] There are some interesting normative innovations in the African (Banjul) Charter, most notably the addition of and emphasis on collective or 'peoples' '' rights (Articles 19–24),[12] such as the rights to peace and development and the particularly prominent place the charter gives individual duties (Articles 27–29).

The Banjul Charter creates an African Commission on Human and Peoples' Rights, allows for interstate complaints, and even envisions the receipt of individual communications. But all these provisions are quite vague, and there is no reporting system, no judicial organ, or any other mechanism for authoritative regional enforcement decisions. The best we can say at this early date is that the commission, which held its first meeting in 1986, may have a limited opening to establish itself as a (weak) monitoring body. And our experience with the American and European regimes suggests that we should not expect much of the African regime.

---

11. For a good review of the background, provisions, and problems of the African Charter, see Kannyo 1984, Gittleman 1984, and Ojo and Sessay 1986.

12. The African Charter at least does clearly distinguish between human rights (rights of individuals) and the rights of peoples. Compare Chapter 8, section 1, above, and Donnelly 1985b.

The regional organizational environment in Africa is extremely unpromising. The OAU is not only highly politicized but also the most deferential of all regional organizations to sovereignty. Although this is quite understandable, given the weak states and strong subnational loyalties in most of black Africa, there is no reason to expect the OAU to deviate from its standard practice in an area as sensitive as human rights. And previous efforts at regional and even subregional cooperation in other issue areas have not been very successful. The prospects are no better when we look at national practice. Over the last twenty years, the human rights record of the typical African country has been about average for the Third World, despite lurid and relatively overreported aberrations, such as Idi Amin and "Emperor" Bokassa. Nonetheless, in the absence of strong pressure by a regional hegemon, the national human rights record of the typical African government suggests a high degree of aversion to international monitoring. Furthermore, the low level of autonomous economic, social, and political organization in most African states suggests that this situation is unlikely to be changed soon through mass popular action.

Even the currently unclear procedures of the African regime, though, are far more developed than those in Asia and the Middle East. In Asia there are neither regional norms nor decision-making procedures. The Association of South East Asian Nations (ASEAN) is perhaps the most promising subregional organization, but even there the level of cooperation and perceived regional community remains relatively low. The League of Arab States established a Permanent Arab Commission on Human Rights in 1968, but there are no substantive regional human rights norms. The Arab Charter of Human Rights has languished largely ignored since it was drafted in 1971, and the 1979 Draft Arab Covenant on Human Rights seems destined to a similar fate. It is not surprising that the Arab Commission has been notably inactive. Robertson discreetly observes that "rather sparse information is available about the results achieved" (1982: 164). The principal reason for this is that the commission's few concrete activities seem to have involved publicizing the human rights situation in the Israeli-occupied territories (Boutros-Gali 1982). This is hardly a basis for even the weakest of regional regimes.

4. SINGLE-ISSUE HUMAN RIGHTS REGIMES

A different type of "nested" human rights (sub-)regime is represented by universal membership organizations with a limited functional competence and by less institution-bound single-issue regimes. Single-issue regimes establish a place for themselves in the network of interdependence by restricting their activities to a limited range of issues—for example, workers' or women's rights—in order to induce widespread participation in a single area of mutual interest.

A. Workers' Rights

The first international human rights regime of any sort was the functional regime of the International Labor Organization (ILO),[13] established by the Treaty of Versailles. Most of the regime's substantive norms were developed after World War II, including important conventions on freedom of association, the right to organize and bargain collectively, discrimination in employment, equality of remuneration, forced labor, migrant workers, workers' representatives, and basic aims and standards of social policy. Although developed autonomously, these rules can be seen as complementary elaborations and extensions of parallel substantive norms of the global regime.

Since regime norms are formulated in individual Conventions and Recommendations, which states adopt or not as they see fit, there is neither universality nor uniformity of coverage. Nevertheless, states are required to submit all Conventions and Recommendations to competent national authorities to be considered for adoption, and they may be periodically required to submit reports on their practice even with respect to Conventions they have *not* ratified. Most important, periodic reports are required on compliance with ratified Conventions.[14] Reports are reviewed by the highly professional Committee of Experts on the Application of Conventions and Recommendations. Although it may only make "observations," it does so with vigor and considerable impartiality, and committee observations have often induced changes in national practice.

Much of the success of this reporting-monitoring system lies in the ILO's "tripartite" structure, in which workers' and employers' delegates from each member state are voting members of the organization, along with government representatives. With the "victims" represented by national trade union representatives, it is relatively difficult for states to cover up their failure to discharge their obligations, especially if some national workers' representatives adopt an internationalist perspective and question

13. For general discussions of human rights in the ILO, see Haas 1970; Valticos 1982; Swepson 1984; Wolf 1984; and Haas 1964: chaps. 9, 11, 12.
14. There is a procedure for interstate complaints, but it is rarely used. Of more importance is the special complaint procedure for freedom-of-association cases arising under Conventions 87 and 98, which works through national and international trade union complaints, reviewed by the Governing Body's Standing Committee on Freedom of Association. See Haas 1964: chap. 12.

practices in countries where labor is less free. The very issue of workers' rights has also been important to the strength and success of the ILO regime, providing a reasonable degree of ideological homogeneity across a now genuinely universal membership. Western, Soviet bloc, and "socialist" Third World regimes have quite different interpretations of the meaning of "freedom of association" and other relevant norms, but all face serious internal and ideological constraints on overt noncompliance. Along with the relatively high level of autonomy and neutrality of the monitoring system, this has been crucial to maintaining a relatively strong regime.

To the extent that these factors of organizational structure and ideological appeal explain the success of the ILO's functional human rights regime, the prospects for other functional regimes seem dim. Tripartism has not been and almost certainly will not be replicated in other organizations. Furthermore, very few other separate human rights issues possess the near universal appeal of workers' rights.

B. Racial Discrimination

The issue of racial discrimination does have such appeal. The 1964 International Convention on the Elimination of All Forms of Racial Discrimination crimination provides a clear and powerful extension and elaboration of the global regime's norms against racial discrimination, but its implementation provisions are fairly weak. The Committee on the Elimination of Racial Discrimination, a body of experts established under the Convention, has very narrowly interpreted its powers to "make suggestions and general recommendations based on the examination of the reports and information received from the States Parties" (Article 9(2)). Furthermore, the interstate complaint procedure has never been utilized, and scarcely a dozen states have authorized the committee to receive communications from individuals. Even the information-exchange elements of the reporting procedure are not without flaws; the public examination of reports, while sometimes critical, is less penetrating than in the Human Rights Committee.

Much of the explanation of this weakness lies in the very different institutional environments of the ILO and the political organs of the United Nations. Most ILO Conventions are truly technical instruments regulating working conditions—for example, hours of work, minimum age, weekly rest and holidays with pay, seafarers' identity documents, radiation protection, fishermen's medical examinations, and exposure to benzene—so that most of the work of the Committee of Experts deals with relatively uncontroversial technical matters. In the course of this work, expectations of neutrality are established and reconfirmed, so that when human rights issues are considered they are examined in a relatively depoliticized context as only one part of the work of an essentially technical body of experts. In addition, there are literally hundreds of ILO Conventions and Recommendations, and the organization has existed for more than sixty years. States are therefore often closely tied into a web of interstate, transgovernmental, and transnational relationships centered on the organization. The Racial Discrimination Committee enjoys none of these advantages.

C. Torture

The one other human rights issue with nearly universal appeal is torture. The Convention against Torture and Other Cruel, Inhuman or Degrading Treatment or Punishment was opened for signature on December 10, 1984, and entered into force in the summer of 1987. Part I contains a strong elaboration of norms against torture, and the procedures outlined in Part II are potentially relatively strong. A Committee against Torture will receive and review periodic reports from states parties every four years. Much will depend on how the committee interprets its powers to "make such general comments on the report as it may consider appropriate" (Article 19), but the potential exists for rather strong monitoring. The Convention also contains optional provisions that allow the committee to receive communications analogous to those permitted under the 1503 procedure, as well as interstate complaints and individual communications. Even at this early date we can say that there is a relatively strong declaratory regime on torture that is likely to develop into a notable promotional regime within the next decade (see also Chapter 13, Section 1).

Ongoing promotional activities should also be noted. For example, the U.N. Voluntary Fund for Torture Victims, established in 1981, had by late 1986 made 69 grants totaling nearly $2 million to 46 projects in 25 countries.[15] And the recent Amnesty International campaign on torture has been an important effort by a nongovernmental organization (NGO) to publicize a major problem. Amnesty has a much higher profile than most, but NGO efforts—especially promotional activities, such as publicity, information gathering, and local monitoring—can be of considerable significance in the day-to-day operations of all the regimes we have considered.

D. Women's Rights

The final major single-issue human rights regime has to do with women's rights, traditionally something of a stepchild in the field of human rights. While racial discrimination is considered in the U.N. Commission

---

15. See U.N. document A/41/706 and earlier reports cited therein.

on Human Rights and throughout the U.N.-centered regime, sexual discrimination has been largely segregated in the U.N. Commission on the Status of Women.[16] In the last decade, though, there has been a substantial normative and procedural evolution of the women's rights regime, and women's rights issues have moved closer to the mainstream of international human rights discussions.

The Commission on the Status of Women, a subsidiary body of ECOSOC established in 1947, has played a role in norm creation very similar to that played by the Commission on Human Rights, having drafted a variety of specialized treaties, such as the 1952 Convention on the Political Rights of Women, as well as the major general treaty in this area, the 1979 Convention on the Elimination of Discrimination against Women. The commission has also undertaken various promotional activities, and in 1984 it began studying individual communications. Although it is still too early to say how this procedure will operate, the lack of a mandate to monitor practices in individual countries is likely to restrict the process to very general promotional activities.

In some ways more promising is the reporting procedure under the Convention on the Elimination of Discrimination against Women, which entered into force on September 3, 1981, and has been ratified by more than ninety states. It appears that the Committee on the Elimination of Discrimination against Women, which has meet annually since 1982, will function much as the Human Rights Committee (although without the optional complaint procedures). Like other treaty-based promotion and monitoring bodies, though, the committee may only consider conditions in countries that are parties to the Convention. The weaker powers of the commission are therefore of continuing importance. As in the global regime, there is a political trade-off between the strength of a set of procedures and their coverage.

The recent strengthening of the women's rights regime can be traced primarily to the changing awareness of women's issues in the 1970s, a process of perceptual change that at the international level centered around the designation of 1975 as International Women's Year and the associated World Conference in Mexico City. In conjunction with political and "con-

---

16. Even in U.N. human rights organs, subtle denigrations of women's rights still occur regularly—for example, the Secretariat's referral of family separation communications to the Commission on the Status of Women, as if they involved women's issues only (see E/1984/15 par. 69), and the Human Rights Committee's lumping of questions of family life and sexual discrimination in its review of issues considered under the Optional Protocol (see A/39/40).

sciousness raising" activities of national women's movements, a major international constituency for women's rights was created; a growing set of regime makers and takers emerged, while potential breakers were deterred from active opposition either by domestic ideological stands or by the emerging international normative consensus. The 1985 follow-up conference in Nairobi also seems to have played an important role in solidifying and deepening this international consensus.

5. THE EVOLUTION OF HUMAN RIGHTS REGIMES

What, if anything, can we say in general about the nature, creation and evolution of international human rights regimes? Table 5 presents a summary overview of the regimes discussed above, seen at ten-year intervals from 1945 to 1985. The most striking pattern is the near complete absence of international human rights regimes in 1945, in contrast to the presence of several in all the later periods. Human rights has become an international issue area in the postwar era. We can also note the gradual strengthening of most international human rights regimes over the last thirty years. But even today promotional regimes are the rule. The only exceptions are the regional regimes in Europe and the Americas and workers' rights, and all three are "special cases."

Once states accept norms stronger than nonbinding guidelines, declaratory regimes readily evolve into promotional regimes; if the regime's norms are important or appealing enough for states to commit themselves to them, then it is difficult to argue against promoting their further spread and implementation. But the move to implementation or enforcement involves a major qualitative jump that most states strongly resist, and usually successfully. Regime evolution may be gradual and largely incremental within declaratory and promotional regimes (and perhaps within implementation and enforcement regimes as well), but there seems to be a profound discontinuity in the emergence of implementation and enforcement activities. Promotional regimes require a relatively low level of commitment. However, the move to an implementation or enforcement regime requires a major qualitative increase in the commitment of states. This commitment is rarely forthcoming. Most of the growth in international human rights regimes has therefore been "easy" growth that does not naturally lead to further growth.

The one partial exception that cannot be explained by special environmental factors is the monitoring procedure of the Optional Protocol to the International Covenant on Civil and Political Rights, but barely three dozen

Table 5. Change in international human rights regimes, 1945–1985

	1945	1955	1965	1975	1985
Global regime	None	Declaratory	Strong declaratory	Promotional	Strong promotional
Norms	None	Guidelines	Strong guidelines	Standards with exemptions	Standards with exemptions
Procedures	None	Weak promotion	Promotion	Strong promotion	Strong promotion/weak monitoring
			Regional human rights regimes		
European regime	None	Implementation	Implementation/enforcement	Enforcement	Enforcement
Norms	None	Guidelines/regional norms	Regional norms	Regional norms	Regional norms
Procedures	None	Promotion/monitoring	Monitoring/regional decisions	Regional decisions	Regional decisions
Inter-American regime	None	Declaratory	Weak promotional	Promotional	Strong promotional/enforcement
Norms	None	Guidelines	Guidelines	Standards with exemptions	Regional norms
Procedures	None	None	Promotion	Monitoring	Monitoring/regional decisions
African regime	None	None	None	None	Declaratory
Norms	None	None	None	None	Standards with exemptions
Procedures	None	None	None	None	None
Asia and the Middle East	None	None	None	None	None

Single-issue regimes

	Promotional	Promotional/ implementation	Promotional/ implementation	Promotional/ implementation	Promotional/ implementation
Workers' rights					
Norms	Weak standards	Standards with exemptions	Strong standards with exemptions	Strong standards with exemptions	Strong standards with exemptions
Procedures	Promotion/ monitoring	Promotion/monitoring	Promotion/monitoring	Promotion/monitoring	Promotion/monitoring
Racial discrimination	None	None	Declaratory	Strong promotional	Strong promotional
Norms	None	None	Guidelines	Strong standards with exemptions	Strong standards with exemptions
Procedures	None	None	None	Promotion/monitoring	Promotion/monitoring
Women's rights	None	Declaratory/promotional	Declaratory/promotional	Declaratory/promotional	Strong promotional
Norms	None	Guidelines	Guidelines	Guidelines	Standards with exemptions
Procedures	None	Promotion	Promotion	Promotion	Promotion/weak monitoring
Torture	None	None	None	Weak declaratory	Strong declaratory
Norms	None	None	None	Guidelines	Standards with exemptions
Procedures	None	None	None	None	None/promotion

countries are covered by this procedure. The weak monitoring of the 1503 procedure presents perhaps the greatest opportunity for making the jump to implementation or enforcement, given the relatively subtle nature of the required changes. Experience with the procedure to date, however, provides no evidence that this is likely. The torture regime has some very promising procedures, but they will apply only to some states with respect to a single right.

We have already considered some of the central factors that explain this pattern of limited growth, emphasizing both awareness and power, which usually are created or mobilized by conceptual changes in response to domestic political action (e.g., women's rights) or international moral shock (e.g., the global regime or torture). Such awareness and power typically function by galvanizing support for the creation or growth of a regime and delegitimizing opposition, which may make moral interdependence more difficult for states to resist. But we should also stress the importance of national commitment, cultural community, and hegemony.

National commitment is the single most important contributor to a strong regime; it is the source of the often mentioned "political will" that underlies most strong regimes. If a state has a good human rights record, then not only will a strong regime appear relatively unthreatening, but the additional support it provides for national efforts is likely to be welcomed. The European regime's unprecedented strength provides the most striking example of the power of national commitment.

The importance of cultural community is suggested by the fact that the only enforcement regimes are regional. In the absence of sociocultural and ideological consensus, strong procedures are likely to appear too subject to partisan use or abuse to be accepted even by states with good records and strong national commitments.[17] For example, opponents of stronger procedures in the global human rights regime and in single-issue regimes include major countries from the First, Second, and Third Worlds with good, mediocre, and poor national human rights records alike. The very scope of all but the regional regimes undercuts the relative homogeneity that seems almost necessary for movement beyond a promotional regime.

Finally, we must stress the importance of dominant power and hegemony, which should be kept analytically distinct. Beyond mere dominant power, hegemonic leadership usually requires ideological hegemony, a

17. The United States presents an exaggerated version of such fears, most strikingly in the U.S. Senate's resistance to, for example, the Genocide Convention and the International Covenant on Civil and Political Rights, with which U.S. law and practice already conform in almost all particulars. These fears, in a less extreme form, are common and widespread.

crucial element in the acceptance of, or at least acquiescence in, the authority of the hegemon. The effective exercise of even hegemonic power usually requires not merely dominating material and organizational resources, but also an ideological justification sufficiently powerful to win at least acquiescence from nonhegemonic powers.

Leaders require followers; regime makers need takers. The reasons for taking a regime may be largely accidental or external to the issue, but sometimes the reasons for taking a regime are connected with the ideological hegemony of the proposed project: Ruggie's (1982) account of "embedded liberalism" and the importance of the ideology of the welfare state in the creation of postwar economic regimes might be read in this way. The seemingly inescapable ideological appeal of human rights in the postwar world thus is an important element in the rise of international human rights regimes. Power, in the sense that the term traditionally has had in the study of international politics, still is important, but true hegemony often is based on ideological "power" as well. We might even argue that the ideological hegemony of human rights was more important than dominant material power.

A hegemonic idea such as human rights may actually draw power to itself; power may coalesce around, rather than create, hegemonic ideas, such as human rights and the regimes that emerge from them. For example, the overriding ideological appeal of the idea of workers' rights has been crucial to the success of the ILO. In Europe, the "hegemonic" power behind the very strong European regime came not from any single dominant state but from a coalition built around the ideological dominance of the idea of human rights. The ideological hegemony of human rights is essential to explaining the creation of an African human rights regime in the face of the OAU's notorious respect for even the tiniest trappings of sovereignty. And the emergence of the global human rights regime cannot be understood without taking account of this impulse, discussed above in terms of perceived moral interdependence.

But hegemonic power does ultimately require material power, and even hegemonic ideas have a limited ability to attract such power. Hegemonic ideas can be expected to draw acquiescence to relatively weak regimes, but beyond promotional activities (that is, once significant sacrifices of sovereignty are required) something more is needed. In other words, hegemony too points to the pattern of limited growth observed above.

The evolution toward strong promotional procedures can be expected to continue, but we can expect states to resist, usually successfully, further growth and efforts to cross over to implementation and enforcement activities. There seems to be no reason to expect significant qualitative change in the short run or medium run. The relatively easy phase of growth has largely passed, and the same factors that explain it suggest relative stagnation or only the slowest future growth. We thus have little reason to expect that the 1995 column of Table 5 will show many significant changes from 1985. But we must not forget how far we have come since 1945.

12

Human Rights and Foreign Policy

Much international action on behalf of human rights takes place in the international forums discussed in the preceding chapter, but many states also pursue international human rights objectives in their bilateral foreign policy, and even a state's participation in international human rights regimes rests on national foreign policy decisions. Therefore, we need to consider how and why states pursue international human rights concerns in their foreign policies.[1]

1. HUMAN RIGHTS: A LEGITIMATE CONCERN OF FOREIGN POLICY?

John Vincent begins the introduction to his recent volume *Foreign Policy and Human Rights* by noting: "There is no obvious connection between human rights and foreign policy" (1986b: 1). In fact, there are three standard arguments against making the connection, which I will call the "realist," the "statist" (or "legalist"), and the "relativist" (or "pluralist") arguments (compare Vincent 1986b: 1–2). The *realist* holds that human rights should not be pursued in national foreign policy because foreign policy is and must always be about the national interest defined in terms of power. The *statist* considers an active concern for the human rights practices of other states inconsistent with the fundamental principle of state sovereignty. The *relativist* views an international human rights policy as a form of moral imperialism that shows inadequate respect for cultural and historical diversity. I argue that although these arguments point to problems

1. For convenience and focus I draw my examples from U.S. foreign policy.

in overemphasizing human rights in foreign policy, they do not establish that the human rights practices of foreign governments are an illegitimate concern of foreign policy.

A. The Realist Argument

Realism, a doctrine about the nature of international relations and the constraints this imposes on foreign policy, holds that international politics is a struggle between power-maximizing states in an environment of anarchy. But international anarchy, the absence of rule (government) at the level of international politics, does not by itself lead to such a conclusion. Equally important is the realist view of other states as acquisitive, power-maximizing, potential (or real) enemies. Faced with such states in an anarchic environment, a concern for power must override just about everything else. To act as anything other than a power maximizer—for example, to pursue goals such as justice or to act out of motivations such as compassion—would leave oneself open to, even invite, attack.

In such a world, self-help is the only help a state can expect. Therefore, power, the ultimate basis of effective self-help, must be the overriding concern of foreign policy. But the accumulation of power, even if intended to be purely defensive, will appear to other states as a new and dangerous threat. In response, they will be impelled to increase their power, which will threaten other states, who will respond by efforts to increase their power, who will respond, and so on. Students of international politics refer to this situation as "the security dilemma" (Herz 1976: chap. 2; Jervis 1978). For the realist, foreign policy, to use Hans Morgenthau's famous formulation, is (must be) about the "[national] interest defined in terms of power" (1954: 5). An intrinsic concern for human rights in foreign policy, as opposed to using human rights to further the national interest defined in terms of power, would be a dangerous mistake.

Most realists are not ruthless defenders of evil or even amorality; in fact, their realism is almost always reluctant. For example, Morgenthau often stressed the unavoidable moral content and implications of *all* human action.[2] But the statesman, because of the nature of his office and the realities of international politics, simply cannot afford to *act* on the basis of moral considerations; morality is appropriate to individual relations but not

---

2. "Man is a political animal by nature; he is a scientist by choice or chance; he is a moralist because he is a man" (1946: 168). "The moral law is not made for the convenience of man, rather it is an indispensable precondition for his civilized existence" (1962a: 373). "To do justice and to receive it is an elemental aspiration of man" (1970: 61). "All human actions in some way are subject to moral judgment. We cannot act but morally because we are men" (1979: 1).

to the relations of states.[3] Thus one of Reinhold Niebuhr's best-known works is entitled *Moral Man and Immoral Society*, emphasizing the disjunction between the individual world of moral relations and the world of collective action, which is dominated by power. Morgenthau typically spoke of this in terms of tragedy.[4] This tragedy, the necessary amorality—even immorality—of foreign policy, is for the realist an unavoidable and enduring fact of international relations:

> Government is an agent, not a principal. Its primary obligation is to the *interests* of the national society it represents, not to the moral impulses that individual elements of that society may experience. . . . The interests of the national society for which government has to concern itself are basically those of its military security, the integrity of its political life and the well-being of its people. These needs have no moral quality. They are the unavoidable necessities of national existence and therefore are subject to classification neither as "good" or "bad." (Kennan 1985–86: 206)

Both academic realists and their brethren in foreign offices have therefore attempted to excise such moral concerns as human rights from foreign policy—or, where they have already been excised, keep them excluded.

But even if we agree that power must be the cardinal concern of foreign policy, this does not mean that power must be the *sole* concern of foreign policy. And it is an empirical question whether the pursuit of other concerns is in fact compatible with the cardinal concern of power. Realism provides no a priori reason to exclude a concern for human rights from foreign policy. If true, realism does show that it may be dangerous to overemphasize human rights,[5] but that is quite a different matter. For example, Morgenthau argues that "the principle of the defense of human rights cannot be consistently applied in foreign policy because it can and

3. "I stick to the fundamental principle that lying is immoral. But I realize that when you are dealing in the context of foreign policy, lying is inevitable. In private affairs, however, you do not deceive others, especially friends" (Morgenthau 1979: 10–11). "The moral dilemma of foreign policy is but a special and—it is true—particularly flagrant case of the moral dilemma which faces man on all levels of social action. Man cannot help sinning when he acts in relation to his fellow man" (Morgenthau 1962a: 319).

4. "Christian ethics demands love, humility and the abnegation of the self; man as a natural creature seeks the aggrandizement of self through pride and power. It is the tragedy of man that he is incapable, by dint of his nature, to do what Christian ethics demands of him" (1962b: 15; compare 1962a: 375).

5. For example, it immediately reveals such statements as Carter's claims that the American commitment to human rights must be "absolute" and that human rights provided the "soul" of U.S. foreign policy to be little more than mystifying rhetorical exuberance.

must come in conflict with other interests that may be more important than the defense of human rights in a particular circumstance'' (1979: 7). But this is true of just about *every* objective of foreign policy. We do not, however, hear realists railing against pursuing economic interests, or friendly diplomatic relations, or cultural contacts, or the principle of *pacta sunt servanda*, because they will inevitably conflict with other interests that in some circumstances must take priority. And we should not accept such arguments with respect to human rights.

Realists typically argue as if human rights and other moral concerns never could be part of the national interest. For example, Kennan, in drawing the contrast between the national interest and morality, speaks of "our interest rather than just our sensibilities" (1985–86: 209), and in a passage quoted above he contrasts the national interest with "the moral impulses that individual elements of that society may experience." Such arguments, which assume that national interests can never include a moral interest, rest on unsupported stipulations rather than theoretical, let alone empirical, arguments. The most that realists may legitimately claim is that moral interests are often incompatible with considerations of national power. That, however, is a much weaker claim.

Realism provides no good theoretical ground for excluding human rights from foreign policy before the fact. In certain (contingent) circumstances it may be unwise to pursue human rights, but that must be determined empirically, case by case. Realists simply are not entitled to categorically exclude human rights or any other concern—economic, social, cultural, or moral—as a legitimate goal of foreign policy.

B. The Statist (Legalist) Argument

International relations is structured around the principle of sovereignty, which grants a state exclusive jurisdiction over its own territory and resources, including its population. Sovereignty in turn implies nonintervention in the internal affairs of other states. The statist or legalist argues that human rights must be excluded from foreign policy because what a state does with respect to its own nationals on its own territory—which is what we usually are concerned with when we discuss human rights violations—is on its face an archetypal matter of sovereign national jurisdiction and thus of no legitimate concern to other states. Where the realist is concerned with the realities of power in an environment of international anarchy, the statist stresses the principal widely accepted limits on the pursuit of power—namely, sovereignty and the traditional body of international law that flows from it. Where the realist argues that it is unwise to pursue human rights in foreign policy, the statist argues that it contravenes the fundamental structural and normative principles of international politics.

The statist argument, like the realist argument, does rest on an important insight into international relations. International politics is at its core the politics of sovereign states. However much we may want to emphasize transnational and transgovernmental relations, even today states are the primary actors and international relations is principally the relations of sovereign states. However much we may talk of world public order, and however much Third World states may complain of the biases and shortcomings of traditional international law, international law is at its core a law of sovereignty. And states in the First, Second, and Third Worlds alike regularly insist on the primacy of sovereignty, especially when their own sovereign interests and rights are at stake.

But although sovereignty is the starting-point of international law, it is not the end-point. In fact, international law is for the most part the body of restrictions on sovereignty that have been accepted by states through the mechanisms of custom and treaty. And over the last forty years an extensive body of international human rights law has been developed, making human rights a legitimate subject in international relations even from a strict legalist position, because sovereign states have chosen to make them so.

The weakness of existing international implementation and enforcement mechanisms might allow the statist to argue that incorporating human rights into foreign policy still contravenes the fundamental principle of nonintervention. And in practice the vast majority of states whose human rights practices are called into question, either in multilateral forums such as the U.N. Commission on Human Rights or in bilateral relations, make precisely such an argument, even when the same states are quite willing to raise the issue of human rights in other countries. However, intervention involves "dictatorial interference in the domestic or foreign affairs of another state which impairs that state's independence" (Friedmann 1971: 40). The threat or use of force in order to influence another state's policy clearly is intervention. Substantially debilitating economic coercion also probably is sufficiently dictatorial to be called intervention. But there are numerous instrumentalities of foreign policy that do not involve intervention—for example, diplomatic representations and granting (or withdrawing) preferential trade agreements. Such means can be used on behalf of human rights as legitimately as they can be used on behalf of other goals of foreign policy.

All foreign policy involves efforts to influence the policy of other countries. Intervention occurs only when that influence is exercised through strongly coercive, essentially dictatorial means. So long as such means are avoided, statism and the principle of nonintervention provide no ground for excluding human rights concerns from foreign policy.

C. The Relativist (Pluralist) Argument

Viewed as a way of protecting one's own state from outside inter-ference, statism fits nicely with realism, but many proponents of a strong principle of nonintervention rest their ''statism'' on a relativist argument that emphasizes the principle of self-determination or a commitment to international pluralism. A country's social and political order should be, on its face, entirely a matter of domestic jurisdiction; in human rights terms, it reflects (or at least ought to reflect) the exercise of basic human rights such as the right to political participation. Each society, acting collectively and independent of external coercion, ought to be allowed to choose its own form of government, and within a certain range of freedom the autonomous choices of a free people should be respected. A similar conclusion can be reached by stressing the positive value of cultural diversity or respect for the values of other peoples and cultures.

Realists often make similar relativist arguments in their attack on human rights in foreign policy. For example, Morgenthau speaks of ''the issue of what is now called human rights—that is, to what extent is a nation entitled and obliged to impose its moral principles upon other nations?'' (1979: 4). Similarly, Kennan argues that ''there are no internationally accepted stan-dards of morality to which the U.S. government could appeal if it wished to act in the name of moral principles'' (1985–86: 207). The reply to such arguments is essentially the same as that made to the legalist argument above: states, including virtually all socialist and Third World states, have regularly and explicitly proclaimed their commitment to the human rights enumerated in the Universal Declaration and the Covenants. Therefore, for the United States or any other country to act on behalf of internationally recognized human rights is not to impose American or Western values on other countries, but to use U.S. influence to bring the practice of other governments more into line with *their own* professed values (which we share).

There *are* authoritative international human rights norms. So long as human rights policy is based on these norms, it does not reflect moral imperialism. In fact, failure to insist on compliance with internationally recognized human rights norms risks a type of reverse racism that is no less serious for being unintentional. The standards of internationally recognized human rights are minimal standards of decency, not luxuries of the West:

It is not by chance that the most important international instrument in this field is entitled the *Universal* Declaration of Human Right, and was adopted without a single dissentient vote. The assertion was that the standards laid down could and should be attained in any country. It was never expected that any state is too small, too remote or too poor to be expected to attain them. (Luard 1981: 21)

We cannot stand by idly and watch torture, disappearances, arbitrary arrest and detention, racism, anti-Semitism, repression of trade unions and churches, debilitating poverty, illiteracy, and disease in the name of diversity or respect for cultural traditions. None of these practices deserves our respect, even if it is traditional (which most frequently is not the case). What Arthur Schlesinger says of civil and political rights holds true for almost all internationally recognized human rights: it is "hard to believe that the instinct for political and civil freedom is confined to the happy few in the North Atlantic littoral" (1979: 521). To act as if internationally recognized human rights are an exotic Western luxury is to display not cultural sensitivity but indefensible moral elitism (compare Part III above).

The relativist argument does remind us that even universal standards need to be tailored in their implementation to reflect particular cultural and historical circumstances.[6] For example, it should caution the United States against the misplaced formalism of using multiparty elections as the sole or even principal measure of political participation. Like realism and statism, however, relativism fails to establish the inappropriateness of pursuing human rights in foreign policy. But we still have not yet considered a positive argument for making the link between human rights and foreign policy.

D. Linking Human Rights and Foreign Policy

Although countries that choose to pursue human rights in their foreign policy are likely to have somewhat different reasons for doing so, in the case of the United States it is easy to advance moral, historical, political, and national interest arguments in support of the linkage. Moral arguments for linking human rights and foreign policy focus on the moral imperatives of universal human rights. If human rights are the rights one has simply because one is human, then they are the rights of *all* human beings, whether they are citizens of the United States or not. National governments may have the *primary* responsibility for implementing internationally recognized human rights in their own countries, but if human rights are para-

6. This position, which I call "weak universalism," is defended in Chapter 6.

mount moral rights, they impose at least some sort of moral obligations on all people, not just fellow nationals. The realities of a world of sovereign states may limit legitimate action on behalf of the human rights of foreigners to means short of intervention, but the moral realities of the pervasive violation of universal human rights demand at least some active response.

The historical arguments focus on the central place of human rights in the American political tradition:

> The United States was founded on the proclamation of "unalienable" rights, and human rights ever since have had a peculiar resonance in the American tradition. Nor was the application of this idea to foreign policy an innovation of the Carter Administration. Americans have agreed since 1776 that the United States must be a beacon of human rights to an unregenerate world. The question has always been how America is to execute this mission. (Schlesinger 1979: 505)

William F. Buckley is typically more acerbic and a bit more accurate in noting that the United States "has had cyclical romances with the notion of responsibility for the rights of extranationals" (1980: 776). This responsibility has been expressed in two principal forms; the American mission has, at different times and to different Americans seemed to demand two very different strategies (compare Mayall 1986: 165ff.). On the one hand, America has been seen as a beacon, the proverbial city on the hill, whose human rights mission was to set an example for a corrupt world. This strand of the American tradition can be traced back at least to Washington's Farewell Address, and in its extreme forms leads to neutralism and isolationism (compare Gilbert 1961). On the other hand, the American mission has been seen, in much more crusading terms, to require positive action abroad: The United States must teach not simply by its domestic example but by active international involvement on behalf of human rights. This strand of the American tradition is no less venerable, and it is the strand that has been predominant in the contemporary revival of concern for human rights.[7] Whether this crusading sense of mission is a good thing or not, it is an important and deep-seated element in the U.S. approach to foreign policy.

The political argument flows from a combination of the historical and moral arguments. Given these moral and historical self-understandings, it

---

7. The cyclical nature of the American commitment to international action on behalf of human rights abroad which Buckley identifies can perhaps best be seen as an oscillation between these two competing conceptions of the American mission.

is difficult for an American government to ignore the concern of its citizens for the human rights impact of U.S. foreign policy. This is especially true in light of the powerful reactions against the occasional "realist" episodes in American foreign policy, such as the Nixon-Kissinger prosecution of the war in Vietnam to its bitter and bloody end, or the sale of arms to Iran (and the illegal diversion of funds to the contras) by Poindexter, North, and the self-anointed realists in their network.

The historical, moral, and political arguments all justify linking human rights and foreign policy in terms of the fact that the sovereign people *want* to pursue human rights in U.S. foreign policy. We can also make a national-interest argument that focuses on the long-run costs of too close an association with rights-abusive regimes in the Third World, a point to which we will return below. Vincent (1986b) reminds us that the connection between human rights and foreign policy is not obvious. In the case of the United States, though, there are powerful reasons for making it, and a number of other countries, such as Canada, the Netherlands, and Norway, have come to a similar conclusion.

2. DICTATORSHIPS AND DOUBLE STANDARDS: WHICH RIGHTS TO PURSUE?

Having chosen to pursue human rights in one's foreign policy, one must next select the rights to be pursued. I have already presented a variety of arguments above for using the list of human rights in the Universal Declaration and the Covenants. Jeane Kirkpatrick and the Reagan administration, however, have given the standard conservative arguments against economic and social rights a new twist in their application to foreign policy, arguing for the support of right-wing dictatorships and virtually reducing the struggle for human rights to a struggle against the Soviet Union and "communism"[8] (1979).

Kirkpatrick adopts a distinction initially developed by Arendt (1951) and Friedrich and Brzezinski (1956). She sharply distinguishes "totalitarian" governments, such as Nazi Germany and Stalinist Russia, which seek to control all aspects of social life (typically through a mass-mobilizing vanguard party), virtually eliminating the distinction between public and private life, from "authoritarian" governments, such as Batista's Cuba,

---

8. For a similar although much less developed effort to link (or reduce) U.S. action on behalf of human rights to action against totalitarian regimes, see Kissinger 1978: 161–63. Compare also Lord 1984: 132, who argues that "human rights policy in a nonliberal world" must begin with "the disestablishment of economic and social rights."

Somoza's Nicaragua, or Mobutu's Zaire, which wield despotic power but
do not seek to remake all of society according to an ideological blueprint
and thus leave free a substantial realm of private activity (at least for those
who do not directly challenge the power of the ruling dictatorship). She
then argues that because the abuses of totalitarian regimes are both more
severe and more difficult to remedy, the United States should focus its
international human rights efforts principally on totalitarian regimes. But
even granting Kirkpatrick the distinction between totalitarian and authoritarian and accepting her narrow definition of human rights, which includes
only civil and political rights (plus the right to property), this policy
argument fails.

Even looking only at civil and political rights, the average human rights
record of totalitarian regimes simply is not clearly worse than that of
authoritarian regimes. The principal "totalitarian" regimes in the Third
World are Cuba, Vietnam, Ethiopia, Angola, Mozambique, and, according to those on the political right who have adopted Kirkpatrick's argument, Nicaragua.[9] Laos is a minor country that should be added to the list
for completeness. The most recent ratings of these countries by Freedom
House, the conservative human rights monitoring group, are reproduced in
Table 6. Freedom House rates countries separately on political rights and
civil liberties on scales running from 1 (most free) to 7 (least free). The
average scores for the seven countries in Table 6 are 6.43 and 6.71 (13.14
for the two ratings combined). This reflects an extremely poor performance
on civil and political rights.

Compare these ratings with those in Table 7, which contains all the other
Third World countries that Freedom House classifies as "not free"[10]—that
is, the full set of strongly authoritarian regimes. I have placed the authoritarian regimes in Table 7 in two groups. Group A contains twenty countries
that individually and as a group were rated no better than the average
totalitarian regime in Table 6, with average ratings of 6.80 and 6.60 on
political rights and civil liberties (13.40 for the two combined). Group B
contains the remaining fifteen countries, which have scores equal to Cuba's
and worse than Nicaragua's. When we combine the two groups, the ratings
of 6.51 and 6.29 show that authoritarian regimes are actually slightly worse
at protecting political rights and only marginally better at protecting civil

9. I consider North Korea to be more a personalist dictatorship, closer to Taiwan in the
1950s than to the other countries on this list. I exclude China because it is clearly an
exception, not really "Third World" in the ordinary sense of that term. Kampuchea and
Afghanistan are not included because they are under foreign occupation.

10. Except those in the preceding note and South Yemen, a regime that largely defies
classification.

Table 6. Freedom House ratings of principal "totalitarian" Third World regimes, 1986–1987 (on a scale of 1 [most free] to 7 [least free])

	Political rights	Civil liberties
Angola	7	7
Cuba	6	6
Ethiopia	7	7
Laos	7	7
Mozambique	6	7
Nicaragua	5	6
Vietnam	7	7
Average	6.43	6.71

SOURCE: Gastil 1987.

liberties. In other words, even considering only civil and political rights, as Kirkpatrick would have us do, systematic differences simply do not exist.

The performance of, say, Ethiopia[11] is as bad or worse than virtually all authoritarian regimes—and most totalitarian regimes as well. But if we consider such authoritarian regimes as Uganda under Amin (or the second Obote regime), Chile under Pinochet, Argentina during the Dirty War, Equatorial Guinea under Macias Nguema, Indonesia in the 1960s (or during the late 1970s in East Timor), or El Salvador or Guatemala during the height of the disappearances, then even at its worst Sandinista Nicaragua looks positively attractive. The standard ways in which totalitarian and authoritarian regimes violate civil and political rights may differ systematically, as may their justifications, but there is no systematic difference in the level of respect for civil and political rights.

This leaves Kirkpatrick with only two remaining arguments. One stresses national interest: many authoritarian regimes are American "friends," whereas all totalitarian regimes are in the Soviet camp. This is an argument about integrating human rights with other concerns of foreign policy, a subject that will be addressed in section 4 below. The other argument, more relevant to our concerns at the moment, contends that authoritarian but not totalitarian regimes contain within them the potential for democratization. This is a plausible, if extremely controversial, claim, but from it Kirkpatrick manages to draw foreign policy conclusions that can only be called bizarre.

Numerous authoritarian regimes have undergone successful democrati-

---

11. Cambodia under Pol Pot presents an even more grizzly case, but given the American policy of supporting Pol Pot in the United Nations and elsewhere, it would be perverse to use this as a standard of comparison.

Table 7. Freedom House ratings of "strongly authoritarian" Third World regimes, 1986–1987 (on a scale of 1 [most free] to 7 [least free])

	Political rights	Civil liberties
Group A		
Benin	7	7
Burkina Faso	7	6
Burma	7	7
Burundi	7	6
Central African Republic	7	6
Chad	7	7
Congo	7	6
Equatorial Guinea	7	7
Ghana	7	6
Guinea-Bissau	6	7
Iraq	7	7
Malawi	6	7
Mali	7	6
Mauritania	7	6
Niger	7	6
Sao Tomé and Principe	7	7
Saudi Arabia	6	7
Somalia	7	7
Syria	6	7
Zaire	7	7
Average	6.80	6.60
Group B		
Algeria	6	6
Cameroon	6	6
Cape Verde Islands	6	6
Comoros	6	6
Djibouti	6	6
Gabon	6	6
Guinea	7	5
Libya	6	6
Nigeria	7	5
Oman	6	6
Rwanda	6	6
Seychelles	6	6
Suriname	6	6
Tanzania	6	6
Togo	6	6
Average	6.13	5.87
Groups A and B (average)	6.51	6.29

SOURCE: Gastil 1987.

zation. In Europe we can point to Spain, Portugal, and Greece in the 1970s. In Asia, the Philippines and South Korea today may be hovering on the brink of successful transitions. In Africa, Senegal has probably made the transition (although if it was authoritarian in the 1970s the authoritarianism was relatively mild), and there are hopeful signs in Uganda and a number of other countries. In Latin America the democratic civilian government in Argentina seems fairly stable, and such democratizing countries as Brazil have not taken major steps backward, despite severe economic pressures. We can, however, point to no case in which a totalitarian regime has undergone a democratic transition (except Nazi Germany, where the transition was imposed from outside after defeat in a war).

These facts, however, are not explained by the internal natures of the regimes in question. For example, it is quite plausible to argue that democratization would have been achieved in both Czechoslovakia and Poland if it had not been for the fact or threat of Soviet invasion. The relative imperviousness to structural transformation of at least some totalitarian regimes may be due more to external intervention than to anything else. Furthermore, our experience with totalitarian regimes in the Third World is extremely limited; we have only a bit more than a decade of totalitarian rule in Vietnam, Ethiopia, Angola, and Mozambique, and only about twenty-five years of experience in Cuba. We can point to literally dozens of authoritarian regimes that have lasted this long or longer.

But let us grant Kirkpatrick that authoritarian, but not totalitarian, regimes hold out a reasonable hope of democratization from within. What follows for U.S. human rights policy? It would seem that the United States should focus its efforts on *authoritarian* regimes, the regimes that have a chance of being democratized. Unless we want to confine our human rights policy to impotent symbolic gestures, which is all that we can do (short of invasion) against totalitarian regimes if we accept Kirkpatrick's account of the nature of these regimes, we must do exactly the opposite of what Kirkpatrick recommends!

There still may be good reasons to support authoritarian regimes, but these can only be realist reasons of national interest. If our concern is with human rights, or even just with civil and political rights, the categorical distinctions of the "Kirkpatrick Doctrine" simply do not stand up to scrutiny. Foreign policy ought to pursue something like the full range of rights of the Universal Declaration.

3. WHAT MEANS SHOULD BE USED?

The question of means to be used would seem to be relatively unproblematic: to pursue human rights goals we should use the same means that are used to pursue other foreign policy objectives. Depending on the circumstances, these may range from silently waiting and hoping for the best, to the threat or use of force. Evan Luard provides a fairly broad list of means that have been used in the pursuit of human rights objectives:

confidential representations, joint representations with other governments, public statements, support for calls for international investigation, initiation of calls for investigation, cancellation or postponement of ministerial visits, restrictions on cultural and sporting contacts, embargoes on arms sales, reductions in aid, withdrawal of ambassadors, cessation of aid, breaking diplomatic relations, and trade sanctions (1981: 26–27). To this list we should add aiding legal opposition groups, aiding illegal nonviolent opposition movements, aiding armed opposition movements, and invasion.

It is extremely difficult to talk about appropriate means in the abstract, because decisions about means should be made with respect to particular cases and after a thorough review of the interests and values at stake, the available policy instruments, and their likely consequences. In U.S. policy, however, as in the policy of most other countries that have chosen to pursue an active international human rights policy, the three principal means have been ''quiet diplomacy'' (confidential representations), public statements, and granting or withholding foreign aid.

A. Public versus Quiet Diplomacy

One of the Reagan administration's central themes, especially in its early years, was insistence on ''quiet diplomacy'' as the principal and in many cases the sole appropriate means to pursue human rights goals in foreign policy.[12] On their face, however, private representations alone would seem largely impotent; at best they could be expected to lead to minor, largely cosmetic modifications.

Governments rarely engage in the types of serious and systematic human rights violations that provoke the diplomatic concern of other states unless they feel that something very important is at stake—usually their control over society or its resources. To expect that they will stop these violations simply because they are asked to by another state is the height of folly. ''Experience has shown that it is precisely the spotlight of international concern that exerts restraining effect on arbitrary government'' (Schlesinger 1979: 525). As one participant from the Carter administration put it, ''U.S. readiness to take stronger action, should its representations fail, did

---

12. Except, of course, in the case of totalitarian regimes, where extremely public and often intentionally inflammatory diplomacy was often much preferred, including (in the case of Nicaragua) providing aid to armed revolutionaries and terrorists, and direct (covert) participation in the warlike act of mining harbors. And not even quiet diplomacy was very seriously pursued in some cases: ''In practice, the Reagan Administration was, time and again, the noisy public apologist for 'friendly' governments that engaged in gross abuses of human rights'' (Americas Watch et al. 1984: 3).

not always guarantee the desired results but made it more possible'' (R. Cohen 1982: 220). Token gestures might be made in order to attempt to improve the tenor of relations in the face of forceful private verbal protests, but it is politically implausible to imagine that quiet diplomacy alone, without at least the threat of more forceful public action, will produce anything more than symbolic gestures.

This is not to deny the importance of even symbolic gestures, especially since one of the most common such gestures is the release of prominent political dissidents. Quiet diplomacy, under both the Carter and Reagan Administrations,[13] has helped bring about the release of certainly hundreds of political prisoners and has ameliorated the conditions of detention of many more. These are real and important achievements, but they have had little or no impact on the general human rights situations in these countries and rarely can be expected to lead to further progress. It might even be argued that many of the apparent successes of quiet diplomacy are attributable not to quiet diplomacy alone but to the combination of private representations and (actual or potential) public actions.

B. Human Rights and Foreign Aid

In addition to confidential and public verbal pressures, the principal means used to pursue human rights in U.S. foreign policy has been conditioning foreign aid on human rights practices. Against the wishes of the Nixon, Ford, Carter, and Reagan administrations alike, Congress has mandated a link between rights and aid in bilateral economic assistance, bilateral security assistance, and U.S. participation in multilateral aid provided through international financial institutions.[14] This is the one area of human rights in U.S. foreign policy that has been fairly thoroughly studied, especially during the Carter administration.

The conclusions of most studies are not heartening. For example, Carleton and Stohl find that in both the Carter and the Reagan administrations "there is a gulf between human rights rhetoric and human rights action" (1985: 219).[15] In the Carter period they find no statistically significant correlations between either economic or security assistance and human

---

13. The Carter administration did not rely solely on public diplomacy. In fact, Roberta Cohen, who worked on human rights in the Carter State Department, argues that "the foundation of the Carter policy was quiet diplomacy. This meant raising the human rights issue vigorously in diplomatic channels" (1982: 217).

14. See, e.g., Weissbrodt 1977 and Franck 1981. For an extensive discussion of Congress's role in U.S. human rights policy, see Forsythe 1988.

15. Compare Stohl, Carleton, and Johnson 1984 for a similar assessment of the Nixon and Ford records, and Carleton and Stohl 1987.

rights practices as measured by Freedom House, Amnesty International, or the annual State Department Country Reports (1985: table 1). During the Reagan administration, the only significant correlation between human rights and aid occurs with the rankings the State Department Country Reports, but because these differ dramatically from both the "conservative" Freedom House rankings and the relatively "liberal" Amnesty International reports, Carleton and Stohl conclude that this reflects Reagan administration efforts to bring official human rights evaluations in line with aid requests, rather than conditioning aid on human rights practices (1985: 218).

Stephen B. Cohen, Deputy Assistant Secretary of State for Human Rights and Security Assistance in the last years of the Carter administration, presents a similar picture with respect to U.S. security assistance.[16] He stresses the often effective bureaucratic resistance of career Foreign Service officers, including self-interested interpretations of the law and distortions of information (1982: 257–60), resulting in a final policy that, despite all the rhetoric, "exhibited a remarkable degree of tentativeness and caution" (1982: 264) with respect to halting aid on human rights grounds:

> Relatively few governments were considered to be "engaged in a consistent pattern of gross (human rights) violations." Security assistance was actually cut off to even fewer, because other U.S. interests were often found to outweigh human rights concerns under the exception of "extraordinary circumstance." Moreover, in some instances, the Carter Administration adopted a highly strained reading of the statute. . . . In other cases, the language was simply disregarded, so that decisions violated even the letter of the law. (S. Cohen 1982: 264)[17]

The Carter administration certainly did more than its predecessors (see, e.g., Schoultz 1981; R. Cohen 1982), but when measured against its own rhetoric, as well as against U.S. legislation, "the record of implementation appears much more modest" (S. Cohen 1982: 276). But although the Carter record was mixed, there was at least sporadic effort to act on behalf of human rights,[18] while the Reagan administration consistently, force-

16. For a more radical account of the relationship between security assistance and human rights, an account that suggests that the relationship is largely inverse, see Klare and Arnson 1981 and Herman 1982.

17. Carleton and Stohl (1985: 222) similarly stress the use of the "extraordinary circumstances" exception and the creative interpretation of "a consistent pattern of gross violations" in producing a policy where, on the whole, there is no significant correlation between human rights practices and U.S. aid.

18. Buckley's description of the Carter approach involving a "random emphasis on human rights" (1980: 784) is perhaps cruel, but not entirely inaccurate.

fully, and publicly resisted both the letter and the spirit of U.S. human rights legislation, "openly def(ying) many of these laws" (Americas Watch et al. 1984: 12) and demonstrating a consistent and more than occasionally successful intent "to flout, circumvent, or bend the meaning of a number of human rights laws" (Lawyers Committee et al. 1986: 8). And when it did finally act on human rights concerns (except in the case of Soviet clients), this was usually only as a result of congressional pressure (as in El Salvador) or as a last-minute face-saving gesture (as in the Philippines).

It is difficult to find countries that have done much more than the United States. Canada has undertaken few concrete steps on behalf of human rights; aid is only rarely affected by human rights considerations, and arms sales almost never (Keenleyside 1988; Regehr 1988). Much the same is true of Great Britain and the other European countries, with the partial exception of the Netherlands (see Baehr 1982) and Norway (see Skalnes and Egeland 1986). And human rights considerations do not seem to play a part in the foreign policy of the Soviet Union and its allies.

C. "Positive Nonintervention":
Toward a More Aggressive Human Rights Policy

There is much more that might legitimately be done on behalf of human rights abroad. Just as aid may be given more or less freely, at the decision of the giver, so too trade, investment, and other economic relations are a standard source of international influence that might be exerted on behalf of human rights, especially by a country as wealthy and as powerful as the United States.[19] Where economic sanctions might threaten the survival or basic prosperity of the target nation, the prohibition of intervention might apply, but in most cases bilateral economic relations are not essential to the economic well-being of either party. Therefore, even breaking economic relations entirely will almost always fall below the threshold of impermissible intervention.

But if the impact really is so limited, why bother? There may be a number of moral reasons for acting. For example, the moral force of major human rights violations may demand that all available options be pursued; material complicity can be thus eliminated; and even symbolic action is often worthwhile. Furthermore, if other countries engage in similar sanctions, the overall impact may be more significant.[20] Similar arguments can

19. For a strong argument advocating using international economic relations (especially trade) both more broadly and in a more positive manner in order to influence human rights practices abroad, see Alston 1982.

20. Economic sanctions and boycotts are especially attractive because the potential for partisan abuse is low. Because there are considerable economic incentives to cheat on a

be made for political noninvolvement with rights-abusive regimes. Even international public opinion is not entirely without force. Some countries are able to exercise considerable political influence, especially in the relatively frequent cases of oppressive regimes that depend heavily on the support of a major power.

Therefore a strategy of what might be called "positive nonintervention"—thorough noninvolvement with regimes guilty of major systematic violations of human rights—shows considerable promise; at minimum it would eliminate complicity in human rights violations perpetrated by others. In fact, "positive nonintervention" may represent the best possible basis for an active, effective human rights policy that combines high moral and legal standards with a healthy degree of realism. By taking massive human rights violations wherever they occur to be a particularly powerful prima facie argument for positive nonintervention, or at least for the gradual phasing out of relations with a rights-abusive regime, positive nonintervention would represent an important new departure for American human rights policy and for the human rights policy of just about every other country as well.

Such a strategy would involve major changes in current practice. Perhaps the most important change would be the virtual elimination of "human rights" arguments for direct support of major human rights violators. No longer could repressive dictatorships be supported as the "lesser of two evils," or at least there would be a strong presumption against such arguments. The burden of proof would be shifted to those claiming that competing national interests should take priority. As a result, these interests would have to be more clearly specified, and the ways in which they deserve priority made clearer and more explicit. Under a doctrine of positive nonintervention, human rights goals would be placed initially at the head of the list so that they would not be lost in the policy process. This would at least help to clarify the true nature and substance of policy, and it might even reduce the frequency with which human rights concerns are sacrificed to other policy objectives.

4. INTEGRATING HUMAN RIGHTS INTO FOREIGN POLICY

Human rights objectives often will conflict with other objectives of foreign policy. Resolving such conflicts is an especially important matter

---

boycott, substantial compliance would signal true international consensus, whereas self-interested boycotts will fail, with the costs being borne primarily by the boycotters.

because the depressing record of past action—along with the fact that the differences between the Carter and Reagan policies, despite their seemingly diametrically opposed starting points, can be seen largely as matters of degree or consistency (compare Mower 1987)—might suggest that concrete action on behalf of human rights is in practice extraordinarily problematic, whatever its attractions in theory.

Human rights are but one concern of foreign policy, and the objective of promoting and preserving human rights may conflict with the national interest more broadly conceived. The relationship between human rights and other national interests, however, is neither as clear nor as simple as realists and other critics make it out to be. In fact, a more extensive commitment to human rights in foreign policy may in some cases make an important *contribution* to the realization of even national security goals.

In numerous instances, the human rights violations of foreign governments have contributed to setbacks for U.S. foreign policy. One of the main reasons for the "loss" of Nicaragua was the arbitrary and corrupt rule of the Somoza regime, with its wide array of human rights violations. If the United States had not created and then supported the Somoza family dictatorship over half a century, it might never have had to deal with a Sandinista government. Likewise, the real cause of the "loss" of Angola was the colonial policy of the U.S.-backed military dictatorship in Portugal. And in Iran, the rise to power of the Ayatollah can be explained only by the revulsion for the Shah, another major American "friend" in the Third World. The United States was more fortunate in the Philippines, but the New People's Army, which is causing significant political problems for the new democratic regime, almost certainly would not have been a force to be reckoned with except for the Marcos dictatorship, which the United States supported.

There is a profound tension between long-run and short-run interests. In many cases the short-run advantages of overlooking the human rights violations of "friendly"[21] governments are more than counterbalanced by the long-run risks and costs of radical revolution induced in part by the very human rights violations ignored by Washington. By tying future U.S. interests in a country to an abhorrent and not particularly stable type of government, the United States almost assures that when today's "friendly" leader becomes tomorrow's enemy of the people, or just another exiled

---

21. "Friendly" usually means anticommunist; if a regime shares this single value, it often seems that, as far as the United States is concerned, it is able to flout all other values with impunity. The topic of the confusion of ideology with both morality and the national interest is a fascinating one of obvious relevance but well beyond our scope here.

dictator, its opponents will have the inside track in the new government, often leaving the U.S. despised and without influence.

Human rights are not *merely* moral concerns. Morality and reality are not necessarily incompatible, and whether they are complementary, competing, or completely unconnected concerns is an empirical question. Sometimes a country can afford to act on its human rights concerns, other times it cannot. In each case, the determination must be made after assessing the facts. There is no simple rule—either realist or moralist—that can provide adequate guidance.

Politics involves compromise, both to accommodate multiple and sometimes inconsistent objectives and to cope with the resistance of a world that is not always responsive to our desires. Human rights, like all other political goals, must sometimes be compromised. For example, because of other interests in the relationship between the United States and the Soviet Union, as well as the power and autonomy of the Soviet Union, not much can be done about Soviet violations of human rights, whether we are in a period of détente or cold war. In the area of human rights as in all other areas of foreign policy, prudence requires major trade-offs and a sense of moderation in what we aspire to achieve. But differing conditions and capabilities must be taken into account in such a way that the resulting policy does not seem inconsistent or biased. The Reagan administration's violent assault on Nicaragua for human rights violations certainly no worse than those of such U.S. clients as Chile and Zaire, is a particularly salutary reminder of the need for consistency and intellectual coherence in any legitimate human rights policy.

If variations in the treatment of human rights violators are to be part of a consistent policy, human rights concerns must be explicitly and coherently integrated into the broader framework of national foreign policy. A human rights policy must be part of, not tacked onto or draped over, a country's overall foreign policy if it is to achieve either domestic or international legitimacy or effect. Difficult decisions must be made about the weight to be given to human rights, and they need to be made in general, as a matter of principle, and as early as possible. Ad hoc responses to immediate problems and crises are almost sure to lead to inconsistencies, both in appearance and in fact.

A loosely hierarchical ordering of foreign policy goals and values must be undertaken. Broad objectives—for example, "national security," "economic interests," "human rights"—must be disaggregated into concrete policy goals. These particular, concrete interests must then be at least roughly ranked—for example, as primary, secondary, and peripheral objectives. This must be done both for human rights concerns and for (all) other competing concerns, and the results must be cross-tabulated, so that when a question of trade-offs does arise, a framework for making at least an initial assessment will be in place. By contrast, actual practice seems to resemble a situation in which any claim of "national security," however weak or implausible, is taken to override any human rights concern, no matter how important.

What is required, in other words, are a structure and rules for making trade-offs. These rules are undeniably difficult to formulate with mathematical precision, but without them "trade-offs" will remain literally unprincipled, and in practice the language of "trade-offs" and "compromises" will usually be little more than a cover for the thoughtless sacrifice of human rights to any and all other (real or alleged) concerns of foreign policy. Hard cases, gray areas, fuzzy boundaries, and exceptions are unavoidable; they may even abound. But unless the effort is taken seriously, the resulting policy is likely to appear baseless or inconsistent, and probably will be so in fact. We can even suggest a simple empirical test of the sincerity and legitimacy of a state's commitment to human rights in its foreign policy: until we see a country willing, in practice, to accept at least small costs in its pursuit of human rights concerns, there is no reason to take even the most fervent professions of commitment seriously.

Like all other policy goals, the real test of commitment is how much one is willing to pay. In the United States and in most other countries, the willingness to pay has been vanishingly small; in practice, human rights have not been integrated into foreign policy, but sacrificed in the name of foreign policy. This is both bad morality and bad foreign policy.

13

Implementing Human Rights:
The Priority of National Action

What has been the practical impact of the multilateral and bilateral instruments and actions considered in the preceding chapters? International action has had, and continues to have, a significant impact on the fate of human rights, but its role is ultimately subsidiary. The fate of human rights—their implementation, abridgement, protection, violation, enforcement, denial, or enjoyment—is largely a matter of national, not international, action. This implies a further particularity to universal human rights, a national particularity in the way international norms are put into practice.

1. THE LIMITS OF MULTILATERAL ACTION

The Convention against Torture and Other Cruel, Inhuman, or Degrading Treatment or Punishment, which entered into force in 1987, provides a reference point for evaluating the strengths and weaknesses of international and regional human rights regimes, which rely principally on reporting and communications (complaints). The emerging international regime against torture, centered on the Convention, not only contains the strongest enforcement measures of any international (excluding regional) human rights regime, but also makes use of most of the mechanisms that other bodies use.

A. The Torture Convention: An Illustration
The Torture Convention establishes an international monitoring system based on the Committee against Torture, a body of ten independent experts serving in their personal capacity that will review quadrennial

reports on national implementation. The Convention also established three stronger *optional* implementation procedures.

Article 21 of the Convention allows states to recognize the competence of the Committee against Torture to consider "communications" (complaints), received from another party that has made such a declaration. Similar interstate complaint procedures in the Civil and Political Covenant and the Racial Discrimination Convention have never been used. Torture is so universally condemned that we might expect an occasional complaint, but for the most part Article 21 is likely to remain a paper formality. The other two optional procedures, however, have considerable promise.

Article 22 permits states to authorize the committee to receive "communications from or on behalf of individuals subject to its jurisdiction" alleging torture. Admissible communications shall be examined, written or oral statements from the state in question solicited, and the committee, at the conclusion of its confidential investigation "shall forward its views to the State Party concerned and to the individual"—that is, it may make judgments of compliance or noncompliance with the obligations imposed by the Convention. Although there is no way to enforce such judgments, this is as strong as any international implementation procedure yet established.[1]

The final optional provision is Article 20, which permits the committee to consider any "reliable information" it may receive "which appears to it to contain well-founded indications that torture is being systematically practiced in the territory of a State Party." A confidential inquiry, undertaken with the cooperation of the state in question, may be carried out by one or more members of the committee, acting on its behalf, and the committee shall transmit the findings of the inquiry to the state, "together with any comments or suggestions which seem appropriate in view of the situation" and may even include a summary of its findings in its annual report.

Article 20 deals with *situations* where torture is systematically practiced, rather than the individual and even isolated cases considered under Article 22. The procedure should therefore appear less threatening to states, which should increase adherence. In addition, the focus on situations should direct attention to the most serious violations. And in contrast to Articles 21 and 22, where states must "opt in," a party is automatically covered under the procedures of Article 20 unless it explicitly "opts out" with a declaration at the time of signature, ratification, or accession (Article 28). Further-

---

1. Unless explicitly noted to the contrary, I exclude regional procedures when referring to "international" action in this chapter.

more, while the declarations under Articles 21 and 22 may be withdrawn at any time, the option not to participate in Article 20 is available only at the time of ratification.

Although it is too soon for an assessment of the impact of these procedures, a preliminary and predictive evaluation is possible, and probably even profitable, on the basis of similar procedures in other human rights organs. Given the strength of the Torture Convention, such an evaluation will serve as a general assessment of the limits of established multilateral procedures.

B. International Reporting Procedures

The model for the reporting procedure established in Article 19 is the International Labor Organization's monitoring of compliance with ILO Conventions and Recommendations, which has previously been emulated by the Human Rights Committee, the Committee on Economic, Social, and Cultural Rights, the Committee on the Elimination of Racial Discrimination, and the Committee on the Elimination of Discrimination against Women (see Chapter 11). But such a reporting procedure will yield only what the reporting state wishes.

Committees cannot always even assure that the required reports are submitted. Should a state submit even the most pro forma of reports, including little more than pious generalities and extracts from its constitution and statutes, it will have formally discharged its reporting obligation. States need not respond to particular questions asked during the public review of the report, let alone provide responses that the questioner or even the committee as a whole considers adequate. And there is no formal follow-up procedure (other than review of the next scheduled report) unless the state initiates it with some form of supplemental report or information, which is likely to be reviewed on an ad hoc or informal basis.

Although reporting is often called "enforcement," to call it even "implementation" probably is stretching the language too far. The international human rights obligations of states are implemented, if at all, through national action. Like most obligations in international law, international human rights obligations ultimately rest on the good faith of states; to pretend otherwise is to confuse aspiration with action, legal rules with practice. Reporting does not even provide a strong system of international monitoring: there is no organized system for acquiring independent information; reports are considered according to a predefined schedule, rather than as the circumstances of state behavior require; no effective follow-up procedures are provided; and the committees may only raise questions, not make even unenforceable judgments of compliance.

Whatever pressure such a committee can exert rests on its ability to embarrass states by drawing international attention to apparent violations or inadequacies in reports that might seem to be attempts to cover up questionable or culpable practices. Such subtle pressure may in some cases have an effect: for both domestic and international reasons, most states are concerned with how their human rights practices are perceived internationally. But even shame is ultimately dependent on a sort of good faith on the part of the violator. Reporting-questioning procedures in the field of human rights are therefore likely to have even a marginal impact only as a supplement to sincere and dedicated national efforts. But they can serve both as a spur to and a check on national efforts.

Perhaps the most important contribution of mandatory periodic reporting is the occasion that drafting the report provides for a periodic national review of a state's own practice. If a country is serious about its reporting obligation, such reviews should help to guard against complacency and resultant shortcomings in practice. Inadequacies and areas for improvement may be uncovered, and the occasion of the next report is likely to serve as a target for remedial action. A purely national reporting system might in theory accomplish all of these purposes, but independent international scrutiny offers one more level of checks and is likely to provide an additional spur to action.

Periodic national reviews of practice in the course of preparing a report also may serve to strengthen the force of particular substantive provisions. For example, the systematic review of interrogation and detention procedures and practices required by Article 11 of the Torture Convention should be placed on nothing less than a four-year cycle, corresponding to the reporting cycle. Similarly, the training procedures required by Article 10 will be placed under a cycle of periodic review if the reporting obligation is undertaken with full seriousness. In general, whenever states are required to look carefully at their practices, as they must in the course of conscientiously preparing a report, the relevant treaty provisions may play a constructive role in furthering the cause of human rights.

Periodic reporting may also provide the occasion for national improvements in information gathering and processing that then serve as the basis for policy reforms—for example, by highlighting local problems or fostering the spread of knowledge about innovative or particularly effective local efforts. Furthermore, the review process itself is likely to increase the awareness and attention of responsible public officials, which should produce even more and better information. Reporting may even further *international* information exchange, allowing states to learn from one another's experiences. This could be greatly encouraged if such monitoring bodies as the committee used their authority to make general comments on reports in order to highlight points of broader international interest in innovative national practices or commonly encountered difficulties.

It appears that the Committee against Torture could have at least as much of an impact through its review of reports as any of its counterparts, and not simply because it will be able to learn from their experience. Being a committee of independent experts, even if all members prove not to be equally independent or expert, should assure the maximum possible impartiality. Independent experts, who do not have skeletons in their own closets or other relationships with foreign states to consider, are also most likely to be thorough and probing in their questioning.

The Convention is silent on how the reports shall be ''considered'' by the committee. This will be worked out when the committee adopts its own rules of procedure and, most important, in practice in the early years of its work. Experience with other bodies, however, indicates that two issues are crucial: the sources of information used and the interpretation given to the phrase ''general comments on the report'' (Article 19(3)). If the committee were to consider only officially available information, the integrity of the review process would be seriously compromised by the incompleteness and bias of official information. At the outset of the work of the Human Rights Committee, an attempt was made to restrict it to official sources, but this effort failed (Fischer 1984: 145–47) and members have been able to use information from any source they deem reliable. This precedent should be decisive for the Committee against Torture. The fact that questions are asked by individual members, not by the committee as a whole, allows maximum latitude in the use of unofficial information, without contravening the terms of the committee's mandate.

The committee's understanding of ''general comments'' and what it considers to be ''appropriate'' comments will be another crucial indicator of its seriousness. This is one of the most controversial aspects of the Convention. Consensus could not be achieved in the Working Group that drafted the Convention; the final formulation arose from last-minute amendments in the Third Committee of the General Assembly. The Torture Committee is explicitly allowed to make general comments *on the report*. By contrast, the Human Rights Committee is authorized only to make ''general comments,'' which in practice has been interpreted to mean comments that do not address the substance of particular reports (Jhabvala 1984: 87, 92–94; Fischer 1984: 149). The Committee against Torture also is explicitly authorized to make such general comments *as it may consider appropriate*. Notions of propriety will vary widely among committee members, and the general practice of consensual decision-making suggests that the interpretation adopted is likely to represent a least common denominator, but there is a chance that the committee as a whole might make substantive comments on some reports. This would be a notable advance over all other established reporting procedures.

Another area that bears watching is the committee's practice with respect to parties' obligations to submit "such other reports as the Committee may request" (Article 19(1)). Requiring reports on serious situations *between* reporting cycles could be a useful supplement to Article 20 (communications on situations of systematic torture), or even a partial substitute for states that opt out of Article 20. It would also address the obvious problem of states avoiding scrutiny in the four-year intervals between reports. The likely constraint on such a use of this power is acquiring the information that would be needed to request such a supplemental report if the state in question does not recognize the committee's competence under Article 20. Some members are certain to argue that the committee as a whole has no authority to take official cognizance of the sort of unofficial information that would suggest the need for a supplemental report, but such an innovative use of the reporting mechanism is not entirely out of the question.

The way such a committee exercises its powers of review may nonetheless influence national practice. The more thorough the questioning, the less likely it is that a state will be able to hide its shortcomings. In at least some instances we can even expect that practices that cannot be covered up will be reformed. Furthermore, the more impartial the committee, the more likely it is to receive open and honest reports; even states with good records and strong national commitments are less likely to participate in or cooperate with procedures and committees that are perceived as biased. The need to induce and maintain state participation and cooperation limits the extent to which a committee can push states: an overly aggressive committee may alienate some states and thus lose its opportunity to have any impact at all in these countries, but an efficient, well-respected, and savvy committee may be able at least occasionally to tip the scales in national policies. Such an impact may prove impossible to pinpoint or disaggregate, but we should expect it to be there in some instances.

Finally, we need to consider the problem of the proliferation of human rights reporting procedures. The burden on scarce bureaucratic resources, especially in Third World countries, must be a serious concern, particularly for a single-right convention, such as that on torture. This concern is reflected in the Torture Convention's four-year reporting cycle (in contrast to the two-year cycle of most prior human rights treaties) and in the fact that reports after the first need cover only "any new measures taken" (Article 19(1)). However necessary these changes may be from a strictly practical perspective, both are likely to reduce to utility of the reporting process by reducing both the scope and the frequency of national review. Whether the reduced administrative burden is worth such costs is difficult to say before the fact, and may not even be clear after several years of experience. The issue is likely to arise in the case of future conventions, though, so special attention should be given to reports in the second and third cycle. If an excessively high proportion of second and third reports amount to little more than statements that there have been no new measures or developments, these innovations in the Convention against Torture probably should be held to be a poor model for future human rights conventions and the reporting burden will have to be addressed in another fashion.

In any case, the role of international monitoring bodies is essentially supplemental. In certain circumstances, international reporting systems can have a minor impact on human rights practices. Conversely, the absence of reporting systems may make it slightly easier for states to get away with violating human rights. But in the end, reports are just that—reports, on national practice. National practice is the key. And that practice, in almost all cases, can at best be only marginally influenced by even the strongest international reporting system.

C. Communications (Complaint) Procedures

The original model for Article 20, which allows consideration of communications that indicate systematic torture, is the "1503 procedure" in the U.N. Commission on Human Rights (see Chapter 11, section 2.A). The Convention against Torture is the first international human rights *treaty* to include such a procedure, even on an optional basis. There is some reason to hope that the procedures under Article 20 will be less cumbersome than the 1503 procedure. The members of the Committee against Torture are independent experts rather than instructed delegates, as in the Commission on Human Rights, the committee is a much smaller body and authorized to carry out an investigation by one or more members acting as an ad hoc committee, and its narrow focus on torture may induce states to allow it to take a more flexible approach.

But even for participants the committee's role under Article 20 will be one of encouragement and moral suasion, involving at most the mobilization of national shame and international public opinion. Before an inquiry is begun, the state in question must be consulted. Then it must be given the opportunity to participate in any investigation, which shall be completely confidential. Once the inquiry is concluded, and before a summary of the proceedings can be released publicly, the state must again be consulted. Throughout the entire process, a cooperative resolution to the problem is sought, and at the end the only real sanction available to the committee is whatever additional publicity its report may provide. But if torture is being systematically practiced, the government is likely to feel itself in some sense under siege and thus be decidedly unreceptive to external pressure, not to mention that a government that systematically tortures its own people is not likely to be overly concerned with international public opinion.

The fact that the committee is unlikely to be very effective in the most serious cases does not indicate that the procedure is without value. The treatment of Equatorial Guinea and Uruguay under the 1503 procedure, in which public action came after a change of government, suggests a possible after-the-fact role for the committee. In such circumstances, international scrutiny may be useful in helping the new regime to get on the right track. Of no less importance is the possible impact of scrutiny under Article 20 in less extreme cases. Between 1978 and 1986, situations in at least thirty countries were confidentially considered under the 1503 procedure (Tolley 1987: 124–32). As a result of confidential pressure, in at least a few of these cases, some small changes must have been made in national policy. We might hope for a similar impact—once more, the use of moral suasion and the threat of international publicity to encourage national action—from Article 20, or similar procedures that might later be established elsewhere. These are modest hopes, but they suggest a real if limited value for even such a hedged, optional procedure. And as is so often the case, this was both the best possible at the time and better than nothing—which, after all, is what Article 20 will replace.

The procedures under Article 22 for considering individual communications are the strongest in the Convention. The Committee against Torture is authorized to consider each case "in the light of all information made available to it by or on behalf of the individual and by the State Party concerned." Furthermore, the committee is explicitly authorized to state its views on the case, and because Article 22 deals with particular individuals instead of general situations, any findings by the committee will be especially difficult for a guilty state to ignore, while remedial action (or retaliation against the victim) can be relatively easily monitored.

Experience suggests, however, that the strength and the coverage of international human rights procedures vary inversely. Less than half the parties to the Civil and Political Covenant have accepted the authority of the Human Rights Committee to receive individual communications, and less than one-tenth of the parties to the Racial Discrimination Convention have permitted individual communications under that instrument. Increased strength is likely to bring decreased participation; when the obligations they would undertake become more than symbolic, states contemplating or engaging in questionable practices usually exempt themselves. This is perhaps the single most significant limitation of multilateral human rights procedures: the states most likely to commit violations that most cry out for international action are precisely the states least likely to participate in strong international procedures.

We also should be wary of the excessive individualism implicit in an overemphasis on individual complaint proceedings. Such procedures are completely dependent on the receipt of admissible communications, which in turn depend not only on a state's formal participation in the procedure but also on the ability of victims (or their advocates) to get information into the hands of the relevant committee. This means that proceedings under Article 22 are likely to overemphasize prominent individuals and cases in relatively open countries or countries with good overall human rights records. Certainly every individual who is helped is a valuable success story for international procedures and a person who has his or her rights violated in a relatively open country, or even in a country that has a generally exemplary human rights record, is not any less deserving of international protection. Nonetheless, individual complaint procedures can be expected to help directly only a relative handful of individuals. For example, the Human Rights Committee, which deals with the full range of personal, legal, civil, and political rights, during its first nine years (1977–86) completed consideration of less than one hundred communications, from Canada, Colombia, Finland, Italy, Madagascar, Mauritius, Sweden, Suriname, Uruguay, and Zaire—hardly a representative sample of violators of civil and political rights.

Furthermore, even a large number of individual complaints to even the most impartial and aggressive of international monitoring bodies will not address the real problem of torture, or any other violation of human rights. Action on individual complaints can at best address the symptoms of the underlying problem. Protecting people against torture or other abuses is not so much a matter of providing international remedies as it is a matter of altering national practices that allow or even encourage human rights violations. True protection against human rights violations rests on fundamental *national* political changes. International monitoring is almost certain to be a largely peripheral factor in bringing about such changes.

Excessive judicialism is the other pitfall of an overemphasis on individual complaint procedures. In fact, the quasi-judicial nature of such proceedings actually obscures their real impact. The review of individual complaints is essentially a mechanism to encourage national cooperation and action—that is, an effort to try to convince, perhaps shame, a state to mend its ways. Recalcitrant states can ignore international committees with impunity, and they regularly do.

2. THE LIMITS OF BILATERAL ACTION

When considering international action on behalf of human rights, one reason to begin with multilateral activity is that the normative consensus worked out in the United Nations provides a context for bilateral action. Another no less important reason is that while we can trace intensive multilateral activity back over forty years to the very beginning of the United Nations, human rights has been an active concern of the national foreign policies of most countries for scarcely fifteen years. For example, U.S. legislation, which has focused on linking foreign aid and arms sales to human rights practices in recipient countries, goes back only to 1973 (see, e.g., Weissbrodt 1977; Vogelgesang 1980), and with the partial exception of the Carter years (1977–80), the executive branch has generally opposed even that. Canada's efforts are even more recent, and no more forceful (see Matthews and Pratt 1988). Even such countries as Norway and the Netherlands, who have gone the furthest in their efforts to pursue human rights concerns in their foreign policy, can trace these endeavors back not much more than a decade (see, e.g., Baehr 1982). And human rights do not appear to have had any place at all in the foreign policies of the Soviet bloc states.

A. The Possibilities of Bilateral Action

Given this history, we might be tempted to say that until recently the human rights impact of bilateral action has been nil. This is true if we look at actions directly undertaken in the name of human rights, but policies undertaken for other reasons often have significant human rights consequences. For example, efforts to foster "democracy" and "development," which have been a part of the foreign policies of most developed countries over the past forty years, may in some cases have helped to increase the enjoyment of both civil and political rights and economic and social rights. Actions by the United States to protect the "free world" from "communism," however, have had a devastating impact on human rights in such countries as Guatemala, Chile, South Korea, Indonesia, Zaire, and South Africa. Likewise, aid programs in the 1950s and 1960s that focused on aggregate growth and "modernization" have in many instances actually impeded the enjoyment of economic, social, and cultural rights in recipient countries.

Bilateral relations seem to provide a much greater range of opportunities—and dangers—for international action on behalf of human rights. It is virtually impossible to produce examples in which multilateral action has had a similar influence, whether for good or evil, on human rights conditions. States, particularly powerful states, have more resources at their disposal than international organizations do. States control, and thus can manipulate for the purpose of their human rights policies, access to markets, resources, and foreign aid. At least some states can make use of the desire of other countries for cordial diplomatic relations or political cooperation in order to exert pressure on behalf of human rights. And the extraordinarily scrupulous concern for sovereignty characteristic of virtually all international organizations and supervisory bodies is less pronounced in the bilateral foreign policy of some states. Although intervention is no less illegal in bilateral relations, states much more frequently choose to ignore or override the prohibition in their bilateral policies.

B. Humanitarian Intervention: The Dangers of Bilateral Action

This combination of greater resources and a greater willingness to use them suggests the possibility of more effective international action through bilateral means, but it also presents serious dangers to human rights, as the example of humanitarian intervention makes clear.[2] "Humanitarian intervention" can be defined as intervention (in the strict sense of dictatorial coercive interference in the internal affairs of another state) in order to remedy mass and flagrant violations of the human rights of foreign nationals by their own governments.[3] Even in this narrow sense, though, humanitarian intervention may involve a great variety of responses to a wide range of types of human rights violations.

For simplicity, we might divide the provocations into "genocide" (understood in a fairly loose sense to mean massive, systematic official human rights violations, including killing a significant fraction of a given population or of an identifiable racial, ethnic, or national group) and other violations. Similarly, we might divide interventionary responses into those that involve military measures and those that do not. The result is the typology in Figure 4. Setting aside for the moment the questionable motives of the interveners, examples of each type would be:

Type 1: The Indian invasion of East Pakistan/Bangladesh

Type 2: Canadian trade and aid sanctions against Amin's Uganda

Type 3: U.S. involvement in the Spanish-American War (to the extent that it was in response to human rights violations in Cuba)

Type 4: U.S. economic subversion of the Allende regime in Chile

I shall concentrate here on types 1 and 2 (military and nonmilitary re-

2. For alternative accounts of humanitarian intervention, see, e.g., Lillich 1967, Matthews and Pratt 1985, and Slater and Nardin 1986.

3. Humanitarian intervention is thus very different from rescue missions on behalf of one's own nationals threatened or held abroad. Compare Lillich 1970: 60–61, Bowett 1974: 45–46, and Fairley 1980: 32.

Figure 4. Typology of humanitarian intervention

Human rights violation:

	"Genocide"	Other
Military response	Type 1	Type 3
Nonmilitary response	Type 2	Type 4

sponses to "genocide"), which are the cases that are most likely to be justifiable.

The central place of the principle of nonintervention in international law hardly needs emphasis; sovereignty is the foundation of international law, and nonintervention expresses the correlative duty to respect the sovereignty of other states. Thus, proponents of the doctrine of humanitarian intervention must show that humanitarian intervention is a recognized exception to the general rule. Because it is not permitted by any human rights treaty, an argument for the legality of humanitarian intervention must rest principally on custom, the other principal source of international law.

The standard arguments for the customary legality of humanitarian intervention rely heavily on nineteenth-century European examples, especially actions against Turkey,[4] but even a casual student of history should be shocked, or at least amused, by the notion that nineteenth-century Europe was the classic locus of the practice of humanitarian intervention. And postwar practice is even less supportive of (unilateral military) humanitarian intervention. For example, the alleged humanitarian motives of the Soviet Union in Hungary and Czechoslovakia, and of the United States in Vietnam and the Dominican Republic, have met with well-deserved and nearly universal ridicule. Humanitarian motives probably played an important part for at least some of those involved in Congo crisis, but the original Belgian intervention was at best a rescue mission with a very large dose of self-interest, and later "interventions" were at the invitation, or at least with the consent, of the generally recognized government and thus not really intervention in the strict sense of coercive interference. The 1970s

4. Stowell 1921 provides one of the most comprehensive surveys of alleged instances of humanitarian intervention. See also Fonteyne 1974. Brownlie (1963: 340) argues that there is only one genuine case of pre-twentieth-century humanitarian intervention.

did produce two major instances of apparently humanitarian intervention—Bangladesh and Uganda—but even here self-interest was a significant factor; the Indian intervention in Bangladesh even resulted in the partition of its archenemy, Pakistan.

The moral case for humanitarian intervention is very strong. Simply because atrocious violations of human rights take place overseas hardly seems sufficient moral reason to turn one's back. ''Surely to require a state to sit back and watch the slaughter of innocent people in order to avoid violating blanket prohibitions against the use of force is to stress black-letter at the expense of far more important values''; in fact, it is ''a classic example of throwing the baby out with the bathwater'' (Lillich 1967: 344, 347). Even Michael Walzer, who presents a powerful moral argument for nonintervention on ''pluralist'' grounds (see Chapter 12, section 1.C), allows intervention in response to human rights violations that shock the moral conscience of most people (1977: 101–8). Critics of the legal doctrine of humanitarian intervention also usually find humanitarian intervention to be a sound moral principle (e.g., Franck and Rodley 1973: 278–79, 304; Hassan 1981: 910).

So long as we include the costs of intervention in any particular moral evaluation, I have no desire to challenge such moral arguments. Practical considerations, however, clearly suggest that humanitarian intervention should not be sanctioned as a general norm. Overwhelming evidence from sad experience suggests that the doctrine of humanitarian intervention, whatever its moral attractions, is in practice likely to be just one more excuse for self-interested interventions by the powerful against the weak. Because unilateral intervention, whether for humanitarian or other purposes, is a policy instrument principally available to the strong against the weak, humanitarian intervention will become politically corrupted by discrimination; it will not be applied against the powerful or the well connected. In trying to defend humanitarian intervention, Lillich argues that ''it is a realistic assumption that no state with the capabilities to act will allow its own nationals and the nationals of other states to be killed or injured abroad'' (1967: 324–25). If this were true, concerns over discrimination could be largely eliminated. In fact, though, the assumption is outrageously unrealistic.

Even genocide usually meets with international inaction, for reasons ranging from countervailing economic and security interests to simple lack of interest. In the last twenty years we can point to a cycle of barbarous atrocities in Burundi, the decimation of Cambodia under Pol Pot and his successors, the death of between one-fifth and one-third of the population of East Timor during its forcible incorporation into Indonesia, and the systematic massacre of Indians in Paraguay and Guatemala, among other countries. Humanitarian intervention was not even attempted in any of these cases.

What will prompt states to act? Necessary conditions seem to include very low costs, the absence of Cold War concerns, and an unusually high level of popular interest. Unless even massive killings overseas are in some compelling way "brought home" *and* competing security, political, economic, and ideological interests are absent, opportunities for humanitarian intervention are almost always not seized. Furthermore, unless there are also clear and considerable selfish national interests to be furthered, "humanitarian" intervention almost certainly will not take place. This is underscored by the actions of India in Bangladesh, Tanzania in Uganda, and France in deposing "Emperor" Bokassa in the Central African Empire. In practice, humanitarian intervention is likely to be restricted to actions against weak, notorious, and relatively peripheral countries. It is plausible to argue that this is better than nothing at all, which is the only practical alternative; significant numbers of people have benefited even from these mixed-motive interventions. Nonetheless, the systematic discrimination implicit in any practical system of humanitarian intervention greatly reduces its attractiveness.

The most serious political problem with humanitarian intervention arises from the fact that many allegedly humanitarian interventions are likely to have no humanitarian concern at all. This is particularly true of the actions of the superpowers, the countries most able and most likely to consider intervention in the largest number of potential cases. Whether we look at the Soviet Union in Hungary, Czechoslovakia, Afghanistan, or Poland, or the United States in Guatemala, the Dominican Republic, postrevolutionary Nicaragua, or Grenada, what we see is the extraordinarily tenuous nature of the claims of humanitarian concern. In fact, in such cases as the Soviet invasion of Czechoslovakia and its threatened invasion of Poland, or the U.S. overthrow of the Arbenz regime in Guatemala and the Reagan campaign against Sandinista Nicaragua, intervention has been to *reverse* improvements in the human rights situation. Such *antihumanitarian* intervention is more the norm than the exception.

The noble aims of those who on moral grounds would counsel sanctioning the principle of humanitarian intervention are likely to be subverted by precisely the moral defects they attempt to reform. The legalization of humanitarian intervention is almost certain to face the fate of other attempts to legislate morality: at best it will be evaded, at worst it will be abused. Whether domestic or international, law can hold a community to standards it generally accepts and respects but by which individuals occasionally find it difficult to abide. It can also help protect the community against outlaws and provide some assurance to individuals who comply that others will not be able to use their compliance to unfair advantage. Law cannot, however, make the majority of people or states better than they truly want to be; it must take its subjects as they are, in the sense of the best that they are willing to work to become. Law can serve a hortatory function, but it will be effective only if it is but a few steps ahead of its subjects. The prohibition of humanitarian intervention begins from and insists on remaining constrained by this fundamental political fact.

There are costs in refusing to push too far beyond the existing international consensus. In the case of humanitarian intervention, these costs center on the seeming sacrifice of justice to power. But would legalizing unilateral humanitarian intervention really promote justice? Almost certainly not. Instead, self-interest would be further promoted, and the name of justice would be cruelly abused. The central political fact about allegedly humanitarian interventions usually is their nonhumanitarian, often even antihumanitarian, motivation. Such interventions represent perhaps the greatest danger of foreign policy action (allegedly) undertaken on behalf of human rights.

C. The Power to Help and the Power to Harm

The record of positive foreign policy achievements in the field of human rights is sparse (Chapter 12), but to look only at inaction is to miss much of the impact of national foreign policies on human rights abroad. Consider, for example, the often profoundly negative human rights impact of U.S. foreign policy decisions undertaken on the basis of security, economic, or ideological considerations. Most Latin American dictatorships are the direct or indirect result of U.S. foreign policy. The United States has chosen to be "constructively engaged" with South Africa—very constructively, from the South African point of view. And despite its considerable responsibility for the prior dictatorships, the United States played a peripheral role in the democratization of the Philippines, Argentina, Spain, and Portugal. The Soviet record is just as bad—consider Afghanistan, Ethiopia, Kampuchea, and the whole of Eastern Europe. And most other countries have produced less harm more out of a lack of power and opportunities for intervention than as a result of a notably more moral foreign policy.

Like most moral considerations, human rights are rarely the bases for positive foreign policy action, except when that action is otherwise beneficial. By contrast, security, economic, political, and ideological considerations are the principal bases of foreign policy in almost all countries.

When human rights goals conflict with these objectives, human rights almost always lose out. States ignore human rights violations or act in ways that harm human rights much more often than they act strongly on behalf of human rights abroad because it is more often in their security, economic, political, or ideological interest to do so.

Even more troubling is the relatively great capacity of external action to harm the human rights situation in another country. There seems to be a profound and troubling asymmetry in the relative efficacy of bilateral international action on behalf of and against human rights: it is much easier to produce great harm than to provide major help. Over and over again we have seen dictatorships effectively propped up by foreign support (at least in the medium-run)—for example, in Poland, Zaire, the Shah's Iran, and Marcos's Philippines—but there are few examples of regimes that respect the full range of internationally recognized human rights that owe their start, let alone their continued existence, to external support.[5] Democratic rule requires popular support and participation and thus can rarely be established through external action, but dictatorship requires only sufficient force to repress opposition. As the fates of such countries as Chile, Guatemala, Poland, and Hungary so sadly illustrate, such force is much easier to acquire as the result of foreign support or intervention. A government that respects human rights must be principally the result of internal political action. A government that violates human rights can owe its existence in significant measure to external forces.

The theoretical potential in bilateral action should not be ignored. Bilateral actors have more resources at their disposal, and operate with fewer constraints, than almost all multilateral organizations. If they choose, countries can exercise a considerable range of foreign policy resources on behalf of human rights. This is especially true of relatively powerful regional actors, such as the United States in Latin America, the Soviet Union in Eastern Europe, or France in francophone West Africa. Such positive actions may have a small but still significant impact on human rights abroad. Typically, however foreign policy resources have been exercised on behalf of human rights only sporadically, if that. And there is a great potential for powerful nations, especially the United States and the Soviet Union, to use their power to undermine human rights in foreign countries.

5. The only striking counterexamples are countries that were decisively defeated in war, such as Japan and Germany. Even the U.S. intervention to protect the results of the 1978 election in the Dominican Republic, which is probably the most important positive U.S. bilateral action on behalf of human rights in at least a dozen years, reveals the essentially secondary and supportive role of even regional hegemons.

This suggests that the greatest foreign policy contribution of the super-powers to human rights might lie in self-restraint, in avoiding actions that actively support or encourage rights-violating regimes.[6] If all countries, and particularly all major powers, were to avoid support for and complicity with repressive regimes—that is, if positive nonintervention were to become the norm—bilateral action could have a more than marginal impact on human rights abroad. At the very least, positive nonintervention would return the fate of human rights to a national struggle between dictators and their citizens, which is where the issue really belongs and where any lasting success must ultimately rest.

3. THE LIMITS OF INTERNATIONAL ACTION

Human rights are ultimately a profoundly *national*, not international, issue. In an international system where government is national rather than global, human rights are by definition principally a national matter. States are the principal violators of human rights and the principal actors governed by international norms. Thus the probable impact of international action is limited. The likelihood of international implementation and enforcement is also reduced because international action on behalf of human rights rests on perceived moral (rather than material) interdependence. Other states are not directly harmed by a government's failure to respect human rights; the immediate victims are that government's own citizens. Therefore, the self-interested incentives of other states to retaliate are low, or at least intangible. Furthermore, "retaliation" is particularly difficult. The only leverage available, beyond moral suasion, must be imported from other issue areas, such as trade or aid. This makes retaliation relatively costly and increases the risk of escalation. In addition, because the means of retaliation are not clearly and directly tied to the violations, its legitimacy is likely to be seen as more questionable.

Even in the best of circumstances, respecting human rights is extremely inconvenient for a government, and the less pure the motives of those in power, the more irksome human rights appear. Who is to prevent a government from succumbing to the temptations and arrogance of position and power? Who can force a government to respect human rights? The only plausible candidate is the people whose rights are at stake.

Foreign actors may overthrow a repressive government. With luck and skill, they may even be able to place good people in charge of finely crafted

6. Compare Shue's emphasis on the special importance of duties to avoid, by one's own actions, denying others their rights (1980: 51ff.). This provides a rather ironic twist to the standard conservative emphasis on "negative" rights.

institutions based on the best of principles. They may provide tutelage, supervision, and monitoring; moral and material support; and protection against enemies. All this is extremely unlikely, but even if we do attribute such unrealistically pure motives and unbelievable skill and dedication to external powers, a regime's ultimate success—its persistence in respecting, implementing, and enforcing human rights—will depend principally on *internal* political factors.

A government that respects human rights is almost always the legacy of persistent national political struggles against human rights violations. Most governments that respect human rights have been created not from the top down but from the bottom up. Paternalism, whether national or international, is unlikely to produce respect for human rights. The struggle for international human rights is, in the end, a series of national struggles. International action can support these struggles, or it can frustrate and sometimes even prevent them. International action is thus an important factor in the fate of human rights, but not the most important factor.

This does not mean that we should give up on international action. Few states press at the limits of the possibilities of international action either in their bilateral relations or in their activities in international organizations. But we must recognize that there *are* major limits to international action and turn our attention to realistic international objectives.[7]

It is also important to emphasize the limits of international action because the academic study of human rights has been dominated by students of international law and politics[8] and because policy-oriented discussions of human rights in North America, and to a lesser extent in Europe, have focused predominantly on human rights practices abroad (especially in the Soviet bloc and the Third World) and on the ability of Western governments to influence them. If my arguments above are correct, such scholarly efforts have been misdirected, at least in part. The study of human rights must in the final analysis rest most heavily on the study of *comparative* politics, not international politics.

There are a variety of historical and sociological reasons for this misdirection. The international normative consensus was worked out in the United Nations, which is studied almost exclusively by students of interna-

7. The disillusionment provoked by the Carter administration, which came into power claiming that human rights were the "soul" of U.S. foreign policy when in fact they were but one of many competing foreign policy objectives, underscores the importance of having realistic goals.

8. This is striking in the two principal human rights bibliographies, Center for the Study of Human Rights 1983 and Friedman and Sherman 1985. In my own field of political science, there are probably as many political philosophers as students of comparative politics writing explicitly on human rights.

tional law and organization, giving them an advantage over their colleagues in other fields. International lawyers have played a major role in drafting the legal instruments, giving them a similar advantage. The distressing tendency toward disciplinary exclusivity and interdisciplinary blindness in much academic work then played a major role in keeping the study of human rights rather narrowly confined—until politics, largely in the person of Jimmy Carter, brought it to the forefront of attention. But because the Carter human rights campaign was almost exclusively international, not national, the relative overemphasis on international action was actually strengthened.[9] Furthermore, students of comparative politics, law, and sociology could go about their work quite adequately without ever making explicit reference to internationally recognized human rights. Much of that work is indeed of central importance to the study of human rights, but because it has not been cast in such terms it has not been widely drawn upon by those who dominate the scholarly community in the field of human rights (principally internationalists, not comparativists).

I do not suggest that the international dimensions of human rights have been overstudied, but it is clear that the *national* dimensions have been woefully *under*studied. Two principal types of national-level work seem especially important: detailed case studies of human rights practices in particular countries, and explicitly comparative studies of practices in two or more countries.

Single-country studies have the advantage of allowing greater depth and detail. Furthermore, all other factors being equal, it is easier to do a single-country study than a multiple-country study. But single-country studies are too easily lost in the flood of publications, known only to other country specialists, and there are notorious problems in aggregating the lessons, or even just the information, of separate single-country studies. This suggests the importance of explicitly comparative studies. The cost of comparative work is likely to be much less detail and a less sure command of the material. But unless we are to say that every case is unique—in which case there is not much of general value to be learned—the explicit search for patterns and their underlying causes is absolutely essential. The comparison may involve pairs of countries (as in Chapter 10); a cluster of countries chosen on the basis of region (e.g., Howard 1986), regime type, or level of development; cross-national aggregate data studies (e.g, Arat

9. We might also add that, in the United States, deep-seated attitudes of American exceptionalism, combined with a belief that what occurs in the United States is almost by definition respect of human rights, also plays a significant role. Most Americans apparently believe that "human rights" problems exist only in places that must be reached by flying over large bodies of salt water.

1986; Henderson 1982; Park 1980, 1987); or some other basis of comparison. The key is to address directly and in a comparative fashion the central question: why do some societies widely respect human rights while others systematically violate them?

We should not stop studying the international dimensions of human rights, let alone give up pursuing human rights goals in national foreign policies and through international and regional regimes. But we must not forget that international mechanisms are at best supplemental to national endeavors. Furthermore, even specialists in international relations cannot successfully carry out studies of human rights independent of the work of students of national or comparative politics; even when the focus of our work is on the international dimensions of human rights, we must pay greater attention to the interaction of national and international factors in the success or failure of international initiatives. International factors are but a small and subsidiary part of the picture.

Thus this volume ends, appropriately, by once more emphasizing the interaction between the universality and the particularity of human rights. The moral universality of human rights, which has been codified in a strong set of authoritative international norms, must be realized through the particularities of national action.

References

Abi-Saab, Georges. 1980. "The Legal Formulation of a Right to Development." In Dupuy 1980.

Adelman, Irma. 1975. "Growth, Income Distribution, and Equity-Oriented Development Strategies." *World Development* 3 (February–March): 67–76.

———. 1980. "Economic Development and Political Change in Developing Countries." *Social Research* 47 (Summer): 213–34.

———, and Cynthia Taft Morris. 1973. *Economic Growth and Social Equity in Developing Countries*. Stanford, Calif.: Stanford University Press.

———, Cynthia Taft Morris, and Sherman Robinson. 1976. "Policies for Equitable Growth." *World Development* 4 (July): 561–82.

———, and Sherman Robinson. 1978. *Income Distribution Policy in Developing Countries: A Case Study of Korea*. Stanford, Calif.: Stanford University Press (for the World Bank).

Ahluwalia, Montek S. 1976. "Income Distribution and Development: Some Stylized Facts." *American Economic Review (Papers and Proceedings)* 66 (May): 128–35.

———, Nicholas G. Carter, and Hollis B. Chenery. 1979. "Growth and Poverty in Developing Countries." *Journal of Development Economics* 6 (September): 299–341.

Ajami, Fouad. 1978. *Human Rights and World Order Politics*. New York: Institute for World Order. Reprinted in Richard Falk, Samuel S. Kim, and Saul H. Mendlovitz, eds., *Toward a Just World Order*. Boulder, Colo.: Westview Press, 1982.

All Africa Council of Churches, World Council of Churches Human Rights Consultation. 1976. "Factors Responsible for the Violation of Human Rights in Africa." *Issue* 6 (Winter): 44–46.

Almond, Gabriel A. 1970. *Political Development: Essays in Heuristic Theory*. Boston, Mass.: Little, Brown.

Alston, Philip. 1981. "Prevention versus Cure as a Human Rights Strategy." In International Commission of Jurists, *Development, Human Rights, and the Rule of Law*. Elmsford, N.Y.: Pergamon Press.

———. 1982. "International Trade as an Instrument of Positive Human Rights Policy." *Human Rights Quarterly* 4 (May): 155–83.

———. 1984. "Conjuring up New Human Rights: A Proposal for Quality Control." *American Journal of International Law* 78 (July): 607–21.

———. 1987. "Out of the Abyss: The Challenges Confronting the New United Nations Committee on Economic, Social, and Cultural Rights." *Human Rights Quarterly* 9 (August): 332–81.

———. 1988. "Making Space for New Human Rights: The Case of the Right to Development." *Harvard Human Rights Yearbook* 1 (Spring): 3–40.

Alves, Maria Helena Moreira. 1985. *State and Opposition in Military Brazil*. Austin: University of Texas Press.

Americas Watch, Helsinki Watch, and the Lawyers' Committee for International Human Rights. 1984. ". . . *In the Face of Cruelty": The Reagan Administration's Human Rights Record in 1984*. New York: Americas Watch, Helsinki Watch, and the Lawyers' Committee for International Human Rights.

Amnesty International. 1981. *Republic of Korea: Violations of Human Rights, an Amnesty International Report* (ASA 25/22/81). London: Amnesty International.

Anon. 1986a. "Bihar: Agrarian Movement in Jehanabad." *Economic and Political Weekly* 21 (May 10): 813–15.

Anon. 1986b. "Bihar: Arwal Massacre—A Government Conspiracy? Report of an Investigation." *Economic and Political Weekly* 21 (May 31): 949–52.

Apter, David E. 1965. *The Politics of Modernization*. Chicago: University of Chicago Press.

Arat, Zehra F. 1986. "Human Rights and Democratic Instability in Developing Countries." *Policy Studies Journal* 15 (September): 158–72.

Arblaster, Anthony. 1984. *The Rise and Decline of Western Liberalism*. Oxford: Basil Blackwell.

Arendt, Hannah. 1951. *The Origins of Totalitarianism*. New York: Harcourt, Brace.

Asante, S. K. B. 1969. "Nation Building and Human Rights in Emergent Africa." *Cornell International Law Journal* 2 (Spring): 72–107.

Asia Watch Committee. 1985. *Human Rights in Korea*. New York: Asia Watch Committee.

Atal, Yogesh. 1968. *The Changing Frontiers of Caste*. Delhi: National Publishing House.

Austin, John. 1954. *The Province of Jurisprudence Determined*. New York: Noonday Press.

Baehr, Peter. 1982. "Concern for Development Aid and Fundamental Human Rights: The Dilemma as Faced by the Netherlands." *Human Rights Quarterly* 4 (February): 39–52.

Baloyra, Enrique A. 1986. "From Moment to Moment: The Political Transition in Brazil, 1977–1981." In Wayne A. Selcher, ed., *Political Liberalization in Brazil*. Boulder, Colo.: Westview Press, 1986.

Ban, Sung Hwan, Pal Young Moon, and Dwight H. Perkins. 1980. *Rural Development*. Cambridge, Mass.: Council on East Asian Studies, Harvard University.

Bay, Christian. 1977. "Human Needs and Political Education." In Ross Fitzgerald, ed., *Human Needs and Politics*. Rushcutters Bay, N.S.W., Australia: Pergamon Press, 1977.

———. 1980. "Peace and Critical Knowledge as Human Rights." *Political Theory* 8 (August): 293–318.

——. 1981. *Strategies of Political Emancipation*. Notre Dame, Ind.: University of Notre Dame Press.

——. 1982. "Self-Respect as a Human Right: Thoughts on the Dialectics of Wants and Needs in the Struggle for Human Community." *Human Rights Quarterly* 4 (February): 53–75.

Bayley, David H. 1964. *Public Liberties in the New States*. Chicago: Rand McNally.

Bedau, Hugo Adam. 1979. "Human Rights and Foreign Assistance Programs." In Brown and MacLean 1979.

Beddard, Ralph. 1980. *Human Rights and Europe: A Study of the Machinery of Human Rights Protection of the Council of Europe*. 2nd ed. London: Sweet and Maxwell.

Beitz, Charles. 1981. "Economic Rights and Distributive Justice in Developing Societies." *World Politics* 33 (April): 321–46.

Berlin, Isaiah. 1969. "Two Concepts of Liberty." In *Four Essays on Liberty*. London: Oxford University Press.

Beteille, André. 1965. *Caste, Class, and Power: Changing Patterns of Stratification in a Tanjore Village*. Berkeley: University of California Press.

——. 1969. *Castes, Old and New: Essays in Social Structure and Social Stratification*. Bombay: Asia Publishing House.

——. 1979. "*Homo Hierarchicus, Homo Equalis.*" *Modern Asian Studies* 13 (no. 4): 529–48.

——. 1983. *The Idea of Natural Inequality and Other Essays*. Delhi: Oxford University Press.

——, ed. 1983. *Equality and Inequality: Theory and Practice*. Delhi: Oxford University Press.

Bhagwati, Jagdish. 1966. *The Economics of Underdeveloped Countries*. New York: McGraw-Hill.

Bhatt, Anil. 1975. *Caste, Class, and Politics: An Empirical Profile of Social Stratification in Modern India*. Delhi: Manohar Book Service.

Borgstrom, Bengt-Erick. 1977. "On Rank and Hierarchy: Status in India and Elsewhere." *Archives européennes de sociologie* 18 (no. 2): 325–33.

Bouglé, Célestin. 1971 (1908). *Essays on the Caste System*. Cambridge: Cambridge University Press.

Boulding, Kenneth E. 1958. *Principles of Economic Policy*. Englewood Cliffs, N.J.: Prentice-Hall.

Boutros-Gali, B. 1982. "The League of Arab States." In Vasak and Alston 1982.

Bowett, Derek W. 1974. "The Interrelation of Theories of Intervention and Self-Defense." In John Norton Moore, ed., *Law and Civil War in the Modern World*. Baltimore, Md.: Johns Hopkins University Press.

Breman, Jan. 1985. " 'I Am the Government Labour Officer . . .': State Protection for Rural Proletariat of South Gujarat." *Economic and Political Weekly* 20 (June 15): 1043–55.

Brietzke, Paul H. 1985. "Consorting with the Chameleon, or Realizing the Right to Development." *California Western International Law Journal* 15 (Summer): 560–606.

Brown, Peter G., and Douglas MacLean, eds. 1979. *Human Rights and U.S. Foreign Policy: Principles and Applications*. Lexington, Mass.: Lexington Books.

Brownlie, Ian, ed. 1981. *Basic Documents on Human Rights*. 2nd ed. New York: Oxford University Press.

Buchheit, Lee C. 1978. *Secession: The Legitimacy of Self-Determination*. New Haven, Conn.: Yale University Press.

Buckley, William F., Jr. 1980. "Human Rights and Foreign Policy: A Proposal." *Foreign Affairs* 58 (Spring): 775–96.

Bull, Hedley. 1977. *The Anarchical Society: A Study of Order in World Politics*. New York: Columbia University Press.

Burlatsky, F. M., et al. 1982. *The Rights of the Individual in Socialist Society*. Moscow: Progress Publishers.

Butterfield, Herbert, and Martin Wight, eds. 1966. *Diplomatic Investigations*. London: Allen and Unwin.

Buultjens, Ralph. 1980. "Human Rights in Indian Political Culture." In Thompson 1980.

Callaghy, Thomas M. 1980. "State-Subject Communication in Zaire: Domination and the Concept of Domain Consensus." *Journal of Modern African Studies* 18 (September): 469–92.

Canak, William. 1984. "The Peripheral State Debate: State Capitalist and Bureaucratic-Authoritarian Regimes in Latin America." *Latin American Research Review* 19 (no. 1): 3–36.

Cardoso, Fernando H. 1986. "Entrepreneurs and the Transition Process: The Brazilian Case." In O'Donnell, Schmitter, and Whitehead 1986 (vol. 3 of paperback ed.).

——, and Enzo Faletto. 1979. *Dependence and Development in Latin America*. Berkeley: University of California Press.

Carleton, David, and Michael Stohl. 1985. "The Foreign Policy of Human Rights: Rhetoric and Reality from Jimmy Carter to Ronald Reagan: A Critique and Reappraisal." *Human Rights Quarterly* 7 (May): 205–29.

——. 1987. "The Role of Human Rights in U.S. Foreign Assistance." *American Journal of Political Science* 31 (November): 1002–18.

Cassese, Antonio. 1972. "The Admissibility of Communications on Human Rights." *Revue des droits de l'homme / Human Rights Journal* 5: 375–93.

——, and Edmond Jouve. 1978. *Pour un droit des peuples: Essais sur la Déclaration d'Alger*. N.p.: Berger-Levrault.

Chakravarti, Anand. 1983. "Some Aspects of Inequality in Rural India: A Sociological Perspective." In Beteille, ed., 1983

Chakravarti, Uma. 1985. "Towards a Historical Sociology of Stratification in Ancient India: Evidence from Buddhist Sources." *Economic and Political Weekly* 20 (March 2): 356–60.

Channa, V. C. 1979. *Caste: Identity and Continuity*. Delhi: B.R. Publishing Corp.

Chatterjee, Satischandra. 1950. *The Fundamentals of Hinduism: A Philosophical Study*. Calcutta: Das Gupta and Company.

Chethimattam, John B. 1971. *Patterns of Indian Thought*. Maryknoll, N.Y.: Orbis Books.

Chkhidvadze, V. 1980. "Constitution of True Human Rights and Freedoms." *International Affairs* (Moscow), October, pp. 13–20.

Claude, Richard Pierre. 1976. *Comparative Human Rights*. Baltimore, Md.: Johns Hopkins University Press.

Cline, William R. 1975. "Distribution and Development: A Survey of the Literature." *Journal of Development Economics* 1 (no. 4): 359–400.

Cobbah, Josiah A. M. 1987. "African Values and the Human Rights Debate: An African Perspective." *Human Rights Quarterly* 9 (August): 309–31.

Cohen, Roberta. 1979. "Human Rights Decision-Making in the Executive Branch: Some Proposals for a Coordinated Strategy." In Kommers and Loescher 1979.

———. 1982. "Human Rights Diplomacy: The Carter Administration and the Southern Cone." *Human Rights Quarterly* 4 (May): 212–42.

Cohen, Stephen B. 1982. "Conditioning U.S. Security Assistance on Human Rights Practices." *American Journal of International Law* 76 (April): 246–79.

Colclough, Christopher. 1982. "The Impact of Primary Schooling on Economic Development: A Review of the Evidence." *World Development* 10 (March): 167–86.

Collier, David, ed. 1979. *The New Authoritarianism in Latin America*. Princeton, N.J.: Princeton University Press.

Collier, Ruth Berins. 1982. "Popular Sector Incorporation and Political Supremacy: Regime Evolution in Brazil and Mexico." In Hewlett and Weinert 1982.

Commissioner for Scheduled Castes and Scheduled Tribes. 1981. *Report: 1979–80 and 1980–81 (Twenty-Seventh Report)*. New Delhi: Government of India Press.

Coomaraswamy, Radhika. 1982. "A Third-World View of Human Rights." *UNESCO Courier* 35 (August–September): 49–52.

Cranston, Maurice. 1964. *What Are Human Rights?* New York: Basic Books.

———. 1973. *What Are Human Rights?* London: The Bodley Head.

Das, Arvind N. 1986. "Bihar: Landowners' Armies Take over Law and Order." *Economic and Political Weekly* 21 (January 4): 15–18.

Dasgupta, Surendra Nath. 1969 (1922). *A History of Indian Philosophy*. Volume 1. Cambridge: Cambridge University Press.

Davis, Marvin. 1976. "A Philosophy of Hindu Rank from Rural West Bengal." *Journal of Asian Studies* 36 (November): 5–24.

deSchwinitz, Karl. 1964. *Industrialization and Democracy: Economic Necessities and Political Possibilities*. New York: The Free Press.

Domínguez, Jorge I. 1979. "Assessing Human Rights Conditions." In J. I. Domínguez et al., *Enhancing Global Human Rights*. New York: McGraw-Hill.

Donnelly, Jack. 1980. "Natural Law and Right in Aquinas' Political Thought." *Western Political Quarterly* 33 (December 1980): 520–35.

———. 1982. "How Are Rights and Duties Correlative?" *Journal of Value Inquiry* 16 (no. 4): 287–94.

———. 1985a. *The Concept of Human Rights*. New York: St. Martin's Press; London: Croom Helm.

———. 1985b. "In Search of the Unicorn: The Jurisprudence of the Right to Development" and "The Theology of the Right to Development: A Reply to Alston." *California Western International Law Journal* 15 (Summer 1985): 473–509, 519–23.

———. 1986. "International Human Rights: A Regime Analysis." *International Organization* 40 (Summer): 599–642.

———, and Rhoda E. Howard, eds. 1987. *International Handbook of Human Rights*. Westport, Conn.: Greenwood Press.

——, and Rhoda E. Howard. 1988. "Assessing National Human Rights Performance: A Theoretical Framework." *Human Rights Quarterly* 10 (May): 214–18.

Dumont, Louis. 1970. *Religion, Politics, and History in India*. Paris and The Hague: Mouton Publishers.

——. 1980. *Homo Hierarchicus: The Caste System and Its Implications*. Complete revised English edition. Chicago: University of Chicago Press.

Dupuy, René-Jean, ed. 1980. *Académie de Droit International de la Haye, Colloque 1979: Le Droit au développement au plan international*. Alphen aan den Rijn: Sijthoff and Noordhoff.

Dutta, Nilanjan. 1986. "Bihar: Arwal Massacre—Part of Government Plan." *Economic and Political Weekly* 21 (July 5): 1146–47.

Dworkin, Ronald. 1977. *Taking Rights Seriously*. Cambridge, Mass.: Harvard University Press.

——. 1985. *A Matter of Principle*. Cambridge, Mass.: Harvard University Press.

Egorov, Anatolii Grigorevich. 1979. "Socialism and the Individual: Rights and Freedoms." *Soviet Studies in Philosophy* 18 (no. 2): 3–51.

Enke, Stephen. 1963. *Economics for Development*. Englewood Cliffs, N.J.: Prentice-Hall.

Epstein, Edward C. 1984. "Legitimacy, Institutionalization, and Opposition in Exclusionary Bureaucratic-Authoritarian Regimes: The Situation of the 1980s." *Comparative Politics* 17 (October): 37–54.

European Commission of Human Rights. 1984. *Stocktaking on the European Convention on Human Rights*. Strasbourg: European Commission of Human Rights.

Evans, Peter. 1979. *Dependent Development: The Alliance of Multinational, State, and Local Capital in Brazil*. Princeton, N.J.: Princeton University Press.

Ewin, R. E. 1987. *Liberty, Community, and Justice*. Totowa, N.J.: Rowman and Littlefield.

Fairley, H. Scott. 1980. "State Actors, Humanitarian Intervention, and International Law: Reopening Pandora's Box." *Georgia Journal of International and Comparative Law* 10 (Winter): 29–63.

Farer, Tom J., ed. 1980a. *Toward a Humanitarian Diplomacy: A Primer for Policy*. New York: New York University Press.

——. 1980b. "Toward a Humanitarian Diplomacy: A Primer for Policy." In Farer 1980a.

——. 1985. "Human Rights and Human Wrongs: Is the Liberal Model Sufficient?" *Human Rights Quarterly* 7 (May): 189–204.

Feinberg, Joel. 1980. *Rights, Justice, and the Bounds of Liberty: Essays in Social Philosophy*. Princeton, N.J.: Princeton University Press.

Feitcher, Georges-André. 1975. *Brazil since 1964: Modernisation under a Military Regime*. London: Macmillan Company.

Fernandes, Florestan. 1966. "Economic Growth and Political Instability in Brazil." In Raymond Sayers, ed., *Portugal and Brazil in Transition*. Minneapolis: University of Minnesota Press.

Fields, Gary. 1977. "Who Benefits from Economic Development? A Reexamination of Brazilian Growth in the 1960s." *American Economic Review* 67 (September): 570–82.

———. 1980. *Poverty, Equality, and Development*. New York: Cambridge University Press.

Fischer, Dana D. 1982. "Reporting under the Covenant on Civil and Political Rights: The First Five Years of the Human Rights Committee." *American Journal of International Law* 76 (January): 142–53.

———. 1984. "International Reporting Procedures." In Hannum 1984.

Fishlow, Albert. 1972. "Brazilian Size Distribution of Income." *American Economic Review* 62 (May): 391–402.

Fonteyne, Jean-Pierre L. 1974. "The Customary International Law Doctrine of Humanitarian Intervention: Its Current Validity under the U.N. Charter." *California Western International Law Journal* 4 (Spring): 203–70.

Forsythe, David P. 1983. *Human Rights and World Politics*. Lincoln: University of Nebraska Press.

———. 1988. *Human Rights and U.S. Foreign Policy: Congress Reconsidered*. Gainesville: University of Florida Press.

Foxley, Alejandro. 1981. "Stabilization Policies and Their Effect on Employment and Income Distribution: A Latin American Perspective." In William R. Cline and Sidney Weintraub, eds., *Economic Stabilization in Developing Countries*. Washington, D.C.: Brookings Institution.

Franck, Thomas. 1981. " 'Congressional Imperialism' and Human Rights Policy." *The Yearbook of World Affairs 1981*. Boulder, Colo.: Westview Press.

———, and Nigel S. Rodley. 1973. "After Bangladesh: The Law of Humanitarian Intervention by Military Force." *American Journal of International Law* 67 (April): 275–305.

Frank, Andre Gunder. 1969. *Capitalism and Underdevelopment in Latin America: Historical Studies in Chile and Brazil*. New York: Monthly Review Press.

Frankel, Charles. 1978. "Human Rights and Foreign Policy." *Headline Series*, no. 241.

Fraser, Donald D. 1979. "Congress' Role in the Making of International Human Rights Policy." In Kommers and Loescher 1979.

Frieden, Jeffrey A. 1987. "The Brazilian Borrowing Experience: From Miracle to Debacle and Back." *Latin American Research Review* 22 (no. 1): 95–131.

Friedman, Julian R., and Marc I. Sherman, eds. 1985. *Human Rights: An International and Comparative Law Bibliography*. Westport, Conn.: Greenwood Press.

Friedmann, Wolfgang. 1971. "Intervention and International Law." In Louis G. M. Jaquet, ed., *Intervention in International Politics*. The Hague: Martinus Nijhoff.

Friedrich, Carl J., and Zbigniew K. Brzezinski. 1956. *Totalitarian Dictatorship and Autocracy*. Cambridge, Mass.: Harvard University Press.

Furtado, Celso. 1963. *The Economic Growth of Brazil*. Berkeley: University of California Press.

Galanter, Marc. 1984. *Competing Equalities: Law and the Backward Classes in India*. Berkeley: University of California Press.

Gallie, W. B. 1968. "Essentially Contested Concepts." In *Philosophy and the Historical Understanding*. New York: Schocken Books.

Gastil, Raymond D., ed. 1987. *Freedom in the World: Political Rights and Civil Liberties, 1986–1987*. Westport, Conn.: Greenwood Press (for Freedom House).

Gautam, Om P. 1982. "Human Rights in India." In Schwab and Pollis 1982.

Gerschenkron, Alexander. 1962. *Economic Backwardness in Historical Perspective.* Cambridge, Mass.: Harvard University Press.

Gewirth, Alan. 1984. *Human Rights: Essays on Justification and Applications.* Chicago: University of Chicago Press.

Ghose, Ajit, and Keith Griffin. 1980. "Rural Poverty and Development Alternatives in South and Southeast Asia: Some Policy Issues." *Development and Change* 11 (October): 545–72.

Gilbert, Felix. 1961. *To the Farewell Address: Ideas of Early American Foreign Policy.* Princeton, N.J.: Princeton University Press.

Gittleman, Richard. 1984. "The Banjul Charter on Human and Peoples' Rights: A Legal Analysis." In Welch and Meltzer 1984.

Goldstein, Robert Justin. 1983. *Political Repression in Nineteenth-Century Europe.* New York: Barnes and Noble.

———. 1987. "United States of America." In Donnelly and Howard 1987.

Goodel, Grace. 1985. "The Importance of Political Participation for Sustained Capitalist Development." *Archives européenne de sociologie* 26 (no. 1): 93–127.

Goodin, Robert E. 1979. "The Development-Rights Tradeoff: Some Unwarranted Economic and Political Assumptions." *Universal Human Rights* 1 (April): 31–42.

Graefrath, Bernhard. 1982. "The Right to Development in a World-Wide Debate." *GDR Committee for Human Rights Bulletin*, no. 1, pp. 11–13.

———. 1983. "Implementation of International Standards on Human Rights." *GDR Committee for Human Rights Bulletin*, no. 3, pp. 3–42.

Gramsci, Antonio. 1971. *Selections from the Prison Notebooks of Antonio Gramsci.* Edited by Quintin Hoare and Geoffrey Nowell Smith. New York: International Publishers.

Gray, John. 1986. *Liberalism.* Minneapolis: University of Minnesota Press.

Greenwold, Stephen Michael. 1975. "Kingship and Caste." *Archives européennes de sociologie* 16 (no. 1): 49–75.

Griffin, Keith, and Jeffrey James. 1981. *The Transition to Egalitarian Development: Economic Policies for Structural Change in the Third World.* New York: St. Martin's Press.

Gros Espiell, Hector. 1979. "The Evolving Concept of Human Rights: Western, Socialist, and Third World Approaches." In B. G. Ramcharan, ed., *Human Rights: Thirty Years after the Universal Declaration.* The Hague: Martinus Nijhoff.

Gupta, A. R. 1984. *Caste Hierarchy and Social Change.* New Delhi: Jyotsna Prakashan.

Gupta, Dipankar. 1980. "From Varna to Jati: The Indian Caste System, from the Asiatic to the Feudal Mode of Production." *Journal of Contemporary Asia* 10 (no. 3): 249–71.

Haas, Ernst B. 1964. *Beyond the Nation State.* Stanford, Calif.: Stanford University Press.

———. 1970. *Human Rights and International Action: The Case of Freedom of Association.* Stanford, Calif.: Stanford University Press.

———. 1980. "Why Collaborate? Issue Linkage and International Regimes." *World Politics* 32 (April): 357–405.

Haggard, Stephan, and Chung-In Moon. 1983. "The South Korean State in the International Economy: Liberal, Dependent, or Mercantile?" In John Gerard Ruggie, ed., *The Antinomies of Interdependence*. New York: Columbia University Press.

Haggard, Stephan, and Beth A. Simmons. 1987. "Theories of International Regimes." *International Organization* 41 (Summer): 491–517.

Hakim, Khalifa Abdul. 1955. *Fundamental Human Rights*. Lahore: Institute of Islamic Culture.

Han, Sung-Joo. 1988. "South Korea in 1987." *Asian Survey* 28 (January): 52–61.

Hannum, Hurst, ed. 1984. *Guide to International Human Rights Practice*. Philadelphia: University of Pennsylvania Press.

Haquani, Zalami. 1980. "Le Droit au développement: Fondements et sources." In Dupuy 1980.

Harkin, Tom. 1979. "Human Rights and Foreign Aid: Forging an Unbreakable Link." In Brown and MacLean 1979.

Hart, H. L. A. 1955. "Are There Any Natural Rights?" *Philosophical Review* 64: 175–91.

Hasan, Parvez. 1976. *Korea: Problems and Issues in a Rapidly Growing Economy*. Baltimore, Md.: Johns Hopkins University Press (for the World Bank).

———, and D. C. Rao, eds. 1979. *Korea: Policy Issues for Long-Term Development*. Baltimore, Md.: Johns Hopkins University Press (for the World Bank).

Hassan, Farooq. 1981. "Realpolitik in International Law: After Tanzanian-Ugandan Conflict 'Humanitarian Intervention' Reexamined." *Willamette Law Review* 17 (Fall): 859–912.

Hayek, F. A. 1960. *The Constitution of Liberty*. Chicago: University of Chicago Press.

[Heaps, David.] 1984. *Human Rights and U.S. Foreign Policy: The First Decade, 1973–1983*. New York: American Association for the International Commission of Jurists.

Heilbroner, Robert. 1963. *The Great Ascent*. New York: Harper and Row.

Henderson, Conway. 1982. "Military Regimes and Rights in Developing Countries: A Comparative Perspective." *Human Rights Quarterly* 4 (February): 110–23.

Herman, A. L. 1976. *An Introduction to Indian Thought*. Englewood Cliffs, N.J.: Prentice-Hall.

Herman, Edward S. 1982. *The Real Terror Network: Terrorism in Fact and Propaganda*. Boston, Mass.: South End Press.

Herz, John. 1976. *The Nation-State and the Crisis of World Politics*. New York: David McKay.

Hewlett, Sylvia Ann. 1980. *The Cruel Dilemmas of Development: Twentieth-Century Brazil*. New York: Basic Books.

———, and Richard S. Weinert, eds. 1982. *Brazil and Mexico: Patterns in Late Development*. Philadelphia, Pa.: Institute for the Study of Humane Issues.

Hicks, Norman L. 1984. "Is There a Trade-off between Growth and Basic Needs?" In Pradip K. Ghosh, ed., *Third World Development: A Basic Needs Approach*. Westport, Conn.: Greenwood Press.

Hiebert, Paul G. 1982. "India: The Politicization of a Sacred Society." In Carlo Caldarola, ed., *Religions and Societies: Asia and the Middle East*. Berlin: Mouton Publishers.

Higgins, Rosalyn. 1984. "The European Convention on Human Rights." In Meron 1984.

Hirschman, Albert O. 1981. *Essays in Trespassing: Economics to Politics and Beyond.* Cambridge: Cambridge University Press.

Hoffmann, Stanley. 1981. *Duties Beyond Borders: On the Limits and Possibilities of Ethical International Politics.* Syracuse, N.Y.: Syracuse University Press.

Horowitz, Asher, and Gad Horowitz. 1988. *"Everywhere They Are in Chains": Political Theory from Rousseau to Marx.* Scarborough, Ont.: Nelson Canada.

Horowitz, Irving Louis. 1982. *Beyond Empire and Revolution: Militarization and Consolidation in the Third World.* New York: Oxford University Press.

Houtart, François, and Genevieve Lemercinier. 1980. *The Great Asiatic Religions and Their Social Functions.* Louvain-la-Neuve: Centre de Recherches Socio-Religieuses, Université Catholique de Louvain.

Howard, Rhoda E. 1978. *Colonialism and Underdevelopment in Ghana.* London: Croom Helm.

———. 1983. "The Full-Belly Thesis: Should Economic Rights Take Priority over Civil and Political Rights?" *Human Rights Quarterly* 5 (November): 467–90.

———. 1984a. "Evaluating Human Rights in Africa: Some Problems of Implicit Comparisons." *Human Rights Quarterly* 6 (May): 160–79.

———. 1984b. "Women's Rights in English-Speaking Sub-Saharan Africa." In Welch and Meltzer 1984.

———. 1986. *Human Rights in Commonwealth Africa.* Totowa, N.J.: Rowman and Littlefield.

Huntington, Samuel P. 1968. *Political Order in Changing Societies.* New Haven, Conn.: Yale University Press.

———, and Joan M. Nelson. 1976. *No Easy Choice: Political Participation in Developing Countries.* Cambridge, Mass.: Harvard University Press.

Hutton, J. H. 1963. *Caste in India: Its Nature, Function, and Origins.* 4th ed. Bombay: Oxford University Press.

Hyden, Goran. 1983. *No Shortcuts to Progress: African Development Management in Perspective.* Berkeley: University of California Press.

Ishaque, Khalid M. 1974. "Human Rights in Islamic Law." *Review of the International Commission of Jurists* 12 (June): 30–39.

Ishwaran, K. 1980. "Bhakti Tradition and Modernization: The Case of *Lingayatism.*" *Journal of Asian and African Studies* 15 (no. 1–2): 72–82.

Jansen, Marius B. 1984. "Democracy vs. Centralism (Panel Discussion)." In Michio Nagai, ed., *Development in the Non-Western World.* Tokyo: United Nations University.

Jervis, Robert. 1978. "Cooperation under the Security Dilemma." *World Politics* 30 (January): 167–214.

Jhabvala, Farrokh. 1984. "The Practice of the Covenant's Human Rights Committee, 1976–82: Review of State Party Reports," *Human Rights Quarterly* 6 (February): 81–106.

Johnson, Harry G. 1962. *Money, Trade, and Economic Growth.* Cambridge, Mass.: Harvard University Press.

Joshi, Barbara. 1982. "Whose Law, Whose Order?: 'Untouchables,' Social Violence, and the State in India." *Asian Survey* 22 (July): 676–87.

Kannyo, Edward. 1984. "The Banjul Charter on Human and Peoples' Rights: Genesis and Political Background." In Welch and Meltzer 1984.

"K.B." 1985. "Andhra Pradesh: Indravelli 1985." *Economic and Political Weekly* 20 (May 25): 906–7.

Keenan, Edward L. 1980. "Human Rights in Soviet Political Culture." In Thompson 1980.

Keenleyside, Terry. 1988. "Human Rights and Foreign Aid in Canadian Policy." In Matthews and Pratt 1988.

Kennan, George F. 1985–86. "Morality and Foreign Policy." *Foreign Affairs* 64 (Winter): 205–18.

Keohane, Robert O. 1982. "The Demand for International Regimes." *International Organization* 36 (Spring): 325–55.

———. 1984. *After Hegemony*. Princeton, N.J.: Princeton University Press.

———, and Joseph S. Nye. 1977. *Power and Interdependence: World Politics in Transition*. Boston, Mass.: Little, Brown.

Keyes, Charles F., and E. Valentine Daniel, eds. 1983. *Karma: An Anthropological Inquiry*. Berkeley: University of California Press.

Khadduri, Majid. 1946. "Human Rights in Islam." *The Annals* 243 (January): 77–81.

Khil, Young Whan, and Dong Suh Bark. 1981. "Food Policies in a Rapidly Developing Country: The Case of South Korea." *Journal of Developing Areas* 16 (October): 47–70.

Khushalani, Yougindra. 1983. "Human Rights in Asia and Africa." *Human Rights Law Journal* 4: 403–442.

Kim, C. I. Eugene. 1981. "The Military-Civil Fusion as a Stable Political Model for Third World Nations." In Claude Heller, ed., *The Military as an Agent of Social Change*. Mexico City: El Colegio de México.

Kim, Kwang Suk, and Michael Roemer. 1979. *Growth and Structural Transformation*. Cambridge, Mass.: Council on East Asian Studies, Harvard University.

Kirkpatrick, Jeane J. 1979. "Dictatorships and Double Standards." *Commentary* 68 (November): 34–45.

———. 1981. "Establishing a Viable Human Rights Policy." *World Affairs* 143 (Spring): 323–34.

———. 1982. "Human Rights and Foreign Policy." In Fred E. Baumann, ed., *Human Rights and American Foreign Policy*. Gambier, Ohio: Public Affairs Conference Center of Kenyon College.

Kissinger, Henry A. 1978. "Continuity and Change in American Foreign Policy." In Said, ed., 1978.

Klare, Michael T., and Cynthia Arnson. 1981. *Supplying Repression: U.S. Support for Authoritarian Regimes Abroad*. Washington, D.C.: Institute for Policy Studies.

Klein, Martin. 1987. "Senegal." In Donnelly and Howard 1987.

Klenner, H. 1984. "Freedom and Human Rights." *GDR Committee for Human Rights Bulletin*, no. 10, pp. 13–21.

Kolenda, Pauline. 1978. *Caste in Contemporary India: Beyond Organic Solidarity*. Menlo Park, Calif.: Benjamin/Cummings Publishing Company.

Kommers, Donald P., and Gilburt D. Loescher, eds. 1979. *Human Rights and American Foreign Policy*. Notre Dame, Ind.: University of Notre Dame Press.

Krasner, Stephen D. 1978. "United States Commercial and Monetary Policy: Unravel-

ling the Paradox of External Strength and Internal Weakness." In Peter J. Katzen-
stein, ed., *Beyond Power and Plenty*. Madison: University of Wisconsin Press.

———, ed. 1983. *International Regimes*. Ithaca, N.Y.: Cornell University Press.

Krueger, Anne O. 1979. *The Developmental Role of the Foreign Sector and Aid*.
Cambridge, Mass.: Council on East Asian Studies, Harvard University.

Kuo, Shirley W. Y., Gustav Ranis, and John C. H. Fei. 1981. *The Taiwan Success
Story: Rapid Growth with Improved Distribution in the Republic of China*. Boulder,
Colo: Westview Press.

Kuper, Leo. 1981. *Genocide: Its Political Use in the Twentieth Century*. New Haven,
Conn.: Yale University Press.

Kuznets, Simon. 1955. "Economic Growth and Income Inequality." *American Economic Review* 45 (March): 1–28.

———. 1963. "Quantitative Aspects of the Economic Growth of Nations, VIII: The
Distribution of Income by Size." *Economic Development and Cultural Change* 11
(January): 1–80.

Lafer, Celso. 1984. "The Brazilian Political System: Trends and Perspectives." *Government and Opposition* 19 (Spring): 178–87.

Lamounier, Bolivar. 1984. "Opening through Elections: Will the Brazilian Case Be a
Paradigm?" *Government and Opposition* 19 (Spring): 167–77.

Laquer, Walter, and Barry N. Rubin, eds. 1979. *The Human Rights Reader*. New York:
New American Library.

Lawyers Committee for Human Rights and The Watch Committees. 1986. *The Reagan
Administration's Record on Human Rights in 1985*. New York: Lawyers Committee
for Human Rights and The Fund for Free Expression for The Watch Committees.

Lee, Eddy. 1979. "Egalitarian Peasant Farming and Rural Development: The Case of
South Korea." *World Development* 7 (April): 493–517.

Legesse, Asmarom. 1980. "Human Rights in African Political Culture." In Thompson
1980.

Lemos, Ramon. 1986. *Rights, Goods, and Democracy*. Newark: University of Dela-
ware Press.

Leng, Shao-chuan. 1980. "Human Rights in Chinese Political Culture." In Thompson
1980.

Le Vine, Victor T. 1980. "African Patrimonial Regimes in Comparative Perspective."
Journal of Modern African Studies 18 (December): 657–74.

Lieberam, Ekkehard. 1979. "Criticism of Bourgeois Attacks on Basic Rights in
Socialism." *GDR Committee for Human Rights Bulletin*, no. 3, pp. 12–23.

Lillich, Richard B. 1967. "Forcible Self-Help by States to Protect Human Rights."
Iowa Law Review 53 (October): 325–51.

———. 1970. "Forcible Self-Help under International Law." *Naval War College Review* 22: 56–66.

"Limburg Principles on the Implementation of the International Covenant on Economic, Social, and Cultural Rights." 1987. *Human Rights Quarterly* 9 (May): 122–
36 (UN document number E/CN.4/1987/17 Annex).

Linz, Juan J., and Alfred Stepan, eds. 1978. *The Breakdown of Democratic Regimes*.
Baltimore, Md.: Johns Hopkins University Press.

Lipset, Seymour Martin. 1959. "Some Social Requisites for Democracy: Economic

Development and Political Legitimacy.'' *American Political Science Review* 53 (March): 69–105.

Lo, Chung-Shu. 1949. ''Human Rights in the Chinese Tradition.'' In UNESCO 1949.

Locke, John. 1967 (1689). *Second Treatise of Government*. In Peter Laslett, ed., *Two Treatises of Government*. Cambridge: Cambridge University Press.

Lomasky, Loren. 1987. *Persons, Rights, and the Moral Community*. New York: Oxford University Press.

Lopatka, Adam. 1979. ''On the Notion of Human Rights.'' *GDR Committee for Human Rights Bulletin*, no. 4, pp. 5–11.

Lord, Carnes. 1984. ''Human Rights in a Nonliberal World.'' In Marc F. Plattner, ed., *Human Rights in Our Time: Essays in Memory of Victor Baras*. Boulder, Colo.: Westview Press.

Luard, Evan. 1981. *Human Rights and Foreign Policy*. Oxford: Pergamon Press (for the U.N. Association of Great Britain and Northern Ireland).

MacCallum, Gerald C., Jr. 1973. ''Negative and Positive Freedom.'' In Richard E. Flathman, ed., *Concepts in Social and Political Philosophy*. New York: Macmillan Company.

MacIntyre, Alisdair. 1981. *After Virtue*. Notre Dame, Ind.: Notre Dame University Press.

Macpherson, C. B. 1962. *The Political Theory of Possessive Individualism*. Oxford: Oxford University Press.

———. 1980. ''Introduction.'' In John Locke, *Second Treatise of Government*. Indianapolis, Ind.: Hackett Publishers.

Mahadevan, T. M. P. 1967. ''Social Ethics and Spiritual Values in Indian Philosophy.'' In Moore 1967.

Mandelbaum, David G. 1970. *Society in India*. Berkeley: University of California Press.

Manglapus, Raul. 1978. ''Human Rights Are Not a Western Discovery.'' *Worldview* 4 (October): 4–6.

Mansfield, Harvey C., Jr. 1978. *The Spirit of Liberalism*. Cambridge, Mass.: Harvard University Press.

Manu. 1886. *The Laws of Manu*. Translated by G. Buhler. Oxford: Clarendon Press.

Marasinghe, Lakshman. 1984. ''Traditional Conceptions of Human Rights in Africa.'' In Welch and Meltzer 1984.

Markovitz, Irving Leonard. 1977. *Power and Class in Africa*. Englewood Cliffs, N.J.: Prentice-Hall.

Marks, Stephen P. 1981. ''Emerging Human Rights: A New Generation for the 1980s?'' *Rutgers Law Review* 33 (Winter): 435–52.

Marriott, McKim. 1960. *Caste Ranking and Community Structure in Five Regions of India and Pakistan*. Monograph Series, no. 23. Poona: Deccan College.

Martin, Rex. 1980. ''Human Rights and Civil Rights.'' *Philosophical Studies* 37: 391–403.

Martins, Luciano. 1976. *Pouvoir et développement economique: Formation et évolution des structures politiques au Brésil*. Paris: Editions Anthropos.

Marx, Karl. 1975. *Collected Works*. New York: International Publishers.

Mason, Edward S., Mahn Je Kim, Dwight H. Perkins, Kwang Suk Kim, and David C.

Cole. 1980. *The Economic and Social Modernization of the Republic of Korea.* Cambridge, Mass.: Council on East Asian Studies, Harvard University.

Matthews, Robert, and Cranford Pratt. 1985. "Human Rights and Foreign Policy: Principles and Canadian Practice." *Human Rights Quarterly* 7 (May): 159–88.

——, eds. 1988. *Canadian Foreign Policy and Human Rights.* Montreal: McGill-Queens University Press.

Mawdudi, Abul A'la. 1976. *Human Rights in Islam.* Leicester: Islamic Foundation.

Mayall, James. 1986. "The United States." In Vincent 1986b.

M'Baye, Kéba. 1980. "Le Droit au développement." In Dupuy 1980.

McDonough, Peter. 1981. *Power and Ideology in Brazil.* Princeton, N.J.: Princeton University Press.

McKeown, Timothy J. 1983. "Hegemonic Stability and Nineteenth-Century Tariff Levels in Europe." *International Organization* 37 (Winter): 73–91.

Melden, A. I. 1977. *Rights and Persons.* Berkeley: University of California Press.

Meron, Theodor, ed. 1984. *Human Rights in International Law: Legal and Policy Issues.* Oxford: Clarendon Press.

Michie, Barry H. 1981. "The Transformation of Agrarian Patron-Client Relations: Illustrations from India." *American Ethnologist* 8 (February): 21–40.

Miller, Stefania Szlek. 1988. "Canadian Foreign Policy and Human Rights: The Polish Case." In Matthews and Pratt 1988.

Milne, A. J. M. 1986. *Human Rights and Human Diversity: An Essay in the Philosophy of Human Rights.* Albany: State University of New York Press.

Mises, Ludwig von. 1985 (1928). *Liberalism in the Classical Tradition.* San Francisco, Calif.: Cobden Press.

Mitra, Kana. 1982. "Human Rights in Hinduism." *Journal of Ecumenical Studies* 19 (Summer): 77–84.

Mojekwu, Chris E. 1980. "International Human Rights: The African Perspective." In Jack L. Nelson and Vera M. Green, eds., *International Human Rights: Contemporary Issues.* Stanfordville, N.Y.: Human Rights Publishing Group.

Moore, Barrington, Jr. 1966. *Social Origins of Dictatorship and Democracy.* Boston, Mass.: Beacon Press.

Moore, Charles A., ed. 1967. *The Indian Mind: Essentials of Indian Philosophy and Culture.* Honolulu: University of Hawaii Press.

Moore, John Norton. 1967. "Comments." *American Society of International Law, Proceedings* 61: 76.

Morawetz, David. 1981. *Why the Emperor's New Clothes Are Not Made in Colombia: A Case Study of Latin American and East Asian Manufactured Exports.* Staff Working Paper no. 368. Washington, D.C.: World Bank.

Moreira, Marcilio Marques. 1984. "Political Liberalization and Economic Crisis." *Government and Opposition* 19 (Spring): 153–66.

Morgenthau, Hans J. 1946. *Scientific Man versus Power Politics.* Chicago: University of Chicago Press.

——. 1954. *Politics among Nations: The Struggle for Power and Peace.* 2nd ed. New York: Alfred A. Knopf.

——. 1962a. *Politics in the Twentieth Century*, Vol. 1: *The Decline of Democratic Politics.* Chicago: University of Chicago Press.

———. 1962b. *Politics in the Twentieth Century*, Vol. 3: *The Restoration of American Politics*. Chicago: University of Chicago Press.

———. 1970. *Truth and Power: Essays of a Decade, 1960–1970*. New York: Praeger Publishers.

———. 1979. *Human Rights and Foreign Policy*. New York: Council on Religion and International Affairs.

Morriss, Bruce R. 1967. *Economic Growth and Development*. New York: Pitman Publishing.

Morsink, Johannes. 1987. "Review of Jack Donnelly, *The Concept of Human Rights*." *Human Rights Quarterly* 9 (August): 438–43.

Mouzelis, Nicos P. 1986. *Politics in the Semi-Periphery: Early Parliamentarism and Late Industrialization in the Balkans and Latin America*. New York: St. Martin's Press.

Mower, A. Glenn, Jr. 1987. *Human Rights and American Foreign Policy: The Carter and Reagan Experiences*. Westport, Conn.: Greenwood Press.

Nadvi, Syed Muzaffar-ud-Din. 1966. *Human Rights and Obligations (in the Light of the Qur'an and Hadith)*. Dacca: S. M. Zahhirullah Nadvi.

Nanda, Ved P. 1987. "Keynote Address." Conference on Human Rights and Development in South Asia, State University of New York at Buffalo, March 6.

Nardin, Terry. 1983. *Law, Morality, and the Relations of States*. Princeton, N.J.: Princeton University Press.

Narveson, Jan. 1981. "Human Rights: Which, If Any, Are There?" In J. Roland Pennock and John W. Chapman, eds., *Human Rights*. New York: New York University Press.

Nickel, James W. 1987. *Making Sense of Human Rights: Philosophical Reflections on the Universal Declaration of Human Rights*. Berkeley: University of California Press.

Nikhilananda, Swami. 1958. *Hinduism: Its Meaning for the Liberation of the Spirit*. New York: Harper and Brothers.

Nolan, Cathal. 1988. "Canada at the Commission on Human Rights." In Matthews and Pratt 1988.

Nozick, Robert. 1974. *Anarchy, State, and Utopia*. New York: Basic Books.

Nugent, Jeffrey B., and Robin Walther. 1982. "Short-Run Changes in Rural Income Inequality: A Decomposition Analysis." *Journal of Development Studies* 18 (January): 239–69.

O'Donnell, Guillermo. 1973. *Modernization and Bureaucratic Authoritarianism: Studies in South American Politics*. Berkeley, Calif.: Institute of International Studies.

———, Phillipe C. Schmitter, and Lawrence Whitehead, eds. 1986. *Transitions from Authoritarian Rule: Prospects for Democracy*. Baltimore, Md.: Johns Hopkins University Press.

O'Flaherty, Wendy Doniger, ed. 1980. *Karma and Rebirth in Classical Indian Traditions*. Berkeley: University of California Press.

Ojo, Olusola, and Amadou Sessay. 1986. "The O.A.U. and Human Rights: Prospects for the 1980s and Beyond." *Human Rights Quarterly* 8 (February): 89–103.

Organ, Troy Wilson. 1974. *Hinduism: Its Historical Development.* Woodbury, N.Y.: Barron's Educational Series.

———. 1975. *Western Approaches to Eastern Philosophy.* Athens: Ohio University Press.

Organski, A. F. K. 1965. *The Stages of Political Development.* New York: Alfred A. Knopf.

Overholt, William H. 1978. *The Future of Brazil.* Boulder, Colo.: Westview Press.

Packenham, Robert A. 1986. "Capitalist Dependency and Socialist Dependency: The Case of Cuba." In Jan F. Triska, ed., *Dominant Powers and Subordinate States: The United States in Latin America and the Soviet Union in Eastern Europe.* Durham, N.C.: Duke University Press.

Pagels, Elaine. 1979. "The Roots and Origins of Human Rights." In Alice H. Henkin, ed., *Human Dignity: The Internationalization of Human Rights.* New York: Aspen Institute for Humanistic Studies; Dobbs Ferry, N.Y.: Ocean Publications.

Paine, Thomas. 1945. *The Collected Writings of Thomas Paine.* Edited by Philip S. Foner. New York: Citadel Press.

Pandeya, R. C. 1986. "Human Rights: An Indian Perspective." In UNESCO 1986.

Park, Han S. 1980. "Human Rights and Modernization: A Dialectical Relationship." *Universal Human Rights* 2 (January–March): 85–92.

———. 1987. "Correlates of Human Rights: Global Tendencies." *Human Rights Quarterly* 9 (August): 405–13.

Paukert, Felix. 1973. "Income Distribution at Different Levels of Development: A Survey of Evidence." *International Labour Review* 108 (August–September): 99–125.

Piscatori, James P. 1980. "Human Rights in Islamic Political Culture." In Thompson 1980.

Pollis, Adamantia. 1982. "Liberal, Socialist, and Third World Perspectives on Human Rights." In Schwab and Pollis 1982.

———, and Peter Schwab, eds. 1980. *Human Rights: Cultural and Ideological Perspectives.* New York: Praeger Publishers.

Pomerance, Michla. 1982. *Self-Determination in Law and Practice: The New Doctrine of the United Nations.* The Hague: Martinus Nijhoff.

Prachand, S. L. M. 1979. *Mob Violence in India.* Chandigarh: Abhishek Publications.

Putambekar, S. V. 1949. "The Hindu Concept of Human Rights." In UNESCO 1949.

Pye, Lucian W. 1966. *Aspects of Political Development.* Boston, Mass.: Little, Brown.

Rabkin, Rhoda. 1987. "Cuba." In Donnelly and Howard 1987.

Rajaraman, Indira. 1976. "Data Sources on Income Distribution in Bangladesh, India, Pakistan, and Sri Lanka: An Evaluation." *Review of Income and Wealth* 22 (September): 223–38.

Rao, D. C. 1978. "Economic Growth and Equity in the Republic of Korea." *World Development* 6 (March): 383–96.

Rawls, John. 1971. *A Theory of Justice.* Cambridge, Mass.: Harvard University Press.

Regehr, Ernest. 1988. "Arms Sales and Human Rights." In Matthews and Pratt 1988.

Reiter, Randy B., M. V. Zunzunegui, and José Quiroga. 1986. "Guidelines for Field Reporting of Basic Human Rights Violations." *Human Rights Quarterly* 8 (November): 628–53.

Remmer, Karen L. 1985. "Redemocratization and the Impact of Authoritarian Rule in Latin America." *Comparative Politics* 17 (April): 253–75.

Renteln, Alison Dundes. 1985. "The Unanswered Challenge of Relativism and the Consequences for Human Rights." *Human Rights Quarterly* 7 (November): 514–40.

Richards, Gordon, 1986. "Stabilization Crises and the Breakdown of Military Authoritarianism in Latin America." *Comparative Political Studies* 18 (January): 449–85.

Richman, Paula, and Michael Fisher. 1980. "Sources and Strategies for the Study of Women in India." *Journal of Ethnic Studies* 8 (Fall): 123–41.

Riggs, Fred W. 1963. "Bureaucrats and Political Development: A Paradoxical View." In Joseph LaPalombara, ed., *Bureaucracy and Political Development*. Princeton, N.J.: Princeton University Press.

Robertson, A. H. 1982. *Human Rights in the World*. 2nd ed. New York: St. Martin's Press.

Robock, Stefan H. 1975. *Brazil: A Study in Development Progress*. Lexington, Mass.: Lexington Books.

Roett, Riordan. 1984. *Brazil: Politics in a Patrimonial Society*. 3rd ed. New York: Praeger Publishers.

Rogers, Gerry B. 1978. "Demographic Determinants of the Distribution of Income." *World Development* 6 (March): 305–18.

Roxborough, Ian. 1979. *Theories of Underdevelopment*. London: Macmillan Company.

Ruffin, Patricia. 1982. "Socialist Development and Human Rights in Cuba." In Schwab and Pollis 1982.

Ruggie, John Gerard. 1982. "International Regimes, Transactions, and Change: Embedded Liberalism in the Postwar Economic Order." *International Organization* 36 (Spring): 379–415.

Said, Abdul Aziz. 1978. "Pursuing Human Dignity." In Said, ed., 1978.

——, ed. 1978. *Human Rights and World Order*. New York: Praeger Publishers.

——. 1979. "Precept and Practice of Human Rights in Islam." *Universal Human Rights* 1 (April): 63–80.

——. 1980. "Human Rights in Islamic Perspectives." In Pollis and Schwab 1980.

Saksena, S. K. 1967. "The Individual in Social Thought and Practice." In Moore 1967.

Sandel, Michael. 1984. *Liberalism and Its Critics*. New York: New York University Press.

Sanson, H. 1980. "Du droit des peuples sous-développés au développement au droits des hommes et des communautés à être soi, non seulement par soi, mais aussi par autres." In Dupuy 1980.

Sawczuk, Konstantyn. 1979. "Soviet Juridical Interpretation of International Documents on Human Rights." *Survey* 24 (Spring): 86–91.

Schlesinger, Arthur, Jr. 1979. "Human Rights and the American Tradition." *Foreign Affairs* 57 (no. 3): 503–26.

Schmitter, Phillipe C. 1974. "Still the Century of Corporatism?" *Review of Politics* 36 (January): 85–131.

Schoultz, Lars. 1981. *Human Rights and United States Policy toward Latin America*. Princeton, N.J.: Princeton University Press.

Schwab, Peter, and Adamantia Pollis, eds. 1982. *Toward a Human Rights Framework*. New York: Praeger Publishers.

Senart, Emile. 1975 (1896). *Caste in India: The Facts and the System*. New Delhi: Ess Ess Publications.

Shah, Vimal P., ed. 1980. *Removal of Untouchability: Proceedings of a Seminar*. Ahmedabad: Gujarat University Press.

Shapiro, Ian. 1986. *The Evolution of Rights in Liberal Theory*. Cambridge: Cambridge University Press.

Sharma, Miriam. 1985. "Caste, Class, and Gender: Production and Reproduction in North India." *Journal of Peasant Studies* 12 (July): 57–88.

Shatrunga, M. 1985. "Andhra Pradesh: Police Killing of Political Activists in Kondapur." *Economic and Political Weekly* 20 (April 27): 748–49.

Shelton, Dinah L. 1984. "Individual Complaint Machinery under the United Nations 1503 Procedure and the Optional Protocol to the International Covenant on Civil and Political Rights." In Hannum 1984.

Shivji, Issa G. 1976. *Class Struggles in Tanzania*. London: Heinemann.

Shue, Henry. 1979. "Rights in the Light of Duties." In Brown and MacLean 1979.

——. 1980. *Basic Rights: Subsistence, Affluence, and U.S. Foreign Policy*. Princeton, N.J.: Princeton University Press.

Sinari, Ramakant A. 1970. *The Structure of Indian Thought*. Springfield, Ill.: Charles C. Thomas.

Sinha, Umesh. 1985. "Bihar: Teaching the Landless a Lesson." *Economic and Political Weekly* 20 (March 2): 343–44.

Skalnes, Tor, and Jan Egeland, eds. 1986. *Human Rights in Developing Countries, 1986*. Oslo: Norwegian University Press.

Skocpol, Theda. 1979. *States and Social Revolutions*. Cambridge: Cambridge University Press.

Slater, Jerome, and Terry Nardin. 1986. "Nonintervention and Human Rights." *Journal of Politics* 48 (February): 86–96.

Snidal, Duncan. 1985. "The Limits of Hegemonic Stability Theory." *International Organization* 39 (Autumn): 579–614.

Soedjatmoko. 1985. *The Primacy of Freedom in Development*. Lanham, Md.: University Press of America.

Sohn, Louis B., and Thomas Buergenthal, eds. 1973. *Basic Documents on International Protection of Human Rights*. Indianapolis, Ind.: Bobbs-Merrill.

Somerville, John. 1949. "Comparison of Soviet and Western Democratic Principles, with Special Reference to Human Rights." In UNESCO 1949.

Srinivas, M. N. 1966. *Social Change in Modern India*. Berkeley: University of California Press.

——. 1977. "The Changing Position of Indian Women." *Man*, n.s. 12 (August): 221–38.

Stackhouse, Max L. 1984. *Creeds, Society, and Human Rights: A Study in Three Cultures*. Grand Rapids, Mich.: William B. Eerdmans.

Starck, Christian. 1982. "Europe's Fundamental Rights in Their Newest Garb." *Human Rights Law Journal* 3: 103–40.

Stein, Arthur A. 1984. "The Hegemon's Dilemma: Great Britain, the United States, and the International Economic Order." *International Organization* 38 (Spring): 355–86.

Stewart, Frances. 1985. *Basic Needs in Developing Countries*. Baltimore, Md.: Johns Hopkins University Press.

Stohl, Michael, David Carleton, and Steven E. Johnson. 1984. "Human Rights and U.S. Foreign Assistance: From Nixon to Carter." *Journal of Peace Research* 21 (no. 3): 215–26.

Stowell, Ellery C. 1921. *Intervention in International Law*. Washington, D.C.: John Byrne Co.

Strauss, Leo. 1953. *Natural Right and History*. Chicago: University of Chicago Press.

Swepson, Lee. 1984. "Human Rights Complaints Procedures of the International Labor Organization." In Hannum 1984.

Tabendeh, Sultanhussein. 1970. *A Muslim Commentary on the Universal Declaration of Human Rights*. London: F. T. Goulding and Company.

Taylor, Charles. 1979. "What's Wrong with Negative Liberty." In Alan Ryan, ed., *The Idea of Freedom: Essays in Honour of Isaiah Berlin*. Oxford: Oxford University Press.

Taylor, Lance, Edmar L. Bacha, Eliana Cardoso, and Frank J. Lysy. 1980. *Models of Growth and Distribution for Brazil*. New York: Oxford University Press (for the World Bank).

Thapar, Romila. 1966. "The Hindu and Buddhist Traditions." *International Social Science Journal* 18 (no. 1): 31–40.

Thomas, Clive Y. 1984. *The Rise of the Authoritarian State in Peripheral Societies*. New York: Monthly Review Press.

Thompson, E. P. 1963. *The Making of the English Working Class*. New York: Vintage Books.

Thompson, Kenneth W., ed. 1980. *The Moral Imperatives of Human Rights: A World Survey*. Washington, D.C.: University Press of America.

Tolley, George S., Vinod Thomas, and Chung Ming Wong. 1982. *Agricultural Price Policies and the Developing Countries*. Baltimore, Md.: Johns Hopkins University Press (for the World Bank).

Tolley, Howard, Jr. 1987. *The United Nations Commission on Human Rights*. Boulder, Colo.: Westview Press.

UNESCO. 1949. *Human Rights: Comments and Interpretations*. London: Allan Wingate.

———. 1986. *Philosophical Foundations of Human Rights*. Paris: UNESCO.

Valticos, Nicolas. 1982. "The International Labor Organization." In Vasak and Alston 1982.

Vasak, Karel. 1982. "The Council of Europe." In Vasak and Alston 1982.

———. 1984. "Pour une troisième génération des droits de l'homme." In C. Swinarski, ed., *Essays on International Humanitarian Law and Red Cross Principles in Honour of Jean Pictet*. The Hague: Martinus Nijhoff.

———, and Philip Alston, eds. 1982. *The International Dimensions of Human Rights*. Westport, Conn.: Greenwood Press.

Vincent, R. J. 1986a. *Human Rights and International Relations*. Cambridge: Cambridge University Press (for the Royal Institute of International Affairs).

——, ed. 1986b. *Foreign Policy and Human Rights*. Cambridge: Cambridge University Press (for the Royal Institute of International Affairs).

Vogelgesang, Sandra. 1978. "What Price Principle: U.S. Policy on Human Rights." *Foreign Affairs* 56 (July): 819–41.

——. 1980. "Domestic Politics Behind Human Rights Diplomacy." In Farer 1980a.

Wai, Dunstan M. 1980. "Human Rights in Sub-Saharan Africa." In Pollis and Schwab 1980.

Wallerstein, Immanuel. 1974. *The Modern World System*. New York: Academic Press.

Walzer, Michael. 1977. *Just and Unjust Wars*. New York: Basic Books.

——. 1980. "The Moral Standing of States: A Response to Four Critics." *Philosophy and Public Affairs* 9 (Spring): 209–29.

Weber, Max. 1946. *From Max Weber: Essays in Sociology*. Edited by Hans Heinrich Gerth and C. Wright Mills. New York: Oxford University Press.

Weichelt, Wolfgang. 1979. "Some Observations on the Notion of Human Rights." *GDR Committee for Human Rights Bulletin*, no. 2, pp. 3–15.

Weissbrodt, David. 1977. "Human Rights Legislation and United States Foreign Policy." *Georgia Journal of International and Comparative Law* 7, Supplement, pp. 231–87.

——. 1981. "The Influence of Interest Groups on the Development of United States Human Rights Policies." In Natalie Kaufman Hevener, ed., *The Dynamics of Human Rights in U.S. Foreign Policy*. New Brunswick, N.J.: Transaction Books.

——. 1986. "The Three 'Theme' Special Rapporteurs of the U.N. Commission on Human Rights." *American Journal of International Law* 80 (July): 685–99.

Welch, Claude E., and Ronald I. Meltzer, eds. 1984. *Human Rights and Development in Africa*. Albany: State University of New York Press.

West, James M., and Edward J. Baker. 1988. "The 1987 Constitutional Reforms in South Korea: Electoral Procedures and Judicial Independence." *Harvard Human Rights Yearbook* 1 (Spring): 135–77.

White, Benjamin. 1979. "Political Aspects of Poverty, Income Distribution, and Their Management: Some Examples from Rural Java." *Development and Change* 10 (January): 91–114.

Wiarda, Howard J. 1982. "Democracy and Human Rights in Latin America: Toward a New Conceptualization." In Howard J. Wiarda, ed., *Human Rights and U.S. Human Rights Policy*. Washington, D.C.: American Enterprise Institute.

Wieruszewski, Roman. 1988. "The Evolution of the Socialist Concept of Human Rights." *SIM Newsletter / Netherlands Quarterly of Human Rights* 6 (no. 1): 27–37.

Wolf, Francis. 1984. "Human Rights and the International Labor Organization." In Meron 1984.

Wolin, Sheldon. 1960. *Politics and Vision*. Boston, Mass.: Little, Brown.

World Bank. 1981. *World Development Report 1981*. New York: Oxford University Press.

——. 1982. *World Development Report 1982*. New York: Oxford University Press.

——. 1984. *World Development Report 1984*. New York: Oxford University Press.

——. 1986. *World Development Report 1986*. New York: Oxford University Press.

——. 1987. *World Development Report 1987*. New York: Oxford University Press.

——. 1988. *World Development Report 1988*. New York: Oxford University Press.

Yamane, Hiroko. 1987. "Approaches to Human Rights in Asia." In Rudolf Bernhardt and John Anthony Jolowicz, eds., *International Enforcement of Human Rights*. Berlin: Springer-Verlag.

Yamani, Ahmad Zaki. 1968. *Islamic Law and Contemporary Issues*. Jidda: Saudi Publishing House.

Young, Oran. 1980. "International Regimes: Problems of Concept Formation." *World Politics* 32 (April): 331–56.

——. 1986. "International Regimes: Toward a New Theory of Institutions." *World Politics* 39 (October): 104–22.

Zakaria, Fouad. 1986. "Human Rights in the Arab World: The Islamic Context." In UNESCO 1986.

Zimmer, Heinrich. 1951. *Philosophies of India*. London: Routledge and Kegan Paul.

Zolberg, Aristide R. 1966. *Creating Political Order: The Party-States of West Africa*. Chicago: Rand McNally.

Zuijdwijk, Ton J. 1982. *Petitioning the United Nations: A Study in Human Rights*. Aldershot, Hampshire: Gower.

Index

Aboriginal rights, 152–54
Adelman, Irma, 170n.12
African Charter on Human and Peoples' Rights, 217
Ajami, Fouad, 41–42
Autonomy, 68–73, 83–87

Basic rights, 37–45
Bay, Christian, 17
Bedau, Hugo Adam, 33, 34, 41
Being right (versus having a right), 9–10
Brazil, 166–69, 181–82, 198–200
Buckley, William F., 236, 244n.18

Carleton, David, and Michael Stohl, 243–44
Caste, 125–42
    class, and political violence, 139–41
    essential features, 127–32
    flexibility and rigidity, 132–34
    human nature and, 135–36
    and politics, 136–42
Cohen, Roberta, 242–44
Cohen, Stephen B., 244
Commission on Human Rights (U.N.), 206–8
Commission on the Status of Women (U.N.), 222
Committee against Torture, 221, 252–58
Committee on the Elimination of Discrimination against Women, 222
Committee on the Elimination of Racial Discrimination, 220
Communism, 55–57, 77–80, 237–41
Communitarian societies, 75–87
Convention against Torture, 221, 250–57
Corporatism, 80–82
Cranston, Maurice, 26, 31–34, 89n.3
Cultural relativism, 3–4, 60–65, 109–24, 135–37, 143ff., 160, 234–35

internal versus external judgments, 114–16, 136–37
types, 109–18
Cultural rights, 154–60

Development (economic)
    and legitimacy, 194–200
    stages, 191–94
    strategies, 163–66, 178–81, 185–87
Development dictatorship, 82–83
Development-rights trade-offs, 163–202
    in Brazil, 166–69, 181–82
    conventional wisdom about, 163–66, 169, 179–80
    "growth first" strategy, 179–81
    inclusion and exclusion, 185–87
    in Korea, 170–78, 181–84
    liberty, 165, 184–202
    needs and equality, 166–80
Duties (and rights), 50–57, 72, 126, 145
Dworkin, Ronald, 10, 68

Economic and social rights, 26, 28–37, 84–86, 96, 101–4, 166–83, 237–41
Entitlement. See Having a right
Equal concern and respect, 68–73, 87, 101, 103, 105
Equality trade-off, 164–83
European Commission of Human Rights, 213–14
Exclusionary regimes, 185–86

Fascism, 81
Feinberg, Joel, 10, 15
1503 Procedure, 206–7, 226, 256–57
Foreign aid, 243–45

Gilbert, Felix, 236

Graduation (newly industrializing countries), 193–98
Group rights, 149–54

Having a right, 9–12
versus enjoying its substance, 38–40, 79, 84–87
Hegemony (and international regimes), 216–17, 226–27
Howard, Rhoda E., ix, 66, 124, 137n.13
Human dignity, 2–3, 17–18, 25–27, 41, 49–87, 113–14, 121–24, 135
Humanitarian intervention, 260–64
Human nature, 17–19, 21–23, 111–12, 130, 135–36
Human rights
caste and, 125–42
collective, 19–21, 143–54
communitarianism and, 75–87
complaints (international), 206–10, 214, 216, 256–58
concept of, 9–27, 50n.1
and development, 163–202
economic and social rights, 26, 28–37, 166–83, 237–41
evolution of lists of, 25–31
and foreign aid, 243–45
and foreign policy, 41–44, 229–49, 259–66
and human dignity. *See* Human dignity
inalienability, 19
interdependence and indivisibility, 28–45
international consensus on, 42–43, 58, 113, 121–22
international norms, 23–25
and liberalism, 66–106
non-Western conceptions, 2, 49–65
African, 53–54
Chinese, 54–55
Indian, 125–37
Islamic, 50–53
Soviet, 55–57, 77–80
regimes. *See* International human rights regimes; *entries for particular types*
reporting on (international), 208–10, 214, 219–21, 252–56
"seatbelt" metaphor, 64–65
source, 16–19
special features, 12–16
subjects, 19–21
substance, 38–40, 79, 84–87
third generation, 143–47
See also Rights
Human Rights Committee, 208–10, 254, 257–58

Individualism (individual rights), 19–21, 57–60, 69–71, 84–87, 90–100, 147–52, 156–58
Industrialization, 192–93
Inter-American Commission of Human Rights, 216
Interdependence (and international regimes), 211–13
International Human Rights Covenants, 24–25, 205–6 (1966–)
International human rights regimes, 205–28
African, 217–18
European, 213–15
evolution of, 210–13, 223–28
global, 206–13
Inter-American, 215–16
racial discrimination, 220–21
torture, 221, 250–58
women's rights, 221–23
workers' rights, 219–20
International Labor Organization, 216
Intervention. *See* Nonintervention
Ishaque, Khalid, 51

Kennan, George F., 231–32, 234
Keohane, Robert O., 210, 213
Khadduri, Majid, 51–52
Khushalani, Yogindra, 49, 126
Kirkpatrick, Jeane J. 237–41
Korea, South (R.O.K.), 170–78, 181–84
basic needs, 171–72, 175
income distribution in, 170–71
industrialization strategy, 174–75
repression in, 176, 184, 189, 200
rural development, 172–73
Krasner, Stephen D., 205n.1, 210

Legalism (statism), 232–34
Legesse, Asmarom, 53, 57–58
Leng, Shao-Chuan, 54
Liberalism, 68–75, 84–106
versus minimalism, 73–75, 88–89, 97–100
radical (social democratic) conception, 73, 89–90, 100–106
Liberty trade-off, 165, 184–202
Lo, Chung-shu, 54–55
Locke, John, 14n.3, 21, 26, 88–106
economic and social rights, 96, 101–4
natural law, 89–90, 94, 96, 98, 102
property, 93–100, 102
self-preservation, 91–92
state of nature, 89–90

Macpherson, C. B., 91, 93, 94, 98–100
Matthews, Robert O., and R. Cranford Pratt, 41, 43

Minimal (nightwatchman) state, 73–75, 97–100

Modernization, 187–92

Moral interdependence, 211–13, 266

Morgenthau, Hans, 230–32, 234

Nardin, Terry, 41n.13

Natural law, 55n.4, 113

Needs trade-off, 164–83

Negative rights, 33–34, 100–101, 105, 266n.6

Newly industrializing countries (NICs), 193–98

Nickel, James, 9n.1

Niebuhr, Reinhold, 231

Nonintervention, 232–34, 245–46, 260–64

positive, 245–46, 266

Nozick, Robert, 74, 89n.3

Paternalist regimes, 186–87

Peoples' rights, 143–49

Pollis, Adamantia, 49, 60–62, 88

Possession paradox, 11, 13–14, 18–19

Possessive individualism, 93–100, 102n.20

Privacy, 83–87

Property, right to, 25n.12, 26–27, 29–30, 31n.4, 72–75, 93–100

Quiet diplomacy, 242–43

Realism, 230–32

Regimes

international, 205–6ff.

types. *See entries for particular types*

Repression (and development), 184–202

contingency of, 185–87, 189–91, 200–202

during industrialization, 192–93

legitimacy, 194–98

newly industrializing countries and, 193–98

structural transformation, 187–88, 191–92

Righteousness (versus rights), 9–10

Rights

assertive exercise, 11

basic, 37–45

and benefits, 11, 40, 54, 58, 79, 84

claims, 9–15, 105

direct enjoyment, 11

and duties, 50–57, 72, 126, 145

enforcement, 11–12, 15–16

and entitlement, 9–12, 15

manifesto sense, 15

nature of, 9–12

negative, 33–34, 100–101, 105, 266n.6

objective enjoyment, 11

positive (legal), 14–16

possession paradox, 11, 13–14, 18–19

standard threats to, 26, 64–65, 113–14, 122, 159

(enjoying the) substance of, 38–40, 79, 84–87

as "trumps," 9–10

See also Aboriginal rights; Economic and social rights; Group rights; Human rights; Individualism; Peoples' rights

Ruggie, John Gerard, 227

Said, Abdul Aziz, 52

Schlesinger, Arthur, 235–36, 242

Self-determination, 111, 147–49, 153, 234–35

Shue, Henry, 26, 33–34, 38–40, 42, 44n.17, 72, 79, 100, 266n.6

Soviet Union, 55–57, 77–80

Standard threats (to rights), 26, 64–65, 113–14, 122, 159

Statism (legalism), 232–34

Thurman, Robert, 64

Totalitarian regimes, 236–41

Traditional society, 49–55, 57–60, 75–77, 113–14, 118–21, 123, 126, 152–54

(1) Universal Declaration of Human Rights, 4, (1948) 24–25, 34–36, 171–73, 205–6

Universality (of human rights)

international normative, 1–2, 4–5, 23–25, 27, 42–43, 121–22

moral, 1, 4, 49

U.S.S.R., 55–57, 77–80

Vincent, R. J., 229, 237

Wai, Dunstan, 53

Walzer, Michael, 262

(1) and (2) together = The International Bill of Human Rights

Library of Congress Cataloging-in-Publication Data

Donnelly, Jack.
  Universal human rights in theory and practice / Jack Donnelly.
    p. cm.
  Includes index.
  ISBN 0-8014-2316-3 (alk. paper) — ISBN 0-8014-9570-9 (pbk. : alk. paper)
  1. Civil rights. 2. Human rights. 3. Cultural relativism. I. Title.
JC571.D75   1989   323—dc20   89-7057

International Human Rights Covenants
    The International Covenant Econ., Social and Cultural Rights